JESUS
THE SON OF
GOD

Other Titles by the Author

Ambten in de apostolische kerk: Een exegetisch mozaïek
De bergrede: Reisgids voor christenen
Bijbelse taal? De samenhang tussen inhoud en taal van de bijbelse open-baring
Christus op aarde: Zijn levensbeschrijving door leerlingen en tijdgenoten (English edition: *Christ on Earth: The Gospel Narratives as History*)
Emancipatie en bijbel: Kommentaar uit 1 Korinthe 11
The Future of the Bible
Die geschichtliche Einordnung der Pastoralbriefe
Het huwelijk gewogen: 1 Korinthe 7
Het lezen van de bijbel: Een inleiding
Lucas: Het evangelie als voorgeschiedenis
Marcus: Het evangelie volgens Petrus
Matteüs: Het evangelie voor Israël
"Na veertien jaren": De datering van het in Galaten 2 genoemde overleg te Jeruzalem
De oorsprong van de kerk te Rome
Het raadsel van Romeinen 16: De apostel Paulus en het onstaan van de kerk te Rome
De tekst van het Nieuwe Testament
De toekomst van de bijbelvertaling
Wie maakte de bijbel? Over afsluiting en gezag van het Oude en Nieuwe Testament

JESUS
THE SON OF
GOD

The Gospel Narratives as Message

Jakob van Bruggen

Translated by
Nancy Forest-Flier

Baker Books

A Division of Baker Book House Co
Grand Rapids, Michigan 49516

Originally published as *Het evangelie van Gods zoon: Persoon en leer van Jezus volgens de vier evangelien*

© 1996 by Uitgeversmaatschappij J. H. Kok B. V., Kampen, Netherlands

English translation © 1999 by Baker Book House Company

Published by Baker Books
a division of Baker Book House Company
P.O. Box 6287, Grand Rapids, MI 49516-6287

Printed in the United States of America

Library of Congress Cataloging-in-Publication Data

Bruggen, J. van, 1936–
    [Evangelie van Gods Zoon. English]
    Jesus the Son of God : the Gospel narratives as message / Jakob van Bruggen ; translated by Nancy Forest-Flier.
      p. cm.
    Includes bibliographical references (p.) and indexes.
    ISBN 0-8010-2216-9 (pbk.)
    1. Jesus Christ—Person and offices. 2. Jesus Christ—Teachings. 3. Bible. N.T. Gospels—Theology. I. Title.
    BT202.B76713 1999
    232.9′01—dc21   99-16926

For information about academic books, resources for Christian leaders, and all new releases available from Baker Book House, visit our web site:
                         http://www.bakerbooks.com

Contents

Introduction

This book is about the message of the Gospel narratives. We can look at the Gospels from two angles. On the one hand, they offer us the more or less chronological *biography* of Jesus of Nazareth, as developed in my book *Christ on Earth*.

The Gospels, however, present us also with the *message* of the narratives—a message that is, in fact, a Person: Jesus the Son of God! He himself is the Good News. This is the focus of this volume. The two books complement each other, but they can also be read independently from each other.

We become acquainted with the message of the Son of God through the same Gospels that tell us about his history. His message is not a philosophy but a Person and a History. This is the guiding premise of this book. It has been written after the completion of commentaries on each of the four Gospels (published in Dutch), and it brings together the key themes of the Gospel narratives. The result is a book that is not a systematic description, as might be found in a biblical theology, but rather a discussion of issues that come up in our reading of the Gospels.

We observe Jesus living in a Jewish environment—how does this background affect his words and deeds? We see the emergence of the great prophet John the Baptist—where and how does he fit in? We read about the preaching of the kingdom of God and about healings—what was the function of this theme and of the miracles? We find particular expressions—what does it mean when Jesus calls himself "the Son of Man," and how do we interpret the various honorific titles for Jesus, such as "Son of David," "the Prophet," and "the Christ"? What is ultimately the significance of the trajectory of his life, of his being rejected and crucified? Did Jesus really form a new community? Did he teach about the future?

Answers to these many questions are presented in this book, organized in such a way that the story of the message is not obscured by the categories of a strictly systematic approach. The book can be used both as a guide, leading the reader into the message of the Gospel narratives, and as a textbook, directing the reader to information on specific issues.

The message of the four Gospels is normative for our understanding of later developments in faith and theology. In recent centuries a virtually impenetrable forest of views and interpretations has sprung up around Jesus, allowing little light to shine through. It is my hope that this book may help us discern in the distant first century the Light that seeks to reach us today with its radiance.

Jakob van Bruggen
Kampen, Netherlands
Pentecost 1999

Abbreviations

CBQ	*Catholic Biblical Quarterly*
FRLANT	Forschungen zur Religion und Literatur des Alten und Neuen Testaments
JSNTSup	Journal for the Study of the New Testament Supplement Series
KJV	King James Version
LXX	Septuagint (ancient Greek translation of the Old Testament)
MT	Masoretic Text (Hebrew Old Testament)
NIV	New International Version
NRSV	New Revised Standard Version
WUNT	Wissenschaftliche Untersuchungen zum Neuen Testament

1

The Stage Set:
The Jews of the First Century

What do we know about the background of Jesus' ministry, of the faith and the way of life of the people of Israel in Palestine during the first century? We will approach this subject from four angles:

1. The commonly accepted image of "the Jews" in the first century A.D. and its problems
2. The various groups and factions within the Jewish nation
3. The characteristics of Jewish religiosity after the exile
4. The contribution made by the New Testament writings

This detailed chapter is in fact only an introduction to the actual subject of this book. Although it can be skipped, the interested reader will find a number of topics here that are an integral part of the backdrop against which the chapters that follow must be read.

1.1 The First-Century Jewish Context

The focus of the Gospels is the ministry of Jesus. But this ministry takes place in the midst of the Jewish people. The situation of the Jews in Palestine during the first century A.D. constitutes the context for everything he said and did. An understanding of this background, this stage set, is therefore essential if we are to fully understand his ministry.

When Jesus' listeners heard terms such as "righteousness of the Pharisees and the teachers of the law," "Elijah," "the prophet," "the Christ," or "the kingdom of heaven," their first association was with meanings these terms had *before* Jesus began using them. When they saw Jesus cast out demons, they understood it in terms of what they already knew about demonic possession. No matter how new the message of Christ was, it was tuned to his listeners' wavelength. And the rift between Jesus and the Pharisees was at least in part determined by what the Pharisees were before Jesus arrived on the scene.

Any interpretation of the Gospels therefore makes use, consciously or unconsciously, explicitly or implicitly, of the image one has formed of the Jewish setting, which functions as an explanatory backdrop for the Gospel events that take place in the foreground. For this reason it is important to study the formation of this image in some detail. A distorted view of the backdrop can throw the whole picture out of focus.

1.1.1 The Commonly Accepted Image

It is not surprising that through the centuries New Testament exegetes have, to a greater or lesser degree, again and again sought enlightenment among the Jews and have steeped themselves in their teaching and history. In the works of Jerome in the ancient church, as well as in the works of the medieval Parisian Franciscan Nicholas of Lyra, we find data derived from Judaism used in the interpretation of Gospel texts. John Lightfoot in the seventeenth century was more systematic and explicit in establishing the points of contact between the Gospel text and the Jewish background.[1] At the beginning of the twentieth century, Paul Billerbeck compiled an almost exhaustive collection of possible points of contact between the New Testament and Jewish literature, specifically rabbinical literature.[2] This coincided with a growing interest in Jewish pseudepigraphal literature, which has often been handed down in Christian adaptations. Translations of this literature into English[3] and German[4] also appeared at the beginning of the twentieth century, and the discovery of new documents at Qumran led to a veritable flood of text editions in this field, culminating in, among others, the English translation edited by Charlesworth.[5] Ancient Jewish literature is much more accessible now than it was in earlier centuries, so it is not surprising that the past hundred years have seen the publication of several comprehensive surveys of the history and religion of the Jewish people before and during the New Testament era.[6]

---

1. J. Lightfoot, *A Commentary on the New Testament from the Talmud and Hebraica*, vols. 1–4 (Grand Rapids: Baker, 1979).

2. H. L. Strack and P. Billerbeck, *Kommentar zum Neuen Testament aus Talmud und Midrasch*, vols. 1–4 (Munich: Beck, 1926–28). Vols. 5–6 ed. J. Jeremias and K. Adolph (Munich: Beck, 1963).

3. R. H. Charles, ed., *The Apocrypha and Pseudepigrapha of the Old Testament in English*, 2 vols. (Oxford: Clarendon, 1913).

4. E. Kautzsch, ed., *Die Apokryphen und Pseudepigraphen des Alten Testaments*, 2 vols. (Tübingen: Mohr, 1900).

5. J. H. Charlesworth, ed., *The Old Testament Pseudepigrapha*, 2 vols. (Garden City, N.Y.: Doubleday, 1983–85).

6. For history see E. Schürer, *The History of the Jewish People in the Age of Jesus Christ (175 B.C.–A.D. 135)*, new English version, rev. and ed. G. Vermes, F. Millar, M. Black, and M. Goodman, 3 vols. (Edinburgh: Clark, 1973–87). For religion and theology from non-

For a time it even seemed that the background could be reconstructed with greater certainty than ever before. Since the middle of the nineteenth century a kind of consensus had been developing, especially in the practice of exegesis. A generally accepted, overall picture developed in which first-century Judaism was seen as having been legalistic or casuistic, often in a formal or external manner. According to this consensus, there were many Jews in Jesus' day who put their hope for national recovery in the person of the coming Messiah, the new king of the end times. The Pharisees imagined that they could speed his coming through "moral rearmament." The Zealots added earthly weapons. Both groups avoided the tax collectors as representatives of the Roman enemy and oppressor.

Against this background, Jesus is then seen as the reformer who leads the people from the distortion of casuistry to the true meaning of the law, which culminates in love. He appears misunderstood precisely because he would not cooperate in the establishment of a program of national recovery, and his friendship with tax collectors even made him religiously suspect.

This consensual backdrop and its characterization of Jesus as a *reformer* of the Jewish religion is reflected in widely divergent interpretations. It is the point of departure for those who, in their liberal understanding of Jesus, regard him as no more than a kind teacher of love. But it also provides a basis for those who see Jesus as the Son of God, who leads Israel from the servitude of legalism to the freedom of redeemed children. Thus, in a variety of ways, the *contrast* between the dark backdrop and the central character of the Gospels is highlighted. Jesus is presented as the *better Jew* or the *heavenly Prophet*, a *protest figure* within the Judaism of his time.

1.1.2 More Sources, a Less-Focused Image

But how confident can we be about this reconstruction of the Jewish world? Was the Jewish context really as dark as is often tacitly assumed? Some people are disturbed by such a question. They believe that it is *thanks to this dark Jewish background* that the light of Jesus is able to shine forth. The stage set simply *cannot* be brightly lit, since it would then fail to act as a foil for the figure of Jesus. Doesn't the need

---

rabbinical sources, see W. Bousset, *Die Religion des Judentums im späthellenistischen Zeitalter*, 3d ed., ed. H. Gressmann, Handbuch zum Neuen Testament 21 (Tübingen: Mohr, 1966). For religion and theology from rabbinical sources, see G. F. Moore, *Judaism in the First Centuries of the Christian Era: The Age of the Tannaim*, 3 vols. (Cambridge, Mass.: Harvard University Press, 1927–30). For religious life see E. P. Sanders, *Judaism: Practice and Belief, 63 B.C.E.–66 C.E.* (London: SCM, 1992).

for contrast call for a somber background? Sometimes it seems as if the hostile picture of the teachers of the law is necessary for the contrasting presentation of the disciples as a circle of friends. The contrast so evident in illustrated children's Bibles and in the Gospel-related visual arts in general would be a study in itself. But we must realize that a stage set is quite different from a shadow; the shape of a shadow is determined by the shape of the object that casts it, but a stage set has a shape all its own and deserves to be assessed on its own terms.

So much has been published in the past several decades about the diversity that existed within the Judaism of the first century that the usefulness of the commonly accepted, popularized image is called into question from a number of directions.[7] Mention should be made of the *broadening* of the picture that has resulted from the discovery of the previously unknown Qumran documents, which may have originated in the monastic-type Qumran (Essene?) community. Furthermore, the sources that were known before, including the targums, have been studied much more comprehensively.[8] All this has made it increasingly difficult to maintain a uniform picture of first-century Judaism. Rather, there are now a number of discrete images.

In addition, the *methodology* used for studying the rabbinic sources has come under discussion. Today, far greater attention is paid to the age of the many data accumulated in the Mishnah and the Talmud. Especially the work of Neusner on the Pharisees, among other topics, should be mentioned here. All this has led to significant fragmentation in the work of historic reconstruction.[9] Instead of a clear, organically evolved image, we are faced with a collection of patches of color against a fuzzy background.

This change in method is linked with the realization that earlier reconstructions were often heavily indebted to a certain *philosophy of history*. At present, scholars are much less inclined to subsume all the data under a model of historical evolution. The diversity of facts and data may not allow for a logical, coherent picture at all! The grand vision of progress of the nineteenth-century historians has been replaced by the pursuit of a modest, pragmatic inventorying of the data.

Another point to be considered is that the prevailing negative picture of the Jewish people of the first century is closely linked with a view of the Old Testament that is not altogether free from *anti-Semitic*

---

7. J. W. Doeve, *Vertekende Beelden. Over de selectie van de bronnen bij de beoefening der Judaïstiek van de eeuwen rondom het begin onzer jaartelling* (Leiden: Brill, 1963).

8. M. McNamara, *Palestinian Judaism and the New Testament*, Good News Studies 4 (Wilmington, Del.: Glazier, 1983).

9. P. S. Alexander, "Rabbinic Judaism and the New Testament," *Zeitschrift für die neutestamentliche Wissenschaft* 74 (1983): 237–46.

influences. In the nineteenth century, Old Testament scholars developed a source hypothesis that saw the older, prophetic religion of the Israelites as developing, via the Priestly Codex of the time of Ezra and Nehemiah, into a rigid, legalistic, and nationalistic "Jewish religion." The first-century Pharisees, with their casuistic and exclusionary practices of ritual purity, are then the exponents of this perverted form of religion. Jesus supposedly wanted to liberate the people from the oppressive yoke of the Jewish religion and to lead them back to the prophetic and less nationalistic faith of ancient Israel.

This widely accepted concept is less self-evident than it seems. Its historical sources do not clearly support it, and it also has nonhistorical roots in a specific *view* of history. For this reason it is necessary to take a closer look at all the different panels that together form the stage set for Jesus' ministry in Israel.[10]

1.2 The Various Jewish Groups

It is not surprising that the influence of this long-held view of Judaism was often reflected in the descriptions of the various groups that existed within the Hebrew population. The legalistic tendency resurfaced in the descriptions of the Pharisees, the nationalistic tendency in that of the Zealots. The resulting image of these groups in turn reconfirmed the existing overall picture.

But now that this unified picture has lost its prominence in the past few decades, the changes in methodology with regard to the use of sources and the broader attention paid to the diversity of these sources have been felt in many areas.

1.2.1 Pharisees

Because of their confrontation with Jesus, the Pharisees play a major role in the New Testament; they seem, in fact, to be the dominant group. Therefore they also deserve extra attention in a book on the gospel of Christ. In this chapter a few points are summarized. For a more in-depth study of this group, see appendix 1.

As soon as we try to form a picture of the Pharisees, we run into the problem of sources mentioned above. For a long time it was common to recognize "Pharisaism" in a wide range of writings on the basis of the commonly accepted view of the Pharisees. Thus the Psalms of Solomon (first century B.C.) were often cited to demonstrate the mentality of the Pharisees at that time. But the Pharisees are not mentioned at all in

10. Compare L. L. Grabbe, *Judaism from Cyrus to Hadrian* (London: SCM, 1994), chap. 8.

these psalms, so it is highly questionable whether this is indeed a typical Pharisaic document. In more recent literature, scholars justifiably have limited themselves to those sources that explicitly mention the party of the Pharisees. They have also limited themselves to documents from the first century, or to documents that can still supply reliable information about this period. This results in a severe curtailment of the source material: the historical books of the New Testament (first century), the writings of the Jewish historian Josephus (end of the first century), and passages from the rabbinic literature (third and following centuries).

Another matter up for discussion besides the choice of sources is the methodology used in studying them. Whereas scholars in the past were often inclined to consult the various writings and to extract "facts" as though they were neutral elements that could quickly be fused into a unified historical picture, the practice today is to pay much more attention to the unique qualities of each source and how these qualities affect the "facts." Thus Neusner applies the historical-critical method (in use in biblical studies for some time before) to the rabbinic sources, and Mason has produced a separate study on Josephus and the Pharisees.

All this work has not resulted in a new unanimity—except for the general abandonment of the image of the Pharisees as a legalistic, nationalistic, and hypocritical group. A comparison of the studies of Rivkin and Neusner on the rabbinic writings reveals ideas so strongly divergent that they cast doubt on the suitability of rabbinic sources for providing a balanced picture of the first-century Pharisees. The Pharisees are often mentioned in later discussions, but only in passing and not systematically. The historian Josephus, however, gives us a more contemporary and broader perspective. He reveals the Pharisees as a respectable party consisting of people who were extremely precise in their observation of the law and the oral tradition, but who at the same time held in esteem the gift of prophecy in their midst and were known for their mildness and humanitarian attitudes. As a politician, Josephus objected to their inflexibility, which made them less-than-likely candidates for political compromise. Nowhere, however, does he present a picture of the Pharisees that might fit the later categories of the Reformation period, when the Pharisees were seen as a group whose main focus was their doctrine of justification—which was clearly the opposite of the Lutheran doctrine of justification by faith alone. Rather, like the other parties in Israel, their primary concern was *lifestyle*—how to live and survive as a Jew in the first century. Ethics and jurisprudence were predominant. Here the Pharisees, as the most meticulous of the groups, enjoyed much popular support, especially in the cities. The result was that many leaders who did not subscribe to the rules of the

Pharisees had to follow these rules when it came to jurisprudence, lest they find themselves in conflict with the people. As far as their specific "doctrine" was concerned, they differed from the Sadducees in their belief in God's providence and in the resurrection of the just.

The New Testament supports this picture, when we pay attention to the general information about the Pharisees we find there. It would be methodologically incorrect to consider the many passages concerning the conflict between the Pharisees and Jesus as simply neutral "facts," and to place them on the same level as all the other available information. We need not assume that the New Testament writers formed their picture of the Pharisees in retrospect. The picture of the Pharisees was already during Jesus' lifetime unique *in the conflict situation*. The Pharisees did not oppose him as a matter of course. They felt that they ought to take action because Jesus, in their eyes, had crossed the line of blasphemy. In the beginning they acted (in their ignorance) in good faith. If Jesus had not been the Son of God but simply a presumptuous individual, there would have been little to blame the Pharisees for. Their great (and, by persevering in it, fatal) error in their appraisal of the Christ of God has incorrectly been used as the basis for the reconstruction of the party in general. This in effect nullifies the impact of the astonishing thing that happened: with their faithfulness to the law and their belief in the resurrection, the Pharisees were closer to Jesus than any of the other parties; how could *they* become his most fervent opponents? Many of Jesus' sharp statements against the Pharisees were not directed at them because they had always been a bad party, but rather because their rejection of God's envoy now turns this best of groups into the worst.

1.2.2 Sinners

The Gospels reveal that there was a particular group of people living in Israel that could simply be identified as "the sinners" (Luke 6:32–34). Many of the reproaches against Jesus include references to them. Jesus is portrayed as a friend and dinner companion of "the sinners." They are often mentioned in the same breath as the tax collectors (Matt. 9:10–11; 11:19; Luke 15:1–2).

Jesus himself also talks about this group, but with kindness rather than scorn: "For I have not come to call the righteous, but sinners" (Matt. 9:13; compare Luke 15:7–10).

What criterion was used to define this group? Recent studies of Judaism during the New Testament period reveal several different opinions. The most important is that the group known as "sinners" was in fact *defined by the presence of the Pharisees* (see sec. 1.2.4, where this view is also applied to the tax collectors). Here we go back to the topic of the previous section. Jeremias writes that the Pharisees regarded those who were not strict observers of the law as a "mob that knows nothing of the law."[11] Anyone who was part of this ignorant and ritually or morally impure people was thus a "sinner" or on a level with sinners. The term thus does not refer to people who were contemptuous of the God of Israel and who lived lives in direct conflict with the regulations of God's law—which was the Old Testament concept of a sinner: someone who failed to keep the norms set forth in the Torah.

In the Judaism of Jesus' day, a much broader notion of "sinner" had developed. Anyone who did not act in the manner prescribed by the Pharisees (which was much more detailed than the Torah) was to be condemned as "sinner," as "lawless" (in the Pharisaical sense of the word). These people are excluded! Jesus speaks of these same people in much more positive terms when he calls them "the poor." What made his behavior so offensive was that he treated the excluded people as if they still belonged to the community.

Sanders has written a detailed refutation of the notion that "sinners" would have been the equivalent of the "mob that knows nothing of the law."[12] He also refutes the idea that the laws of ritual purity of the Pharisees constituted the line of demarcation between them and the "sinners." A popular modern picture of the Pharisees of the first century— that of a small introverted sect with a number of rules that aimed at imposing priestly purity on every Jew—cannot be defended on the basis of a contrasting image of "sinners." And in the New Testament, the irritation evoked by Jesus' association with "the sinners" was not limited to the Pharisees. This irritation was shared by the general population (Luke 7:34; 19:7). The category "sinners" must therefore be seen as not dependent on the category "Pharisees."

We should understand "sinners" to refer to people whose religious or moral behavior caused them to be out of step with a people who (with various degrees of strictness and with diverging religious convictions) wanted to serve the God of Israel. Thus heterogeneous groups such as rich tax collectors and adulterous women could both fit in the category "sinners" (Luke 7:37, 39; Matt. 21:31–32).

The reason why Jesus concerned himself with "sinners" will be discussed in section 7.1.2. His love for them, however, cannot be placed against a specifically Pharisaic backdrop, as if concern for "sinners"

11. J. Jeremias, *New Testament Theology* (London: SCM, 1971), 111ff.
12. E. P. Sanders, *Jesus and Judaism* (London: SCM, 1985), 174–211. See also D. A. Neale, *None but Sinners: Religious Categories in the Gospel of Luke*, JSNTSup 58 (Sheffield: JSOT Press, 1991).

could be interpreted as nothing more than overtly *anti-Pharisaic* behavior.

1.2.3 Zealots

Whereas the Pharisees are often used to help depict Jesus as a reformer among a people bent under the weight of legalism and joyless casuistry, the Zealots have more than once been cited to demonstrate that on the nonspiritual plane Jesus was also clashing with aggressive nationalism. According to Pickl, all of Jesus' teaching was geared to detaching his disciples from this prevailing this-worldly, political messianic expectation.[13] Others are of the opinion that the Gospels cover up the actual situation[14] and that Jesus was even sympathetic toward the Zealots,[15] or that at most he differed on the means by which he sought to liberate his people.[16] Is it correct to take into account in some way the role of Zealotism in the reconstruction of the Jewish background of the Gospels?[17]

Religious nationalism undeniably surfaced later in the first century, during the Jewish War (A.D. 66–70), although for a thorough understanding of this episode the social and economic factors that led to turmoil and revolt must also be taken into account. Furthermore, Josephus, in his account of the Jewish War, more than once mentions a group that called itself Zealots, and he shows that the years prior to the war were marked by turmoil and incidents.

But is there evidence that during the first half of that century, at the time of John the Baptist and Jesus, there was an influential party of Zealots in addition to the familiar Pharisees, Sadducees, and Essenes? And can we, for example, view the Beatitudes on the meek and the peacemakers as an implicit polemic against many revolution-minded Jews in Palestine at the time of the Sermon on the Mount?

Tacitus, the second-century Roman historian who never missed an opportunity to say unfavorable things about the Jews, makes a striking remark about this period—the reign of Emperor Tiberius—in the Jew-

13. J. Pickl, *The Messias* (St. Louis: Herder, 1946).

14. S. G. F. Brandon, *The Fall of Jerusalem and the Christian Church: A Study of the Effects of the Jewish Overthrow of A.D. 70 on Christianity*, 2d ed. (London: S.P.C.K., 1978).

15. S. G. F. Brandon, *Jesus and the Zealots: A Study of the Political Factor in Primitive Christianity* (Manchester: Manchester University Press, 1967).

16. R. Eisler, *Iesous Basileus Ou Basileusas: Die messianische Unabhängigkeitsbewegung vom Auftreten Johannes des Täufers bis zum Untergang Jakobs des Gerechten, nach der neuerschlossenen "Eroberung von Jerusalem" des Flavius Josephus*, 2 vols. (Heidelberg: Winter Universitätsbuchhandlung, 1929–30).

17. E. Bammel and C. F. D. Moule, eds., *Jesus and the Politics of His Day* (Cambridge: Cambridge University Press, 1984).

ish region. He states succinctly, "Sub Tiberio quies" (Peace under Tiberius!).[18] This does not suggest national turmoil. Thus, when the Gospels are silent about Zealotism and aggressive nationalism, it may mean that these phenomena did not play a significant role at the time.

Nonbiblical sources tell us that there was one turbulent *year* at the *beginning* of the first century. When Archelaus, one of Herod the Great's three successors, was removed by the emperor in A.D. 6, a central region of the Jewish region (Judea, Idumea, and Samaria) came under the direct jurisdiction of the imperial governor. This brought with it a total administrative change. Until then, this area had been under a vassal king and enjoyed relative independence. Now it came under *direct* Roman governance, which meant that direct imperial taxes would have to be raised as well.

So the imperial legate and his troops were sent from Syria to Jerusalem to carry out the massive reorganization. The legate's orders were to deal with the vast private estate of Archelaus and to supervise the reorganization of the government. In connection with this change, a (regional) registration of property and persons was held to obtain current data for the governmental takeover. These Roman measures provoked much resistance. In Jerusalem the result was a revolt under the leadership of Judas of Galilee (or of Gaulanitis) and Zadok the Pharisee. The revolution was crushed with a great massacre.

In a sense, this revolt of A.D. 6 can be regarded as a spark that would later flare up with far more intensity in the Jewish War. But there were few of these sparks in the decades immediately after the revolt itself. Gamaliel expressed the view that prevailed during the fourth decade of the century: such revolts were bound to fail. He said, "After him, Judas the Galilean appeared in the days of the census and led a band of people in revolt. He too was killed, and all his followers were scattered" (Acts 5:37). If the Pharisee Gamaliel could calmly address the whole Sanhedrin in this way without fear of contradiction, it clearly indicates that the influence of Judas the Galilean *during the years of John the Baptist and Jesus* was slight or nonexistent. After the violent uprising of A.D. 6, the Jewish region enjoyed a few decades of "peace."

This peace did not come to an end until King Agrippa died in A.D. 44. Not only had he been allowed to take over the territories of Antipas and Philip, but he had also been handed the administration of the central region (Judea, Samaria, and Idumea). From A.D. 41 to 44 there was once again a king (of their own) in Jerusalem, a king who managed to make himself popular with the people. So in A.D. 44, when the emperor placed the *entire country*, and not only the central region, under direct Roman

18. Tacitus, *Histories* 5.9.

control, it came as a heavy blow. Life under a Roman governor was no longer a regional exception—it had become a nationwide reality. This revived the mentality of the year A.D. 6. The country became agitated and remained so during the next two decades, until total war broke out in A.D. 66.

In this third quarter of the first century, agitating elements played a more prominent role in the life of the people, which led to reprisals against the Jews in Rome.[19] Whether the instigators of the various incidents in Palestine were motivated by religious, nationalistic, or socioeconomic concerns is not important here. What should be noted is that seeing this national tension as a factor of significance during the time of Jesus' ministry is *to date it too early*.

But something does not seem quite right with this observation. Doesn't the name of one of Jesus' disciples, *Simon the Zealot* (Luke 6:15; Acts 1:13), suggest that there were Zealots in Jesus' time who were already known by that name and who were even found among Jesus' disciples? Here we run into the problem that the Greek word *zēlōtēs* does not just mean "follower of the party of the so-called Zealots." Its normal meaning is "enthusiast." In the New Testament we find various word combinations that have to do with someone's *enthusiasm* for something, but the word *zēlōtēs* in those combinations does not have the slightest connection with membership in a Zealot party.[20] That a certain Simon is given the *nickname zēlōtēs* may refer to his being a devoted and fervent, perhaps even somewhat fanatic, character: Simon the Striver or Simon the Fanatic. The sons of Zebedee were similarly called "Sons of Thunder."[21]

We may interpret the nickname *zēlōtēs* as a reference to membership in the Zealot party only if *during those years* "Zealot" was as clearly a reference to membership in a party as "Pharisee" and "Sadducee"—but that is not the case. The party name "Zealots" does not appear anywhere in the Gospels. In the meantime, the conviction has been gaining ground that the title "Zealot" was not linked with a *party* until the year A.D. 44.[22]

19. J. van Bruggen, *De oorsprong van de kerk te Rome*, Kamper Bijdragen 3 (Groningen: de Vuurbaak, 1967).

20. Acts 21:20 (*zēlōtai* for the law); 22:3 (Paul the *Pharisee* [!] calls himself a *zēlōtēs* of God, "as any of you are today"); 1 Pet. 3:13 (who is going to harm you if you are *zēlōtai* to do good?); see also 1 Cor. 14:12; Titus 2:14.

21. For this Simon of Cana, see J. van Bruggen, *Christ on Earth: The Gospel Narratives as History* (Grand Rapids: Baker, 1998), sec. 8.9.

22. M. Borg, "The Currency of the Term *Zealot*," *Journal of Theological Studies* 22 (1971): 504–12. M. J. J. Menken, "De 'zeloten': Een overzicht," *Vox theologica* 45 (1975): 30–47. H. Guevara, *La resistencia judia contra Roma en la epoca de Jesus* (Meitingen: Meitinger, 1981). R. A. Horsley, "The Zealots: Their Origin, Relationships, and Importance in the Jewish Revolt," *Novum Testamentum* 28 (1986): 159–92.

Josephus uses the term *Zealots* only during the years of the Jewish War. In his description of the "fourth party" that began with Judas the Galilean,[23] he says that this movement valued freedom above all else and would tolerate no human masters lording it over them. Nowhere, however, does he apply the name "Zealots" to this group. It is also clear that he pays more attention to Judas the Galilean because he sees something *beginning* here that will *later* prove to become disastrous on a much larger scale. Thus he writes that *the people* began to suffer from the sickness of this fourth party during the time of Governor Gessius Florus (right before the outbreak of the Jewish War).[24] This seems to indicate not only that the name "Zealots" was unknown during the first half of the first century, but also that Judas the Galilean's desire for freedom and the movement he started still did not exercise any significant influence on the people at that time. Josephus traces the rise of a so-called fourth party to Judas the Galilean *from the later perspective* of the Jewish War. Gamaliel (around A.D. 33) sees Judas as one of the failed insurgents from the past. Josephus feels that it is important to explain to his readers that the passion for freedom that characterized the Jewish War, with all its dreadful consequences, did not have its origins in the three traditional Jewish parties but was the terrible fruit of something begun by Judas the Galilean, which Josephus now calls a "fourth party," even though it was less a new *party* than a new *mindset*. This fourth movement was in total agreement with the Pharisees and differed only in its desire for freedom.[25] By speaking of a new "party" or "movement," Josephus tries to keep outsiders from seeing the Jewish War as an outgrowth of "normal" Judaism. This is why he points to the rise of Judas the Galilean as the beginning of the fourth movement, even though there is nothing at all to tell about the party during the following decades—it is as if it does not exist. Josephus's intent behind the early dating of the origins of the new movement is thus to keep his readers from concluding that the mentality that would later produce groups like the Zealots (especially *during* the Jewish War) was a common Jewish mentality during the first century that merely found some extreme modes of expression during the war. Josephus's autobiography clearly reveals how little the "fourth movement" resembled a real party in comparison with all the others in the decades before the Jewish War.[26] When he was sixteen years old, Josephus devoted himself to learning about all the parties that were active among the Jewish people at the

23. Josephus, *Antiquities* 18.1.1–6 §§1–25.
24. Ibid., 18.1.6 §25.
25. Ibid., 18.1.6 §23.
26. Josephus, *Life* 2 §§10–12.

time; he mentions only three (Pharisees, Sadducees, and Essenes). This was in about A.D. 53. Apparently there was no reason at that point to become acquainted with a fourth party. The historical connection to which Josephus points, between Judas the Galilean and the Jewish War, should not tempt us to suspect that there was a fourth "party" of any real significance during the intervening decades.

Some scholars view the *robbers* or *bandits* mentioned in the New Testament and in the writings of Josephus as politically and religiously motivated guerrilla fighters who in fact were the "Zealots" from the period between A.D. 6 and A.D. 70. Thus the robbers on the cross and certainly Barabbas were in their view actually Zealots.[27] But this theory confuses two things. First, it was not until after A.D. 44 that we see forms of banditry that begin to resemble Zealotry. And second, there were always bandits who had nothing to do with religion or politics. Barabbas is called a "bandit" (*lēstēs*) in John 18:40 (NRSV); if he had been a *Zealot* and *as such* a popular favorite, it would have been strange for Peter to stand in the forum before the entire population a few months later and calmly call him a *murderer* (Acts 3:14; compare Luke 23:19). Neither could the two "robbers" (*lēstai*) on the cross (Mark 15:27) have been popular Zealot guerrilla fighters; they were actually criminals (Mark 15:28; Luke 23:33), one of whom even admitted that they *deserved* crucifixion (Luke 23:41)! Josephus tells how Eleazar, the robber chieftain who had been active for twenty years, was arrested by Felix, the governor.[28] Here we see the leader of a gang of bandits who had already been active during the time of Barabbas, but there is not a trace of religious passion or political objectives in this man. Josephus relates that it was not until the *late fifties* of the first century that gangs of bandits, who had been active for decades, started intimidating people in order to build up resistance *against the Romans*.[29] Until then, the main tensions had been between the Jews on the one hand and the *Samaritans* (!) and the inhabitants of the *Greek cities* on the other. Because the Romans kept intervening, the agitation began to be turned on these "protectors" of the hated Samaritans and the ethnic Greeks.[30]

In conclusion, it can be said that no Zealots existed during the time of John the Baptist and Jesus, and that there was no active and anti-

---

27. K. H. Rengstorf, "λῃστής," in *Theological Dictionary of the New Testament*, ed. G. Kittel, trans. G. W. Bromiley (Grand Rapids: Eerdmans, 1967), 4:257–62; M. Hengel, *The Zealots: Investigations into the Jewish Freedom Movement in the Period from Herod I until 70 A.D.*, trans. D. Smith (Edinburgh: Clark, 1989).

28. Josephus, *Jewish War* 2.13.2 §253.

29. Ibid., 2.13.6 §§264–65.

30. For Josephus's description of the gangs of bandits, also see R. A. Horsley, "Josephus and the Bandits," *Journal for the Study of Judaism* 10 (1979): 37–63.

Roman religious nationalism. That this nevertheless is so often assumed can be blamed on the blending of facts that simply have nothing to do with each other (gangs of bandits and nationalism), a too early date for "Zealot" as the name of a party, and an overrating of the connection that Josephus makes between the Jewish War and the disturbances under Judas the Galilean (the beginning of the "fourth party").

So if it cannot be proven that Zealotry was a significant factor in the lives of the people during the earthly ministries of John the Baptist and Jesus, then the main reason for accusing the people of that period of this-worldly nationalism is no longer valid. The preaching of the Baptist tells us that Abraham's children needed to be warned against a false sense of self-confidence, but neither John nor Jesus confronts any tendencies to seek liberation from the Romans, or even to establish the kingdom of God on earth, by means of an earthly struggle. Thus we have every reason to believe that most Jews knew full well how to tell the difference between seeking solutions for earthly political or economic problems and the expectation of the coming of the LORD God and his kingdom of peace. Even during the Jewish War the two are never seen as identical, even though religious self-confidence made some people blind to the prevailing military reality during the war.

1.2.4 Tax Collectors

While the Zealots appear to have played no role at all during Jesus' life on earth, the presence of the tax collectors and the disparaging attitude of the people toward them seem to prove that anti-Roman sentiments did indeed exist. Tax collectors are often seen as Roman collaborators; after all, they collected taxes on behalf of the ruling power.[31] Is this not the reason why Jesus was resented for maintaining friendly contact with them? The people's hostile attitude toward these middlemen working for the foreign occupier then shows the extent to which Zealot ideology had spread throughout the population.[32] Because the tax collectors as a social group appear rather frequently in the Gospels, this panel from the early first-century Jewish stage set deserves special attention.

The first question is: what was the function of these tax collectors? Herrenbrück devoted an extensive study to this subject[33] and concluded

---

31. E. M. Smallwood, *The Jews under Roman Rule: From Pompey to Diocletian*, Studies in Judaism in Late Antiquity 20 (Leiden: Brill, 1976), 151.

32. M. Hengel, *Die Zeloten: Untersuchungen zur jüdischen Freiheitsbewegung in der Zeit von Herodes I. bis 70 n.Chr.*, 2d ed., Arbeiten zur Geschichte des antiken Judentums und des Urchristentums 1 (Leiden: Brill, 1976), 144.

33. F. Herrenbrück, *Jesus und die Zöllner: Historische und neutestamentlich-exegetische Untersuchungen*, WUNT 2/41 (Tübingen: Mohr, 1990).

that often too little distinction is made between the wealthy Roman *publicani* and the lesser tax leaseholders who worked in the former Hellenistic states of the East. The Roman *publicani* were responsible for collecting taxes within a very large area (an entire province of the empire) that were to be paid directly to Rome. They were not part of the indigenous population but belonged to the Roman nobility.

In the regions of the former Hellenistic states (in particular Egypt and Syria), the *tax leaseholder* had been a familiar figure for centuries. He must have been a wealthy man, because the leased taxes had to be paid in advance, but he did not necessarily have to be a member of the very wealthy class, to which the *publicani* always belonged. These small tax leaseholders were from the indigenous population. They could lease the right to collect one or more of the many kinds of taxes for a smaller region (usually a city), and they were allowed to make a profit percentage on the prepaid, leased taxes they collected.

It would be incorrect to describe the Jewish tax collectors in Palestine as Roman collaborators. The taxes to be paid directly to Rome were not leased to them. They were responsible for the taxes collected for the city government or for the vassal king. The tax collectors in Galilee and Perea leased taxes from Herod Antipas, but this made them at most friends of the Herodians; they certainly were not Roman collaborators. So the negative attitude that the Pharisees had toward them must have stemmed from other causes.

Herrenbrück believes that the negative attitude toward tax collectors did not spring from any sense of nationalism but was rather a consequence of the ideal of holiness that was espoused by the Pharisees at that time. Herrenbrück agrees with Neusner and others on the position of the Pharisees during the first century (compare sec. 1.2.1). The Pharisees, they argue, held the tax collectors in contempt because they did not join them in advocating a more extensive, priestly sort of holiness for the entire population. We must agree with Herrenbrück that in the Gospels the disdain for the tax collectors is mainly attributed to the Pharisees. Viewed in isolation, this could indicate that their negative attitude was the result of something that was specific to the Pharisees. Yet we see at times that the entire population is negatively disposed toward specific tax collectors (Luke 19:7). In addition, the question must be raised whether the Pharisees' objection to the tax collectors did not stem from *the law itself* rather than from any of their own, more detailed interpretations of the law. After all, the whole tax leasing system was based on the charging of *interest*. By investing his capital with the authorities, the tax collector was granted the right to recover this capital (which in fact was an advance or loan on behalf of the taxpayers) by collecting taxes *with interest*. He received no salary for his work; his only income was the interest he earned on his capital. But when this interest was in effect charged against and paid by his fellow Israelites, as part of their taxes, it was a violation of the law (Deut. 23:19–20). The idea behind this prohibition of interest must have been concern for the poor of the community. But how often the tax collector made his claim for taxes (plus interest) even in the face of poverty and need! So when Zacchaeus says, "I give half of my possessions to the poor," it is hardly an act of altruism but rather an active righting of wrongs committed. In addition, the collection system was vulnerable to corruption, as we see in the second "restitution" of this converted tax collector: "If I have cheated anybody out of anything, I will pay back four times the amount." The fact that this is a *general* fault of all tax collectors is evident from the statement by John the Baptist: "Don't collect any more than you are required to" (Luke 3:13). This appeal by the Baptist is certainly aimed at corruption, but it may also have been an appeal against charging *interest*. We have several indications that the tax collectors were generally regarded as men who were none too honest in their financial dealings and who failed in their religious duties toward their less fortunate fellow citizens.

There was thus a straight line connecting the specific group of sinners known as tax collectors, with their economic crimes, to other trespassers of the law such as robbers and adulterers (Luke 18:11), sinners (Matt. 9:11; 11:19; Luke 15:1–2), and prostitutes (Matt. 21:31–32). These were the "sick" members of a society that wanted to live a healthy life under the law of Moses, and thus they were in need of "repentance" (Luke 5:32).

In chapter 7 we will take a closer look at the significance of Jesus' ongoing contact with tax collectors (see sec. 7.1.2). In this chapter on the Jewish setting we may conclude that the tax collectors are presented, not as Roman collaborators, but as one of the categories of sinners within the population. Because they belonged to the propertied class and could afford to hold banquets, Jesus' association with them is rather striking and conspicuous.

1.2.5 Teachers of the Law

The reader of the Gospels frequently encounters the "teachers of the law," which might give the impression that they formed a separate group *in addition to* groups such as the Pharisees and the Sadducees. But that was not the case. The Pharisees and Sadducees were parties between which one could choose. The teachers of the law, on the other hand, served a particular function—they practiced a profession. They could have been followers of any one of the parties in Israel. Thus we read about "teachers of the law who were Pharisees" (Acts 23:9; compare Mark 2:16), meaning *that portion* of the teachers of the law who, along with the elders and chief priests, made up the Sanhedrin. Furthermore, it appears that not all of the teachers of the law belonged to the party of the Pharisees. Some scholars regard them as the theological minds behind this party,[34] which would mean that the entire group known as teachers of the law belonged to the party of the Pharisees. But "Pharisees" and "teachers of the law" should be seen as neither equivalent nor identical.[35] While many teachers of the law may have given their support to the party of the Pharisees, there is still a difference between them. On one occasion, after Jesus had given the Pharisees a sharp rebuke, one of the teachers of the law responded with, "Teacher, when you say these things, you insult us also." So he answers, "And you experts in the law, woe to you" (Luke 11:45–46). This discussion reveals both the similarity and the difference between the two groups: similarity, because it was the party of the Pharisees that supported a strict application of the law; difference, because party and profession did not coincide.

The fact that the teachers of the law are often mentioned along with the chief priests (Matt. 2:4; 20:18; 21:15), or with the chief priests and elders (Matt. 16:21), or with the elders (Matt. 26:57; 27:41; Acts 4:5; 6:12) proves that they all were part of the ruling upper class.

The most common designation for these teachers of the law in the New Testament is the Greek word *grammateus*. This is a common word that as a rule means "clerk, higher official" (compare Acts 19:35). For Greek readers, the association of *grammateus* with "government" would have been more obvious than for English-speaking Bible readers, who are more likely to think of a theologian than a government official when reading about "teachers of the law." Jewish tomb inscriptions tell us that the word *grammateus* could also refer to a man with a certain function in the synagogue community.[36]

It cannot be denied that the *grammateis* who appear in the Gospels were in fact specialists in the constitution of Israel (the Torah). It is probably not accidental that for his Greek readers Luke rather frequently alternates *grammateus* with *nomikos* ("expert in the law, jurist") or with *nomodidaskalos* ("teacher of the law"; compare Luke 5:17

34. S. Westerholm, *Jesus and Scribal Authority*, Coniectanea Biblica, New Testament Series 10 (Lund: Gleerup, 1978).

35. D. R. Schwartz, "Scribes and Pharisees, Hypocrites: Who Are the 'Scribes' in the New Testament?" in *Studies in the Jewish Background of Christianity*, WUNT 60 (Tübingen: Mohr, 1992), 89–101.

36. P. W. van der Horst, *Ancient Jewish Epitaphs: An Introductory Survey of a Millennium of Jewish Funerary Epigraphy (300 B.C.E.–700 C.E.)*, Contributions to Biblical Exegesis and Theology 2 (Kampen: Kok Pharos, 1991), 91–92.

[*nomodidaskaloi*] with 5:21 [*grammateis*]; Acts 5:34 [*nomodidaskalos*]; Luke 7:30 [*nomikoi*]).

In the Greek translation of the Old Testament, the word *grammateus* appears regularly and means "foreman, clerk": the foremen in Egypt (Exod. 5:6, 10, 14, 15, 19) and in the desert (Num. 11:16, "officials" in NIV). In the time of the kings, these *scribes* belong to the leading circles of the royal household. We first see these officials applying their expertise to knowledge of the law of the LORD in Ezra. Ezra was called "a teacher well versed in the Law of Moses" (Ezra 7:6, 11–12). From the words of the Persian king, we see that this specialized knowledge was still being combined with the older function of the government official: "Provide with diligence whatever Ezra the priest, a teacher of the Law of the God of heaven, may ask of you" (Ezra 7:21).

In Sirach 38:24–39:11 (second century B.C.) we find a hymn in praise of the work of the *grammateus* (the "scribe"): he devotes himself to the study of the law of the Most High. While others are involved in practical labor and are occupied with material things, he concentrates on the immaterial. Therefore his place is in the public assembly, and he occupies the judge's seat. Sirach's description is a cross between the image of a Hellenistic philosopher and the memory of a prominent lawyer-statesman such as Daniel.

When the people of Israel lost their national independence, the "royal scribe" evolved into an "authority on religious matters." Although the Levites had traditionally been responsible for providing instruction in the law, it is not clear whether all the teachers of the law were members of the tribe of Levi and perhaps also served frequently as priests. In a letter written by Antiochus III (second century B.C.), we find evidence of a governing body the Jews were permitted to maintain: "the council of the elders and priests and *grammateis* of the temple and the temple singers."[37] Here the "scribes" seem to belong to the administrative stratum of the people and are connected with the temple. Elsewhere Josephus mentions a *grammateus* of Captain Eleazar (around A.D. 62). This "scribe" was apparently a son of the high priest Ananias or Ananus.[38] So at least *some* of the "scribes" came from the priestly tribe of Levi.[39]

It is curious that outside the New Testament there is no direct information concerning these teachers of the law *as a social group* within the Judaism of the time.[40] Therefore it is not impossible that a shift in per-

---

37. Josephus, *Antiquities* 12.3.3 §142.
38. Ibid., 20.9.3 §§208–9.
39. Schwartz ("Scribes and Pharisees, Hypocrites") has even come to the conclusion that all the teachers of the law were *Levites*.
40. A. J. Saldarini, *Pharisees, Scribes, and Sadducees in Palestinian Society* (Edinburgh: Clark, 1989).

spective has taken place within the New Testament—whenever the "legal experts" gather around the controversial teacher Jesus, we can easily get the impression that they were a well-defined *social group*, when as a rule this may not have been the case. The legal experts who served as administrators in the Sanhedrin may well have belonged to a completely different social group (the administrators) than the legal scholars who served as teachers for the public (in the role traditionally filled by the Levites).

Because of their designation as "scribe" or "clerk," these functionaries may well have been primarily regarded as notaries, lawyers, and legal authorities who were entrusted with the drawing up of religiously sound contracts (letters of divorce, title deeds, annual calendars of festivals, etc.). Since the entire economic and social sphere of life was regulated by the law of Moses, the "scribe" would first of all have to have been a specialist in *religious* law, so that competence in the Scriptures and the work of a "scribe" went hand in hand.

Even though we have very little information about the training, social position, and job description of the "teachers of the law," it is nevertheless important to recognize how much value the people in Jesus' day attached to those who could knowledgeably discuss the law of the LORD (Matt. 7:29; 23:2–3) and who could draw up contracts that were religiously sound in form and content. This seems to indicate that the entire population (with the exception of the tax collectors and sinners) was more than ready to accept the ancient national Scriptures of Moses as rule and guide for life.

1.2.6 Herodians

The *Herodians* are mentioned several times in the Gospels. Because the word *Hērōdianoi* does not appear anywhere else, it is not easy to tell whether it refers to friends and relatives of the Herodian family or to a party whose main thrust was the reunification of all of Palestine under a vassal monarch from the Herodian dynasty.

Hoehner discusses this group in detail.[41] He regards them as partisans of the Herodian dynasty and sees a close connection with the Boethusians, a small Saducean group, which then explains why we read of "the yeast of the Sadducees" in Matthew 16:6 and "the yeast of Herod" (some manuscripts read "of the Herodians") in Mark 8:15.[42]

---

41. H. W. Hoehner, *Herod Antipas*, Society for New Testament Studies Monograph Series 17 (Cambridge: Cambridge University Press, 1972), 331–42.

42. He claims that support for this connection between the house of Herod and the Boethus group within the Sadducees is based on the fact that (Herod) Agrippa I appointed a high priest from the Boethus family in the year 38. It is still possible, however, that Jesus issued his warning against both the Sadducees and the partisans of Herod because both had begun working against him.

The Herodians certainly wielded political influence. When the Pharisees wanted to kill Jesus, they contacted this group (Mark 3:6), and when they went to Jesus to ask about paying taxes to Caesar they brought the Herodians with them (Matt. 22:16).

The reason their presence is so important in re-creating the backdrop of the Gospels is that it reveals how large segments of the Jewish population in Palestine (including Galilee, where Jesus lived and spent the greater part of his life) did not live under direct Roman rule during these years but were governed by fellow Jews from the house of Herod. So it is unlikely that the people as a whole were dominated by anti-Roman sentiments and were disappointed when Jesus did not agree with them. Much more important is the relationship of John the Baptist and Jesus to the Herodian dynasty.

1.2.7 Other Groups: Sadducees, Essenes, Chief Priests, Elders

For a balanced picture of the Jewish population in New Testament times, a few other groups must be mentioned. But in the context of this book about the teachings of Christ, it is not necessary to discuss them in great detail because they occupy little or no space in the Gospels. The most interesting question is, in fact, why these groups are not more prominent.

This applies first of all to the *Sadducees*. It is known that as a party they had fewer scruples than the Pharisees in the administration of justice, that they had more followers among the wealthy, and that they rejected the teaching about the resurrection and belief in angels. It is difficult to determine whether this group had been more influenced by the Hellenistic culture than the Pharisees. Actually, we know next to nothing about the Sadducees.[43] Josephus, no admirer of the Sadducees, does not provide a continuous historical picture of this party.[44] There is no proof for the commonly accepted view that they refused to acknowledge any oral tradition and limited themselves to a literal explanation of the Torah.[45] They are not a particularly striking presence in the Gospels because, while their dismissive point of view regarding

---

43. G. G. Porton, "Diversity in Postbiblical Judaism," in *Early Judaism and Its Modern Interpreters*, vol. 2 of *The Bible and Its Modern Interpreters*, ed. R. A. Kraft and G. W. E. Nickelsburg (Philadelphia: Fortress, 1986), 57–80.

44. E. Main, "Les Sadducéens vus par Flavius Josèphe," *Revue biblique* 97 (1990): 161–206.

45. J. Le Moyne, *Les Sadducéens*, Études bibliques (Paris: Gabalda, 1972). A. J. Saldarini, *Pharisees, Scribes, and Sadducees in Palestinian Society* (Edinburgh: Clark, 1989). G. Stemberger, *Pharisäer, Sadduzäer, Essener*, Stuttgarter Bibelstudien 144 (Stuttgart: Katholisches Bibelwerk, 1991).

the "matter of John the Baptist and Jesus" was the same as that of the Pharisees (Matt. 3:7–9; 16:6, 11–12), they were less vocal in their opposition.

When the apostles were being persecuted because of the disturbances their teaching was causing in *Jerusalem*, we see the Sadducees take action twice, together with the priestly class (Acts 4:1; 5:17). Were these Sadducees more concerned about peace in the temple city than about correct doctrine in Galilee? Whatever the case, their differences with the Pharisees were of little importance where the New Testament is concerned, because they formed a united front with this party against the prophet John and Jesus the Christ.

Another group that played a role in the Judaism of those days but is not mentioned at all in the New Testament is the *Essenes*. The Essenes had long been known from the writings of Josephus, Philo, and Pliny the Elder. The discoveries in Qumran suddenly thrust them into the limelight. The Essenes were a type of religious order who lived according to their own rule, a community of men with pacifist tendencies who forswore private property, paid much attention to ceremonies of ritual purification, and followed extensive rules guiding mutual relationships among those who had entered the community.[46]

Is this group perhaps never mentioned in the New Testament because John the Baptist and other disciples of Jesus were originally members of this group? This suggestive question will be discussed in chapter 2 (secs. 2.2.1 and 2.2.3) in connection with the specific connections that have been proposed between the New Testament material and Qumran and the Essenes, especially the extent to which the prophet John and his baptism can be traced back to this movement. Because, as will be shown, these proposed connections cannot be sub-

---

46. For the source material see G. Vermes and M. D. Goodman, eds., *The Essenes: According to the Classical Sources*, Oxford Centre Textbooks 1 (Sheffield: JSOT Press, 1989), and for an extensive description see Schürer, *History of the Jewish People in the Age of Jesus Christ*, rev. ed., 2:555–90. Although the dating of the documents found at Qumran has not been disputed, it is most likely that the bulk of the material was pre-Christian (W. H. Rose, "De 'Leraar der Gerechtigheid': Johannes, Jakobus, of X? De datering van de Dode-Zeerollen en de vroegchristelijke kerk," in *Een sprekend begin: Opstellen aangeboden aan Prof. Drs. H. M. Ohmann*, ed. R. ter Beek et al. [Kampen: Kok, 1993], 186–99). T. S. Beall discusses the similarities and differences between Josephus and the Dead Sea Scrolls regarding the Essenes (*Josephus' Description of the Essenes Illustrated by the Dead Sea Scrolls*, Society for New Testament Studies Monograph Series 58 [Cambridge: Cambridge University Press, 1988]). The work by Laperrousaz is devoted especially to the Essenes of Qumran (E. M. Laperrousaz, *Les Esséniens selon leur témoignage direct*, Religions et Culture [Paris: Desclee, 1982]). García Martínez sees the Qumran sect as the result of a schism within the greater Essene party (F. García Martínez and J. Trebolle Barrera, *The People of the Dead Sea Scrolls: Their Writings, Beliefs, and Practices*, translated from Spanish [Leiden: Brill, 1995]).

stantiated, it seems more likely that the Essenes had relatively little impact on the population and that this is why they are not mentioned in the New Testament (Philo estimates their number at around four thousand).

Josephus wrote extensively about the Essenes because his sympathies lay largely with this "third party." The same is true for Philo, who was personally interested in the lifestyle and philosophy of the Therapeutae, a group related to the Essenes. But Jesus directed his attention toward the people in all the synagogues of Galilee and Judea. There is no indication whatsoever that he was trying to convert people to the specific lifestyle of the Essenes. This does not rule out the possibility that there was agreement between Jesus' teaching and certain elements that *happened* also to be part of Essene teaching (warnings about riches, emphasis on sharing with others, etc.), but these elements are not presented as specifically Essene.

However important our knowledge of this group is for demonstrating that the Jewish world at that time was highly diverse, the Essenes do not qualify as a separate panel in the backdrop of the New Testament stage. So it is understandable that the Essenes, of whom scholars have always been aware through the writings of Josephus and Philo, have never been regarded as important to the study of the New Testament. This small group managed to attract the attention of many New Testament scholars during the second half of the twentieth century mainly due to the findings at Qumran. Because of these findings, the written information about this group (assuming that the Qumran community was Essene) suddenly became an object of attention. (Pixner's hypothesis is striking; he claims that there was even an Essene district in Jerusalem and that Jesus spent his last stay in Bethany in an Essene neighborhood.)[47]

Although the Old Testament seems to indicate that important decisions were made and carried out by the *elders* and the *chief priests* in Jerusalem, we do not get the impression that they determined the spiritual climate during that period. We meet them in the New Testament as one of the groups within the Sanhedrin (Matt. 16:21; Mark 14:53, 55). At decisive moments, the high priest and other members of the high-priestly line (Acts 4:6) appear to take charge of the action against Jesus in Jerusalem (Matt. 26:57; John 11:47, 49, 57), and later against the apostles and their disciples (Acts 5:17–18; 9:1–2). Nevertheless, it is

---

47. B. Pixner, "Das Essener-Quartier in Jerusalem," and "Bethanien bei Jerusalem—eine Essener-Siedlung?" in *Wege des Messias und Stätten der Urkirche: Jesus und das Judenchristentum im Licht neuer archäologischer Erkenntnisse*, ed. R. Riesner (Giessen: Brunnen-Verlag, 1991), 180–207, 208–18.

clear that the elders and chief priests did not constitute an independent religious group. Rather, they provided the people with administrative leadership and bore the responsibility for the highest judicial decisions and for the day-to-day routine in the temple. Their contribution consisted mainly in *maintaining* the spiritual status quo, rather than primarily *determining* it.

McLaren and Goodman agree that the chief priests and elders exercised the sociopolitical leadership during the first century. While McLaren concludes that the position of the Pharisees during that time was therefore marginal,[48] Goodman argues that, on the contrary, the political and social leaders at that time were the ones who occupied a marginal place within their own population.[49] Sanders contends that first-century Judaism as a whole should be described from the vantage point of the priestly class, since the temple service was the focus of the religious praxis of common Judaism,[50] but Hengel has suggested that although Judaism looked like a priestly state *from the outside*, the reality was determined by many other factors.[51] Not least among these factors was the influence of the law-abiding Pharisees, who determined the climate within which the administrators wanted to (or had to) operate.[52] This is apparent from the writings of the New Testament; it was the Pharisees who took action against Jesus in Galilee, and the chief priests in Jerusalem added strength to this action in the form of a trial before the Sanhedrin.

We get the same picture from the writings of Josephus: when Annas the younger, a Sadducee high priest, deviated from a strict interpretation of the law in a trial he was conducting against James, the brother of Jesus, in A.D. 62, the citizens of Jerusalem, who were strict observers of the law, forced him to step down under pressure from Agrippa.[53] Archaeological finds also seem to indicate that the Pharisees were extremely influential among the people, for example with regard to the use of stone jugs wherever ritual purity was important.[54]

48. J. S. McLaren, *Power and Politics in Palestine: The Jews and the Governing of Their Land 100 B.C.–A.D. 70*, JSNTSup 63 (Sheffield: JSOT Press, 1991), 224.

49. M. Goodman, *The Ruling Class of Judaea: The Origins of the Jewish Revolt against Rome A.D. 66–70* (Cambridge: Cambridge University Press, 1987), 46.

50. E. P. Sanders, *Judaism: Practice and Belief*.

51. M. Hengel and R. Deines, "E. P. Sanders' 'Common Judaism,' Jesus and the Pharisees," *Journal of Theological Studies* 46 (1995): 51–67.

52. M. Pelletier, *Les Pharisiens: Histoire d'un parti méconnu* (Paris: Editions de Cerf, 1990), 236–42.

53. Josephus, *Antiquities* 20.9.1 §§199–203.

54. R. Deines, *Jüdische Steingefässe und pharisäische Frömmigkeit: Ein archäologisch-historischer Beitrag zum Verständnis von Joh 2,6 und der jüdischen Reinheitshalacha zur Zeit Jesu*, WUNT 2/52 (Tübingen: Mohr, 1993).

1.3 Jewish Religiosity

Even though we have limited ourselves in the preceding sections to groups that are in any way important to the background of the New Testament, we still find that the Judaism of that period cannot easily be characterized in a few short sentences. There was great diversity. Anyone who takes the trouble to read the works of Josephus will discover that the picture is even more colorful than the preceding pages might suggest.

But is it not possible to find a few points that all Jews had in common and that can be considered typical of *all* groups? Although generalizations are dangerous, we want to hazard an attempt. It is worth the trouble to look at the Judaism of that time *from the outside*. How was it *different* from its non-Jewish surroundings, and what were the *lines of demarcation*?

This allows us to focus our attention on the fact that after the exile the Jews were not the only inhabitants of Palestine. They lived among all kinds of non-Jews, and this made it necessary for them to preserve a clear identity if they were to avoid being absorbed into the other cultures in Palestine. This potential loss of Jewish identity had been a real threat on several occasions, such as the time of Nehemiah, who strongly opposed cooperating with the Samaritans in the fifth century B.C., and the time of the Maccabean revolt, which was primarily a religious war against the policies of cultural and religious synthesis of the Syrians and the Hellenized high priests in the second century B.C.

During the New Testament period, the Jews living in the region of the former twelve tribes had to deal mainly with the gentile population of the Hellenistic cities on Palestinian soil and with the Samaritans who occupied the region between Judea and Galilee.

The Jewish people differed from the Greeks in that they possessed ancient religious documents, the Holy Scriptures. They distinguished themselves from the Samaritans by the central place the temple in Jerusalem occupied in their lives. These two focal points unified all Jews and created a sense of future-oriented expectation among the people.

In this section we will, for the sake of clarity, separately address these three interrelated aspects, which concern the people's past, present, and future: (1) reverence for the ancient Scriptures; (2) the central position of the temple in Jerusalem; (3) the expectation of what was to come.

1.3.1 Reverence for the Ancient Scriptures

The centrality of Israel's ancient holy books (the books of Moses, the Prophets, and the Writings) is evident in the presence of teachers of the law and of synagogues.

The fact that lawyers and teachers in Israelite society were actually experts in the law of Moses and the customs of the fathers reveals the extent to which all social intercourse stood under the authority of the ancient Scriptures (see sec. 1.2.5). This is borne out by the readings from the books of Moses on every Sabbath in every synagogue in the world (Acts 15:21). Regardless of how much is unclear about the origin and spread of synagogues, we do know that by the time of the New Testament they had been built in every city and village where there was a sufficient number of Jews. When Jesus wanted to reach the *people*, he had only to make a tour of *their synagogues*. And the same was true for Paul as he traveled through the Diaspora. These synagogues were places for gathering and celebration, but first and foremost they were buildings where the scrolls containing the Law and the Prophets were kept and opened (Acts 13:14–15).

The Scriptures became the Magna Carta of Israel. Whereas King Jehoiakim had destroyed the scroll of Jeremiah by burning it, a few centuries later the Maccabean resistance fighters risked their lives when the Torah scrolls were damaged by the Syrians.

There was a danger that in later centuries this central position of the law would be assessed incorrectly. After the Protestant Reformation, much attention was given to the place of the law in the justification of sinners. But it is an anachronism to assume that the Jews of Jesus' time esteemed the law so highly because they regarded it as a means of justification. Their way of respecting these ancient writings can best be seen in a few first-century documents in which Jews try to explain to others what God's laws mean to them.

Josephus wrote about it to the Gentile Apion. And Philo, who lived in the city of Alexandria, where Jews and Greeks formed the two most important population groups, tried within the context of Greek culture to explain the riches the Jews possess in their Mosaic laws.

In reading these very different documents, one is struck by the fact that the law of Moses is clearly not discussed in the context of justification. Instead, the law is presented as the source of ancient wisdom, the document whose age surpasses all gentile writings and that opens the door to real virtue. The law introduces us to the *true* God, the Creator. The Torah liberates from all idolatry and nurtures charity. Whereas all nations have been misled, Israel is the caretaker, on behalf of the world, of the truth found in the Holy Scriptures. The Jews thus are not a group of strange people with strange customs, as many think; on the contrary, they have the message of the true God for the entire world. They are not out to harm non-Jews—they are interested only in *benefiting* them. Thus Israel is the light of the nations, thanks to the law. In Romans 2:17–20 Paul puts it this way:

Now you, if you call yourself a Jew; if you rely on the law and brag about your relationship to God; if you know his will and approve of what is superior because you are instructed by the law; if you are convinced that you are a guide for the blind, a light for those who are in the dark, an instructor of the foolish, a teacher of infants, because you have in the law the embodiment of knowledge and truth . . .

1.3.2 The Centrality of the Temple in Jerusalem

Although ever since Sinai, Israel had a dwelling place for the LORD in its midst, there were periods when this dwelling place was nowhere near the center of people's lives. During the time before the monarchy, the tabernacle stood in ruins for a lengthy period and the ark had been taken away or stored somewhere. The first temple, planned by David and built by Solomon, underwent periods under the later kings when its interior and the sacrificial rites were badly neglected or modernized according to heathen practices; there even were times when the doors remained locked.

After the return of a number of Jews from exile we see, not a restoration of national autonomy, but permission to form a temple nation within the Persian, and later the Ptolemaic, empire. Events were guided in such a way that after the exile attention had to be *concentrated* on the temple and the sacrificial rites. As a result, at the beginning of our era, the temple had more or less become the central "palace" for the believing population—the dwelling place of their invisible king! Herod the Great understood this all too well when (despite many problems with the priests) he insisted on such a tremendous renovation and expansion of the second temple that the result was in effect a completely new building. The fact that this renovated temple was regarded as one of the wonders of the world and a tourist attraction for people from many countries contributed in no small measure to the fact that all Israel regarded this place as the center of their own religion.[55]

All Jews throughout the world paid an annual temple *didrachma* (temple tax). Many people tried to attend the feasts. The law proceeded from the temple; this was where the teachers of the law were trained and where the annual calendar of feasts was drawn up.

It was obvious to every visitor that this was the beating heart of Judaism. A multilingual sign at the entrance gate that opened onto the innermost forecourt of the temple made clear that every non-Jew who dared to enter would immediately be put to death.[56] The difference be-

---

55. For a broad description of the temple cult see E. P. Sanders, *Judaism: Practice and Belief,* 47–189.

56. See van Bruggen, *Christ on Earth,* sec. 14.6.4.

tween non-Jew and Jew was visible at this dividing wall. Jews and proselytes were allowed to approach the true, faceless God, but Gentiles
had to stay outside. Only Israel was the nation of the true God, adopted
by him!

So it is understandable that the plans of Gaius Caesar (Caligula) to
erect a statue in this temple threw all of Judaism into the greatest turmoil around the year A.D. 40. Philo, in *Embassy to Gaius* (esp. 36–41
§§276–329), makes this very clear: anyone who touches the temple of
the true God attacks the very heart of the Jewish people. Better to die
than to allow such a sacrilege!

It is no accident that Jesus' ministry in Jerusalem began with a sign
in the temple (John 2:13–25) and ended with a demonstrative action in
the same temple area (Mark 11:15ff.). And within the highly pluralistic
Judaism that permitted all sorts of teachings, the greatest possible commotion ensued whenever the temple was maligned or appeared to have
been desecrated (Mark 14:58; Acts 6:13; 21:28).

The temple in Jerusalem set the Jews apart from the Samaritans,
whose traditional temple site had been on Mount Gerizim, until it was
destroyed by the Jews in 128 B.C. Since then, however, the Samaritans
stubbornly refused to conform to the worship in Jerusalem (John 4:20).
Because the Samaritans shared both their tradition and the Torah with
the Jews, they can in a sense be called an Israelite sect,[57] and the bitter-
ness between the Jews and the Samaritans was considerable. Jesus was
never accused of wanting to be a "Greek," but it was suggested that he
was a Samaritan sympathizer (John 8:48), a suggestion that was made
just when he called into question the Jewish identity as "Abraham's descendants": the temple in Jerusalem showed that *the Jews* were the true
descendants, not the Samaritans!

1.3.3 Hope for the Future

A people who possess the truth in the law and access to God in the
temple have expectations of the future. Josephus writes that living according to the law of God does not reward one with silver or gold; sometimes it even costs an individual his or her life. But those who live this
way expect that God will give them *a better life.*[58] The prophets also gave
every reason to expect some kind of future.

But what form did those expectations take? Did many people expect
the restoration of an earthly, Jewish kingdom ruled by Davidic kings?
Did they expect a messiah? In the first section of this chapter we noted

---

57. J. D. Purvis, "The Samaritans and Judaism," in *Early Judaism and Its Modern Interpreters*, 81–98.

58. Josephus, *Against Apion* 2.30 §218.

that we often work from a rather simplistic premise: the Jews all longed for a messiah who would come to liberate them from the Romans.

One could devote an entire study to the future expectations of the Jews at the beginning of that era.[59] Here we must clearly distinguish two separate issues. First, was there a *clear* and *uniform* concept of the expected future, including a well-defined idea of a coming redeemer? Second, was that future expectation something that *dominated* all of life?

1.3.3.1 EXPECTATION AND VARIATION

The expectation of a coming final judgment, the resurrection of the righteous, and a new dispensation (the "world to come") was nearly universal. We encounter these notions in 2 Maccabees, and they are part of the beliefs of the Pharisees, among others. From the fact that the Sadducees rejected the resurrection of the righteous, however, we conclude that there was not total agreement on this point.

There was as little uniformity in the concept of this future and how this future would be reached as there is in modern, Christian eschatological concepts such as the resurrection of the body and the new earth. In the so-called apocalyptic writings we find widely divergent presentations of the ultimate future, and in all likelihood we should not regard these as competing eschatological dogmas but as concepts that can stand side by side because of their unifying center in the Old Testament promises.

This end-time expectation also included the expectation of a coming figure. Apart from any specific names or concepts, it cannot be denied that a coming redeemer was part of the common Jewish expectations for the future.

But even here we see all sorts of variation in specifics. There is no uniform, sharply defined picture (the people at Qumran may even have expected *two* messiahs). That the Messiah will deprive Israel's enemies of their power does not mean, however, that the concept of the Messiah embodies an earthly kind of liberation ideal projected onto the future. It is striking that the various rebel leaders are not called *Messiah*. This confirms that God's anointed is a figure belonging to God's future—not a political but an eschatological figure. The horizontal time line of the Jewish people will be intersected by a redeemer, anointed by God, who enters history from the dawning of the end time—but the people's own political and social struggles will not lead to the emergence of a messiah who will lead them into the future. At most, the

---

59. G. S. Oegema, *De messiaanse verwachtingen ten tijde van Jezus: Een inleiding in de messiaanse verwachtingen en bewegingen gedurende de hellenistisch-romeinse tijd* (Baarn: Ten Have, 1991).

struggles will result in good generals, liberating leaders, and reigning kings.[60]

1.3.3.2 DOMINANT OR DORMANT?

Generally speaking, eschatological expectations are not a dominant theme in the works of Josephus and Philo. They dominate the apocalyptic literature, but it is questionable whether this necessarily implies the existence of a *separate* apocalyptic trend within Judaism. It is also possible that this *aspect* of the Jewish faith did not play a major role in daily life. Similarly, there are many Christian groups who pay much attention to theoretical chiliastic speculations but who do not allow these ideas to control their daily lives.

The historical books about Judaism during the New Testament era do not suggest a climate of great unrest. The apocalyptic writings show that there were expectations among the people of a future ushered in by God and of a world liberator from the house of David, anointed by God.

1.4 The Stage Set as Depicted in the Gospels

Thus the long-accepted picture of a legalistic, nationalistic, and political-messianic Judaism, although it continues to exercise strong influence (sec. 1.1.1), not only begins to fade (sec. 1.1.2) but can no longer be defended in the face of the facts (secs. 1.2 and 1.3). There are no clear traces of a religious process of deformation that is supposed to have led to the perverted religion of a formal and casuistic Judaism. Nor can we say that the lives of the people were dominated by fierce nationalism. There is no evidence of an earthly, anti-Roman messianic expectation.

Yet during the time of Jesus' ministry on earth, there clearly appears to be a heightened expectation among the people of a coming figure (a messiah). We also see a religious clash between Jesus and the leaders. How is this possible?

1.4.1 Distortion?

In the twentieth century, many studies have appeared that assume that the New Testament actually modified or "colorized" the reality of Jesus' time from the perspective of later developments. In the Gospels, so the argument goes, later Christians, with obscured vision, looked back at the Jewish world of the synagogue, which by that time had become their enemy. This explanation is applied to the picture of the

---

60. More detailed descriptions of the expectation regarding a future redeemer can be found in chap. 5 (see sec. 5.2: "David's Son and Lord"; and sec. 5.3.3: "Messianic Expectations in Judaism").

Pharisees, for example, which is said to be far too negative,[61] and to John the Baptist, a prophet of repentance from the circle of the Essenes, who is said to have been recast as a forerunner and witness of Jesus Christ.[62] Teachers of the law are said to have been distorted in the light of a later Christianity that had done away with the law. The title "Son of Man" was wrenched from its former context and made the equivalent of the title "Christ," while both titles would thereafter be revalued on the basis of the Hellenistic reverence for the Lord who is present in the cult.[63]

It is a fact that the Gospels as religious documents are not impartial, but this does not ipso facto rule out the possibility that they provide us with objective information about their own time and Jesus' opponents. An exegesis of the texts and a comparison with the extrabiblical data will show us whether and to what extent any distortion has taken place.

That this distortion is now often accepted a priori is the result of the view, dominant for more than a century, of the literary development of the Gospels. If these descriptions of Jesus' life were a result of the later editing of secondary and primary traditional material by third parties, as many scholars today believe, then the real facts are indeed obscured in the mists of these later developments of the tradition.

We cannot enter into a detailed discussion of the development of the Gospels here.[64] However, sufficient support can be found in the actual tradition of the first centuries for accepting the Gospels as primary documents of eyewitnesses such as Matthew and John, or as an almost stenographic report of the preaching of Peter (Mark), while Luke's purpose, according to his prologue, is to incorporate historically verified facts into his Gospel (in the Book of Acts he appears to have been an eyewitness to part of the history he wrote about).[65] Instead of putting the New Testament on trial while depriving it of its right to speak for itself

61. See, among others, J. H. A. van Tilborg, "The Jewish Leaders in Matthew" (doctoral thesis, University of Nijmegen, 1972).

62. G. Lindeskog, "Johannes der Täufer: Einige Randbemerkungen zum heutigen Stand der Forschung," *Annual of the Swedish Theological Institute* 12 (1983): 55–83.

63. W. Bousset, *Kyrios Christos: A History of the Belief in Christ from the Beginnings of Christianity to Irenaeus*, translated from German (1913) (Nashville: Abingdon, 1970). R. Bultmann, *Theology of the New Testament*, trans. K. Grobel (New York: Scribner, 1951–55). For a broader discussion, see sec. 4.2.2.

64. For a more detailed discussion, see van Bruggen, *Christ on Earth*, secs. 1.1–1.3.

65. For a more detailed discussion, see the introductory sections of the Gospel commentaries in Commentaar op het Nieuwe Testament, 3d series: J. van Bruggen, *Matteüs: Het evangelie voor Israël*, 2d ed. (Kampen: Kok, 1994); idem, *Marcus: Het evangelie volgens Petrus*, 2d ed. (Kampen: Kok, 1992); idem, *Lucas: Het evangelie als voorgeschiedenis* (Kampen: Kok, 1993); and P. H. R. van Houwelingen, *Johannes: Het evangelie van het Woord* (Kampen: Kok, 1997).

in our search to discover what the Jews of that time thought and believed, we should give the Gospels a place in the witness stand, beside the rabbinical writings and the pseudepigrapha. These documents should be considered key witnesses, because they are closer in time to the events they describe than any other source. Granted that the New Testament was not written primarily as a source of information about early-first-century Judaism, it still contains so much firsthand direct and indirect information that it can legitimately be called as a key witness.

1.4.2 Connection

After careful analysis, focusing primarily on the nonconfrontational passages, the information in the New Testament appears to confirm or supplement information from other sources.

1.4.2.1 NATIONALISTIC RELIGION?

We find confirmation in the Gospels that there is no trace of outspoken nationalism either among the crowds or among their leaders. We *do* find a question as to whether it is lawful to pay taxes to Caesar, but that was a trap set to make it possible to hand Jesus over to the Romans (Luke 20:23). It is striking that the questioners were not for a moment afraid of enthusiastic popular support if Jesus were to repudiate the tax. Apparently the mood was not explosively nationalistic in those days!

And when the crowds wanted to make Jesus king (John 6:15), it was not in the context of an insurrection against the Romans but rather in the framework of a revolt against Herod Antipas, who had killed John the Baptist and from whose territory most of the people came. It was for a good reason that the Pharisees, in their actions against Jesus, more than once allied themselves with the *Herodians* (Mark 3:6; Matt. 22:16). But more important is the fact that people did not begin by being *against* an existing king or emperor; rather, after the miracle of the loaves and fishes they wanted to somehow express their belief that Jesus was really the Prophet who was to come into the world, so that he had an inherent right to royal honor (John 6:14).

Even in his contacts with the tax collectors, it appears that Jesus did not evoke irritation by associating with friends of the *Romans* but rather by eating with people whose influential position was not a good example of a pure life lived according to the law. The same naturally holds true for his contacts with "sinners."

In addition, when Jesus' disciples argue with him, it is not based on nationalism (as if they expected that he was about to establish an anti-Roman, earthly empire), but on their lack of comprehension about the path of suffering leading to the kingdom of heaven.

If the nationalistic model had not been introduced into the interpretation of the New Testament *from the outside* and read into the texts, it would never have been deduced from the Gospels alone!

1.4.2.2 Legalistic Pharisees?

Is the question of legalism any different? Is not their perceived legalistic attitude the great black mark against the Pharisees in the New Testament?

It does seem to be the case. But if we focus on the nonconfrontational parts of the Gospels, we actually see a confirmation of the same positive picture of the Pharisees that is found in extrabiblical sources. There is indeed a profound conflict between the Pharisees and Jesus, but it is not based on their teachings or precepts.[66]

The line between Jesus and the Pharisees is drawn when a man from Nazareth claims to be God's Son. This is a new situation that generates its own, unique kind of conflict. But the Pharisees' role in this conflict is that of guardians of the law, and their actions are directed against alleged blasphemy (for a more detailed discussion, see appendix 1, on the Pharisees).

1.4.2.3 Earthly Expectations?

The Gospels show that there were *general* expectations as to what would happen in the future. There was the expectation of an *Anointed* of God, of *the* Son of David, of the arrival of *the* prophet. And before the arrival of this end-time figure, Elijah would come.[67]

---

66. For a broader discussion, see van Bruggen, *Matteüs*.

67. Magi visiting Jerusalem ask about the "one who has been born king of the Jews." Herod then asks the teachers of the law where "the Anointed" would be born, and they tell him Bethlehem, on the basis of Micah 5 (Matt. 2:2–4). The angel who appeared to the shepherds could assume that they understood what he was talking about when he announced the coming of "the Anointed, the Lord" in the town of David (Luke 2:11). Simeon knows what is meant when he is promised that he will not die before seeing the Anointed of the Lord (Luke 2:26). When John the Baptist begins his ministry, the people wonder if he is the Christ (Luke 3:15), and a commission of inquiry from Jerusalem asks if he is Elijah or the prophet (John 1:21). John answers that he is neither (John 1:24). Apparently it was considered possible that the prophet and the Christ would be two separate people (John the Baptist himself considers the possibility that another was to be expected in addition to Jesus the Christ; Matt. 11:2–3). When the people talk about Jesus, we find that they had an expectation of an "Anointed One" prior to his coming (John 7:26–27, 31, 42). Even the Samaritan woman knows that an "Anointed One" is to come: "He will explain everything to us" (John 4:25, 29). The leaders prohibit anyone from acknowledging Jesus as "the Anointed" (John 9:22), and before the Sanhedrin they ask him if he sees himself as "the Anointed One, the Son of God" (Matt. 26:63). This title implies in any case a kingship over the Jews (Matt. 27:11, 29, 37; Luke 23:2). It relates to *the* Son of David (Matt. 22:42; 12:23; 21:9). The people identify Jesus as *the* prophet who was to come (Matt. 21:11; John 6:14–15), even though, according to the pattern of their expectations, that identification was in principle not the only possible one (John 7:40–41).

But nowhere is this expectation linked with earthly political aspirations. The Anointed One is the Son of God. He ushers in the end times and he will remain forever (John 12:34). He gives new revelation (in his role as prophet), ushers in David's kingdom of peace (as king of the Jews), and brings consolation and redemption to Israel (Luke 2:25, 38). He is the Savior of the world (John 4:42). The title "Son of David" does not have a political ring; it is the cry of the needy (the blind, etc.). It does not make the crowds in Jerusalem run for their weapons; rather, it makes them grab the palm branches that they had been saving in their homes for the coming Feast of Tabernacles (John 12:12–15). In short, the messianic expectation is colored by the promises and the prophecies (John 1:45, 49)—not by the short-term options of an anti-Roman mentality.

1.4.3 New Elements

But even if there is in principle no conflict between the image of first-century Judaism outside the New Testament and that inside the New Testament, this should not blind us to some remarkable phenomena in the New Testament that have no parallel in extrabiblical sources. This applies to two things in particular: the heightened state of preparedness for God's future and the major influence of a prophetic revival.

1.4.3.1 REVITALIZED EXPECTATIONS

The existing general expectations concerning the future were strongly *intensified* during the period of Jesus' life. When the Magi came to Jerusalem, Herod's consulting the teachers of the law about the birthplace of the Christ seemed like theological archival work. And people like Simeon, Anna, and all who expected "redemption" for Jerusalem (Luke 2:38) seemed to be a relatively small group.

But later, when Jesus began his ministry in Palestine, the *entire nation* began actively to wonder whether the old future expectations were *now* being fulfilled through this man as the Christ (John 7:26). They were asking whether the Son of David had come (Matt. 12:23). The dormant, generalized expectations suddenly came alive.

1.4.3.2 A PROPHETIC REVIVAL

The groundwork for all this had been laid by the overpowering influence of a new prophet, John the Baptist. It is impossible to get a proper perspective on the period of the Gospels without including this historical figure who was the gateway to Jesus' ministry.

For this reason, we devote the next chapter to the question of what was so extraordinary about the years A.D. 27–33. At that time, a short-lived but extremely important historical phenomenon took place. Because it was so short, there is little reverberation in later, more distant historical sources. But because of its intensity, its impact during the years of Jesus' ministry is significant. When the curtain rises around the year 30, the stage appears to be illuminated by a striking new light source. The change in atmosphere during the years that follow is the result of the work of the greatest of all prophets: John the Baptist.

2

The Stage Lighting: John the Baptist

This chapter deals with the person and the preaching of John the Baptist. For the time around the year A.D. 30, we must supplement our picture of the general Jewish stage set discussed in the preceding chapter with a sketch of the sudden changes brought about during those years by the imposing prophet John the Baptist. At precisely the time when Jesus began his ministry in Israel, the Jewish stage was affected by very special lighting. A description of the historical context of Jesus' ministry would be woefully inadequate if the focus were limited to Judaism in general without paying attention to the exceptional situation in which this Judaism found itself for a time when the people fell under the Baptist's spell.

2.1 John's Influence

2.1.1 Under the Prophet's Spell

From the desert, John addressed the entire nation. It is remarkable how rapidly this message from the wilderness got a firm hold on the people. John's voice reaches the farthest corners of the land, and all strata of society. He moves everyone, no matter who they are. The people are baptized in large numbers for the repentance of sins. The leaders of the people, who refuse baptism, nevertheless travel to the wilderness to listen and observe. A fact-finding commission consisting of priests and Levites is sent from the temple to report on the ministry of this priest's son. His blunt preaching, without respect of persons, even throws the court of Herod Antipas into a state of commotion. When the king finally has John put in prison, he continues to consult John with deepest respect. Suddenly the entire nation, from border to border and from the most exalted to the most humble, stands in the spotlight of this man from the desert.[1]

---

1. See Matt. 3:1–2, 5–7 (Mark 1:4–5; Luke 3:3, 7, 10–15; John 1:19–28; 3:23; Acts 13:24); 11:7–9 (Luke 7:24–26, 29); 14:3–5 (Mark 6:17–20; Luke 3:18–20).

48

Even after John is beheaded through Herodias's intrigues, the memory of his person and his ministry continues to have a hold on the people. They hold him in high esteem. The leaders dare not say anything against the Baptist—John is unassailable as a prophet in Israel. And when a few years later Herod suffers a defeat in the battle against Aretas, the father of his former wife whom he had sent away in favor of Herodias, the people immediately draw a connection with the murder of John. God is avenging the blood of his prophet![2]

Because the people remained under the spell of his preaching and baptism after his death, we see that John's influence even extended beyond the borders of Palestine. Decades later, Paul encounters some of the Baptist's disciples in the city of Ephesus (Acts 19:1–5). And Apollos, from Alexandria in Egypt, appears to be familiar with the baptism of John; he used it as the basis for his preaching in Ephesus about Jesus (Acts 18:24–25). This incidental information tells us that even people far away in the Diaspora had come (and remained) under the spell of John the Baptist.

In later periods we come across several baptismal sects, smaller groups scattered here and there. This could be used as an argument against John's ministry as initially involving *the whole nation*. However, we must remember that, just as in Ephesus, the traces left by John were erased by the gospel of Jesus (see next section). But whatever traces of John remain prove that the Baptist's impact was such that people here and there continued to attach more value to this great prophet than to his even greater successor.[3]

2.1.2 A Prophetic Eclipse

In the reconstruction of the historical context for Jesus' ministry, a curious phenomenon now takes place: the most influential factor of

2. See Matt. 21:26, 32; Mark 11:32; Luke 20:6. See also Josephus, *Antiquities* 18.5.2 §§116–19 (discussed in J. van Bruggen, *Christ on Earth: The Gospel Narratives as History* [Grand Rapids: Baker, 1998], sec. 6.5). For Josephus on John, see also J. Ernst, *Johannes der Täufer: Interpretation—Geschichte—Wirkungsgeschichte* (Berlin: de Gruyter, 1989), 253–63; R. L. Webb, *John the Baptizer and Prophet: A Socio-Historical Study*, JSNTSup 62 (Sheffield: JSOT Press, 1991), 31–45; J. P. Meier, "John the Baptist in Josephus: Philology and Exegesis," *Journal of Biblical Literature* 111 (1992): 225–37; and for Josephus on the *baptism* of John, see R. Schütz, *Johannes der Täufer*, Abhandlungen zur Theologie des Alten und Neuen Testaments 50 (Zürich: Zwingli, 1967), 13–27 (in confrontation with Schlatter).
3. For a discussion of the baptismal sects, see Ernst, *Johannes der Täufer*, 349–84. In an extensive study, Backhaus has shown that there are no traces of a separate community founded by John beside or in opposition to that of Jesus and his disciples (modern exegesis incorrectly reads many parts of the Gospels as implicit controversies with such a Johannine community). The later baptismal sects did make John the Baptist their honored prophet, but he was not their founder. K. Backhaus, *Die "Jüngerkreise" des Täufers Johannes: Eine Studie zu den religionsgeschichtlichen Ursprüngen des Christentums*, Paderborner theologische Studien 19 (Paderborn: Schoeningh, 1991).

that time more or less disappears from view after the fact. During Jesus' life on earth, John the Baptist was popularly regarded as a more authoritative figure than Jesus (even after John was beheaded). The man from Nazareth stood in the shadow of the prophet from the desert. After Pentecost, however, many begin to believe in Jesus. He grows in esteem, and as he moves into the foreground, John's importance begins to fade in a kind of prophetic eclipse. Even though this is entirely in line with John's preaching ("He must increase, but I must decrease"), it nevertheless opens the door to a distortion of the historical perspective. Now that Christ is shining high in the heavens as the risen sun of righteousness, the light of the pale moon seems to be of limited significance. But when Jesus walked the earth in the night of his humiliation, the scene was brightly lit by the full moon: John the Baptist!

Thus when reading the Gospels from a historical perspective, we must try to enter into this time of Jesus' humiliation, the time of his assuming "the very nature of a servant." This was when John was still more and Jesus less, a period in which the leaders dared to slander Jesus before the crowds but dared not say a single word against John. In addition, the people first judged Jesus by measuring him against the Baptist's message, while Jesus presented himself as the one announced by this great and authoritative prophet. Many of Jesus' statements and many of the terms he uses are, as we will see in the following chapters, related to the message of the Baptist.

Early in Jesus' ministry it becomes evident that he, through his disciples, is baptizing more people than John himself (John 3:22, 26; 4:1–2). There is clearly a connection between him and John—baptism—but he is becoming the greater. When Jesus withdraws to Galilee (John 4:3) after John's arrest (Matt. 4:12–17) and continues his ministry without baptizing, people do not regard him as a quickly rising *colleague* of John, but as the person who was to come *after John*. Because of John's imprisonment and death, the great prophet is kept in reverent memory, and Jesus becomes the center of attention—but he also becomes an increasingly controversial figure.

We see just how dominant the memory of the Baptist continued to be when some people understand Jesus to be *the resurrected John* (Mark 6:14; Luke 9:7; Matt. 16:14).

Jesus himself appealed to the authoritative witness of the great prophet when speaking to the crowds (John 5:33–35), and the people were inclined to believe him on the basis of *John's words* (John 10:41).

The Gospels focus most of their attention on Jesus and put him in the foreground. Yet what they tell us about John the Baptist enables us to realize that the perspective during Jesus' years on earth was different than it would be after Pentecost.

2.1.3 Beheaded by the Evangelists?

Since the beginning of the twentieth century, a great deal of attention has been paid to the significance of John the Baptist.[4] And in the second half of this century, a series of studies on the Baptist have emerged.[5] The question whether John was not at least as important as Jesus appears with increasing frequency in these works. Few scholars go as far as Bernoulli, who claims that "Christianity, as an historic force, is more conceivable without Jesus than without John the Baptist."[6] Even so, there is a tendency to view John as the determining background factor for Jesus, or as his equal. Jesus then is the *disciple* and John the master.

Why does this prophet appear to be a head shorter than Jesus in the Gospels? Because, so the explanation goes, the Evangelists gradually *depicted* John as smaller to fit him into their expanded perspective of the message about Jesus. The Christology that developed later is supposed to have absorbed and incorporated the original prophetic movement.[7] So the great John was, figuratively speaking, actually made a head shorter by the Evangelists of Jesus!

According to Böcher, John and Jesus originally were equal partners (comparable to pairs of rabbis), as an Elijah and a Moses figure respectively.[8] The two witnesses in the streets of the great city in Revelation 11 then are a reminder of this earliest stage. According to Becker, Jesus received his spiritual formation as a disciple of his master, the prophet John. But he further developed John's preaching about judgment by placing the kingdom of heaven in the center as a present eschatological means of escape.[9] Badtke also is of the opinion that Jesus was initially

---

4. A. Schlatter, *Johannes der Täufer*, ed. W. Michaelis (Basel: Reinhardt, 1956; orig. manuscript 1880); M. Dibelius, *Die urchristliche Überlieferung von Johannes dem Täufer*, FRLANT 15 (Göttingen: Vandenhoeck & Ruprecht, 1911); E. Lohmeyer, *Das Urchristentum*, Buch 1, *Johannes der Täufer* (Göttingen: Vandenhoeck & Ruprecht, 1932).

5. C. H. Kraeling, *John the Baptist* (New York: Scribner, 1951); Schütz, *Johannes der Täufer*; J. Becker, *Johannes der Täufer und Jesus von Nazareth*, Biblische Studien 63 (Neukirchen: Neukirchener Verlag, 1972); W. Wink, *John the Baptist in the Gospel Tradition*, Society for New Testament Studies Monograph Series 7 (Cambridge: Cambridge University Press, 1968); Ernst, *Johannes der Täufer*; Webb, *John the Baptizer and Prophet*. For an overview, see also R. L. Webb, "John the Baptist and His Relationship to Jesus," in *Studying the Historical Jesus: Evaluations of the State of Current Research*, New Testament Tools and Studies 19, ed. B. Chilton and C. A. Evans (Leiden: Brill, 1994), 179–229.

6. C. A. Bernouilli, *Johannes der Täufer und die Urgemeinde* (Leipzig: Neue Geist, 1918).

7. G. Lindeskog, "Johannes der Täufer: Einige Randbemerkungen zum heutigen Stand der Forschung," *Annual of the Swedish Theological Institute* 12 (1983): 55–83.

8. O. Böcher, "Johannes der Täufer in der neutestamentlichen Überlieferung," in *Rechtfertigung, Realismus, Universalismus in biblischer Sicht*, ed. G. Müller (Darmstadt: Wissenschaftlicher Buchgesellschaft, 1978), 45–68.

9. Becker, *Johannes der Täufer und Jesus von Nazareth*.

a *disciple* of the Baptist. He claims that the expression "who comes after me" actually meant "who is following me as a disciple."[10] It is then true that John himself later referred to this disciple, Jesus, as the one who was to come, but the other disciples continued to harbor a measure of annoyance against such one-sided attention for this one member of their circle. Wink regards John the Baptist as the beginning of the gospel: through John's teaching Jesus became aware of the nearness of the kingdom, and through John's baptism he learned about his own relationship to this coming of the kingdom.[11] Backhaus offers an extensive discussion (and refutation) of the idea that Jesus was a disciple of John the Baptist.[12]

The problem with all these ideas is that the source material is not being taken seriously. Although the Gospels present themselves as coherent historical reports, they are read as unrelated theologies in historical disguise, from which one can deduce, with a great deal of difficulty and little certainty, a few paltry historical facts.[13] The historical information about the announcement of John's birth by the angel Gabriel and about the prophetic words of his father Zechariah after his birth (Luke 1) are often no longer regarded as the point of departure. Ernst's approach in his highly detailed treatment of the data from the Gospels is typical. He begins by discussing how John the Baptist was successively *viewed* by the *redactor* of Mark, by the hypothetically reconstructed Logia source, and by the *redactor* of Luke. Then follows a separate chapter on "John the Baptist in the Lucan birth story." The foundational beginning of Luke's historical work (Luke 1–2) is thus cut off from the rest of the book and is lined up with other documents that offer us a "picture of John." Ernst even has a chapter titled "The Image of the Baptist in Acts."[14]

But the four Gospels and Acts were not written to rewrite history for the sake of providing a quasi-historical basis for later views; rather, they were written to record the past as it had been *remembered*. Nowhere do the Evangelists offer their own commentary on the Baptist, which would indeed allow us to speak of their "picture of John." Furthermore, their information about John the Baptist is limited because the main character in their writings is Jesus. In addition, Jesus' statements about John the

10. W. B. Badtke, "Was Jesus a Disciple of John?" *Evangelical Quarterly* 62 (1990): 195–204.

11. Wink, *John the Baptist in the Gospel Tradition*.

12. Backhaus, *Die "Jüngerkreise des Täufers Johannes."*

13. E. F. Lupieri, "John the Baptist in New Testament Traditions and History," in *Aufstieg und Niedergang der römischen Welt*, part 2, *Principat*, vol. 26, *Religion* (Berlin: de Gruyter, 1992), 1:430–61.

14. Ernst, *Johannes der Täufer*.

Baptist are often made in passing. So it is methodologically misleading to deduce from the presence or absence of such a statement in a given Gospel that the Evangelist intentionally included, omitted, or suppressed it.

The Evangelists cannot be made accountable for deliberately minimizing John's role, but modern Gospel critics *can* be held accountable for reducing the stature of the Evangelists as narrators of events and as writers of coherent, integral texts. In fact, it argues in their favor that they refused to smooth over or suppress the profound significance of John the Baptist, and that they honestly show how the people felt free to disagree about Jesus while they were united in their respect for the prophet John. If the Evangelists had been involved in a process of historical *revisionism,* in which John had to be reworked to fit into the theology of Christ, they certainly did an awkward, sloppy job.

The apostles themselves saw that Jesus was *greater* than John, yet they do not omit their memories of John. He was the greatest prophet who ever lived! Reverence for God's Son did not make the Evangelists blind to the importance of this witness, who decreased as Jesus increased, but who was nevertheless always so great that he dominates the beginning of the Gospels!

2.2 John's Ministry and Preaching

2.2.1 A Voice in the Wilderness

John came to the people as a desert prophet. He lived in the wilderness "until he appeared publicly to Israel" (Luke 1:80). There, in the desert, the Word of God came to him (Luke 3:2). And when he became a preacher he did not leave this environment but let the people *come to him* in the wilderness to hear him (Matt. 3:1, 5). The practice of baptizing in the Jordan took him to "the country around the Jordan" (Luke 3:3), but although the people were baptized in the river, they still regarded John as the herald from the desert, so much so that Mark can simply say, "And so John came, baptizing in the desert region" (Mark 1:4).

The way John presents himself is unique. There were rebel leaders or prophets who were well known at the time who *took the people with them* into the desert in order to prepare them for further action (compare Acts 21:38), but this is a prophet who *lives* in the wilderness and makes no effort to look for people in their towns or to take them from their houses. Even John's clothing and food support this image: he lives like a Bedouin.[15]

---

15. See J. van Bruggen, *Marcus: Het evangelie volgens Petrus,* 2d ed., Commentaar op het Nieuwe Testament, 3d series (Kampen: Kok, 1992), on Mark 1:6.

The Essenes of Qumran also lived in the desert (according to the most commonly accepted interpretation of the ruins that have been found there), as did hermits such as Bannus, with whom Josephus went on a three-year retreat in the middle of the first century. Should we view John the Baptist against this background?[16] After the discoveries in Qumran, John has more than once been described as a sympathizer[17] or disciple[18] of the Essenes, but this hypothesis is not generally accepted. The differences are too significant:[19]

1. John's clothing and food cannot be understood in terms of what we know about the Essenes.[20] According to Davies, John had to rely on natural products such as honey and locusts in the desert because outside the "monastery" he could not maintain the strict dietary laws of the Essenes.[21] But nowhere in the Gospels are we told that John's desert fare was an emergency measure.
2. John's appeal to the whole population does not fit in with the character of the Essenes as a separatist movement. Brownlee claims that John was an Essene who wanted to make the movement more extroverted.[22]
3. But if we accept this last point, we run into a problem. The appeal to uphold ritual purity, which played such an important role in Qumran, is nowhere to be found in the preaching of the Baptist. In addition, no one is ever invited to join the Essenes by coming to live in the desert.

The strange location for his ministry is something John himself explained to the fact-finding commission of priests and Levites: "John replied in the words of Isaiah the prophet, 'I am the voice of one calling in the desert, "Make straight the way for the Lord"'" (John 1:23). In Isa-

---

16. B. Reicke, "Die jüdischen Baptisten und Johannes der Täufer," in *Jesus in der Verkündigung der Kirche*, Studien zum Neuen Testament und seiner Umwelt A/1, ed. A. Fuchs (Linz: Fuchs, 1976), 76–88.

17. D. Flusser, *Judaism and the Origins of Christianity* (Jerusalem: Magnes, 1988).

18. O. Betz, "Was John the Baptist an Essene?" in *Understanding the Dead Sea Scrolls: A Reader from the Biblical Archaeology Review*, ed. H. Shanks (New York: Random House, 1992), 205–14; L. Goppelt, *Theology of the New Testament*, ed. J. Roloff, trans. J. E. Alsup (Grand Rapids: Eerdmans, 1981).

19. Schütz, *Johannes der Täufer*; H. Stegemann, *Die Essener, Qumran, Johannes der Täufer und Jesus: Ein Sachbuch* (Freiburg: Herder, 1993); J. E. Taylor, *The Immerser: John the Baptist within Second Temple Judaism* (Grand Rapids: Eerdmans, 1977).

20. Ernst, *Johannes der Täufer*.

21. S. L. Davies, "John the Baptist and Essene Kashruth," *New Testament Studies* 29 (1983): 569–71.

22. W. H. Brownlee, "John the Baptist in the New Light of Ancient Scrolls," *Interpretation* 9 (1955): 71–90.

iah 40 the desert is an image for the deplorable condition of the people, who have been taken into exile because of their sins. Thus John takes the people back to the time before the return from exile, the time of the "desert"! It is true that the LORD had the temple rebuilt during the time of Cyrus, so that for several centuries there had once again been a Jewish settlement with its own cultus in Palestine, but John's desert ministry lets it be known that despite all that, their sins had not yet been atoned for and the people were continuing to forfeit their right to stay. People must leave their homes and towns and symbolically return to the desolation of the desert. In this way the prophet calls the people to humble themselves. Each person must relinquish what he has acquired. There is no choice but to obey a voice in the wilderness!

Thus John is a prophet who calls the people as it were to a new exodus. The people must symbolically abandon all that has been built—including the temple—and, needy and destitute, turn to God in the desert.

The first word the voice utters fits this picture: *"Repent"* (Matt. 3:2). John appears like a missionary to the Gentiles. His message hits the people like an earthquake: what is needed is *conversion*, even for the Jews! His baptism requires humility and is called a baptism of *repentance* (Mark 1:4; Luke 3:3; compare Matt. 3:11). It becomes a specific concept among the people: "The Repentance." John asks for fruits that correspond to this repentance (Matt. 3:8; Luke 3:8). The people, who must go out to the desert, find that the established foundation of their lives is taken from them by John—they must seek an altogether new foundation for their lives.

This is apparent when John says in so many words that they cannot depend on their descent from Abraham (Matt. 3:9; Luke 3:8). God can *make* children of Abraham, but *stones* would serve that purpose just as well as the people streaming into the desert. John's preaching shakes the people to the core. This earthquake from the desert robs all believers in Israel of their self-confidence.

Thus the *entire* nation is called on to *confess their sins*. The Jews had the annual Day of Atonement as the day for general contrition and repentance. That was one day per year. John is calling for the *Year* of Atonement. Apparently temple sacrifices are inadequate. Living under the law does not exempt anyone from this confession and repentance—not the crowds (Luke 3:7) and not even the leaders, the Pharisees and Sadducees, with their strict observance of the law (Matt. 3:7). Coming for baptism demands confessing one's sins (Matt. 3:6; Mark 1:5). Thus the way of the LORD is made straight and the obstacles of pride and misplaced self-confidence are removed (Matt. 3:3; Mark 1:3; Luke 3:4–5).

The Year of Atonement is being proclaimed because God himself is about to appear. And when the Holy One comes, everything else will seem unholy. Israel's light must fade, now that the sun of God's righteousness is about to appear! God comes with judgment: the winnowing fork is in his hand. And it will happen very soon; the ax is already at the root of the tree of Israel (Matt. 3:10, 12; Luke 3:9).

The newness of John's ministry lies primarily in its being a great, unique movement of repentance for everyone. This desert prophet makes the people realize that even though they are Abraham's descendants, and despite all the temple sacrifices, what they now stand in need of is a *general amnesty* when the LORD comes to his people—what is required is nothing less than, as it were, a new birth!

2.2.2 The Herald of God's Coming

This baptism of repentance is a baptism *for the forgiveness of sins* (Mark 1:4; Luke 3:3). This does not mean that the baptism itself produces cleansing, but that by hearing God's voice in the desert one is being prepared to participate in the amnesty for sinners. When God comes, he will not only burn the chaff with fire, but he will also gather the grain into his barn. He comes to immerse in the Holy Spirit, and in this way he purifies and sanctifies sinners.

In Isaiah 40, the sounding of the voice in the wilderness is linked with the promise that the LORD himself will appear (Isa. 40:5, 9). He comes to pay for sin (Isa. 40:2) and to tend the tattered flock like a shepherd (Isa. 40:10–11). The fellowship between the holy God and the sinful people will be permanently secure!

John then announces that the kingdom of heaven is near (Matt. 3:2). When the judge comes, the age of mercy will begin for those who are now confessing their sins, which also means the beginning of the age in which they will enter God's world. It would be incorrect to categorize all John's preaching under the heading "the kingdom of God." This term occurs only once in connection with the Baptist. In all four Gospels, however, we find preaching about a *Person close at hand*. Someone is near who will surpass John; he will not baptize with water, but with the Holy Spirit (Matt. 3:11; Mark 1:7–8; Luke 3:16–17; John 1:26–27, 33). Because God *himself* is now coming to judge and to impart his Spirit, it can also be said that the *kingdom of heaven* is at hand. This reality is the result of the arrival of the heavenly king. He is not just "a" more powerful person than John; he is *the More Powerful One* (Mark 1:7; Luke 3:16). John is at this point the most imposing prophet of all times, but God alone is more powerful than all the prophets. And this More Powerful One is coming! John baptizes first of all to reveal *Someone* to Israel (John 1:31).

As the prophet of the great repentance, he leads those who are baptized on a path of hope and expectation. But in doing so he places before them a mysterious riddle. When he shows Isaiah 40 as his passport, it is clear that he intends to announce the coming of Yahweh! How then can he speak of sandals and thongs? Does God wear sandals? Is God coming to Israel as a *man*? The secret of the incarnation is heard for the first time, albeit as a muffled whisper, throughout all of Israel!

The prophet who summons people to the Year of Atonement preaches God's imminent arrival and teaches people to hope in the general amnesty and the new birth, through the Holy Spirit.

2.2.3 Baptist of a Nation

Although the leaders did not heed the call of the prophet of repentance, the nation as a whole went to him for baptism (Mark 1:5; Matt. 3:5; 21:32; Luke 7:29–30; John 3:23–24). By confessing their sins and praying for the one to come, the people are put *in the proper attitude* for the coming of the LORD.

The nature of this baptism is a much-discussed topic. Attempts have been made to trace this rite back to the baths of purification of the Essenes at Qumran or to consider it analogous to proselyte baptism, but on closer inspection such hypothetical derivations are untenable, as might be expected.[23] For the people of that time, John's rite was *new*. Almost immediately he was given a nickname because he immersed people in the Jordan. He becomes generally known as Jochanan the Immerser (even his disciples referred to him this way: Luke 7:20). It is not likely that this nickname would be applied so quickly and easily if John merely did what others were also doing.[24] But John's baptism was unique.[25]

1. The ablutions at Qumran differed from John's rite in essential respects: they were repeated regularly, they occurred in the context of purification, they were only for the members of the group,[26] and they were not performed by another person.[27]
2. It cannot be proven that the baptism of proselytes had already been introduced during the first century[28] and that John then

---

23. Schütz, *Johannes der Täufer*; G. N. Stanton, *The Gospels and Jesus*, The Oxford Bible Series (Oxford: Oxford University Press, 1989).

24. E. Stauffer, *New Testament Theology*, trans. J. Marsh (London: SCM, 1955).

25. Stanton, *The Gospels and Jesus*; Stegemann, *Die Essener, Qumran, Johannes der Täufer und Jesus*; S. Légasse, *Naissance du baptême*, Lectio Divina 153 (Paris: Cerf, 1993).

26. J. Jeremias, "Der Ursprung der Johannestaufe," *Zeitschrift für die neutestamentliche Wissenschaft* 28 (1929): 312–20.

27. Stauffer, *New Testament Theology*.

28. J. Leipoldt, *Die urchristliche Taufe im Lichte der Religionsgeschichte* (Leipzig: Doerffring, 1928); T. F. Torrance, "Proselyte Baptism," *New Testament Studies* 1 (1954–55): 150–54.

adapted it with new significance *within* Israel.[29] According to Taylor, before proselytes could participate in the sacrifices they had to purify themselves with water.[30] This purification rite supposedly remained intact after A.D. 70. Because it was no longer followed by a sacrifice, it acquired the status of a rite of initiation comparable to Christian baptism, especially in the second century, when the prohibition on proselyte circumcision made the purification bath sometimes the only initiation rite that was used. But even if proselyte baptism had been in use before John, there are still considerable differences between the purification bath that was administered before being admitted to the community and the total immersion in the Jordan of people who were already part of Israel.[31]

In order to get a clear understanding of the meaning of John's rite, we must focus more attention on the location of the immersion. John baptizes not only *with water*; he immerses *in the Jordan*. Christian baptism is a baptism in the name of a person (Jesus Christ), but John's baptism is an immersion in a special *river*. People were not immersed "in the name of John"—they were immersed "in the Jordan" (Matt. 3:6; Mark 1:5). This is the river of the entrance into Canaan, through which God once led his people with dry feet into the land they were to occupy. But the prophet of repentance not only compels them to leave all this behind and to go out to the desert—he also *submerges* them in the boundary river. This time they are not spared, as the people in Joshua's day had been; they sink into the river's water.

Immersing (*baptizein*) suggests an action in which something is pushed completely under water *without* being taken out again. We therefore cannot agree with Jeremias that John's baptism is analogous to the *purification* of the whole nation, as had happened at Sinai.[32] Nor can we accept an analogy with temple purification rites, with which John, as a priest's son, would have been intimately familiar.[33] John's rite is described not by verbs such as "purify" or "wash" but by the verb

---

29. T. W. Manson, "John the Baptist," *Bulletin of the John Rylands University Library* 36 (1953–54): 395–412.

30. T. M. Taylor, "The Beginnings of Jewish Proselyte Baptism," *New Testament Studies* 2 (1955–56): 193–98.

31. For the preceding two points, see also the excursus "Origin of Christian Baptism" at the end of chap. 7.

32. J. Jeremias, *New Testament Theology* (London: SCM, 1971); also idem, "Der Ursprung der Johannestaufe."

33. J. Gnilka, "Die essenischen Tauchbäder und die Johannestaufe," *Revue de Qumran* 3 (1961): 185–207; also idem, "Der Täufer Johannes und der Ursprung der christlichen Taufe," *Bibel und Leben* 4 (1963): 39–49.

"submerge." Even if the act were limited to a *symbolic* drowning, it nevertheless speaks the language of a fatal submersion in the Jordan. Abraham's children are like citizens who are being made to turn in their passports and get shot at the border. This ceremony turns them into asylum seekers in their "own" country, foreigners who seek shelter and pardon from the one who is to come.

Just as once a nation was led through the Jordan with dry feet, so now a *nation* is symbolically drowned in the same river. John looks for the *totality* of Abraham's people, as is indicated in several ways. (1) His call is for *everyone* to be immersed and includes a harsh outburst at the leaders who refused. (2) He does not spare the Galilean king, the tetrarch Herod Antipas. (3) His concrete warnings to the crowds, the tax collectors, and the soldiers are intended to bring about a *living together* of the people in love and righteousness.[34]

Thus John wants to prepare this *nation*, these people who have forfeited everything, including their lives, for the amnesty of the heavenly kingdom of the one who is to come.[35]

2.3 Sent by God

John the Baptist struck like a meteorite. Mysterious and imposing, this unknown desert dweller suddenly captured Israel's attention. The people stood in awe of this unexpected presence—it was as though the entire nation had been captured by a new force field. It was a time when everyone's attention was riveted on the future that John was announcing.

Modern biblical scholarship, however, poses the question of the *origin* of this revival in Israel. Is it possible to fit John the Baptist into a known religio-historical framework by describing him as a charismatic apocalyptic or as a passionate Essene looking for renewal? Many nineteenth-century scholars had already settled the Christ question: belief in God's Son, they said, was a later distortion. Jesus was thus demoted to a friendly teacher or protest figure within the Judaism of his day. But what do we do now, in the twentieth century, with John the Baptist? He is a much more recalcitrant figure. Is it for this reason that someone like Conzelmann, in his book on the theology of the New Testament,

---

34. See J. van Bruggen, *Lucas: Het evangelie als voorgeschiedenis,* Commentaar op het Nieuwe Testament, 3d series (Kampen: Kok, 1993), on the exegesis of Luke 3:10–14.

35. Reiser compares the ministry of the Baptist with the vision in Ezekiel 9: a man clothed in linen goes through Jerusalem to find everyone who is sighing and moaning about the atrocities being committed there and puts a mark on their foreheads, by which they will escape the judgment that is following in the man's footsteps (M. Reiser, *Jesus and Judgment: The Eschatological Proclamation in Its Jewish Context,* trans. L. M. Maloney [Minneapolis: Fortress, 1997]).

completely bypasses this prophet and his message?[36] When it comes to John, one can hardly speak of a later theological "promotion" (by whom?), and it is difficult to simply put him back into his own era and dismiss him as a product of the Judaism of that age. Thus this prophet of repentance can disturb the conscience of those who brushed aside faith in God's Son.

2.3.1 A Unique Ministry

Attempts to explain the "phenomenon" of John in terms of the religious history of the Jews of his day have had little result. Reitzenstein suggests a gentile background in his attempt to locate the baptismal rite within the Mandaean baptismal sect, but this is generally considered implausible.[37] The impossibility of a direct connection with the Essenes has already been discussed (see sec. 2.2.1). Descriptions of John as one of the apocalyptists[38] have been disputed[39] and provide no explanation for the baptismal rite that was characteristic of John's ministry, nor for the clear announcement of the coming of the More Powerful One.

Apart from many possible points of contact and overlap with more or less familiar groups from that period, it remains in principle unlikely that John should be understood as a representative of any existing group, sect, or movement. After all, the sources are unanimous in their assertion that his contemporaries experienced him as a unique phenomenon. Who would have been in a better position to push John back into the religio-historical setting from which he came than the hostile leaders of the period? Their knowledge of Jewish matters of the first century was considerably more extensive than that of the best specialists of the twentieth. Yet we see that these leaders are in something of a fix. They are unable to pigeonhole John the Baptist. The fact-finding commission of priests and Levites begins asking desperate questions: "Who are you? Give us an answer to take back to those who sent us. What do you say about yourself?" (John 1:22). And as meticulous members of the party of the Pharisees, they probe more deeply: "Why then do you baptize if you are not the Christ, nor Elijah, nor the Prophet?" (John 1:25). His contemporaries are not able to fit John the Baptist into any existing context; the best they can do is look for a *future* context! Even his quickly acquired nickname, "The Immerser," indicates that everyone considered his activity as something strikingly *new*. As long as the study of religion does not by defini-

---

36. H. Conzelmann, *An Outline of the Theology of the New Testament*, trans. J. Bowden (London: SCM, 1969).

37. R. Reitzenstein, *Die Vorgeschichte der christlichen Taufe* (Leipzig: Teubner, 1929).

38. Stauffer, *New Testament Theology*.

39. Becker, *Johannes der Täufer und Jesus von Nazareth*; Ernst, *Johannes der Täufer*.

tion exclude any new, and possibly divinely inspired, phenomena, scholars would be well advised to treat John the Baptist as a separate chapter instead of relegating him to a paragraph in some other chapter.

2.3.2 John's Birth

John the Evangelist writes, "There came a man who was sent from God; his name was John" (John 1:6). It is not until verse 7 that the Evangelist speaks of this prophet's ministry ("He came as a witness"). In verse 6 he points to the *birth*: God caused a *person* to be born to serve as his missionary (compare the parallel in 1:14: the Word *became* flesh).

This birth is described in more detail in Luke. What John's Gospel merely alludes to, Luke's Gospel makes plain: the birth of John the Baptist was extraordinary. His parents were well past childbearing age, but God let a child be born after it was no longer humanly possible. This drew the attention of everyone in the neighborhood (Luke 1:58): the LORD has shown mercy!

After his speech returns, Zechariah can explain what had taken place before the birth, during his stay in the temple (Luke 1:64). People are told how none other than Gabriel announced the coming of this son born "out of season," and the awestruck inhabitants of the Judean countryside wonder what sort of child this will be (Luke 1:65–66). From the very beginning it is clear that John was sent by God.

The goal of his mission had been stated briefly by Gabriel: "He will go on before the Lord, in the spirit and power of Elijah, . . . to make ready a people prepared for the Lord" (Luke 1:17). The first stage of God's coming is the preparation of a prophet who goes before him as a missionary to Israel.

Because of this beginning, John cannot be reduced to a mere expression of the Judaism of his day. He is a human being conceived beyond the limits of human time. Anyone who wants to classify him must heed the words of an angel who stands in the presence of God. John's birth proved that the world should prepare itself for something entirely new.

2.3.3 The Prophecy of Zechariah

John's father, Zechariah, in answer to many questions (Luke 1:66), is allowed to give voice to a prophecy about his son. John will be called a "prophet of the Most High." He will "go on before the Lord to prepare the way for him." This will happen because the people will learn to understand that the path to the future is opened only by God's amnesty (Luke 1:76–77).

When Zechariah delivered this prophecy, he not only had in mind the message Gabriel had given him in the temple but also knew that the same Gabriel, with abundant promises, had appeared to Mary, who was betrothed to Joseph, a man from the house of David. Zechariah knew about the coming of the Son of God in Mary's womb. Elizabeth, his wife, had already greeted Mary as "the mother of my Lord." She had felt the baby John "leap for joy" in her womb when Mary entered her house (Luke 1:41–44). John arrives before Mary's child; the prophet arrives before the King! This is why Zechariah first says that God "has raised up a horn of salvation for us in the house of his servant David" (Luke 1:69). And only then does he speak about John, who is to go before the Lord.

Zechariah was filled with the Holy Spirit (Luke 1:67). Through his mouth, the Spirit of God teaches Israel how this child should be viewed. John cannot be understood "from below." Who he is, is determined by what the Almighty is coming to do on earth. The prophecy of Zechariah proves that with John a completely new chapter in Israel's history has begun.

2.3.4 The Witness of Jesus

Even the testimony of Jesus about John the Baptist points to John as someone sent from God. John came to the people in "the way of righteousness" and the people had to believe him (Matt. 21:32). Jesus says emphatically, "I tell you the truth: Among those born of women there has not risen anyone greater than John the Baptist" (Matt. 11:11a; compare Luke 7:28a).

Jesus calls John a prophet. Indeed, he is "the Elijah who was to come"—if they are willing to accept it (Matt. 11:14). Jesus here speaks the same message as Gabriel. John is the promised prophet who is to go before the Lord himself "in the spirit and power of Elijah." In Malachi 4:5 we read, "See, I will send you the prophet Elijah before that great and dreadful day of the Lord comes." The appearance of this prophet will be like seagulls who fly ahead of the storm. Anyone who hears the signal (Elijah is here!) can know that God himself is nearby (". . . else I will come and strike the land with a curse"). So the teachers of the law knew that the day of salvation would have to be preceded by the coming of an Elijah (Matt. 17:10).[40] It is Jesus who bestows this honorific on John, whom the teachers of the law have failed to appreciate (Matt. 17:11–13). For anyone who will take note of it, giving the prophet John this title serves as a signal concerning Jesus.

John himself seems to have denied that he was Elijah when questioned by the interrogators from Jerusalem (John 1:21, 24). But this fact-finding commission was thinking of a *revived* or *returned* Elijah.

---

40. Compare D. C. Allison, "Elijah Must Come First," *Journal of Biblical Literature* 103 (1984): 256–58.

Similarly, Jesus was later seen by some as a revived John the Baptist, Elijah, Jeremiah, or one of the prophets (Matt. 16:14). So John is correct in denying that he is Elijah in person. When Jesus later calls him "Elijah," he is not thinking of John as *identical* with the earlier prophet Elijah. We see this later, when Jesus, Peter, and John come down from the Mount of Transfiguration. At that point the disciples have the real Elijah in mind, whom they had just seen—why didn't he stay with them? But Jesus then teaches them that the promised "Elijah" had already come, and the disciples understand that he did not refer to the Elijah who had appeared on the mountain, but to John the Baptist (Matt. 17:10–13). Because he had come as a prophet to fulfill the promise of Malachi 4:6, *John* is the prophet whom we read about in Malachi 4:5, who will appear as an Elijah figure in the spirit and power of Elijah. In terms of personal *identity* John the Baptist is not the same as Elijah, but in terms of his *function* he really is an Elijah who would, as promised, come before the great day of the LORD.

Jesus' testimony also shows us that the explanation of John the Baptist is not to be found in the Judaism of the time. What we see here is an initiative of God, prophesied in his name several centuries earlier by Malachi.

Does Jesus regard this prophet John as the beginning of the new age or as the end of the old dispensation? Some scholars insist that Matthew places him within the new age, while Luke puts him in the previous one.[41] Kümmel contests this, however: he points out that in Luke 16:6, John the Baptist is referred to as the inaugurator of the new age.[42] Ridderbos, however, sees John everywhere depicted as belonging to the period of expectation,[43] while the age of fulfillment does not begin until Jesus.[44]

In Matthew 11:13 we read, "For all the Prophets and the Law prophesied until (*heōs*) John." This must mean that the Law and the Prophets,

41. Jeremias, *New Testament Theology*; Conzelmann, *Outline of the Theology of the New Testament*; Stanton, *Gospels and Jesus*.

42. W. G. Kümmel, "Das Gesetz und die Propheten gehen bis Johannes—Lukas 16,16 im Zusammenhang der heilsgeschichtlichen Theologie der Lukasschriften," in *Verborum Veritas: Festschrift für Gustav Stählin zum 70. Geburtstag*, ed. O. Böcher and K. Haacker (Wuppertal: Theologischer Verlag, 1970), 89–102. See also M. Bachmann, "Johannes der Täufer bei Lukas: Nachzügler oder Vorläufer?" in *Wort in der Zeit: Neutestamentliche Studien*, ed. W. Haubeck and M. Bachmann (Leiden: Brill, 1980), 123–55. O. Böcher ("Lukas und Johannes der Täufer," *Studien zum Neuen Testament und seiner Umwelt* 4 [1979]: 27–44) even suggests that as a disciple of Apollos, Luke was an indirect disciple of John.

43. H. Ridderbos, *The Coming of the Kingdom*, trans. H. de Jongste, ed. R. O. Zorn (Philadelphia: Presbyterian & Reformed, 1962).

44. See also D. A. Carson, "Do the Prophets and the Law Quit Prophesying before John? A Note on Matthew 11.13," in *The Gospels and the Scriptures of Israel*, JSNTSup 104, ed. C. A. Evans and W. R. Stegner (Sheffield: Sheffield Academic Press, 1994), 179–94.

up to and including the coming of John, prophesied in God's name about the coming kingdom of God. The verse stands in a causal relationship to the preceding verse: *"From the days of* John the Baptist until now the kingdom of heaven suffers violence, and violent men take it by force" (Matt. 11:12 KJV). We can understand "the days of John" here to mean the period in which he freely acted as a prophet in Israel. When his activities were halted because of his arrest, the time of the kingdom of heaven began to come under pressure. Both John and Jesus were endangered. Insofar as John was serving as a prophet among the people, Jesus reckons him as belonging to the final period of the Law and the Prophets (he closes off that period as the promised Elijah, who would only be sent at the eleventh hour). But the time of suffering (imprisonment and death) that then followed coincides with the time of Christ, and the suffering of John belongs to the new age of God's mercy.

Luke 16:16 says, "The Law and the Prophets were proclaimed until (*heōs* or *mechri*) John. Since that time, the good news of the kingdom of God is being preached." In Luke the verb phrase "to preach the good news" is also used in reference to John (Luke 3:18), but the preaching of the good news about "the kingdom of God" does not begin until Jesus (Luke 4:43; 8:1). So it makes little difference whether we opt for the reading *mechri* or *heōs*; in both cases John's ministry is included under the "Law and the Prophets."

As a prophet, John the Baptist is the "to be continued" notice at the end of the Old Testament. Jesus' statements are rather shocking to Jewish listeners. To them, the Law and the Prophets had long been a completed book. But now Jesus says that the Law and the Prophets would remain a closed book if people failed to listen to the last spokesman of the Old Testament, John the Baptist. He is not a product of his age; he is the last trumpet call of the Law and the Prophets. John is the last word of the Scriptures that people were accustomed to reading. Anyone with an ear for the law will listen carefully to what this prophet has to say (Matt. 11:15)![45]

2.4 The Forerunner of Jesus of Nazareth

John announces the coming of the LORD: *God* stands at the door as judge. The prophet wants the people to share, through repentance and prayer, in the amnesty for the faithful and in the renewal through filling with the divine Spirit.

---

45. The phrase "more than a prophet," which is often applied to John, is not dealt with here because it most likely refers to Jesus himself (see J. van Bruggen, *Matteüs: Het evangelie voor Israël*, 2d ed., Commentaar op het Nieuwe Testament, 3d series [Kampen: Kok, 1994], for a detailed discussion of Matt. 11:7–10).

At the same time, however, the Gospels include things that John says about Jesus the *man*. How are these statements related to his announcement of *God's* coming?

Lindeskog is of the opinion that John, the prophet of repentance, announced only the approach of *God*, and that Christians later co-opted him by turning him into a forerunner of the *Messiah*. The figure of Jesus was supposedly inserted between John the Baptist and God.[46] Many other scholars also attribute the tension between the eschatological preaching of the Baptist and the appearance of the man from Nazareth to the result of the later appropriation of John the Baptist by the Jesus tradition. According to Enslin, Jesus was never baptized by the Baptist, and it took the execution of the prophet of repentance to convince Jesus that the end was at hand.[47] By later incorporating John the Baptist into their own religious point of view, the followers of Jesus provided themselves with the still-absent Elijah figure and thereby also with a messianic alibi for Jesus.

Böcher also sees John and Jesus as parallel phenomena; only later was John "degraded" to the forerunner of Jesus, making the Christians the heirs of his specific eschatological baptismal rite.[48] Wink is of the opinion that Jesus himself only realized that John was his forerunner by undergoing his baptism.[49] According to Becker, John's preaching lacked the messianic category and any notion of the kingdom of heaven.[50] Because he was acknowledged as the forerunner of Jesus, he was later annexed and made to represent elements that were actually foreign to him.

2.4.1 Preparing the Way for the Sandals of God

John is the prophet who prepares the way for the coming of the LORD himself. The voice in the wilderness, as he calls himself, appealing to Isaiah 40, announces to the people that the LORD, the Shepherd of Israel, is soon to appear. The More Powerful One who is coming is God himself.[51] Many elements in John's preaching point to this: he who will be coming after John will perform acts that are the exclusive prerogative of God, such as the carrying out of the last judgment and the conferring of the Holy Spirit of God.[52]

---

46. Lindeskog, "Johannes der Täufer."
47. M. S. Enslin, "John and Jesus," *Zeitschrift für die neutestamentliche Wissenschaft* 66 (1975): 1–18.
48. Böcher, "Johannes der Täufer in der neutestamentlichen Überlieferung."
49. Wink, *John the Baptist in the Gospel Tradition.*
50. Becker, *Johannes der Täufer und Jesus von Nazareth.*
51. Ernst, *Johannes der Täufer*; Webb, *John the Baptizer and Prophet.*
52. J. H. Hughes, "John the Baptist: The Forerunner of God Himself," *Novum Testamentum* 14 (1972): 191–218.

Yet in John's primary preaching, all of this is already combined with a human characteristic: John says that he is not even worthy to carry the sandals (Matt. 3:11) or untie the sandal thongs of the one who is to come (Mark 1:7). Hughes, referring to Psalms 60:10 and 108:10, suggests that speaking of footwear could be appropriate when talking about God.[53] Reiser also sees in this passage an anthropomorphism parallel to that in Psalm 108:10.[54] But these psalms involve metaphors, while John is speaking in concrete terms. It would certainly have been impossible for Moses on Mount Sinai to have said that he was not worthy to carry or loosen the sandals of Yahweh!

The announcement of God's own coming is paired with the suggestion of a human individual who wears sandals. This mysterious combination, however, is in line with what John already knew. He was awaiting God in human form, as is clear at the baptism of Jesus. Even though he had come to prepare the way of *God*, John had no difficulty at all pointing to a *person* from Nazareth, wearing sandals, as the one to come after him (John 1:27), who would baptize with the Spirit (John 1:33–34). He had also told his disciples ahead of time that a *man* would be coming after him (John 1:30).

John the Baptist had received this attitude toward Jesus from God while in his mother's womb. As an unborn child, he leaped in Elizabeth's womb when "the mother of her Lord" entered the room (Luke 1:41–44). As a small child, he would have heard from his father and mother about the promises the angel Gabriel had made to Mary: "He will be great and will be called the Son of the Most High" (Luke 1:32). And Zechariah, in his prophecy, said to his son John, "And you, my child, will be called a prophet of the Most High; for you will go on before the Lord to prepare the way for him" (Luke 1:76). Zechariah was also thinking of Mary's child, born of the Holy Spirit. This is apparent from the preceding words: "He has raised up a horn of salvation for us in the house of his servant David" (Luke 1:69).

John's concrete expectation is also evident when Jesus comes to be immersed in the Jordan. For the Baptist it is immediately clear that now *Someone greater than himself* is standing before him. This is why at first he refuses to involve Jesus in this humiliating ceremony (Matt. 3:14). He knows that the man standing there is a "man from God" (compare Matt. 1:18: it had become known that Mary was pregnant by the Holy Spirit).

Later, John twice declares to his disciples that he "did not know" Jesus (John 1:31, 33). But this does not mean that he knew nothing about Jesus and the promises attached to him. The prophet is only saying that his testimony is not based on an intimate relationship of two childhood play-

53. Ibid.
54. Reiser, *Jesus and Judgment.*

mates. John grew up in the desert, and Jesus in Nazareth. Rather, John's testimony was based on his *being sent by God to announce the coming of Jesus* (John 1:31) and on the *sign of validation in the form of a descending dove* (John 1:33). John's testimony about Jesus is from heaven!

So after Jesus' baptism, John does not hesitate to refer his disciples to the Greater One who would come after him and who now had actually arrived (John 1:29–37). Joyfully he watches Jesus increase while he steps into the background, into the shadow of this One who comes after him (John 3:26–30).

Later John asks the question, "Are you the one who was to come, or should we expect someone else?" (Matt. 11:3). At that point John continues to recognize the works of Jesus as those of the *Christ*, and he continues to defer to Jesus as his superior. But he has difficulty accepting the fact that the judgment has not come (he himself is now in prison), and he wonders if perhaps he should expect a second figure *besides* Jesus (the Christ), someone who would carry out the announced judgment.[55] But the fact that John has his disciples ask *Jesus* such a question reveals once again that he continues to regard him as the one who was to come after him, the Greater One.

The whole of John's preaching makes it clear that from the very beginning he knew that the LORD God would come to Israel as the son of a human being, the son of a woman. The people of Israel had been told through Isaiah of the promise of an Immanuel, a child who would be born of a woman and who would be called "Wonderful Counselor, Mighty God, Everlasting Father, Prince of Peace" (Isa. 7:14; 9:6). John had grown up knowing that Gabriel had told Mary that *Jesus* would be this child (Luke 1:32–33). That is why he is the one to prepare the way for God, the King who comes in sandals.[56]

2.4.2 Witness to the Lamb of God

In the Gospel according to John, the Baptist is characterized as someone who "came as a witness to testify concerning [the] light" (John 1:7; compare 1:15, 32, 34; 3:26; 5:33). Here the Fourth Gospel uses a terminology all its own, yet its meaning is no different from what has already

---

55. See van Bruggen, *Mattèüs,* for a more extensive treatment of Matt. 11:1–6.

56. Lindeskog ("Johannes der Täufer") and other scholars project the human messianic model of later theology back into the first century, and it is understandable that this results in a tension between the announcement of *God's* coming on the one hand and the arrival of the *Messiah* on the other. But here modern biblical scholarship has to pay the price for assuming that Jesus was only later *made* into God as a result of the *church's* theology. Seen from the vantage point of modern achristological dogma, the gate by which the Gospels are entered (John's ministry) thus finds itself obstructed—which does not argue in favor of the correspondence between this twentieth-century dogma and the facts of history.

been described in the other three Gospels. In John 5:33, when questioned by hostile Jewish leaders, Jesus points to the statement John made about him to the fact-finding commission from Jerusalem. If we go back to 1:18–28, the positive core of this witness turns out to have been the reference to Isaiah 40 and the announcement that John is not worthy to loosen the thong of the sandal of him who is to come (John 1:23, 26–27). It is precisely these two elements that we also find in the Synoptic Gospels. And the combination of the two clearly reveals that the LORD is now going to come to his people in human form. John develops this theme more broadly and meditatively in the prologue to his Gospel ("the Word became flesh"). It is this to which the Baptist is a witness (see John 1:6–7, 15). And the fourth evangelist also provides a few detailed recollections from the time he spent near John the Baptist, as one of his disciples. At that time he saw John point his finger at Jesus as the announced Greater One (John 1:30, 32, 34; 3:26). Thus John the Baptist is a witness, sent by heaven, to the truth that God is appearing as a human being and that the man Jesus is the Son of God (John 1:34).[57]

In the Gospel of John, we read how the Baptist more than once pointed to Jesus as "the Lamb of God who takes away the sin of the world" (1:29; compare 1:36). According to Brown, the lamb here is a ruling and conquering lamb (compare Rev. 5:9), not a sacrificial animal.[58] However, the texts in which the lamb is presented as reigning assume that the reign itself is owed to the *ultimate commitment* like that of a sacrificial lamb. This is why the texts are usually explained as an allusion to the Passover lamb or to a sacrificial lamb in general.[59] Bypassing for the moment the question of how much John the Baptist already knew about the gospel of the Passion, we can at least say that his immersion ceremony in the Jordan deprived the people of whatever trust they may have had in a human sacrificial lamb. At the same time he promised the coming of a divine pardon. In that context, Jesus, the one to come after him, is clearly the person who will somehow open the way to God. He is the lamb who will personally bring about amnesty for the world.

It is striking that, as far as we know, John did not use this term in his public preaching—but he did use it in discussions with his disciples, although only after Jesus was baptized by him. John already had the God-

57. Unlike R. Bultmann (*Theology of the New Testament*, trans. K. Grobel [New York: Scribner, 1951–55]), who regards the prologue sections of John as later insertions, Hooker has clearly shown how this prologue and these very passages together constitute an integrated composition (M. Hooker, "John the Baptist and the Johannine Prologue," *New Testament Studies* 16 [1969–70]: 354–58).

58. R. E. Brown, "Three Quotations from John the Baptist in the Gospel of John," *CBQ* 22 (1960): 292–98.

59. See P. H. R. van Houwelingen, *Johannes: Het evangelie van het Woord*, Commentaar op het Nieuwe Testament, 3d series (Kampen: Kok, 1997).

given knowledge that he would be allowed to see the Spirit descend on the one who was to come, on Jesus. But apparently he was not prepared to see this happen after Jesus had been immersed in the Jordan. This was a shocking experience for the Baptist, but it taught him something about "the path of righteousness." Jesus does say, *"It is proper for us to do this* to fulfill all righteousness" (Matt. 3:15). The path of the one who far outranks John must pass through humiliation. After this lesson, John the Baptist also assigned the name "the *Lamb* of God" to the More Powerful One. The lion comes as a lamb—this is how he brings pardon. Even if at this point John the Baptist did not have a full or clear picture of the suffering and death that were to come, it was clear to him not only that the Word had become flesh but also that it had come in all humility to serve the very people whom the Baptist had denounced.

The Fourth Gospel gives us a succinct characterization of John's public ministry: he is the *witness* of God's coming in the flesh. And this Gospel also provides a supplement to the other Gospels by telling how, through the baptism Jesus wished to undergo, John the Baptist learned to emphasize to his disciples the *humiliation* of the More Powerful One who was to come after him—the *Lamb* of God has come!

2.4.3 Forerunner in Death

We have the impression that John's preaching was more or less smothered by hostile forces. He who by immersion in the Jordan brought symbolic death to the people himself finds literal death in the dungeon of Herod Antipas. The vision of his bloody head on the platter of Herodias and Salome seems like an anticlimax to his impressive ministry. Doesn't this threaten to rob his work of its credibility?

Jesus himself does not take action, however, when John is rendered powerless, humiliated, and killed. Despite the fact that at that time Jesus was displaying his enormous power throughout Israel, he did not even protest John's fate. It is as though nothing strange has happened to the forerunner as far as he is concerned.

Jesus even said that the violence against John is typical of the way of the kingdom. The leaders of the Jewish people are already planning Jesus' death; they are going to do the same thing to him that Herod had done to John. The humble presentation of the kingdom makes it vulnerable and brings it within the grasp of the violent (Matt. 11:12). But this is God's intention. Just as they did not spare the herald, neither will they spare the Son (Matt. 17:12; 21:33–46). Thus, through his imprisonment and death, John the Baptist becomes a *silent witness* for the path to be followed by the one who comes after him. John's role as forerunner includes a violent death. Jesus will follow him as the More Powerful One who rises again, takes away the sin of the world, accomplishes judgment, and floods the people with the Spirit of God. Just as Paul, as the prisoner of Christ, will foreshadow that which awaits the church on earth, so John, by immersion in the waters of the Jordan as the way to submersion in death, is a sign for the way of the Christ.[60]

2.5 A Prophet of the Most High

When Jesus begins his ministry among the Jews in about A.D. 30, he stands on the stage, illuminated by special lighting. The recent ministry of the desert prophet near the Jordan has aroused a new and extraordinary expectation among the people, a kind of expectation that had not been known in the Jewish religious world until then. This fact is of great importance for a proper description of the gospel in its historic context.

2.5.1 John's Continuing Importance

There are many good descriptions in print of Judaism before and during the first century. But what is often missing is a separate discussion of unique aspects of the years during which Jesus ministered. The immersion of so many Jews in the Jordan, which began around A.D. 27, was very disturbing to the people in those years. Confidence was shaken. Certainties began to waver. Great expectations were aroused. People began to look forward to the appearance of the LORD—in human form.

It is consequently completely inadequate to study the religio-historical context of the gospel only in terms of general Jewish categories such as "apocalyptic spirituality," "the Essene community," "popular piety versus secularized leaders," and so on. The most direct religio-historical context for Jesus' ministry is not to be found in the rabbinical material or in the pseudepigrapha. The brief but intense revival that took place during John's time left no traces there. And that is no wonder, considering the rejection of Jesus. More surprising is that when we look at the Jewish source that is closest to the New Testament period, the writer Josephus, we do find a reliable report of the enormous impression John made. As a non-Christian, Josephus limited himself to a brief description. For him as a Jew who does not recognize Christ Jesus, this is a closed chapter—yet even here we find traces of John's ministry.

Any attempt to describe the context for a gospel that, as a new phenomenon, was being preached around the year 30 must focus specifically on *those years* and not lose sight of the specifics by paying attention only to the wider horizon of the *centuries* at the beginning of our

---

60. See van Bruggen, *Matteüs,* for a broader discussion of the statement about violence in Matt. 11:12.

era. In short, careful historical reconstruction demands more detail in the painting of the precise time in which the gospel came.

2.5.2 The Focal Point of the Old Testament

Not only is the *Jewish* background important in describing the gospel of Jesus Christ; the *Old Testament* background also plays a role. But that poses a problem that has been discussed in detail by Hübner.[61] Does the Old Testament *as a whole* move *inevitably* into the New? Is it not true that in the New Testament a limited *selection* from the Old Testament is used for support?

Hübner himself is of the opinion that we should avoid wanting to move from the Old Testament, via a forward development (and reinterpretation), in such a way that we must end up in the New Testament, which would suggest too much continuity. Rather, we must, by analyzing the retrospective selection and interpretation by the authors of the New Testament, establish how the "Old Testament in the New" relates to the "Old Testament as such."

The problem this raises, however, cannot be discussed without taking into account the ministry of John the Baptist. Jesus himself called him the last prophet of the Law and the Prophets. As the *Elijah who was to come*, he is *in* the Old Testament and he still *belongs to* the Old Testament. Because John, like Elijah in the past, is not a *writing* prophet but one who stands on the threshold of the New Testament with the immediacy of the final *word*, we often end up with a distorted perspective. A gulf threatens to form between the Old Testament (up to and including Malachi) and the preaching of Jesus. We must insist on an Old Testament background that extends *up to and includes John*. Then we find that John the Baptist serves as a focusing lens. Various lines from the Old Testament, which when viewed individually do not necessarily all lead directly to Jesus, are now refracted and brought together into a single focus on the expectation of the More Powerful One in human form. A certain openness that still exists in the Law and the Prophets and that resulted in a Judaism with many divergent expectations of the future is now supplemented through God's word to John in the desert and focused on a specific expectation and a more defined figure.

Whenever we try to discuss the way in which the Old Testament relates to the New Testament without taking into account the last Old Testament prophet of Yahweh, we sever an essential connection. To look no further than the line of prophets from Moses to Malachi is to overlook the greatest prophet of the Old Covenant. Psychologically there is

61. H. Hübner, *Biblische Theologie des Neuen Testaments*, vol. 1, *Prolegomena* (Göttingen: Vandenhoeck & Ruprecht, 1990).

much to be said for the idea of making room in the Bible, at the end of the Old Testament—after the four major and twelve minor prophets—for the single greatest prophet of them all. His words, taken from the accounts in the Gospels, could be summarized there. Luke has already composed the introduction: "In the fifteenth year of the reign of Tiberius Caesar—when Pontius Pilate was governor of Judea, Herod tetrarch of Galilee . . . , during the priesthood of Annas and Caiaphas, the word of God came to John son of Zechariah in the desert" (Luke 3:1–2).

To obtain a balanced vision on revelation history and canon, the forgotten prophet of the Old Covenant, John the Baptist, must be restored to *his own, rightful place.*

2.5.3 "And John Is His Prophet!"

There are three great religions of the book: Judaism, Christianity, and Islam. All three recognize the great value of Moses. But Judaism criticizes Christianity for threatening monotheism by confessing Jesus as God's Son, and Islam makes the same criticism. While the Jews rally around Moses, Islam moves on to the great prophet Mohammed. The two religions differ over prophets. But between the two of them and Christianity stands the acknowledgment of a man, Jesus of Nazareth, as "more than a prophet," as true God, Immanuel.[62]

By what right does Jesus elevate himself above Moses and Mohammed? Dare a human being make himself equal to God? Does Jesus not lack a prophet such as Yahweh has in Moses and Allah in Mohammed?

---

62. The Jewish author Y. Kaufmann is of the opinion that the three great religions are not divided by teachings or ethics (within every religion we find the same contradictions between teachings and behavior that can be found among these three religions). The three religions, in fact, part company only on the question of the authority of persons: who *is* Jesus, and is Mohammed an *authentic* prophet? Kaufmann attaches to this the idea that Christianity and Islam were rejected by the Jews and accepted by other peoples because Christianity and Islam, through monotheism, were able to triumph over idols that had been driven from Israel long before. Thus, in a certain sense, Christianity and Islam fulfill the same role for these other peoples that Moses fulfilled for the *nation* of Israel (Y. Kaufmann, *Christianity and Judaism: Two Covenants*, trans. C. W. Efroymson [Jerusalem: Magnes, 1988; a translation of *Golah ve-Nekhar* (1929–30), vol. 1, chaps. 7–9]).

In a study of the historical relationship between Judaism, Judaic Christianity, paganism, and early Islam, Colpe traced the origins of the term "seal of the prophets" (Qur'an, Sura 33.40). He believes that this term arose within Judaic Christianity and served to mark the place of Jesus within Judaism. Mohammed then appropriated the term in order to lay claim to the "prophetic claim to finality" (*prophetische Endgültigkeitsanspruch*) for himself. (C. Colpe, *Das Siegel der Propheten: Historische Beziehungen zwischen Judentum, Judenchristentum, Heidentum und frühem Islam*, Arbeiten zur neutestamentlichen Theologie und Zeitgeschichte 3 [Berlin: Institut Kirche und Judentum, 1990], 243.) According to Colpe, the history of religion cannot decide whether it is presumption when a human being regards himself as the "seal of prophecy," nor can it decide who is eligible for this honor—the Jewish prophets, Christ, Mani, or Mohammed (ibid., 247).

The answer to this question is John the Baptist. Jesus is great (Luke 1:32) and John is his prophet (Luke 1:76)! Christianity's justification vis-à-vis later non-Christian Jews and the even later Muslims can be found in the witness of the greatest prophet God has sent. In its encounter with Jews and Muslims, the Christian religion should point more to the prophet of Christianity—John in the desert. It is no accident that Jews have erased him from their memories, although he belongs to the pre-Christian era in their history, and that the Qur'an mentions this prophet with honor (Sura 3.38–41; 6.85; 19.2–15; 21.90)—but not as the Baptist or as the witness to God's Son.

Jesus himself appeals to the witness of the Baptist (John 5:31–47). He does not come "in his own name"—his credentials are signed by Moses and John! Christian theology cannot function without this prophet, and Christian apologetics must start with him.

3

The Works of God in Israel

In this chapter we address the way in which Jesus presented himself to Israel, specifically when he first began his public ministry. We look at how he initially presented himself, in his first preaching and in his first actions. And we will see that his later speaking and acting include elements that can only be understood as a *reaction* against the attitude of those around him—for instance, his speaking in parables or his denunciation of the unbelieving leaders.

We will discuss Jesus' preaching about the kingdom of heaven (sec. 3.1), his healing of many (sec. 3.2), and his power over nature (sec. 3.3). When the man Jesus does the "works of God," he is not self-seeking but rather denying himself for the sake of the people (sec. 3.4).

On one occasion Jesus himself made the following comment about his ministry: "I have a testimony greater than John's. The works that the Father has given me to complete, the very works that I am doing, testify on my behalf that the Father has sent me" (John 5:36 NRSV; compare 10:25). Jesus makes visible "the work of God" (John 9:3; compare 10:32, 37–38; 14:10), so that these words are an appropriate characterization of his ministry.

3.1 The Gospel of the Kingdom of God

3.1.1 The Central Theme of the Gospels?

Much attention during the past 150 years has focused on the theme of the *kingdom of God* in the Gospels. At the same time there has been less and less interest in some other subjects, such as the life of Jesus, the natures of Christ, and the atoning character of his death—focal points of interest in the ancient church and in the time of the Reformation that have lost much of their significance in contemporary New Testament theology. The questions have shifted from the doctrine *about* Christ to the teaching *of* Jesus.

This shift was accompanied by a religio-historical emphasis on Jesus in the framework of the Judaism of his time. If his ministry took place in the context of a general expectation of the kingdom of God, what ideas of his own did he offer his contemporaries?

According to some, Jesus' teaching about the kingdom of heaven is squarely at odds with the this-worldly, nationalistic expectations of many Jews at that time. Especially in the nineteenth century Jesus was seen as the preacher of a new *spiritual* or *inner* kingdom.[1] According to others the significance of his teaching lay precisely in the fact that he gave a concrete focus to the general Jewish apocalyptic expectations of a heavenly kingdom, bringing an eschatological tension to the time in which his listeners lived. During the first half of the twentieth century, many saw Jesus as the man who called people to make decisive choices with an eschatological dimension. The scholarly discussion revolved mainly around whether he saw the kingdom as an imminent reality,[2] or as actualized,[3] or as in the process of being actualized,[4] or both, in the present and in the future.[5]

It is hardly surprising that the heart of Jesus' teaching has been sought in his preaching of the coming kingdom of God. The phrase

1. A. von Harnack, *What Is Christianity?* with an introduction by R. Bultmann, trans. B. Saunders (Gloucester: Smith, 1957).

2. A. Schweitzer, *The Quest of the Historical Jesus: A Critical Study of Its Progress from Reimarus to Wrede,* with a new introduction by J. M. Robinson, trans. W. Montgomery (London: Black, 1931).

3. C. H. Dodd, *The Parables of the Kingdom,* 2d ed. (London: Nisbet, 1936).

4. J. Jeremias, *New Testament Theology* (London: SCM, 1971).

5. W. G. Kümmel, *Promise and Fulfillment: The Eschatological Message of Jesus,* trans. D. M. Barton (London: SCM, 1961); O. Cullmann, *Salvation in History,* trans. S. G. Sowers et al. (New York: Harper & Row, 1967); H. Ridderbos, *The Coming of the Kingdom,* trans. H. de Jongste, ed. R. O. Zorn (Philadelphia: Presbyterian & Reformed, 1962).

For the history of the research in the twentieth century: W. Willis, ed., *The Kingdom of God in Twentieth-Century Interpretation* (Peabody, Mass.: Hendrickson, 1987).

For the period up to 1960: G. Lundström, *The Kingdom of God in the Teaching of Jesus: A History of Interpretation from the Last Decades of the Nineteenth Century to the Present Day,* trans. J. Bulman (Edinburgh: Oliver & Boyd, 1963); N. Perrin, *The Kingdom of God in the Teaching of Jesus* (London: SCM, 1963); G. E. Ladd, *Jesus and the Kingdom: The Eschatology of Biblical Realism* (London: S.P.C.K., 1966).

For the period after 1960: W. G. Kümmel, *The New Testament: The History of the Investigation of Its Problems,* trans. S. M. Gilmour and H. C. Kee (London: SCM, 1973); L. Goppelt, *Theology of the New Testament,* ed. J. Roloff, trans. J. E. Alsup (Grand Rapids: Eerdmans, 1981); J. Schlosser, *Le Règne de Dieu dans les dits de Jésus,* Études bibliques, 2 vols. (Paris: Gabalda, 1980); B. Chilton, ed., *The Kingdom of God in the Teaching of Jesus,* Issues in Religion and Theology 5 (Philadelphia: Fortress, 1984); B. Chilton, "The Kingdom of God in Recent Discussion," in *Studying the Historical Jesus: Evaluations of the State of Current Research,* New Testament Tools and Studies 19, ed. B. Chilton and C. A. Evans (Leiden: Brill, 1994), 255–80.

For the way the concept functions in the evangelical theology of the twentieth century: E. J. Schnabel, *Das Reich Gottes als Wirklichkeit und Hoffnung: Neuere Entwicklungen in der evangelikalen Theologie* (Wuppertal: Brockhaus, 1993).

kingdom of God or *kingdom of heaven* occurs with great frequency in the Gospels. It is also understandable that the background of "the kingdom of God" is sought in the Judaism of that time. After all, it is striking how little explaining Jesus does when he uses this phrase. He apparently assumes that his listeners already have a concept of what he is talking about and that he can simply go ahead with *further teaching* on this theme.

It has been demonstrated more than once, however, that in the Judaism of the centuries before Christ there was no generally held and well-defined doctrine of the kingdom of heaven. What we *do* find are all sorts of expectations, inspired by the prophets, of a great future in which God will rule over the earth and all injustice or sin will disappear ("the age to come"). But there is nothing to suggest that the "kingdom of God" was a central theme in the world of Judaism. Jeremias calls Jesus' words about the kingdom of heaven a creative process that stems from his own creative language skills.[6]

But the precise background of Jesus' use of "the kingdom of God" escapes us if we fail to recall the climate of expectation that had been created by John the Baptist just before Jesus' ministry began.[7]

3.1.2 John the Baptist and the Kingdom of God

In the Gospels we find the term *kingdom of heaven* only once in connection with John the Baptist, in Matthew's summary of John's preaching: "Repent, for the kingdom of heaven is near" (Matt. 3:2).

Repentance is the central theme in John's preaching. He does not introduce a new theme (the kingdom of God); rather, he makes a fiery appeal to the people because the LORD is coming with judgment and the baptism of the Spirit. The promises of Isaiah and Malachi are about to be fulfilled; let the people prepare themselves for the heralded coming of the LORD—speedily and in faith!

Implicit in John's preaching is the message that when the prophecy of God's coming is fulfilled, the new age, which the prophets had foreseen and which can be described as the "kingdom of heaven" (*basileia tōn ouranōn*) or the "kingdom of God" (*basileia tou theou*), will also dawn. This is the new world order. The nations now are in the grip of Satan (compare Luke 4:5–6), but this will end. The LORD will rule, and his rule will renew the earth. Anyone who refuses to repent will be

6. Jeremias, *New Testament Theology.*
7. In his book about Jesus' proclamation of God's rule, Merklein says that John the Baptist and his preaching about judgment are the "anthropological premise of this proclamation" (H. Merklein, *Jesu Botschaft von der Gottesherrschaft: Eine Skizze*, Stuttgarter Bibelstudien 111, 3d ed. (Stuttgart: Katholisches Bibelwerk, 1989).

blown away like chaff, but the faithful will be suffused with the Holy Spirit.

John the Baptist does not go into great detail about this kingdom of heaven. He is the herald, and it is his job to prepare the people for God's coming. But the wording of Matthew 3:2 suggests that that coming will be the fulfillment of the expected kingdom of peace.

Although we do not find the actual term *kingdom of God* in the Old Testament, the concept is there. We must pay attention to what the Old Testament says about God's rule *in relation to the future*. There are many Old Testament statements about the Creator's permanent kingship over the whole world, but this is not what the term *kingdom of God* relates to.

1. God's kingship as Creator is eternal and can hardly be described as "coming" or "at hand."

2. The Greek word *basileia*, like the Hebrew word *malkut*,[8] means both kingly *rule* and kingly *territory*. These meanings reflect different aspects of the word but are not mutually exclusive. The word *basileia* is not an abstract term for "king*ship*" (which exists apart from the recognition of such a status); it is rather a concrete reference to "kingly *dominion*" (the acknowledged and exercised royal power in a particular territory).

3. Phrases such as "entering the kingdom" or "inheriting the kingdom" or "the kingdom of the Son of Man" are difficult to relate to God's eternal rule over heaven and earth. (Merklein can maintain the meaning of king*ship*—as divorced from any reference to a king*dom*—only by dismissing all statements by Jesus in which *basileia* is connected with a concept in time and space and by regarding them as secondary formulations produced by the later church community.)[9]

4. It is striking that what is being preached is not the coming of the *king* (*basileus*) but the coming of the *kingdom*. Jeremias suggests that *malkuta* (*kingdom*) already existed in the first century as a way of describing God, so that the expression "the kingdom of God is at hand" is the equivalent of "God is at hand."[10] But the addition of "of God" or "of heaven" argues against this; the *kingdom* is distinguished from God himself, so that the word must refer to his *kingdom*, in which everything is subject to him.

---

8. U. Luz, "Basileia," in *Exegetisches Wörterbuch zum Neuen Testament*, ed. H. Balz and G. Schneider (Stuttgart: Kohlhammer, 1980), 1:481–91.

9. Merklein, *Jesu Botschaft von der Gottesherrschaft*.

10. Jeremias, *New Testament Theology*.

5. The phrases "kingdom *of God*" and "kingdom *of heaven*" appear side by side. Although the latter is found only in Matthew, it cannot be understood as an attempt to avoid using the name of God by means of a paraphrase. Matthew regularly uses the phrase *ho theos* for Yahweh, even in statements made by Jesus. He also occasionally uses the expression "kingdom *of God*" (Matt. 12:28; 19:24; 21:31, 43). Apparently these are synonymous expressions, which gives us a clue to the meaning of "*of God.*" It is not one of the earthly kingdoms or spheres of power that is approaching, but the realm of power *from above* that has come to take possession of the earth. *God's* kingdom stands in opposition to the earthly kingdoms. Just as earthly kingdoms have a *territory* or *domain* and as heaven has a *domain*, so also does the kingdom of God have a *domain*. After kingdoms such as Assyria, Babylonia, and Rome comes the kingdom from above, the as yet unseen kingdom where the Lord of Hosts resides and reigns. The *kingdom* "of God" is not *God's eternal dominion as Creator* but *the redeemed domain where his authority holds sway.*

The Old Testament contains not only statements about God's eternal kingship as Creator but also promises of the coming of the Lord ("the day of the Lord") and of a *coming* kingdom and a *coming* king.[11] We are reminded in particular of the prophecy of Daniel.

This prophet lived when the kingdom of Judah and the reigning house of David had been conquered. There was no longer an anointed king of the dynasty of David. When the great world powers, Assyria and Babylonia, had overrun everything, it was Daniel who received the promise, in a variety of forms, that these kingdoms would ultimately be defeated by a new kingdom that would come from heaven. God will establish this kingdom; it will exist forever and will annihilate all other kingdoms (Dan. 2:44). This eternal kingdom will be given to the son of man, who comes with the clouds of heaven into the presence of God (Dan. 7:11–14). A Most Holy One will be anointed, a ruler (Dan. 9:24–26; cf. v. 24 NIV margin). It is still in the distant future, but God will surely make it come about (Dan. 12:8–13).

This presentation of the promises in Daniel stands against the backdrop of a long history of promises about the future. Throughout the history of God's people, Israel, it becomes increasingly clear that God will usher in a better kingdom. Saul, the king the people wanted, is re-

---

11. G. R. Beasley-Murray, *Jesus and the Kingdom of God* (Grand Rapids: Eerdmans, 1986). See also: G. R. Beasley-Murray, "The Kingdom of God in the Teaching of Jesus," *Journal of the Evangelical Theological Society* 35 (1992): 19–30, cf. 31–38.

placed by David, the man after God's heart. And David receives the promise of a great successor who will finally occupy his throne forever. In these promises made to the house of David we find a further focusing of the promises made to Abraham and his descendants. God had promised that he would bless all nations through Abraham. The path to that blessing appears to run through the house of David. And behind the promises to Abraham were even older promises: immediately after the fall there is the pledge that a child born of a woman will kill the serpent. It is a long way from this promise in Paradise, via the narrower focus on Abraham's descendants and the even more specific focus on the house of David, to the promises given to Daniel—at a time when both Abraham's people and David's house seem to have come to an end. Ultimately, the promised future for all nations will be made secure—through the son of man, who receives from God the eternal kingdom. In Jewish apocalyptic literature we find all sorts of future expectations embroidered onto these prophecies. Although a precise and uniform scheme is lacking, the expectation of a future given by God to Israel, and through Israel to all the nations of the earth, is widespread.

When John the Baptist speaks of "the kingdom of heaven," he connects with these Old Testament promises and the expectations among the people that are rooted in these promises. John's unique addition is that he confronts everyone with the nearness of the promise's fulfillment and the need to repent.

In summary, we can say that John the Baptist uses the term "kingdom of heaven" (*basileia tōn ouranōn*) as a corollary of his preaching about the coming of the LORD himself, and that he indicates how that coming will make the expectations of a new order for heaven and earth a reality.

In John's preaching, the term "kingdom of heaven" is not inspired by the rejection of the expectation of an earthly or national kingdom. There is no trace of such a contrast in John; for his listeners it was apparently self-evident that the coming of God's kingdom would not be connected with earthly, human activities—such as driving out the Romans—but rather with the appearance of the LORD himself. There apparently was no need to explain that the kingdom of heaven is something more than and different from a restored kingdom of the Jews, such as had existed for a short time under the Hasmoneans, until about a century before.

The meaning of the term "kingdom of God" as used by John is also not determined by an eschatological fever among certain Jewish apocalyptic groups, but by the concrete and God-commanded preaching about a coming *person*. The soil in which John's preaching about the kingdom of heaven is rooted is to be found not in apocalyptic circles but in the initiative of God and the instructions of his angel Gabriel.

3.1.3 Jesus' Preaching about the Kingdom of God

Jesus' preaching is in line with that of the Baptist. This is very clear in Matthew: John's announcement of the kingdom (Matt. 3:2) is taken up by Jesus (Matt. 4:17): "Repent, for the kingdom of heaven is near." Mark also records Jesus' early preaching: "The time has come. The kingdom of God is near. Repent and believe the good news!" (Mark 1:14). Although Luke does not use the term as such, he does show how from the beginning Jesus regarded his ministry as the fulfillment of Isaiah 61, a chapter that describes the content of the kingdom ("to proclaim the year of the Lord's favor," Luke 4:18–21). And in John we read how, before the arrest of John the Baptist, Jesus joined him in preaching the kingdom of heaven; he tells Nicodemus that without a rebirth "no one can see the kingdom of God" (John 3:3, 5).

So at first glance there seems to be no difference between the preaching of the Baptist and that of Jesus. Nevertheless, an attentive listener in those days would have noticed a striking difference. John links the approaching kingdom with the announcement of the More Powerful One who is to come—an announcement that is absent from Jesus' preaching. What remains is only the nearness of the kingdom. Against the background of the awe-inspiring preaching of John the Baptist, this omission would have been quite striking and significant. John said, "*Someone* is coming, and his coming also ushers in the *kingdom of God*." But now someone *is here* who says, "The kingdom of God is at hand." Apparently nothing more remains to be said about the coming of the More Powerful One, leaving the clear suggestion that the man from Nazareth who has taken over John's theme is *himself* the More Powerful One, whose coming is so closely tied to that of the kingdom of heaven.

In a single passage we read that John the Baptist "exhorted the people and preached the good news to them" (Luke 3:18), but this good news consisted of the *announcement* of the one to come (compare Luke 3:15–17). Jesus preaches the kingdom simply as *good news* (Mark 1:15; Luke 4:18, 43). The kingdom of heaven came *after* John—and *with* Jesus. Within the frame of reference of the Baptist's earlier preaching, Jesus' preaching concerning the kingdom of heaven means that he himself is the God whose coming has been heralded. What we have here is an indirect self-presentation played in a major key.

Initially, this preaching of the *nearness* of the kingdom of heaven, also by Jesus, is not a problem, for the kingdom comes with the king.

Jesus starts dispelling sickness and sin and death (see sec. 3.2)—but the word "near" is never changed into "present" or "now." Later, when the twelve apostles are sent out, Jesus also tells them to announce to Israel that "the kingdom of heaven is near" (Matt. 10:7). It is still something to *be proclaimed* (Luke 9:2). Disciples learn how they are to *pray* for the coming of the kingdom (Matt. 6:10; Luke 11:2). And until the end of Jesus' earthly preaching, we find that the kingdom of heaven is mentioned in combination with future-oriented terms such as "inherit," "enter," and so forth (Matt. 25:34; compare Luke 19:11).

This continued use of the word *near* in the preaching of Jesus does not seem to fit with his claim to be the More Powerful One, announced by John, with whom the kingdom would appear. This is where the Baptist's own question comes in (Matt. 11:2): if Jesus is the one who is to come, then is it not time to begin establishing the kingdom with judgment and with the renewal of heaven and earth? Where is the ax? Where is the fire? Where is the suffusion of the people of God with the Holy Spirit? The mystery is not that Jesus expects a kingdom of heaven, nor that he preaches it as being close at hand, but that *he* seems to have become stuck in the "coming kingdom of God" that simply is not arriving.

Jesus' answer to John the Baptist shows that his teaching consists mainly of making people conscious of *how* the kingdom is coming and *how* people are entering it. Jesus first refers to the many signs and wonders he performs: they legitimize him. Then he makes the profound statement, "Blessed is the man who does not fall away on account of me" (Matt. 11:6). Happy are those who accept Jesus in his majesty *and* in his humiliation. The nearness of the kingdom is not a postponement. It does not mean that the kingdom is still without influence and beyond reach. On the contrary, it is within reach even now. The kingdom of God does not overpower the world, however: the King offers the citizens of this world the right to enter through faith in him. That is why Jesus' style of ministry is truly a gospel—truly Good News. John could only say that the kingdom of heaven is at hand, but Jesus is handing out admission tickets. He opens the doors and begins inviting people in. He himself is the door. He is the one who decides who will inherit the kingdom. The kingdom of heaven is as close as Jesus himself.

He is the guide. Through his suffering, death, and coming again he takes those who are his into the kingdom. The decision is his, and therefore he is the one who separates: those who do not believe in him are judged and thrown into the fire, into outer darkness, where there is gnashing of teeth. Remaining outside Jesus is the same as dwelling in the dark country beyond the borders of the kingdom of heaven. Believing in him is the same as being a citizen and heir to the kingdom of heaven.

In Matthew 12:28 (compare Luke 11:20), we read that *in the person of Jesus* the kingdom of God is presented to his contemporaries. It reaches them through Jesus. Those who do not want to seek it through him will fail to find it.[12]

Much of Jesus' teaching about the kingdom of heaven derives its special effect from the surprising, unexpected things he says about it. In the parables, when the kingdom of heaven is compared to something small like a mustard seed or something ordinary like a fish net, his listeners are challenged to search for the meaning. They learn to better understand the secrets of the kingdom (Matt. 13:11). Jesus' preaching about the kingdom of heaven is in line with both the general expectations of the people and the preaching of the Baptist, but he also reveals *new things* about this kingdom. And those new things have to do with the *path he will use to usher in the kingdom, the path by which people can participate in it*. It appears that entering the kingdom requires both humiliation and exaltation, and that for this reason we must believe in *him* and in his extraordinary work. These secrets are now being revealed, and the keys are being distributed. Jesus' work is in line with prophecy, but the arguments from the Scriptures are preceded by the direct revelation of Jesus himself. What God had kept hidden from the wise and the wealthy is what Jesus is now revealing to children (Matt. 11:25–27). The new element is not the expectation of a kingdom of heaven; rather, it is the revelation of the secret that Jesus' humiliation unlocks the entrance to the kingdom for believers.

The presentation of the kingdom is so humble and modest that mocking Pharisees can ask just *when* is it coming—failing to notice that it is already in their midst (Luke 17:21). Unbelievers still scan the horizon, while the kingdom has already arrived among them. It comes in such a way that it can easily be contradicted and denied.[13]

In summary, Jesus' preaching about the kingdom of heaven makes it impossible to view topics such as his life, his person, and his task as belonging to a secondary Christology, added later by the community to Jesus' simple teaching about the kingdom of God. The way in which he speaks about this kingdom—against the background of John's preach-

---

12. A look at a concordance will convince anyone that the largest portion of Jesus' statements about the kingdom of God are directed toward the future. O. Cullmann (*Salvation in History*, trans. S. G. Sowers et al. [New York: Harper & Row, 1967], 200–209) says three statements are based on a very direct, temporal understanding of the proximity of God's kingdom. For a discussion of these statements (Matt. 10:23; Mark 9:1; 13:30), see below, sec. 8.1. None of these three texts refers to a *period* of temporal proximity.

13. For a more detailed discussion of Luke 17:20–21, see J. van Bruggen, *Lucas: Het evangelie als voorgeschiedenis*, Commentaar op het Nieuwe Testament, 3d series (Kampen: Kok, 1993).

ing and with the authority of a judge—places his own person and his work in the very center of attention.

3.1.4 The Kingdom of Heaven in the Preaching of the Apostles

Jesus charges the Twelve with the preaching of the imminent coming of the kingdom of heaven (Matt. 10:7; 24:14). Thus in Acts, "preaching the kingdom" is a way of characterizing apostolic preaching in general (Acts 8:12; 14:22; 19:8; 20:25; 28:23). Although in the Epistles we regularly find allusions to the preaching of the kingdom (1 Cor. 4:20; Gal. 5:21; 1 Thess. 2:12; James 2:5; 2 Pet. 1:11; etc.), outside the Gospels the frequency with which the kingdom is mentioned drops sharply. In its place the expression *preaching Christ* or *preaching the gospel* gains prominence. This would seem to be a shift in emphasis—from an expected reality to a revered person. But the way in which Jesus taught the secrets of the kingdom of heaven makes this seeming shift more understandable.[14] The formulation of his message is aimed at his immediate context: Jews under the spell of the Baptist. What he taught about himself is therefore also often expressed in the terminology of the coming kingdom.

But in the Diaspora this specific context (Jews under the spell of the Baptist) did not exist. For this reason the horizon, the expected kingdom of heaven, is still present in the Acts and the Epistles, but the path to the kingdom (Christ) is preached more directly and now receives all attention as the trajectory of faith immediately before us.

Paul and Peter view the kingdom of God as the new order that will become a reality on earth when Christ appears. The nearness of this kingdom thus becomes the nearness of the Lord (Phil. 4:5; Rev. 22:12). Faith in Christ, and justification and sanctification as the way to enter, now become the framework within which the dynamic equivalence of what Jesus taught about the smallness of the kingdom, its simplicity, and so forth, is presented. And the reality of the faith connection with the coming kingdom now becomes apparent in the first giving of the Holy Spirit. When Paul says that God has "brought us into the kingdom of the Son he loves" (Col. 1:13), he does not mean that this kingdom is the Christian community. Rather, he is speaking about the indissoluble tie that already exists with the kingdom of heaven. Thus he also says with regard to people who are still living on the earth: "God raised us up with Christ and seated us with him in the heavenly realms in Christ Jesus" (Eph. 2:6). The certainty of the faith of the people who know that

---

14. P. Feine, *Theologie des Neuen Testaments*, 3d ed. (Leipzig: Hinrichs, 1919).

they are already citizens of that kingdom through the Spirit, and who, through this Spirit, already share in its first gifts, does not rule out the fact that entering into this kingdom is still future, so that Paul can write, "The Lord will rescue me from every evil attack and will bring me safely to his heavenly kingdom" (2 Tim. 4:18).

Thus the fact that the concept of "the kingdom of God" is not central in the later development of the teaching of the church is consonant with the flow of history. The early church and the Reformation clearly understood the striking way in which Jesus dealt with the concept of the kingdom of God when they placed at the center the satisfaction by means of Jesus' atoning death and the salvation through God's only Son. Today the gospel of the kingdom of God consists in bestowing the power of faith in Christ. This faith preserves us and lets us inherit the future. The Spirit of God, who already lives in all believers, is the pledge of the promised inheritance, for which we now pray with confidence: "Thy kingdom come."

3.2 Restoring People

3.2.1 Healings

From the start, Jesus' preaching of "the gospel of the kingdom" in the synagogues of Galilee went hand in hand with his "healing every disease and sickness among the people" (Matt. 4:23–24; 9:35; Mark 1:39). Thus Luke characterizes the return to Galilee as a coming "in the power of the Spirit" (Luke 4:14; compare 5:17). These healings are part of a program of *preaching* and must not be isolated from it. The miracles *show* that the kingdom of heaven is really around the corner.[15] Its blessings are already being felt!

This was not simply a matter of people getting well; there were doctors at the time who also accomplished many healings.[16] And miracles were performed by holy people, charismatic figures, and magicians. Stories of healings were associated with the temples of Asclepius. This is why Sanders comments that Jesus' miracles, in and of themselves, have no clear significance.[17] Bystanders could interpret them in a variety of ways. But Sanders overlooks what was unique about Jesus' heal-

15. H. K. Nielsen, *Heilung und Verkündigung: Das Verständnis der Heilung und ihres Verhältnisses zur Verkündigung bei Jesus und in der ältesten Kirche*, Acta theologica danica 22 (Leiden: Brill, 1987).

16. L. P. Hogan, *Healing in the Second Temple Period*, Novum Testamentum et Orbis Antiquus 21 (Freiburg: Universitätsverlag, 1992).

17. E. P. Sanders, *Jesus and Judaism* (London: SCM, 1985), 157–73.

ing activity: the scope of the healings, the speed, and the manner in
which they were performed.

> a. *Scope*. The healings are *universal*. We never read that people were
> sent away unhealed. There is only one example of a case in which
> there was no healing, but that failure was the result of the disci-
> ples' lack of faith—and when Jesus intervenes in the case of the
> demon-possessed boy, there is complete healing after all (Matt.
> 17:14–21). The scope of the healings exceeds all human measure;
> it is boundless and perfect. Some of the cases were considered to-
> tally *incurable* (Matt. 12:22), while in other cases the doctors were
> powerless (Mark 5:26; John 9:32). Leprosy, for which the Old Tes-
> tament had no other treatment than quarantine, is completely
> conquered. Even the dead are raised (Mark 5:35–42; Luke 7:11–
> 17; John 11:37–44; Matt. 27:51–53). The kingdom of heaven,
> where *no one* will ever be ill, really seems to be around the corner.
> All things may yet be well—even death itself must retreat!
>
> b. *Speed*. It is also striking that the recovery takes no time at all. The
> Evangelists often emphasize how the sick recovered *at once*. Pe-
> ter's mother-in-law, healed of a high fever, is immediately well
> enough to take up her household chores. There is only one exam-
> ple of a healing that takes place in two stages, the second coming
> immediately after the first: the blind man whose vision is still
> blurred at first and then becomes sharp (Mark 8:22–26). But this
> delay puts in even sharper focus how immediate and complete
> Jesus' healing is. He does not do things by halves; he heals com-
> pletely! And he helps immediately; even the recovery of this blind
> man is accomplished without further delay.
>
> c. *Manner*. The *manner* of the healings is also striking. Jesus pre-
> scribes no medicines, gives no lifestyle advice, and asks for no
> money (compare Luke 7:21: blind people who were beggars re-
> ceive their sight for nothing). Healing comes from Jesus without
> charge. He is like a fountain of life in Israel. He heals by word or
> by touch—his person alone is sufficient. This is underscored by
> the fact that Jesus demands *faith* when he heals. People must
> have faith in him if they are to be healed. When that faith is ab-
> sent, he cannot do signs and wonders (as in Nazareth, Mark 6:5–
> 6), not because his power is inadequate, but because the gifts of
> heaven are sent only through him, and only to believers.

These special and unique characteristics of Jesus' healings show that
the approach of the kingdom of heaven coincides with Jesus' own coming. Here, too, is a visible demonstration of the difference between John

the Baptist and Jesus. John preached both the proximity of the kingdom of heaven and the coming of the More Powerful One. With Jesus, the latter is omitted (he himself is the More Powerful One), and this omission is now justified by his actions. John performed no miracles (John 10:41), but Jesus makes people whole with a superhuman power. People now must look to *him* for the coming of the kingdom. He *is* the More Powerful One, the LORD, announced by John, who comes to visit his people.

3.2.2 Power over Demons

Casting out demons is part of healing the sick and the damaged, the blind, the lame, and so on (Matt. 4:24; 8:16–17; 10:1; Luke 6:18). As with all his healings, Jesus performs these exorcisms through his word. Other exorcists have to rely on words and formulas to do their work, but Jesus differs from them in that he does not use magical incantations that evoke higher powers. The terms "exorcism" (*exorkismos*) and "exorcize" (*exorkizein*) are not used in conjunction with Jesus' casting out of demons. And whereas the Jewish practitioners can indeed be called *exorkistai* (Acts 19:13), it is not a term that can be applied to Jesus, even though he does comparable things (Luke 11:19). When compared with gentile and Jewish exorcism, it is striking that Jesus simply *orders* the demons to depart *without exorcizing them*. He does not even appeal to the name of the LORD. His own word is enough.

This shows in the reactions of the demons. They do not retreat before powerful incantations or appeals to a higher power, but before Jesus' personality. They know who he is: the Holy One of God, the Son of God (Mark 1:24; 3:11–12). And that is why they throw themselves down before him, make their escape, and turn their victims over to him. Whereas part of the exorcist's art at the time was to discover the *name* of the demon in order to gain power over it, the demons appear willing to give their name to Jesus without being forced to do so, and afterward it turns out that Jesus does not even need the name of the demon in order to cast it out (Mark 5:9).

The reactions of his hearers also show that they realize that Jesus' *person* alone explains his power over the evil spirits. In Capernaum people ask, "What is this? A new teaching—and with authority! He even gives orders to evil spirits and they obey him" (Mark 1:27). And after the healing of a demoniac who was both blind and mute, the people react with astonishment: "Could this be the son of David?" (Matt. 12:23).

Even Jesus' opponents are forced to admit that the secret of this power, unlike that of the Jewish exorcists, does not lie in incantations but in Jesus himself. They try to explain it with the theory that he has a secret pact with Beelzebub, the prince of demons (Matt. 12:24; Mark 3:22).

Jesus himself established the connection between his personal power over the demons and his gospel of the kingdom of heaven that is imminent. Satan has been bound; his spoils have already been carried off (Mark 3:27). Jesus enters the house of "the strong man" and plunders it, showing once again that he is the *More Powerful One* who is to come, as promised by John. Every time he drives out evil spirits by the power of the Holy Spirit, the kingdom of heaven has come to earth and touches people (Matt. 12:28). These exorcisms are like invading troops landing in hostile territory.

Jesus' personal superiority over the evil spirits proves that he is the Christ, the Son of God. He forbids the spirits to proclaim this confession, but his prohibition does not deny the truth of their proclamations as to who he is. Jesus simply will have nothing to do with *this* kind of preacher. He wants *Israel*, rather than the demons, to learn to acknowledge him as the Christ, the Son of the living God, on the basis of these exorcisms (Matt. 12:28–37; Luke 11:20–28), and he wants the people to distance themselves from those leaders who accuse him of being possessed by an unclean spirit (Mark 3:28–30). This is why the evil spirits are given the chance to declare their knowledge of him within the hearing of the Jews, but then are ordered to keep quiet.

3.2.3 The Works of God and the Human Worldview

In recent centuries, scholars have been more emphatic than ever in pointing out that the biblical miracle stories presuppose a particular worldview—a claim that is difficult to deny. A report of exorcism assumes that unclean spirits actually *exist* and that they have conquered their own sphere of influence on earth, specifically in human beings.

According to many in the modern Western world, the existence of devils is simply an outmoded idea, but this Western view creates a problem in reading the New Testament, where devils were definitely *not* outmoded and were only in danger of losing their *territory*. Must a modern worldview that is based mainly on natural laws, immanence, causality, and a measure of anonymous coincidence or fate automatically lead to a denial or reinterpretation of the miracle stories in the Gospels?

In the nineteenth century, frequent attempts were made to treat these stories as actual events but to give them natural explanations so that they are no longer real *miracles*. But this effort to explain away the miracles resulted in some highly improbably "explanations." In the twentieth century, therefore, the accent was placed more on denying the *factuality* of the miracle stories. They were supposedly symbolic, legendary reports that mostly took shape among later Christian communities and were projected back onto the life of Jesus.[18] The miracles are then nothing more than a *mode of expression* that was quite common at the time and was connected with a then generally accepted view of human control over cosmic forces.[19]

In the Gospels, the *reality* of the miracles is abundantly clear. The miracle stories do not represent isolated, extraneous bits of magic in an otherwise mundane story. After all, the miracles are at several points interwoven with what goes on outside the miracle story. (1) The crowds, with all their sick, came flocking to Jesus because they saw *people* who had been healed, not because they had heard stories with no visible effects. (2) Jesus' opponents did not deny the reality of the miracles and found it necessary to come up with alternative explanations. (3) In the

18. W. Schmithals, *Wunder und Glaube: Eine Auslegung von Markus 4,35–6,6a* (Neukirchen: Neukirchener Verlag, 1970).

19. H. C. Kee, *Medicine, Miracle, and Magic in New Testament Times*, Society for New Testament Studies Monograph Series 55 (Cambridge: Cambridge University Press, 1986); M. E. Mills, *Human Agents of Cosmic Power in Hellenistic Judaism and the Synoptic Tradition*, JSNTSup 41 (Sheffield: JSOT Press, 1990).

For the history of miracle criticism, see W. G. Kümmel, *Vierzig Jahre Jesusforschung (1950–1990)*, 2d ed., ed. H. Merklein, Bonner Biblische Beiträge 60 (Weinheim: Beltz Athenäum, 1994); H. van der Loos, *The Miracles of Jesus*, Novum Testamentum Supplement 8 (Leiden: Brill, 1965), 3–113; W. L. Craig, "The Problem of Miracles: A Historical and Philosophical Perspective," in *Gospel Perspectives*, vol. 6, *The Miracles of Jesus*, ed. D. Wenham and C. Blomberg (Sheffield: JSOT Press, 1986), 9–48; G. Maier, "Zur neutestamentlichen Wunderexegese im 19. und 20. Jahrhundert," in *Miracles of Jesus*, ed. Wenham and Blomberg, 49–88.

For a critical discussion of the theory that Jesus' life was patterned after the model of the Greek "superman" (*theios anēr*): B. L. Blackburn, "Miracle Working *Theioi Andres* in Hellenism (and Hellenistic Judaism)," in *Miracles of Jesus*, ed. Wenham and Blomberg, 185–218; E. Koskenniemi, *Apollonius von Tyana in der neutestamentlichen Exegese: Forschungsbericht und Weiterführung der Diskussion*, WUNT 2/61 (Tübingen: Mohr, 1994); J. R. Brady, *Jesus Christ: Divine Man or Son of God?* (Lanham, Md.: University Press of America, 1992).

The theory that Jesus was a magician is analyzed and refuted by E. Yamauchi, "Magic or Miracle? Diseases, Demons, and Exorcisms," in *Miracles of Jesus*, ed. Wenham and Blomberg, 89–184.

Blackburn expands this refutation to include the theory put forward by Vermes that Jesus was a Galilean ḥāsîd, a charismatic wonder-working prophet. (B. L. Blackburn, "The Miracles of Jesus," in *Studying the Historical Jesus: Evaluations of the State of Current Research*, New Testament Tools and Studies 19, ed. B. Chilton and C. A. Evans [Leiden: Brill, 1994], 353–94; compare with C. A. Evans, *Jesus and His Contemporaries: Comparative Studies*, Arbeiten zur Geschichte des antiken Judentums und des Urchristentums 25 [Leiden: Brill, 1995]; G. Vermes, "Jesus the Prophet," in *Jesus the Jew: A Historian's Reading of the Gospels* [Philadelphia: Fortress, 1973], 86–102.)

Finally, for a comparative study on the basis of a morphological structural analysis of the stories, see W. Kahl, *New Testament Miracle Stories in Their Religious-Historical Setting: A Religionsgeschichtliche Comparison from a Structural Perspective* (Göttingen: Vandenhoeck & Ruprecht, 1994).

stories themselves there are often elements that could have been checked by later readers (the references to those whose names appear in the stories: Jairus, Bartimaeus, Mary Magdalene, Malchus, and Lazarus; the disaster with the herd of two thousand pigs near Gadara).

This means that the works of God that Jesus performed also have something to tell us about the world in which we live. It is apparently— even if we may be less aware of it in some cultural contexts—a world in which unclean spirits can torment people with all sorts of diseases and maladies and can even make themselves at home in a person.

The fact is that Jesus' miracles demonstrate a certain link between sickness and demonic possession. On the one hand he appears to be a perfect physician; on the other hand he is a powerful exorcist. The reader of the Gospels whose worldview is devoid of angels and demons can easily be tempted to make a distinction between physician and exorcist. This limits the worldview problem to the passages dealing with demonic possession, while Jesus' healing activity is accepted as the charism of a gifted individual. But even in Jesus' healings we are faced with a worldview in which God takes action against Satan and his unclean spirits.[20]

There is certainly a distinction between the many sick or weak persons and the truly demon-possessed ones, but this might be called the difference between people who are being *besieged and bombarded* (from the outside; *circumsessio*) by the devil, and those whom the devil has *occupied and laid waste* (from the inside; *possessio*).[21]

1. The four detailed stories of *very notable* exorcisms (Mark 1:21–28; 5:1–20; 7:24–30; 9:14–29) might leave us with the impression that the presence of demons can always be recognized by aggressive behavior. The fact is, however, that driving out this aggressive *type* of demon is a spectacular event, whereas driving out other kinds of demons tends to be less spectacular. Thus there are various examples of nonaggressive demoniacs with very different symptoms (the fortune-telling woman in Philippi, Acts 16:16–18; the woman with a debilitating spirit that caused her to be completely bent over, Luke 13:11; the spirits that cause deafness or muteness, Matt. 9:32–33; 12:22; Luke 11:14). Jesus was also accused of being "possessed" (John 8:48–49; Mark 3:30; Matt. 12:24), though there was nothing in his behavior that would make him comparable to the aggressive kind of demons. What all de-

20. Hogan, *Healing in the Second Temple Period.*
21. J. Smit, *De daemoniacis in historia evangelica*, dissertatio exegetico-apologetica (Rome: Pontificii Instituti Biblici, 1913).

mons and "demoniacs" had in common was that they could do no good. For the crowds, this was the only criterion to which they could turn to reject the suggestion that Jesus was "possessed": "These are not the sayings of a man possessed by a demon. Can a demon open the eyes of the blind?" (John 10:21). The demon that inhabits a person thus can sometimes be recognized by the absence of the ability to speak or to use normal language, and usually by the damage it inflicts on the person and sometimes also on the person's environment.

2. Although there is a difference between sickness and demon possession, there is nevertheless something that unites them: both conditions can be "cured" (Matt. 4:23–24; Luke 6:17–18; 7:21). Among the many sick people who are healed, there are those from whom demons depart (Luke 4:40–41; Acts 19:12). Driving out demons and thus restoring people who are in bad shape fulfills the promise that the Servant of the Lord will take away all sickness (Matt. 8:16–17). When the Twelve are sent out, they are given power over all unclean spirits, and because of that power they have "authority to drive out evil spirits and to heal every disease and sickness" (Matt. 10:1). Thus Peter describes Jesus' ministry as follows: "he went around doing good and healing all who were under the power of the devil, because God was with him" (Acts 10:38). He not only refers to the demon-possessed, but to all those who are sick. All of them can be said to be "harassed" (*katadynasteuein*; compare James 2:6). Some are only troubled from the outside; in other cases the unclean spirit has taken up residence within them. Thus it is possible that even a fever is "rebuked" (Luke 4:39).

In the New Testament we do not find two worldviews—the worldview of closed causality in which various clinical diagnoses have their place, and the open worldview of an earth with a heaven, in which angels and spirits play a role. There is only one worldview: that of earth and a heaven. In this worldview God is at war against the devil and his evil spirits. These spirits have managed to get a foothold on earth: they influence people and turn them into liars (John 8:44), damage them, and sometimes even take total possession of them.

From the perspective of this worldview, the unity of the works of God performed by Jesus Christ is more recognizable. Whether healing or driving out demons, he is busy undoing the negative and destructive work of the evil spirits. Satan breaks and destroys; God restores. The hands of the King heal! The kingdom of heaven is now standing at the gates of the human fortress where Satan and his spirits have ensconced themselves.

Jesus heals people and lengthens their lives in order that they may use their time for *faith in him*. Thus they shall inherit the kingdom of heaven. That is why he limits himself to healings and exorcisms. He refuses to become involved as a social worker or as a human judge. On one occasion someone tried to interest him in a question concerning an earthly inheritance, but Jesus did not want to use his power in matters such as this. This story marks the *boundary* of his exercise of power on earth and also demonstrates its goal.[22] Christ liberates people so that they can inherit the kingdom of heaven: this is what his mission is all about.

When the Seventy(-two) are sent out and are allowed to heal the sick, they must add a message to the healings: "The kingdom of God is near you" (Luke 10:9). And when they come back amazed that "even the demons submit to us in your name," Jesus says that he saw Satan fall like lightning from heaven. This means that they should expect severe aggression from the spirits who are on the brink of defeat. But Jesus has given his disciples power "to trample on snakes and scorpions and to overcome all the power of the enemy; nothing will harm you" (Luke 10:17–19).

When the apostles are sent out after the resurrection, they receive signs to accompany their words. These are signs of the victory of Jesus. Driving out evil spirits, taking up snakes, drinking poison, and healing the sick are all of a piece—they are proof that God's opponent is losing both influence and territory.

The apostle Paul himself was an example of the fact that a non-possessed person can be bothered by Satan with sickness or hardship (2 Cor. 12:7–9). The persistence of these hardships in his life confirms that Christ came to do God's work on earth in order to engender faith in God and in his Anointed and to show proof of the *nearness* of the kingdom.

3.3 Authority over Creation

Healings and exorcisms are aimed at *people*. But the world in which these people live also appears to be under the power of Jesus. God's work involves not only the sick and the possessed, but also water, wind, bread, and fish. These so-called nature miracles show Jesus' power over creation. They constitute the frame within which the works on behalf of people and against the demons can be performed. Jesus carries on his ministry in his *own* world.

The "first of his miraculous signs" consisted of *changing* a large amount of water into excellent wine at the wedding at Cana. In this act Jesus "revealed his glory" (John 2:11).

22. See van Bruggen, *Lucas*, on Luke 12:14.

Later Jesus supplies needs even more creatively by *multiplying*—creating—food. He turns five loaves and two fish into enough food for five thousand men, not including women and children. And with seven loaves and a few fish he feeds four thousand men, not including women and children. In both cases more food was left over than there had been at the start! The disciples' lack of faith might have disappeared if they had remembered the totals of these multiplications (Mark 8:17–21)!

Authority over creation is apparent in the way Jesus directs schools of fish in the Sea of Galilee (Luke 5:4–11), a sign that is repeated after Easter (John 21:6–11). On another occasion, Simon is sent to an appointed place and catches a fish with a coin in its mouth, sent by Jesus (Matt. 17:27). Jesus also appears to have power over storms and towering waves. With a word he commands wind and water (Mark 4:35–41), another expression of his power that is exhibited more than once (Mark 6:51). And when he wants to, he even walks on the water across a stormy sea (Mark 6:48).

Among the "nature miracles" is also the only sign performed by Jesus that was not healing but harmful: the fig tree that is cursed by him and withers overnight. The effect of this sign is at odds with what the people are used to seeing Jesus do. It is a unique and grave message for an unbelieving Israel, on whom a healing Savior is lost (Mark 11:12–14, 20–26).

Jesus appears to have control over creation, which raises questions about who he really is (Matt. 8:27). The answer is inescapable: he is God's Son (Matt. 14:33). Peter says the same to the Jews on Pentecost: "Jesus of Nazareth was a man accredited by God to you by miracles, wonders and signs, which God did among you through him, as you yourselves know" (Acts 2:22). And to Cornelius, Peter speaks of "Jesus Christ, who is Lord of all. You know what has happened throughout Judea, beginning in Galilee . . . how God anointed Jesus of Nazareth with the Holy Spirit and power" (Acts 10:36–38).

The gospel of the coming kingdom is brought by the King himself. Not only do his hands heal, but creation listens to his voice!

3.4 The Works of God: For Others Only!

There seems to be something contradictory in the way in which Jesus does God's work. On the one hand his power is unlimited; on the other, he comes as a sometimes needy and weak human creature. This shows up clearly during the temptations in the wilderness: "If you are the Son of God, tell these stones to become bread" (Matt. 4:3). Why does Jesus not do this when he is consumed with hunger after forty days of prayer and fasting? Later he will provide bread and fish for thousands of people out in the wilderness. The comments of the chief priests, teachers of the law, and elders at the foot of the cross point to the same thing: "He saved others, but he can't save himself! He's the King of Israel! Let him come down now from the cross, and we will believe in him. He trusts in God. Let God rescue him now if he wants him, for he said, 'I am the Son of God'" (Matt. 27:42–43).

Jesus suffers from fatigue, he weeps, he is tempted, he more than once escapes attempts on his life, and finally he is arrested and crucified. In all this he is no more than a vulnerable man. Later, Lutheran dogmatics will pose the question whether he "concealed" (*krypsis*) or completely "laid aside" (*kenōsis*) his divine nature. Modern theology makes a distinction between the man Jesus *before* Easter and the Christ, proclaimed to be God's Son, *after* Easter. But neither of these distinctions takes the facts into account.

The reality is that Jesus does give full expression to his divine power in the works he does during his stay on earth, but *always for others and never for himself*. In the midst of the healing and redeeming work of God, there is one person who gives without taking for himself. He abstains and thus his hunger, his fatigue, and his arrest are not the sufferings of a powerless victim but the work of a *free agent*. He does the work of God for the people, but he himself suffers the existence of a powerless human being, tempted by Satan, slandered by enemies, and killed on the cross.

This combination puts the works he does in a special light. The nearness of the kingdom is revealed in the works of God—healing people and exercising power over creation. But the way these works are accomplished shows that the kingdom comes *by way of renunciation and humiliation*. The kingdom comes nearer through the hands of a dying King. This is its hallmark—a mystery that finds expression in the announcements of the Passion and in a number of the parables. In Jesus' ministry, it stands large as life before all.

4

The Self-Presentation
of the Son of Man

From the very beginning, the things that Jesus did and taught were attention getting: God's works were being performed in Israel, and his kingdom was being preached. Even Jesus' *way* of speaking quickly attracted attention. His unusual expressions and surprising stylistic choices did not go unnoticed. And why did he keep calling himself "the Son of Man"? This chapter is devoted to Jesus' way of referring to himself, which he used to send clear signals to his listeners. The people heard a human being speak, but his way of expressing himself belonged to someone who was more than a mere human being.

The first part of this chapter deals with a number of striking characteristics of Jesus' use of language (sec. 4.1). The second part is a detailed discussion of the way he refers to himself as "the Son of Man" (sec. 4.2).

4.1 Jesus' Use of Special Terms

4.1.1 "I Tell You"

It is striking how often Jesus begins a sentence with the words "I tell you." This introductory formula occurs at the point where the prophets normally indicate that the LORD is speaking through them ("Thus says the LORD . . ."). Interestingly, Jesus never uses this prophetic formula—he speaks with his *own* authority. When it is *he* who says something, no appeal to a higher authority is necessary.

Jesus' way of speaking is also different from that of the rabbis, who constantly appeal to the elders, the rabbis of former generations. Their statements are authoritative only when they are supported by tradition. But Jesus has his own voice. He does not lean on the fathers for support.

In fact, he raises his voice to *supersede* the words of Moses. God spoke to the fathers through Moses, and Jesus fulfills that which was spoken by Moses and the prophets, but he also brings new revelation and asks the people to submit to his authoritative words (Matt. 5–7; 11:27–30; Mark 7:14–16; John 12:44–50).[1]

People are shocked by his tone (Matt. 7:28–29; Mark 1:27). He teaches as one with authority and not as the teachers of the law. Jesus speaks as though he were God himself, and his language raises questions. Even in the twentieth century, a Jewish writer considers it a matter of course that Jesus used authoritative backing for the points he makes in the Sermon on the Mount; the fact that such authorities are missing in the Gospels means, according to this writer, that they must have been removed later by the Evangelists in order to present Jesus' authority as exclusive.[2]

4.1.2 "Amen, Amen"

Although Jesus speaks with his own authority ("I tell you"), he does not speak as a solitary individual. This introductory formula is regularly preceded by an "Amen" or "Yes," as if with his words Jesus is *endorsing* the truth rather than presenting it as something brand-new of his own devising.

Jeremias points out that in Jewish literature "amen" is always an affirmative or assenting exclamation that *follows* a statement of praise, a blessing, or a curse.[3] The New Testament communities also use the words "amen" or "yes" to affirm what others have said (1 Cor. 14:16; 2 Cor. 1:20). What is completely new about Jesus' usage is that he *begins* his statements with an "amen" or a "yes." In the Gospel of John, we always find a double "amen" ("Amen, amen, I tell you"; translated "I tell you the truth" in NIV).

Jeremias considers this introductory "amen" a trademark of the authentic words of Jesus.[4] Others feel that this introduction goes back to the charismatics of the oldest church communities, who used an "amen" to pass on to the community whatever they had heard from the Lord in heaven.[5] Some insist that this formula is an aspect of Judaism's visionary-apocalyptic movement, making the "amen statements" one of the formulas used to legitimize prophetic seers.[6] Although Berger

---

1. Compare R. Karpinski, *Exousia: A la base de l'enseignement de Jésus et de la mission apostolique selon S. Matthieu* (Rome: Nilo, 1968).

2. S. Ben-chorin, *Broeder Jezus: De Nazarener door een Jood gezien*, trans. F. van der Heijden (Baarn: Ten Have, 1971), 67 (German ed., 1967).

3. J. Jeremias, *New Testament Theology* (London: SCM, 1971), 43–44.

4. Ibid.

5. V. Hasler, *Amen: Redaktionsgeschichtliche Untersuchung zur Einführungsformel der Herrenworte "Wahrlich ich sage euch"* (Zürich: Gotthelf, 1969).

6. K. Berger, *Die Amen-Worte Jesu: Eine Untersuchung zum Problem der Legitimation in apokalyptischer Rede*, Beihefte zur Zeitschrift für die neutestamentliche Wissenschaft 39 (Berlin: de Gruyter, 1970).

claimed to have found two pre-Christian examples of such an introductory "amen" in the Testament of Abraham,[7] he later qualified his thesis.[8] And Jeremias followed with the renewed assertion that the introductory "amen" occurs only in statements by Jesus and is without extrabiblical parallel.[9]

This extraordinary usage suggests that, though Jesus said very surprising and new things, he in fact *endorses* what is already known and that he *agrees with* what has already been said by or is known to someone else.

Who is the "someone else"? His hearers are faced with an enigma. Some think that Jesus is disturbed, others think he is in league with Beelzebub. But Jesus himself wants people to get the idea that he is making known what is already known by the Father, and that he speaks about what he himself has already seen. He speaks in accordance with what the Father knows and wants to make known through Jesus' ministry. His speaking is a *response*. We see this when Jesus *begins* a sentence with "Yes!" "Yes, Father, for this was your good pleasure. All things have been committed to me by my Father, and no one knows the Father except the Son and those to whom the Son chooses to reveal him" (Matt. 11:26–27). On earth he speaks with a single voice, but his preaching is supported by many voices. His is not a solo ministry: "I stand with the Father, who sent me" (John 8:16). The Son has an open connection with heaven and speaks together with the Father: "I tell you the truth, *we* speak of what *we* know, and *we* testify to what *we* have seen, but still you people do not accept our testimony" (John 3:11; the plural here can hardly be a reference to Jesus and John the Baptist, because shortly thereafter, in John 3:31–32, John emphatically declares that not he but Jesus, who "comes from heaven," testifies on the basis of what "he has seen and heard").

4.1.3 "I Have Come"

Another striking expression is found in Jesus' habit of speaking of his ministry on earth in a general sense as "coming." He acts and speaks in this human world, but he continually gives the impression that he has come *from somewhere else* to do his work here (for example, Matt. 5:17; 10:34; 20:28; Luke 19:10; John 5:43; 12:47).

---

7. Berger, *Die Amen-Worte Jesu.* The examples in the Testament of Abraham are found only in the longer redaction, in a medieval manuscript, which may reflect Christian influences. Besides, we read in chap. 8 of the Testament of Abraham how God affirms *his own (quoted) promises*, and in chap. 20 the personification of death responds in the affirmative to *Abraham's question* whether there is a sudden death.

8. K. Berger, "Die königlichen Messiastraditionen des neuen Testaments," *New Testament Studies* 20 (1973–74): 1–44.

9. J. Jeremias, "Zum nicht-responsorischen Amen," *Zeitschrift für die neutestamentliche Wissenschaft* 64 (1973): 122–23.

This is more explicitly stated in the Gospel of John: Jesus comes *from above* (John 3:31). He himself knows where he comes from, but his opponents have no idea (John 8:14). He came into the world, and he leaves it once again to return to the Father (John 16:28). Thus Paul later confesses, "Christ Jesus *came* into the world to save sinners" (1 Tim. 1:15).

In the context of Jesus' teaching as a whole it is quite clear where he comes from and where he is going, but it is not always explicitly stated. In his speaking there is regularly an appeal to his hearers; because of his miracles and his teaching they see that he is *here*, but they have to ponder his origin. Where does he *come from*?

Behind this usage stands a claim. Jesus is one who is sent. The crowds think they can place him: he is the man from Nazareth and Galilee (John 7:41). For this reason, most people do not feel compelled to recognize him as the Messiah of God: "When the Christ comes, no one will know where he is from" (John 7:27). But Jesus protests forcefully: the people do not know God, who sent him (John 7:28)!

4.1.4 "Greater Than" and "Before"

With a certain regularity, Jesus makes statements about himself in which he calls himself superior to others or says that he existed before they did, specifically mentioning the great men of the past or the patriarchs. Thus he tells the crowds more than once that someone is now in their midst who is "greater than Solomon" or "greater than Jonah" (Matt. 12:41–42; Luke 11:31–32).

His conversation with the Samaritan woman suggests that he is "greater than Jacob" (John 4:12). The way he presents himself to the Jews gives them the impression that he is "greater than our father Abraham" (John 8:53). Abraham and the prophets have died, after all, but Jesus dares to say that whoever keeps *his* word will never taste death (John 8:51). For the Jews this is a confirmation of their suspicion that he is a Samaritan and possessed by an evil spirit (John 8:48, 52). So they ask him, "Who do you think you are?" (John 8:53). This question leads to a discussion in which Jesus finally says, "I tell you the truth . . . before Abraham was born, I am!" (John 8:58).

Only someone who transcends the highest human criteria would describe himself this way. In reaction against this claim, the Jews pick up stones to kill him for blasphemy (John 8:59). They clearly sense Jesus' claim, even though they refuse to honor him as God.

4.1.5 "I Am"

Many of the sayings of Jesus are directly or indirectly aimed at the meaning and significance of his own person. He uses a wide variety of images to indicate who he really is. Apparently he is a "fisher of men" who recruits others into his service (Matt. 4:19). He is the "narrow gate" (Matt. 7:13–14; compare 7:21–23). Jesus is "the shepherd" who has come to save those who are lost (Matt. 18:11–14).

John the Evangelist has preserved several direct images. Jesus calls himself the bread of heaven, the bread of life (6:41, 48, 51), the light of the world (8:12), the gate for the sheep (10:7, 9), the good shepherd (10:11–14), the resurrection and the life (11:25), the way, the truth, and the life (14:6), and the true vine (15:1, 5).

In the indirect statements the image comes first in the form of a parable. The explanations of these parables then make clear that they are told to show who Jesus is and what his work signifies. Behind the sower in the parable stands Jesus himself: he sows the word of God (Luke 8:11). The man who scatters the good seed in the field turns out to be none other than the "Son of Man" (Matt. 13:37–43). The son of the owner of the vineyard who is killed by the tenants is Jesus (Matt. 21:33–46). Similarly, most of the parables, even when they are not explained, offer indirect images of who Jesus is.

The use of these parables and images is typical of his teaching. It encourages listeners not to be satisfied with their image of Jesus—do they know who he *really* is?

4.2 Jesus' Use of "Son of Man"

4.2.1 A Mysterious Self-Designation

All four Gospels indicate that Jesus frequently referred to himself as "the Son of Man"—a somewhat enigmatic term, the more so because in the Gospels it is used only by Jesus himself. It is strictly a self-designation and is used by no one else.

Jesus called himself "Son of Man" from the very beginning of his public ministry (John 1:52; 3:13–14; Mark 2:10, 28; Luke 6:22), and he still used it in his final statement before the Sanhedrin that would condemn him to death: "In the future you will see *the Son of Man* sitting at the right hand of the Mighty One and coming on the clouds of heaven" (Matt. 26:64; Mark 14:62; Luke 22:69).

Jesus used this self-designation throughout his public ministry in Israel. It became characteristic of his speaking. In the four Gospels familiar to us there are more than fifty separate statements in which Jesus calls himself *the Son of Man*.[10]

---

10. The phrase *ho huios tou anthrōpou* occurs thirty-two times in most of the manuscripts of Matthew (thirty times in modern editions: 18:11 and 25:13b are missing); fourteen times in Mark; twenty-six times in most manuscripts of Luke (twenty-five times in

What is striking is the absence of the term "Son of Man" elsewhere in the New Testament. Outside the Gospels it appears only once, in Acts 7:56. Stephen, brought before the Sanhedrin, cries out that he can see the Son of Man standing at God's right hand. This clearly points back to Jesus' own words, spoken before the same Sanhedrin not long before (Matt. 26:64). It is, in fact, a *quoted* self-designation. From the writings of the apostles we know that the term "Son of Man" was never used by others in reference to Jesus; it was used *exclusively* by Jesus as a means of identifying himself.

In Revelation 1:13 and 14:14 there is mention of "someone 'like a son of man'" (indefinite article; compare Dan. 7:13), but here Jesus is compared with a son of man in general; it is not a specific designation or title for him. In Hebrews 2:6, we read about "a son of man" (via a quote from Ps. 8:4: "what is man that you are mindful of him, the son of man that you care for him?"), but this is a reference to humanity in general and not to Jesus personally—the discussion of this passage from the psalm in Hebrews 2:8–9 does not identify Jesus as "Son of Man."

In the Gospels, the only time that other people utter this name is as an echo of Jesus' own words, when people are quoting him. He himself had said, in answer to the crowd's question "Who are you?" (John 8:25), "When you have lifted up the Son of Man . . ." (John 8:28). There is reference to this later, when he was asked, "We have heard from the law that the Christ will remain forever, so how can you say, 'The Son of Man must be lifted up?'" (John 12:34) The phrasing of the question proves that the crowds easily make use of the name Messiah. They have the impression that Jesus wants to be the Messiah, but he talks about tasks that seem strange for a messiah ("be lifted up"), and he uses an unusual name or title ("the Son of Man"). What is behind this strange phrase he keeps using to refer to himself, in a way that does not seem to fit in with what people expect from the Messiah?

Regardless of what the name may mean, it is obvious whom it refers to: Jesus of Nazareth. He himself *is* "the Son of Man." This name occupies the same place in the sentence structure as a personal pronoun would. There are two parallel places in the Gospels where "the Son of Man" alternates with "I" (Matt. 5:11 and Luke 6:22; Matt. 16:21, Mark

---

modern editions: 9:56 is missing); and twelve times in most manuscripts of John (thirteen times in modern editions: 9:35 uses "Son of Man" instead of "Son of God"). In Luke there are nine unique cases not found in the other Gospels (6:22; 9:22; 12:8; 17:22; 18:8; 19:10; 21:36; 22:48; 24:7). In John, all thirteen cases are unique. The total number of cases in Matthew (thirty-two/thirty) plus the unique cases in Luke (nine) and John (twelve/thirteen) add up to fifty-three/fifty-two. These statements are spread fairly evenly across all the periods (before and after John's arrest and during Jesus' ministry in Galilee, journey to Jerusalem, and final week).

8:31, and Luke 9:22). There are also a few places that are not historically parallel but that are comparable in content, in which "Son of Man" as a designation for Jesus also alternates with "I" (for instance, Matt. 10:32–33 and Luke 12:8–9).

When Jesus' audience heard him identify himself in this way, it was not immediately clear to them what he intended to convey by it. He invited them in effect to establish their own connection between this rather striking name and the prevailing expectations. Thus he asks his disciples at Caesarea Philippi, "Who do people say that *I*, the Son of Man, am?" (author's translation).[11] The answers vary ("John the Baptist, Elijah, Jeremiah or one of the prophets"). Only the disciples give the correct answer: "You are the Christ, the Son of the living God" (Matt. 16:13–16). It appears that *for Jesus himself* the designation "Son of Man" is in line with that confession, but that the confession "You are the Christ, the Son of the living God" is not a *necessary* implication of the phrase. Others could attach other ideas to it (by misunderstanding his ministry).

Two things become clear when we begin exploring how Jesus uses this self-designation.

1. The name is striking.
2. It does not fit in naturally with commonly held expectations for the future.

Apparently Jesus wanted to use an uncommon name to attract attention and invite reflection. Why did he choose to do this in this manner? Several answers have been given, but each usually ignores one of two facts. One answer is that the name "Son of Man" was not striking at all; in fact, it was nothing more than an (Aramaic) alias Jesus hid behind. This theory does justice to the fact that the name did not coincide with current expectations for the future, but it fails to appreciate the fact that Jesus' way of referring to himself did attract attention. Another answer is that the term is a common designation for well-defined future expectations regarding "the (expected) son of man." As such this term is striking, all the more so because Jesus appropriates this exalted title for himself. This theory does justice to the striking quality of the name, but it ignores the fact that people in Jesus' day could not easily fit the name into current expectations about the future.

11. On the basis of a few manuscripts, newer translations of 16:13 read as follows: "Who do people say the son of man is?" For a discussion of this point see J. van Bruggen, *Matteüs: Het evangelie voor Israël,* 2d ed., Commentaar op het Nieuwe Testament, 3d series (Kampen: Kok, 1994), on Matt. 16:13.

Because of the large amount of literature on this subject, both arguments deserve further discussion in the next two sections.[12]

4.2.2 A Commonly Used Title?

In the twentieth century it was for a time customary to describe the Christology of the New Testament primarily on the basis of the so-called titles it uses for Jesus. In addition to designations such as *Christ, Lord*, and *Son of David*, the term *Son of Man* was then also discussed in depth as one of the most pivotal characterizations of Jesus.[13] Cullmann even argues for a rewriting of classical Christology by making "Son of Man" its most central concept.[14]

But this approach has come under criticism. The answer to the question *Who is Jesus?* is found not in isolated designations but in sentences and statements in the New Testament. The "titles" derive their value for the most part from the sentences in which they are used.[15]

This criticism, while pointing out the limited possibilities of a specific approach, does not preclude that some titles had significant value in and of themselves. This, according to many, is the case with "Son of Man." This title then is thought to have a rather well-defined meaning in the context of future expectations, since, so the argument goes, in Jewish circles at the time of the New Testament the "Son of Man" was expected as the judge of the end time. Jesus then tied into this expectation when he spoke about the coming of the Son of Man to judge the nations.

12. For an overview of the many opinions and for an exhaustive literature list, see M. Müller, *Der Ausdruck "Menschensohn" in den Evangelien: Voraussetzungen und Bedeutung*, Acta theologica danica 17 (Leiden: Brill, 1984); C. C. Caragounis, *The Son of Man: Vision and Interpretation*, WUNT 38 (Tübingen: Mohr, 1986). For a treatment limited to recent discussions, see A. J. B. Higgins, *The Son of Man in the Teaching of Jesus*, Society for New Testament Studies Monograph Series 39 (Cambridge: Cambridge University Press, 1980), 29–53; W. G. Kümmel, *Jesus der Menschensohn?* Sitzungsberichte der wissenschaftlichen Gesellschaft an der Johann Wolfgang Goethe-Universität Frankfurt am Main 20.3 (Stuttgart: Steiner, 1984); W. O. Walker, "The Son of Man: Some Recent Developments," *CBQ* 45 (1983): 584–607. For an expanded version of this article, see W. O. Walker, "The Son of Man Question and the Synoptic Problem," in *New Synoptic Studies: The Cambridge Gospel Conference and Beyond*, ed. W. R. Farmer (Macon, Ga.: Mercer University Press, 1983), 261–301; J. R. Donahue, "Recent Studies on the Origin of 'Son of Man' in the Gospels," *CBQ* 48 (1986): 484–98.

13. V. Taylor, *The Names of Jesus* (London: Macmillan, 1954); F. Hahn, *The Titles of Jesus in Christology: Their History in Early Christianity*, trans. H. Knight and G. Ogg (London: Lutterworth, 1969).

14. O. Cullmann, *The Christology of the New Testament*, trans. S. C. Guthrie and C. A. M. Hall (Philadelphia: Westminster, 1959).

15. L. E. Keck, "Toward the Renewal of New Testament Christology," *New Testament Studies* 32 (1986): 362–77; D. R. A. Hare, *The Son of Man Tradition* (Minneapolis: Fortress, 1990), 280–82.

Only gradually did the idea take hold that the future judge coincided with the person of Jesus. For Bultmann, the only sayings of Jesus that are authentic are those in which he speaks of the coming Son of Man as though he were speaking about a person distinct from himself.[16] Statements in which Jesus identifies himself with the Son of Man then derive from the Christian communities and are not authentic. Only after Jesus' death was the idea born that the deceased Master would return as the long-awaited Son of Man. In a number of announcements of the Passion, Jesus' death is then linked with this "Son of Man." At a still later stage in the tradition, statements developed in which the Son of Man was also identified with the work of Jesus during his earthly life. Vielhauer goes one step further than Bultmann; according to him Jesus never said a word about "the Son of Man," and the Christian community put words in his mouth after his death, paving the way for the later identification.[17] Higgins is somewhat more moderate than Bultmann; he claims that there are a limited number of authentic statements by Jesus that contain the expectation of a future exaltation in which he as judge would perform the *functions* of the "Son of Man." This is then the starting point for the *identification* of Jesus' person with this Son of Man in the oldest Christian communities.

An important presupposition of these theories is that within the Judaism of Jesus' day there was an expectation of the son of man who would come as judge in the last days. The biblical starting point for that expectation is Daniel 7:13.[18] Daniel's vision of the four (wicked) beasts has the following conclusion:

> In my vision at night I looked, and there before me was one like a son of man, coming with the clouds of heaven. He approached the Ancient of Days and was led into his presence. He was given authority, glory and sov-

16. R. Bultmann, *Theology of the New Testament*, trans. K. Grobel (New York: Scribner, 1951–55). Compare H. E. Tödt, *Der Menschensohn in der synoptischen Überlieferung* (Gütersloh: Mohn, 1959) and H. J. de Jonge, "De visie van de historische Jezus op zichzelf," in *Jezus' visie op zichzelf: In discussie met De Jonge's christologie* (Nijkerk: Callenbach, 1991), 48–64.

17. See also P. Vielhauer, "Gottesreich und Menschensohn in der Verkündigung Jesu," (1963) in *Aufsätze zum Neuen Testament*, Theologische Bücherei 31 (Munich: Kaiser, 1965), 55–91; Walker, "Son of Man: Some Recent Developments," 584–607; Walker, "Son of Man Question and the Synoptic Problem," 261–301; and A. Vögtle, *Die "Gretchenfrage" des Menschensohnproblems: Bilanz und Perspektive*, 2d ed., Quaestiones Disputatae 152 (Freiburg: Herder, 1995).

18. C. Colpe, "ὁ υἱὸς τοῦ ἀνθρώπου," in *Theological Dictionary of the New Testament*, ed. G. Friedrich, trans. G. W. Bromiley (Grand Rapids: Eerdmans, 1972), 8:400–477; C. C. Caragounis, *Son of Man: Vision and Interpretation*; B. Witherington III, *The Christology of Jesus* (Minneapolis: Fortress, 1990); J. J. Collins, "The Son of Man in First-Century Judaism," *New Testament Studies* 38 (1992): 448–66.

ereign power; all peoples, nations and men of every language worshiped him. His dominion is an everlasting dominion that will not pass away, and his kingdom is one that will never be destroyed. (Dan. 7:13–14)[19]

Starting with Daniel 7:13, the expectation developed within Judaism of a coming redeemer—the son of man who appears as a judge. This development is reflected especially in 1 Enoch 37–71 (the Parables) and in 4 Ezra. For a long time there was hardly any doubt that such a Jewish expectation of "the son of man" did exist, and a collection of essays was even published with the title *Jesus and the Son of Man*.[20] But that time has passed; this reconstruction is—rightly—attacked from all sides.[21]

a. Daniel 7:13 speaks of "one like a son of man." A comparison is being made, but the passage does not say that this refers to a human being. The "one like a son of man" in Daniel 7:27 turns out

19. Some see Daniel 7:13 as a prophetic representation of an already existing expectation. Some connect it with the Babylonian myth of the Man: S. Mowinckel, *He That Cometh*, trans. G. W. Anderson (Oxford: Blackwell, 1956; Norwegian original 1951); H. S. Kvanvig, *Roots of Apocalyptic: The Mesopotamian Background of the Enoch Figure and of the Son of Man*, Wissenschaftliche Monographien zum Alten und Neuen Testaments 61 (Neukirchen: Neukirchener Verlag, 1988). Others connect it with a Canaanite myth of a son of god: Colpe, "ὁ υἱὸς τοῦ ἀνθρώπου." Kearns further narrows Colpe's idea by specifying a Syrian Hadad mythology, which was supposedly reworked in the process of Hellenistic syncretism: R. Kearns, *Vorfragen zur Christologie: Morphologische und Semasiologische Studie zur Vorgeschichte eines christologischen Hoheitstitels*, 3 vols. (Tübingen: Mohr, 1978–82). In keeping with H. Lietzmann (*Der Menschensohn: Ein Beitrag zur neutestamentlichen Theologie* [Freiburg: Mohr, 1896]), Kearns is also of the opinion that the son of man myth affected the conceptualization of Jesus by way of *Hellenistic* Judaism and not by way of Daniel 7 and Palestinian Judaism (see R. Kearns, *Das Traditionsgefüge um den Menschensohn: Ursprünglicher Gehalt und älteste Veränderung im Urchristentum* [Tübingen: Mohr, 1986]; compare R. Kearns, *Die Entchristologisierung des Menschensohnes: Die Übertragung des Traditionsgefüges um den Menschensohn auf Jesus* [Tübingen: Mohr, 1988]).

20. R. Pesch and R. Schnackenburg, eds., *Jesus und der Menschensohn: Für Anton Vögtle* (Freiburg: Herder, 1975).

21. M. Casey, *Son of Man: The Interpretation and Influence of Daniel 7* (London: S.P.C.K., 1979); R. Leivestad, "Jesus—Messias—Menschensohn: Die jüdischen Heilandserwartungen zur Zeit der ersten römischen Kaiser und die Frage nach dem messianischen Selbstbewusstsein Jesu," in *Aufstieg und Niedergang der römischen Welt*, part 2, *Principat*, vol. 25, *Religion* (Berlin: de Gruyter, 1982), 1:220–64; B. Lindars, *Jesus Son of Man: A Fresh Examinaton of the Son of Man Sayings in the Gospels in the Light of Recent Research* (London: S.P.C.K., 1983); H. Bietenhard, "Der Menschensohn—*ho huios tou anthrōpou*: Sprachliche und religionsgeschichtliche Untersuchungen zu einem Begriff der synoptischen Evangelien: I. Sprachlicher und religionsgeschichtlicher Teil," in *Aufstieg und Niedergang der römischen Welt*, part 2, *Principat*, vol. 25, *Religion* (Berlin: de Gruyter, 1982), 1:265–350; Walker, "Son of Man: Some Recent Developments"; J. D. G. Dunn, *Christology in the Making: A New Testament Inquiry into the Origins of the Doctrine of the Incarnation* (London: SCM, 1980).

to be a symbol for "the saints, the people of the Most High"; this people will reign forever and all powers will serve them. In contrast to the hostile, worldly human powers that are depicted as beasts stands the chosen people of God, which has a human shape. When this figure is carried to God on the clouds, it is not proof of a theophany. People can also be carried to God on the clouds (Elijah, for example).[22] Daniel 7 does not suggest that the reference here is to an angel[23] or a heavenly figure such as Michael.[24] It can be concluded, as Casey and others have done, that there is nothing here directly referring to or describing the Messiah.

b. It must therefore be assumed that the figure of a "coming son of man" developed within the later Jewish tradition (building on Dan. 7:13). Decisive proof for this can be found in 1 Enoch, supplementary proof in 4 Ezra 13. The few additional bits of information are so scanty and vague that they can only serve to confirm the existence of a "son of man" tradition if the existence of that tradition has first been demonstrated on the basis of other sources (specifically 1 Enoch and 4 Ezra). For this reason we limit ourselves to 1 Enoch 37–71 and 4 Ezra 13.[25] We know that 4 Ezra (= 2 Esdras NRSV) was written at the end of the first century A.D.— that is, after the New Testament. The dating of 1 Enoch 37–71 is disputed. The evidence we have does not support a pre-Christian date. Thus the ideas contained in these writings can only have been influential at the time of the New Testament *if* these ideas are assumed to be older and more influential than the writings from which we learn about them. But even if this were proven true, it would still be difficult to make a connection between these ideas and the New Testament. To the extent that the imagery of a son of man goes back to Daniel 7 (as in 1 Enoch 46.1), it has not led to a title that can breathe on its own. In 1 Enoch, "son of man" always refers back to the figure introduced in 46.1 (*"this* son of man").[26] Similarly, 4 Ezra also fails to demonstrate any development of "one like a son of man" into a real title or technical term.[27]

---

22. Hare, *Son of Man Tradition.*

23. B. D. Chilton, "The Son of Man: Human and Heavenly," in *The Four Gospels 1992*, ed. F. van Segbroeck, Bibliotheca ephemeridum theologicarum lovaniensium 100 (Louvain: Peeters, 1992), 1:203–18.

24. Collins, "Son of Man in First-Century Judaism."

25. For a full discussion of all data, see Casey, *Son of Man,* 99–141.

26. Casey, *Son of Man*; Lindars, *Jesus Son of Man.*

27. G. Vermes, "Jesus the Son of Man," in *Jesus the Jew: A Historian's Reading of the Gospels* (Philadelphia: Fortress, 1973), 160–91; M. Müller, *Der Ausdruck "Menschensohn" in den Evangelien: Voraussetzungen und Bedeutung*, Acta theologica danica 17 (Leiden: Brill, 1984).

We can therefore conclude that there are insufficient grounds for the claim that within pre-Christian Judaism an expectation and a terminology had taken shape around the phrase "son of man." For more details see appendix 2: "The Son of Man in 1 Enoch 37–71 and 4 Ezra 13."

c. The reaction of Jesus' audience also clearly shows that they made no connection between the name he used to identify himself and a prevailing expectation or title. It is unlikely that twentieth-century New Testament scholars with less knowledge of the first century than those who lived during that period would be able to establish better connections.

d. Many of the remarks that Jesus makes in which he uses this form of self-identification do not fit in at all with the idea of a coming judge of the end times. Thus most of Jesus' statements about the Son of Man do not fit in Bultmann's popular hypothesis. But dismissing these statements as spurious in order to maintain the hypothesis is circular reasoning.

e. It is methodologically incorrect to determine the meaning of a self-referential term exclusively on the basis of the statements in which it is uttered. Jesus makes several statements about the coming of the Son of Man, but this does not limit the meaning of "Son of Man" to the future.

f. The hypothesis of a Jewish expectation concerning the coming Son of Man as the background for Jesus' appropriation of this existing honorific cannot in any way explain why the Christian church has *never* chosen to honor or confess him as "Son of Man." According to Conzelmann, "Son of Man" as a creedal name for Jesus was formed by the Palestinian Christian community.[28] But this hypothesis conflicts with the fact that we never encounter the designation "Son of Man" in any creedal statements of the church. If there is one phrase that *cannot* come from church tradition, it is the phrase "Son of Man" applied to Jesus. This fact alone makes it incomprehensible that so many continue to dismiss as church tradition what must undeniably be an authentic word of Jesus himself. Here we are not faced with church tradition but with the highly personal and never imitated way in which Jesus referred to himself.

4.2.3 An Aramaic Idiom?

Can the phrase "son of man" be traced back to Aramaic, the language then in common use? Did it cease to be used because the church

---

28. H. Conzelmann, *An Outline of the Theology of the New Testament*, trans. J. Bowden (London: SCM, 1969).

stopped speaking Aramaic? This is the direction in which the solution has been sought over the centuries.[29]

During the past hundred years (in reaction against various ideas put forward concerning a circulating myth of the Son of Man), many scholars in a variety of ways have insisted that Jesus' use of "Son of Man" deserves a much simpler explanation; that in fact it is nothing more than an *Aramaic* idiom. This is, on the one hand, the argument of Aramaic experts on the basis of the language's characteristics,[30] while it is, on the other hand, substantiated by translating Jesus' words back into Aramaic.[31] In Aramaic, the expression *bar (ʾ)nasha* ("the son of man") or *bar (ʾ)nash* ("a son of man") would have attracted little attention; it was a common way of describing a member of the human race.[32] The phrase can therefore be compared to phrases such as "a son of the prophets"—someone who belongs to the group "prophets." A person could easily have referred to himself as "(this) son of man." Functionally this term is the equivalent of the personal pronoun "I." Using "this son of man" as a way of saying "I" does lend a certain color to the sentence. When scholars attempt to fine-tune this color, opinions begin to differ:

1. Jesus is describing himself as "I" in a way that is somewhat indirect, evasive, and vague.[33]
2. Jesus qualifies himself as belonging to the human race: "I belong to the people."[34]
3. Jesus is speaking ironically about his situation: *"this* son of man" or "a man in my circumstances."[35]

29. D. Burkett, "The Nontitular Son of Man: A History and Critique," *New Testament Studies* 40 (1994): 504–21.

30. A. Meyer, *Jesu Muttersprache: Das galiläische Aramäisch in seiner Bedeutung für die Erklärung der Reden Jesu und der Evangelien überhaupt* (Freiburg: Mohr, 1896); G. Vermes, "The Use of Bar Nash/Bar Nasha in Jewish Aramaic," in *Post-Biblical Jewish Studies*, Studies in Judaism in Late Antiquity 8 (Leiden: Brill, 1975), 147–65.

31. G. Schwarz, *Jesus "der Menschensohn": Aramäistische Untersuchungen zu den synoptischen Menschensohnworten Jesu*, Beiträge zur Wissenschaft vom Alten und Neuen Testament 6/19 (Stuttgart: Kohlhammer, 1986).

32. For illustrations from the Aramaic translation of the Old Testament, see M. Casey, "The Use of the Term *bar (ʾ)nash(ʾ)* in the Aramaic Translations of the Hebrew Bible," *Journal for the Study of the New Testament* 54 (1994): 87–118. For the theory that this Aramaic has been *literally* translated into Greek, see M. Casey, "Idiom and Translation: Some Aspects of the Son of Man Problem," *New Testament Studies* 41 (1995): 164–82.

33. G. Vermes, "The Present State of the 'Son of Man' Debate," in *Jesus and the World of Judaism* (London: SCM, 1983), 89–99; R. Bauckham, "The Son of Man: 'A Man in My Position' or 'Someone'?" *Journal for the Study of the New Testament* 23 (1985): 23–33; Hare, *Son of Man Tradition*.

34. Casey, *Son of Man*.

35. J. P. Brown, "The Son of Man: 'This Fellow,'" *Biblica* 58 (1977): 361–87.

4. Jesus is speaking modestly.[36]

5. Jesus is indeed saying something striking.[37]

A few authors admit the possibility that this self-referential term contained some potential for developing into a special title. According to Lindars, Jesus recognizes his difficult situation as a mission he cannot avoid, and this feeling can later be connected with a messianic title.[38] Leivestad claims that Jesus presents himself as the one person who is predestined to later become the Messiah.[39] According to Chilton, Jesus suggests that as a Son of Man he has something to do with the angels (Luke 12:8–9) and thus his self-reference relates indirectly to a heavenly figure.[40]

Various objections can been raised against this approach:

a. At issue are the meaning and intonation of a linguistic detail of first-century Aramaic. Our sources for Aramaic from that century, however, are too limited and inadequate to reconstruct such a detail with any certainty. Thus, for example, it cannot be positively determined whether there was a difference at that time between the definite and the indefinite use of "son of man." Is *"the* son of man" (*bar [ʾ]nasha*) identical with "*a* son of man" (*bar [ʾ]nash*)? But if so, why then is the definite form ("*the* son of man") always used in what is assumed to be a translation from Aramaic into Greek? Isn't it too easy to dismiss this simply as a translation error?

b. Jesus uses the self-referential term not only as the subject of the sentence but also as the object about which he says certain things. The things he says *about* "this son of man" would have conferred a special status even on an unremarkable pseudonym and must have given his hearers (even in Aramaic) the idea that there is more intended here than merely an expression motivated by modesty.

36. Müller, *Der Ausdruck "Menschensohn" in den Evangelien*; Schwarz, *Jesus "der Menschensohn"*; Bietenhard, "Der Menschensohn—*ho huios tou anthrōpou*"; Hare, *Son of Man Tradition.*

37. G. Dalman, *The Words of Jesus Considered in the Light of Post-Biblical Jewish Writings and the Aramaic Language* (Edinburgh: Clark, 1902; translated from German); P. Fiebig, *Der Menschensohn: Jesu Selbstbezeichnung mit besonderer Berücksichtigung des aramäischen Sprachgebrauches für "Mensch" untersucht* (Tübingen: Mohr, 1901).

38. Lindars, *Jesus Son of Man.*

39. Leivestad, "Jesus—Messias—Menschensohn." Also see V. Hampel, *Menschensohn und historischer Jesus: Ein Rätselwort als Schlüssel zum messianischen Selbstverständnis Jesu* (Neukirchen: Neukirchener Verlag, 1990).

40. Chilton, "Son of Man: Human and Heavenly."

c. Although the phrase Jesus uses to refer to himself is not a common Greek expression, it can still be explained within the context of the Greek language.[41] When Jesus refers to himself not only as a human being but as a "Son of Man," this phrase in Greek refers to his human *birth*. He *appears* not only as a man in his ministry on earth, but he also has a concrete place in the line of human births. He is "human-born." A translator would have thought twice (more likely ten times) before deciding to use this unusual Greek phrase as the equivalent of an Aramaic periphrastic for "I." And translation error due to carelessness is unlikely, given the unusual nature of the Greek phrase.

d. Jesus certainly must have spoken to the crowds in Greek as well, and probably much more often than has long been assumed.[42] If he had used this term originally in Aramaic, then the Greek "translation" (*ho huios tou anthrōpou*) must also stem from him. This phrase can hardly be dismissed as a later translation error if Jesus used it himself in its Greek form. The term must then at least be explained in its Greek form as well (apart from a possible Aramaic origin).

41. In Greek there is the Semiticized expression "sons of men" (Mark 3:28: *hoi huioi tōn anthrōpōn*; translated "men" in NIV). This sort of wording is not entirely unknown in the Greek language ("sons of Achaians" = "Achaians"; "sons of doctors" = "doctors"). The phrase "sons of men" is comparable to the Old Testament term for the prophetic class: "the sons of the prophets," translated "the company of the prophets" in NIV (LXX: 2 Kings 2:3–15; 4:38; 6:1). These "sons of the prophets" are "prophets" themselves (compare LXX: 1 Kings 20:35, "one of the sons of the prophets," with 1 Kings 20:41, "one of the prophets"), or they identify with the prophets (Tobit 4:12 [Alexandrinus]: "for we [Jews] are sons ["the descendants" in NRSV] of the prophets"; as children of prophets, the Jews are obliged to live isolated lives and to marry within the tribe). Whenever one particular prophet is being discussed from among these "sons of the prophets," he is always referred to with a *descriptive phrase*: "one (or a man) of/from the sons ['company' in NIV] of the prophets" (LXX: 1 Kings 20:35; 2 Kings 5:22). However, when Amos says, "I was neither a prophet nor a prophet's son (*huios prophētou*), but I was a shepherd" (Amos 7:14), he makes known that neither he nor his father is a prophet. In this case we do not read "son of the prophets" but "son of a prophet." Thus there is also a difference between *huios anthrōpōn* (someone who belongs to the group "people") and *huios anthrōpou* (someone who is descended from a person, who is born in that line). In both cases the subject is a person, but in the first case the term is generic, in the second the accent is on *lineage*. In Acts 23:6, Paul calls himself "a Pharisee, the son of Pharisees" (*huios Pharisaiōn*; translated "the son of a Pharisee" in NIV). This seems to be a repetition used for the sake of emphasis ("I am a Pharisee, and I consider myself a member of the Pharisee party"). In a large number of manuscripts, however, the word is singular (*huios Pharisaiou*), and in such a case Paul is revealing two things: (1) he himself is a Pharisee; (2) he has been a Pharisee from childhood because his father belonged to this group as well.

42. See the introduction to my commentary on Mark, *Marcus: Het evangelie volgens Petrus*, 2d ed., Commentaar op het Nieuwe Testament, 3d series (Kampen: Kok, 1992), sec. 4.

4.2.4 Old Testament Content?

The expression "Son of Man" cannot have been adopted from the Judaism of that time. Nor can it be explained on the basis of general Aramaic usage. What we thus encounter here is Jesus' own creative use of language. What was his purpose in using this self-designation?

Many nineteenth-century scholars found in this expression proof of the idea that he wanted to be the ideal human being, and that humanity is the key to his teaching. People find in him their role model and example.

In the twentieth century, the dominant idea is that by using this term Jesus hoped to create an original link between his person and one or more elements from the Old Testament.

a. Marshall thinks it possible that Jesus may have been using a common Aramaic phrase that also could be used as a reference to Daniel 7. According to some, it may even have been an intentionally obscuring term, and only eventually would it become clear that Jesus intended to allude to the figure in Daniel 7:13, with which he finally openly identified himself before the Sanhedrin.[43] Thus "the Son of Man" is a temporary, secret title for "the Son of God."[44]

b. Jesus establishes a connection between his person and his forefather Adam, *the* man. He is the promised son of Adam.[45]

c. The terminology is in line with the way in which the phrase "son of man" is often used in Old Testament poetic passages to emphasize a person's lowliness; the accent is then on lowliness before God.[46]

d. Jesus connects with the way the prophet Ezekiel is often addressed as "son of man." This prophet, *as a son of man,* was made a judge in Israel.[47]

e. Burkett even sees (in John) a whole series of Old Testament associations, among them Proverbs 30:1–4 and Jacob's ladder.[48]

43. H. N. Ridderbos, *Zelfopenbaring en zelfverberging: Het historisch karakter van Jezus' messiaanse zelfopenbaring volgens de synoptische evangeliën* (Kampen: Kok, 1946); J. P. Lettinga, "De uitdrukking 'De zoon des mensen,'" in *Almanak Fides Quadrat Intellectum 1955–1957* (Kampen: Kok, 1957), 141–49; Bietenhard, "Menschensohn"; Bauckham, "Son of Man."

44. S. Kim, *The "Son of Man" as the Son of God,* WUNT 30 (Tübingen: Mohr, 1983).

45. J. B. Cortès and F. M. Gatti, "The Son of Man or the Son of Adam," *Biblica* 49 (1968): 457–502; O. Moe, "Der Menschensohn und der Urmensch," *Studia theologica* 14 (1960): 119–29.

46. J. Bowker, "The Son of Man," *Journal of Theological Studies* 28 (1977): 19–48.

47. E. M. Sidebottom, "The Son of Man as Man in the Fourth Gospel," *Expository Times* 68 (1956–57): 231–35; B. Vawter, "Ezekiel and John," *CBQ* 26 (1964): 450–58.

48. D. Burkett, *The Son of Man in the Gospel of John,* JSNTSup 56 (Sheffield: JSOT Press, 1991).

The problem with these solutions is that they still fail to explain why the church did not adopt this creative designation for the Messiah after it had been made apparent.

Neither is it unequivocally clear that Jesus before the Sanhedrin established a direct connection between Daniel 7 and the term "Son of Man" in reference to *himself*. He does not explain his name, but answers the question about being the Messiah, the Son of God (Matt. 26:63). He then speaks *directly* from Psalm 110: he will be seen sitting "at the right hand of the Mighty One." He will also come "on the clouds of heaven," an allusion to Daniel 7, but an *indirect* one (Dan. 7:13 has to do with the movement of someone like a son of man going *up* to heaven—in the clouds—but Jesus is speaking about coming *down* from heaven). And there is still a difference between the *comparison* with a son of man in Daniel 7 and the self-referential term "the Son of Man."

Nor is there clearly a *direct* connection with Adam. Cortès and Gatti appeal to Jesus' use of the definite article: "the son of *the* man" (i.e., the pre-eminent son of the pre-eminent man). But this is incorrect, because in Greek the word *son* used as a definite noun (*the* son) requires that any additional modifier also be given a definite article ("of the man"). To speak of *ho huios anthrōpou* (the son of a man) would not be good Greek. In order to indicate in Greek that the subject is a very special man, one would have to use additional words (for example, "the son of the *first* man" or "the son of the *pre-eminent* man.")

In general, the meaning of a self-referential term cannot be derived from sentences in which it is used as the subject. Added to this is the fact that Jesus referred to himself as the Son of Man in very diverse contexts (relative to his earthly work, his suffering, and his future). "Son of Man" is apparently a self-referential term that does not have a highly specific meaning, so that it can be used in a variety of contexts. It is a name whose raison d'être does not derive from the statements Jesus attaches to it.

4.2.5 *"Son of Man" in Dialogue*

If this term as an original creation cannot be explained on the basis of thematic connections with Old Testament elements, we must conclude that it had little content. True, it is a striking term, but not because of its specific meaning. It is simply too general for that. The term tells us no more than that Jesus is "the descendant of a human being."

But what *is* striking is that Jesus keeps using this rather empty term in connection with statements that refer to superhuman and divine works. There is a peculiar tension in many of Jesus' statements. He calls himself simply "the descendant of a human being," but he goes on to speak of the significance, calling, and future of this human descendant in a way that is completely out of keeping with such a designation. We do not expect that someone who is human-born has also come to us from heaven (John 3:13; 6:62) or that he will be lifted up into heaven (John 3:14; 8:28) and will also return from heaven (John 6:62). It does not seem appropriate for a Son of Man to announce his "coming" (Matt. 10:23; Luke 12:40; Matt. 24:44; 25:13; 26:64) and his "appearing" (Matt. 24:27, 37, 39), at which he will send out angels and be accompanied by them (Matt. 13:37, 41; 16:27–28; 24:30; 25:31). It is contrary to all expectation that a Son of Man should come to judge all the nations of the earth and sit at God's right hand (Matt. 19:28; Luke 21:36). Even so, this is how the Son of Man will be "revealed" (Luke 17:30) when his time comes (Luke 17:22–30). The greatness of what he ascribes to himself is even more striking because he refers at the same time to himself with such a lowly phrase—"Son of Man." It is this paradoxical combination that attracts people's attention. They can imagine that Jesus, who regards himself as the Messiah, will remain forever. But what does it mean that the Son of Man must be lifted up? Who is this Son of Man (John 12:34)? The pieces don't fit!

The designation "Son of Man" does fit very well, however, with what most Jews think of Jesus. They see in him no more than someone of human descent. The unclean spirits that are driven out recognize that he is the "Son of God" (Mark 3:11; Matt. 8:29), but the Jews call him "son of Joseph" (Luke 4:22; John 1:45; 6:42), and that is how he is viewed (Luke 3:23). He is no more than the son of the carpenter, with a mother, with brothers and sisters (Matt. 13:55–56; Mark 6:3).

When Jesus uses the same kind of terminology to refer to himself, is he perhaps echoing the assessment of those around him? He is what they think he is: "the human-born." Not the son of Joseph, to be sure, but that is left out of consideration. For the Jews the important thing is that Jesus is merely a descendant of human beings and that he concurs with this by calling himself "Son of Man." At the same time, however, he shows that his final destination is not on earth (Matt. 8:20) and that he has divine authority, tasks, and qualities. For the Jews, Jesus' place is sufficiently delineated by the designation "the son of Joseph," but for Jesus himself that human lineage appears to imply no limitations or restrictions. It is precisely as the descendant of a human being that he has his great task and future. The end of the matter for the Jews (his human origin) is for Jesus the beginning (his divine work). He can take a platitude from the public and attach a fireworks display of grand pronouncements to it: this person, born of a woman, *is* the Son of God, who is taking his place at God's right hand.

The term used with the *definite* article ("*the* Son of Man") builds on the image of him held by the people around him. *They* said, "A son of man!" He answers, "*The* 'Son of Man' [as you call me] will come on the clouds of heaven." Strictly speaking, this self-referential term is not a freely chosen name, but rather the designation given to him by the people and endorsed by Jesus himself!

In a few cases, this connection is even rather explicit. Philip introduces Jesus to Nathanael as "the son of Joseph, from Nazareth" (John 1:45). For Nathanael it is all too human: "Can anything good come from there?" (John 1:46). When Nathanael then discovers how Jesus knew him with a kind of divine omniscience, he quickly switches to, "You are the Son of God; you are the King of Israel" (John 1:49). Jesus affirms his confession; Nathanael will see even greater things! At the same time it remains true that Jesus is human: the angels will ascend and descend on the "the Son of Man" (John 1:51). Nathanael must realize that the Son of God is truly "the Son of Man, from Nazareth."

John the Baptist had announced that a divine figure would be coming after him and would baptize with the Holy Spirit. When Jesus later appears in their midst with signs and wonders (but still as a human being), the people dismiss his ministry as "just human." They even call him a "gluttonous *man*." Jesus criticizes them for their shortsightedness, but he does acknowledge that he has come as a "Son of Man" (Matt. 11:19). Nevertheless, he must be more than that. John is the greatest "among those born of women" (Matt. 11:11). If Jesus is more than John, he must therefore be *more* than a human being, born of a woman.

On the day when Jesus forgives the sins of the paralytic, the leaders think that he has been *blaspheming*: only God can forgive sins (Mark 2:7), and in their eyes Jesus is no more than the son of Joseph. To this he responds that "the Son of Man" really does have authority on earth to forgive sins (Mark 2:10). Unfortunately, the crowds misunderstand him—they think now that God has given this authority to all people in general (Matt. 9:8). The crowds fail to recognize that the man Jesus is at the same time more than a son of man.

In the night in which Judas delivered his Master into the hands of men, Jesus asks him why he kissed him if all he wanted to do was turn over a mere "son of man" to other human beings (Luke 22:48).

It is understandable that such a term of self-reference would fall into obscurity with Jesus' death and never serve as a designation for him in the church's later prayer and confession. Only in Jesus' constant, conflict-ridden dialogues with the people did it make sense for him to fall in again and again with popular notions about his merely human descent, and he did so only to show that human birth does not preclude but rather makes possible a divine future. It was a time when the disciples were despised for believing in the Son of Man and confessing his name. But Jesus encourages them to remain strong in their faith and not to allow themselves to be dissuaded by those who dismiss Jesus as *nothing more than a man*. Let the disciples fully appropriate the Son of Man incarnate by confessing him and by eating his flesh and drinking his blood (Luke 6:22; 12:8; 18:8; John 6:53; see also John 9:35 in a number of manuscripts). He even promises forgiveness for those who blaspheme against the Son of Man, provided that they will go on to acknowledge that God's Spirit is in him (Matt. 12:32; Luke 12:10). As a Son of Man, he is a temporary sign of God's great future in their midst, as Jonah once was for Nineveh (Luke 11:30). But the self-referential term "Son of Man" becomes defunct as soon as Jesus' humiliation in Israel has come to an end. It is striking that Jesus, in announcing his Passion, keeps referring to himself as the Son of Man, but immediately after Easter replaces it with the title he has received from God: "Christ" (Luke 24:26, 46). His birth from a woman, a human being, was not a limitation for him. It was the path that God's Anointed followed as the Son of Man to seek and save the lost (Matt. 18:11; Luke 9:56; 19:10; Matt. 20:28). That is why the glorification of this Son of Man begins at the moment when his death is approaching (John 12:23; 13:31). It is by being made *man* that God's Son receives the authority to stand in judgment (John 5:27).

The self-referential term "Son of Man" belongs to the way Jesus referred to himself while on earth. Only then did it have a function. The many statements in which he used this term show us that undergoing a real human birth with Mary as mother did not rule out the reality of being God's Son. Indeed, that birth paved the way for his work on earth and later for sitting at God's right hand, until and including his coming as the world's judge. It was on this rejected Son of Man that God set his seal: "God!"[49]

Viewed objectively, the term "the Son of Man" reminds us on the one hand of the real rejection Jesus suffered during his humiliation (to which he had to respond). On the other hand it points positively to the significance of the incarnation. Because the incarnation of the Son of God has everything to do with Adam, with the promise to Eve, with the visions of Daniel, it is possible that the term contains all sorts of oblique references. Precisely because the term is general rather than specific, it can evoke a wide range of associations in a broad range of contexts. Thus in Mark 2:27, Jesus alludes to the creation of Adam and God's giv-

49. See P. H. R. van Houwelingen, *Johannes: Het evangelie van het Woord,* Commentaar op het Nieuwe Testament, 3d series (Kampen: Kok, 1997), on John 6:27.

ing the Sabbath, and he draws a direct conclusion from it for "the Son of Man"—for himself (Mark 2:28). As a "Son of Man" he is also son of Adam! But the extraordinary thing is that Jesus acts as though the law (in this case the law relating to the Sabbath) does not apply to him. Is he a son of Adam in a different sense than the other Israelites? What sort of claim lies hidden in his activity on the Sabbath? In church tradition, at least since the time of Irenaeus, the positive aspect of the term "Son of Man" is understood mainly in connection with the *incarnation*. This is legitimate. But the definite article—*the* Son of Man—posed a problem, since it does not help provide any independent meaning or significance. The phrase is simply part of Jesus' way of referring to himself in reaction to the way others saw him and rejected him as the Son of God. He accepts the challenge: the "Son of Man" lets himself be heard!

5

The Recognition
of the Son of God

The previous chapter examined the ways Jesus referred to *himself*. From his particular way of speaking and his characteristic way of referring to himself we see how he presented himself to Israel as more than a son of man. He invited his listeners to come to their own decision and to arrive at a clear verdict about him. This chapter deals with the positive names and designations *others* gave him in reaction to his self-designation, and how Jesus assessed these characterizations.

5.1 More Than a Prophet

Jesus' work had much in common with that of a prophet: both conveyed heavenly messages to the people. Through inspiration they reached beyond the possibilities of ordinary human speech. Jesus even acted like a teacher with his own authority, so it is understandable that people began to call him a "prophet." This title was bestowed on him in three ways.

a. In the first place, many regard Jesus as *a prophet like other prophets who were around at that time*. Josephus reports that among both the Pharisees and the Essenes there were people who could make reliable statements about the future[1] on the basis of heavenly apparitions.[2] He may have avoided using the word *prophet* because that title had gained a negative connotation around the time of the Jewish War due to the revolutionary "prophets" who had been active among the people. For instance, Josephus tells us that in the first century, popular charismatic leaders arose who acted as "prophets" and gathered people around them, sometimes taking them into the desert to prepare them for some eschatological event that they expected to happen.[3]

---

1. Josephus, *Jewish War* 2.8.12 §159; idem, *Antiquities* 14.9.4 §§174–76.
2. Josephus, *Antiquities* 17.2.4 §§41–45.
3. Josephus, *Jewish War* 2.13.4–5 §§259–62; idem, *Antiquities* 20.5.1 §97; 20.8.6 §§168–70; compare Acts 5:36; 21:38.

Because there were "prophets" in the Jewish world of the first century,[4] it is not surprising that the remarkable ministries of John the Baptist and Jesus cause people to conclude that they are also "prophets." Thus many regard John the Baptist as a prophet (Matt. 14:5; 21:26; compare Mark 11:32; Luke 20:6), and they later apply the same designation to Jesus (Matt. 21:46; Luke 7:39; 24:19; John 4:19; 9:17; compare John 7:52; Matt. 26:68 = Mark 14:65 = Luke 22:64).

When nondisciples sometimes address Jesus respectfully as "rabbi" or "teacher," it is fully in keeping with this tendency to recognize him as a prophet. The title "rabbi" was appropriate only for a theologian with rabbinical training. Jesus, however, was not trained by rabbis. So when people insist on honoring him as a rabbi, they are taking into account the fact that he has "come from God" as a teacher (John 3:2). Even when they only *feign* recognition by using the title "teacher," they are nonetheless suggesting that Jesus is not swayed by men: "You pay no attention to who they are; but you teach the way of God in accordance with the truth" (Mark 12:14). He seems to have been instructed directly by God. His being a "rabbi" is related to his being a "prophet": he owes his insights not to human education but to revelations or visions.[5]

b. Second, there is a group of more devoted admirers who see in Jesus more than a prophetic contemporary. They think he should be placed *on a level with the prophets of old* (Mark 6:15), and they consider him to be a biblical prophet come back to life (Matt. 16:14 = Mark 8:28 = Luke 9:19; Mark 6:15 = Luke 9:8; 7:16 [a great prophet]). Some think specifically of Jeremiah (Matt. 16:14). Others, reasoning along the same lines, see him as a reincarnation of John the Baptist (Matt. 14:2 = Mark 6:14–16 = Luke 9:7–9).

c. Third and last, there are people who see Jesus as *the special and unique prophet of the end times* (most manuscripts of Matt. 21:11 read "This is Jesus, *the* prophet"). They think of Elijah, whose coming as forerunner of the LORD was announced by Malachi (Mal. 4:5–6; Matt. 16:14 = Mark 8:28 = Luke 9:19; Mark 6:15), or of the prophet who was to come into the world (John 6:14; 7:40). The latter is based on the prophecy of Deuteronomy 18:18–19.[6]

---

4. R. Meyer, *Der Prophet aus Galiläa: Studie zum Jesusbild der drei ersten Evangelien* (Leipzig: Wissenschaftlicher Buchgesellschaft, 1940); R. A. Horsley, "Like One of the Prophets of Old: Two Types of Popular Prophets at the Time of Jesus," *CBQ* 47 (1985): 435–63.

5. Compare J. Jeremias, *New Testament Theology* (London: SCM, 1971), 81–84. B. Witherington III (*Jesus the Sage: The Pilgrimage of Wisdom* [Edinburgh: Clark, 1994]) is of the opinion that Jesus was regarded as the personification of Wisdom and that for this reason he was recognized as a teacher or prophet.

6. F. Hahn, *The Titles of Jesus in Christology: Their History in Early Christianity*, trans. H. Knight and G. Ogg (London: Lutterworth, 1969); F. Schnider, *Jesus der Prophet*, Orbis

In Deuteronomy 18:9–22, Moses talks about what will happen after the Israelites enter the Promised Land. He warns Israel not to turn to the teachings and way of life of the pagans, particularly not to astrology and spiritualism (18:9–14). God is not to be approached through the stars or the dead. The people came to know God at Horeb as a consuming and living fire and they shrank from him, afraid for their lives (18:16–17). The LORD judged this anxiety positively. This gap between God and the people, which is not to be bridged by stargazing and soothsaying, will be closed by the LORD himself in a way comparable to what happened in the desert before Israel entered the land. At that time Moses spoke to the people as a mediator. They heard God's word, yet they continued to live. In Canaan the LORD will provide a similar sort of prophet as a mediator (18:15, 18). The decision about life or death, about remaining in the land or being expelled from it, rests with their choice between listening or ignoring this prophet (18:19). What is striking is that the appearance of this prophet will at the same time bring about God's *judgment*.

In 18:20–22, Moses speaks about the possible appearance of prophets who want to seduce the people to worship idols, perhaps even under the guise of having been sent by the LORD. But these pseudo-prophets must be exposed; the signs they announce will not come to pass. These final verses have caused some interpreters to understand the announcement of "the prophet in your midst, like myself" in a *collective* sense, which would mean that the pericope deals with "soothsaying and prophecy" in general and that the promise relates to the coming of true prophets throughout the ages. But these final verses discuss only the *false* prophets and how to recognize them. It is necessary to distance oneself from them in order to be ready for the coming of the promised prophet.

Although the true prophets certainly have their place along the path that leads from Moses to the announced prophet who will be *like Moses*, they are not the fulfillment of the promise about that prophet who is to come. For they lack the one special characteristic—the LORD will implement the words of the prophet who is to come by means of *judgment* (18:19). The true prophets are more or less foreshadowings of the prophet who is to come and whose judgment will bring about a decisive division. Deuteronomy 34:10–12 therefore states that "no prophet has risen in Israel like Moses, whom the LORD knew face to face, who did all

---

Biblicus et Orientalis 2 (Freiburg: Universitätsverlag, 1973). O. Cullmann (*The Christology of the New Testament*, trans. S. C. Guthrie and C. A. M. Hall [Philadelphia: Westminster, 1959]) sees the expectation of "*the* prophet" as a consolidation of various Old Testament data, among them the promise about the coming of Elijah.

those miraculous signs and wonders the Lᴏʀᴅ sent him to do in Egypt. . . . For no one has ever shown the mighty power or performed the awesome deeds that Moses did in the sight of all Israel." The forerunners of the prophet "like Moses" could be despised and rejected without this having any visible effect on the disobedient. But when *the* prophet enters the land, his word will be as effective as that of God, who before the entrance into the Promised Land appeared in fire on Mount Horeb and who judged the people in the desert through Moses.

Thus the words of Deuteronomy 18:17–19 (together with 34:10–12) gave reason during the first century A.ᴅ. to anticipate, after all the true prophets who had already come, the appearance of a special prophet *like Moses*.[7] His word brings the most extreme consequences, both for those who through this prophet listen to the Lᴏʀᴅ and for those who refuse to do so. Thus, in the second century B.ᴄ., the Jewish people decided that Simon Maccabeus would be the permanent ruler and high priest "until a trustworthy prophet should arise" (1 Macc. 14:41). Philonenko sees in this passage an echo of Deuteronomy 18:14, 18 and Numbers 11:17 (Moses as the *trustworthy* prophet).[8] Apparently the people are awaiting the arrival of a special prophet "like Moses."

During that same century a decision as to what to do with the rubble from the desecrated altar is postponed "until a prophet should come to tell what to do" with it (1 Macc. 4:46). The expectation of a coming prophet is also evident in a few documents found at Qumran (1QS 9.10–11: "until the prophet and the anointed of Aaron and Israel come"; compare 4QTest 5–8).[9] In the New Testament we also find a few traces of this kind of expectation during Jesus' time (John 1:21, 24; 6:14; 7:40).

Otherwise the extrabiblical literature does not give cause to think that the expectation of "the prophet" was widespread and occupied a *dominant* place. But this still is no reason to ignore the New Testament data. Deuteronomy 18:17–19 is not the only place in the Old Testament where we find indications of someone who is to come. The Jewish people were confronted by all sorts of pronouncements (about the prophet, about a coming Elijah, about the servant of the Lᴏʀᴅ, about the Son of David, about an Anointed One, and so forth). It was not clear which of

7. Compare P. D. Miller, "Moses My Servant: The Deuteronomic Portrait of Moses," *Interpretation* 41 (1987): 245–55.

8. M. Philonenko, "Jusqu'à ce que lève un prophète digne de confiance (1 Machabées 14,41)," in *Messiah and Christos: Studies in the Jewish Origins of Christianity; Presented to David Flusser on the Occasion of His Seventy-Fifth Birthday,* ed. I. Gruenwald et al., Texte und Studien zum antiken Judentum 32 (Tübingen: Mohr, 1992), 95–98.

9. According to F. García Martínez ("Messianische Erwartungen in den Qumranschriften," *Jahrbuch für Biblische Theologie* 8 [1993]: 203–6), the figure of the expected prophet in Qumran even has a messianic tint.

these pronouncements would in the end be most determinant, and the way the pronouncements related to each other was also vague. The Israelites had enough to nurture hope but too little to give them a clear picture of what lay ahead. So at the time of the New Testament we see within Judaism all sorts of unintegrated elements of eschatological expectations (Elijah? the prophet? the Christ?). It is not impossible that the statement from Deuteronomy 18 occupied a rather secondary, somewhat dormant position among the elements that made up these Jewish expectations. But under the influence of the ministry of John the Baptist, the dormant and less prominent elements in Israel's store of future possibilities were also activated. Thus we see that because of the heightened degree of expectation at the time of John there is also a clear awareness of the promise from Deuteronomy 18. (This passage apparently ceased to be of enduring interest to non-Christian Jews. In later [rabbinic] sources the expectation of "the prophet" does not occupy a clear place.)

How did *Jesus himself* react to the attempts to characterize him as "a prophet," as "one of the prophets of old" or as "the coming prophet"? First, it is clear that he sees himself as the equivalent of a prophet. What happens to him is what happens to the prophet who is not honored in his own country (Matt. 13:57; compare Mark 6:4; Luke 4:24; John 4:44), and like a prophet he must die in Jerusalem (Luke 13:33). Even so, he continually indicates that the designation "prophet" is inadequate when applied to him. He is, indeed, "more than a prophet" (Matt. 11:9 = Luke 7:26).[10] For this reason he can say of himself that he is "greater than Jonah" (Matt. 12:41; Luke 11:32) or "greater than Abraham and the prophets" (John 8:52–58). He is not "one of the prophets or Elijah or Jeremiah" but "the Christ" (Matt. 16:13–17).

After Jesus' ascension, the apostle Peter does apply Deuteronomy 18:18–19 to Jesus (Acts 3:22–23), just as Stephen does later (Acts 7:37). But Peter combines it with *the Christ title* (Acts 3:18, 20). The accent also falls on this promised prophet's *judicial* role, which focuses the eye on the future, when he will return in glory.[11]

---

10. See J. van Bruggen, *Matteüs: Het evangelie voor Israël,* 2d ed., Commentaar op het Nieuwe Testament, 3d series (Kampen: Kok, 1994), on Matt. 11:9.

11. The context of Acts 3:22–23 speaks about Jesus' *return.* At that time he will pass judgment on all who did not turn to him in time. The Messiah's act of judgment (when unbelievers will perish) is deferred by the ascension, so there is still opportunity to believe before the actual judgment takes place, when God will bring his Son into the world as the final judge. In Acts 3:19–21a there is an appeal for timely conversion. The coming age of Christ was foretold by all the holy prophets (3:21b). This reference to the prophets is now elaborated on: (a) by an appeal to Moses as the first prophet (3:22–23), and (b) by a reference to all the other prophets who spoke in the same vein (3:24). The other prophets are thus not seen as the fulfillment of the promise about the coming prophet in

During his stay on earth Jesus did not act as a judge who punishes misdeeds. On the contrary, he was gentle and merciful. He also did not allow himself to be forced into the role of a judge who adjudicates disputes (Luke 12:13–14). When at the feeding of the five thousand the crowds acknowledge Jesus as "the Prophet who is to come into the world" (John 6:14), there is a strong desire to "make him king" (John 6:15). This is not intended as preparation for a revolt against the Romans. The people realize that the promised judge/prophet must be given authority in Israel. He must become his people's judge/king. But the crowds are eager to jump ahead to something for which the time has not yet come. Jesus is indeed the prophet, but for the time being his ministry is one of gentleness. So he escapes the crowds who want to crown him and he goes to the mountain to pray. This helps us understand why the function of "*the* promised judge/prophet" does not gain prominence until the Book of Acts, and then as a clear argument against postponing the decision to choose Christ: he is God's final word for Israel and for the world. After this, sentence will be pronounced and carried out.

We can also understand why Jesus himself did not refer to Deuteronomy 18, although he did not preclude the connection. It is true that he refused the title "one of the prophets," but he did not protest against the possibility of being the prophet who is to come into the world. He could not readily go along with that idea because the people continued to *make a distinction* between this prophet and the Christ (compare John 1:19–25; 7:40–41), while Jesus' coming and the course of his life make it clear that, while Elijah is indeed a separate figure (John the Baptist), "the judge/prophet" and "the Christ" are one. In addition, his juridical role as *the* prophet would be implemented at his return—not during the time of his humiliation.

That is why "prophet" is not the most suitable title for Jesus. Although his work can also be described as prophetic, he is in fact more than a prophet. Islam assigns him a place no higher than that of a prophet, whereas Christians confess him as the Christ, the Son of God. Even modern Christology sometimes defends the theory that Jesus' oldest role was that of prophet, and that the rest was later added by the Christian community, which turned the prophet into a Messiah. This is

---

Deuteronomy 18, but they serve to support what Moses prophesied about the end time (including the coming of *the* prophet). The passage from Deuteronomy 18 is quoted by Peter as pointing to the coming of a *judge*/prophet who is to be the decisive factor: whoever listens to him will be saved, those who refuse will be killed. It was precisely this last and decisive element that was absent from the other prophets. Peter thus relates the promise of the coming judge/prophet to the *return* of Christ as judge!

When Stephen in Acts 7:37 also quotes the words of Deuteronomy 18 about the promised Moses-like prophet, it is after twice characterizing Moses as *judge* (Acts 7:27, 35).

Casey's position in his book with the telling title *From Jewish Prophet to Gentile God*,[12] and Vermes sees Jesus as a wonder-worker/prophet.[13] But such an approach fails to do justice to the totality of available information on Jesus' teaching and ministry. If the ancient Christian church did not accord Jesus the title "prophet," it is not because they failed to recognize the prophetic aspect of his ministry but because they realized that he is much more than a prophet. This realization does justice to the historic sources (the Gospels) and cannot be described as a later super-imposition of a metaphysical Christology on the title "prophet."

5.2 David's Son and Lord

An angel came to Joseph in a dream and announced that Mary's child would be called *Immanuel*, as had been foretold by the prophet Isaiah (Matt. 1:23). This was not the earthly name by which he was commonly known; he was called *Jesus*. Nor do we find the name Immanuel used later by confessing believers. The crowds finally call Jesus "the Son of David," and the disciples acknowledge that he is "the Christ, the Son of the living God." The promise of the angel is nevertheless fulfilled in this confession. Using a variety of names and terms, people came to the realization that God himself had appeared to Israel when Jesus ministered there.

The titles *Son of David* and *Christ, the Son of the living God* are largely synonymous. In using them, people acknowledged that God's dominion had come to them: Immanuel! These titles could be discussed together, since they refer to the fulfillment of the same promises. But because there are differences in accent, we will discuss first the term "Son of David," then the title "Christ," and finally the closely related designation "Son of God."

Some of Jesus' fellow Jews, in reaction to his impressive ministry, refer to him as "(the) prophet," but there are also those who ask themselves whether he might not be "the Son of David." People react with astonishment to his healing of a demoniac who was both blind and mute, and they wonder, "Could this be the Son of David?" While the crowd continues to hesitate (compare John 7:42), there are some individuals who trust him completely and who go to this "Son of David" for help. It is blind people (Matt. 9:27; 20:30–31; Mark 10:47–48; Luke 18:38–39)

---

12. M. Casey, *From Jewish Prophet to Gentile God: The Origins and Development of New Testament Christology* (Cambridge: Clarke; Louisville: Westminster/John Knox, 1991).

13. G. Vermes, "Jesus the Prophet," in *Jesus the Jew: A Historian's Reading of the Gospels* (Philadelphia: Fortress, 1973), 86–102. For an overview of recent publications, see G. Nebe, *Prophetische Züge im Bilde Jesu bei Lukas*, Beiträge zur Wissenschaft vom Alten und Neuen Testament 127 (Stuttgart: Kohlhammer, 1989).

and foreigners (Matt. 15:22) who first give him this title unconditionally. But during the triumphal entry into Jerusalem—after the raising of Lazarus, John 12:17–18—we finally hear these words coming from the crowd: "Hosanna to the Son of David!" (Matt. 21:9), a cry of jubilation that echoes later across the temple area when it is picked up by children (Matt. 21:15).

What did this name mean to people at that time? Apparently it was more than an acknowledgment that Jesus was somehow related to David. They knew his father and mother, his brothers and sisters; the genealogical lines were no secret. If people had wondered whether Jesus was *related to* David," the question would have been easy to answer. But it is highly doubtful whether they would have been so quick to apply the name "Son of David" to some distant relative of the former royal house. Other descendants of Zerubbabel are never called "sons of David." In addition, Jesus is not called "*a* Son of David" but "*the* Son of David." It is a title that indicates that he is the fulfillment of a unique expectation: people were hoping for the appearance of a special and redeeming person from the house of David—"*the* (promised and expected) Son of David." The crowds gradually begin to realize that Jesus is this promised one.

This promised figure is a king, so we also read in the Gospels that the recognition of Jesus as "the Son of David" went hand in hand with honoring him as king (Matt. 21:5; Luke 19:38; John 12:13) and submitting to him as the Lord (the title *Son of David* often occurs in conjunction with the title *Lord*: Matt. 9:27–28; 15:22; 20:30–31).

The foundation for an enduring expectation concerning the house of David had been established centuries earlier, with God's promise to David: his throne would last forever (2 Sam. 7:10–16, 25–29; Ps. 132:11–18). Ethan reminds the Lord of this promise when things seem to be going badly with the royal house (Ps. 89:4–5, 28–52). And the prophets who in the end must announce that Judah's royal house will lose its throne are at the same time instructed to focus the promise to David's house on a future righteous ruler, a shoot from the stump of the tree that has been cut down (Isa. 7:14; 9:1–7 [8:23–9:6 MT]; 11:1–10; 32:1–8; Mic. 5:2–5 [5:1–4 MT]). This servant of the Lord will be a most marvelous king! The more the radiance of David's house grows dim, the more the prophets glorify the coming Son of David (Jer. 23:5–8; Ezek. 34:23–31).[14]

---

14. For an overview of this promise tradition, see D. C. Duling, "The Promises to David and Their Entrance into Christianity—Nailing Down a Likely Hypothesis," *New Testament Studies* 19 (1973–74): 55–77. For the incorporation of these promises into early Judaism, see C. L. Rogers, "The Promises to David in Early Judaism," *Bibliotheca Sacra* 150 (1993): 285–302.

It is striking that Jesus did not present himself directly to the people with the titles *Lord* or *Son of David*; in fact, it is almost as if he were trying to avoid these titles. According to Neugebauer and Farla, Jesus actually rejected the designation "Son of David" (as it was then commonly understood).[15] According to Cullmann, Bauer, and others, he did not reject the title but he did try to distance himself from it because it had become charged with nationalistic and political expectations.[16] But this is doubtful. The Davidic dynasty had been meaningless for centuries; during the centuries preceding Jesus, the Hasmonean family and the Herodians were politically far more important. The expectation of a Son of David is ultimately not political but religious. Believing Jews continued to anticipate the coming of a definitive Savior and Redeemer solely on the basis of God's ancient promises. Thus the crowds at the triumphal entry are not crying for revolt and struggle here below, but for "Peace in heaven and glory in the highest" (Luke 19:38). They expect the coming kingdom of David in the name of the Lord (Mark 11:10). Thus they reach not for sticks and spears but for palm branches: "Hosanna in the highest!" (Matt. 21:8). Jesus has come in God's name, and that is why he is able to perform such astonishing signs and wonders. He cures the lame and the blind in the temple area—and it is then that the children call out "Hosanna to the Son of David." Jesus accepts this as praise ordained by God from the mouths of children and infants (Matt. 21:15–16).[17]

In reaction against the political connotations of the Jewish ideas around the phrase "Son of David," more recent studies have come up

15. F. Neugebauer, "Die Davidssohnfrage (Mark xii 35–7 parr.) und der Menschensohn," *New Testament Studies* 21 (1974): 81–108; P. J. Farla, *Jezus' oordeel over Israël: Een Form- en Redaktionsgeschichtliche analyse van Mc 10,46–12,40* (Kampen: Kok, 1978). For a critical discussion of this theory, see M. de Jonge, "Jesus, Son of David and Son of God," in *Jewish Eschatology, Early Christian Christology, and the Testaments of the Twelve Patriarchs: Collected Essays,* Novum Testamentum Supplement 63 (Leiden: Brill, 1991), 135–44.

16. Cullmann, *Christology of the New Testament*; D. R. Bauer, "Son of David," in *Dictionary of Jesus and the Gospels*, ed. J. B. Green and S. McKnight (Downers Grove, Ill.: InterVarsity, 1992), 766–69.

17. John 6:15—which relates how the crowds want to make Jesus king after the feeding of the five thousand—is also quoted in support of an excessively this-worldly, political messianic expectation. But the starting point for the people is not recognition of Jesus as "Son of David" but recognition of him as "the prophet" (John 6:14). They immediately want to give the judicial, decisive function of the coming prophet a place in Israel by appointing Jesus as judge-king. This has nothing to do with politics or revolution, but with anticipating the exercising of the judicial rights of "*the* prophet" (see sec. 5.1, "More Than a Prophet"). Jesus' contemporaries did not yet know that "the prophet" and "the Christ" would be the same person (see John 7:40–41). Therefore we must not project any actions taken in response to their recognition of Jesus as the prophet onto the expectations of the Son of David.

with an entirely different approach.[18] According to them the title "Son of David" is not messianic but is used by Jesus' contemporaries as a reference to *Solomon*.[19] The teachers of wisdom were not the only ones who appealed to the wisdom and knowledge of Solomon, David's son (a number of wisdom writings are attributed to Solomon). The Jewish magicians also claimed that their magical powers and incantations were derived from a tradition that went back to Solomon.[20] Against this background it is presumably more understandable that the crowds call Jesus "the Son of David" precisely because of his unprecedented miracles and because of his unique power over demons. He is seen as a reincarnated Solomon![21]

These newer perspectives on the background of the term "Son of David" may contain valuable elements, but on the whole they are not convincing.[22] Insofar as Solomon, with his wisdom and insight, serves as a foretaste of the promised Son of David, it is not strange that connections can be made between Jesus and this Son of David. Even Jesus compares himself to Solomon, though he calls himself "greater than Solomon." It is unlikely, however, that the crowds were thinking of Solomon when they began to call Jesus "Son of David." Although Solomon's wisdom had become legendary, there was no expectation of his return (as in the case of Elijah). In addition, the recognition of Jesus as "the Son of David" was indeed *evoked* by his wisdom and his mighty acts (comparable with those of Solomon), but it derives its *content* from the expectation of the coming *kingdom* of David, as we see in the jubilation during the en-

18. E. Lövestam, "Jésus Fils de David chez les Synoptiques," *Studia theologica* 28 (1974): 97–109; K. Berger, "Die königlichen Messiastraditionen des neuen Testaments," *New Testament Studies* 20 (1973–74): 1–44; compare C. Burger, *Jesus als Davidssohn: Eine traditionsgeschichtliche Untersuchung*, FRLANT 98 (Göttingen: Vandenhoeck & Ruprecht, 1970).

19. L. R. Fisher, "Can This Be the Son of David?" in *Jesus and the Historian*, ed. F. T. Trotter (Philadelphia: Westminster, 1968), 82–97; D. C. Duling, "Solomon, Exorcism, and the Son of David," *Harvard Theological Review* 68 (1975): 235–52.

20. Josephus, *Antiquities* 8.2.5 §§42–49; Testament of Solomon; compare E. Schürer, *The History of the Jewish People in the Age of Jesus Christ (175 B.C.–A.D. 135)*, new English version, rev. and ed. G. Vermes, F. Millar, M. Black, and M. Goodman, 3 vols. (Edinburgh: Clark, 1973–87), 3.1:375–79.

21. Somewhat comparable with this idea is the view of M. de Jonge, "Jezus als profetische Zoon van David," in *Profeten en profetische geschriften*, ed. F. García Martínez et al. (Kampen: Kok, 1987), 157–66. According to de Jonge, there was a prophetic image of David in circulation as well as a royal image. In this prophetic image, David was seen as anointed by the *Spirit* as a prophet and an exorcist. Jesus would have regarded himself as the Son of David in this prophetic sense, which would explain why the title *Christ* refers not so much to kingship as to being anointed by the Spirit in order to be a bearer of God's word and work.

22. B. Chilton, "Jesus *ben David*: Reflections on the *Davidssohnfrage*," *Journal for the Study of the New Testament* 14 (1982): 88–112.

trance into Jerusalem. The term thus alludes to the *promises* that were made to David concerning a future *King of Peace* who would be born into his family. "Son of David" and the term *messiah* (Hebrew for *anointed* = Greek *christos*) are interchangeable (see Matt. 22:42; John 7:41–42). The fact that being anointed with the *Spirit*, prophesying, and performing miracles all play a major role in this terminology cannot be separated from the kingship; rather, these aspects should be regarded as a description of the way in which this kingship will be carried out.[23]

For Jesus' contemporaries, therefore, the title "Son of David" implies the as yet unfulfilled promises made to David's house and the prophecies concerning a king coming in God's name. A number of fragments found at Qumran also point in this direction. They show that the expectation of a Davidic messiah went hand in hand with the messianic interpretation of texts such as Genesis 49:10; Numbers 24:17; Isaiah 11:1–5; Jeremiah 23:5–6.[24] The title "Son of David" thus had extraordinary significance for the Jews of Jesus' day. The promised son is, after all, at the same time David's *Lord* (Ps. 110:1). He is the Son begotten of God (Ps. 2), born of a virgin (Isa. 7:14), on whom the Spirit of God will rest (Isa. 11:1–5); his name is "Wonderful Counselor, Mighty God, Everlasting Father, Prince of Peace" (Isa. 9:6), and his origin is "from of old, from ancient times" (Mic. 5:2). People knew the Scriptures well, so the teachers of the law were well aware that the promised Son of David is also "his Lord." But they refuse to see any more than a human being, a "son of man" in *Jesus*. They try in numerous ways to undermine his claim to authority in the days before his death, and Jesus resists their attacks regally and sovereignly. Then, on the last day, he turns to the crowds and asks them why the leaders refuse to recognize his divine authority: aren't the Scriptures quite clear about the Son of David? In rejecting Jesus the leaders are being disloyal to their own source of authority[25]—they do not bow before the divine Scriptures because their hearts are too proud for Jesus of Nazareth.

And this is the sensitive issue: Jesus does carry out his ministry with authority and great miracles, so that he seems to deserve recognition as David's *Lord*, but on the other hand he is unpretentious, humble, and on the way to his death. When the wise men come from the East and arrive in Jerusalem, the teachers of the law tell them that the King of the Jews will be born in Bethlehem (Matt. 2:4–6). Micah 5:1 was a fa-

---

23. Compare H. J. de Jonge's criticism of M. de Jonge (H. J. de Jonge, "De visie van de historische Jezus op zichzelf," in *Jezus' visie op zichzelf: In discussie met De Jonge's christologie* [Nijkerk: Callenbach, 1991], 53–54).

24. García Martínez, "Messianische Erwartungen in den Qumranschriften."

25. See J. van Bruggen, *Marcus: Het evangelie volgens Petrus*, 2d ed., Commentaar op het Nieuwe Testament, 3d series (Kampen: Kok, 1992), on Mark 12:37.

miliar passage. Even so, not one of the teachers of the law travels with the wise men to go to the place and have a look. It seemed inconceivable that the Messiah could arrive so inconspicuously, unnoticed by Jerusalem and only observed by a few pagan astrologers.

The same problem occurs later on a larger scale. Jesus grows up as a boy in Nazareth and conducts his ministry from Galilee, so in Jerusalem he is known as "the Galilean." This is not impressive. No prophet ever came from Galilee (John 7:52). And some of the crowd begin to question whether he can be the Christ. The Messiah was to come "from David's family and from Bethlehem, the town where David lived" (John 7:42). And although Jesus was born in Bethlehem, he never makes much of the fact. It is as though he has chosen to shroud himself in anonymity. Why doesn't he make Bethlehem his home, the base from which he travels through Israel until it is time to go up to the capital? The crowds are not concerned whether Bethlehem was Jesus' birthplace, but they do wonder why Bethlehem has not become the home base for this messianic ministry. The crowds are faced with a difficult puzzle: on the one hand there is the inescapable conclusion that God's Anointed has come down to Israel; on the other hand it is hardly suitable, they feel, that he presents himself as a humble Galilean, that he associates with tax collectors and sinners, and that he talks about preparing to die.

This explains how the crowds who welcome him as the Son of David in Jerusalem later fail to appear at the crucifixion. For Jesus to be taken prisoner does not fit their image of him.[26] David's Son and Lord—in chains? At the cross the statement that Jesus "saved others" goes unchallenged. What is incomprehensible, however, is that the Son of David, the King of Israel, cannot save *himself*. The leaders are quick to suggest that he *cannot* save himself because he is not "the King of Israel," while in reality he can but *chooses* not to.

The designation *"the* King of Israel (of the Jews)" refers to "the promised Son of David." Both terms are used for "the Messiah, the Son of God" (John 1:49; Mark 15:31–32; Luke 19:38; John 12:13). When the wise men from the East ask where the one is who was born "King of the Jews," the teachers of the law immediately think of the promised ruler from Bethlehem mentioned in Micah 5:1. On the day of the crucifixion, the title "King of the Jews" is frequently used by Pilate and the soldiers (Matt. 27:11, 29, 37; Mark 15:9, 12; Luke 23:37; John 19:14–15, 21). It is their way of expressing that Jesus *claims* to be the Savior King of Israel. There are Jews who speak about the "King *of Israel*" (Matt. 27:42; Mark

---

26. K. Berger, "Zum Problem der Messianität Jesu," *Zeitschrift für Theologie und Kirche* 71 (1974): 6.

15:31–32; John 1:49). They use a religiously charged word that refers to the people chosen by God. Outsiders prefer a more pragmatic, political label: "King *of the Jews*." Neither label, however, suggests a political rebel or an earthly pretender to the crown. We see this from Pilate's profound conversations with Jesus. And we see it also from the way the Jewish leaders take up the mockery begun by the Roman soldiers. The soldiers cry out, "If you are the King of the Jews, save yourself" (Luke 23:37). The leaders say, "He saved others, but he can't save himself! Let this Christ, this King of Israel, come down now from the cross, that we may see and believe" (Mark 15:31–32).

The fact that the *Son of David* must first suffer and die makes it understandable that Jesus allowed others to give him this title but did not emphasize it himself *before Good Friday*. After Christ's ascension, however, the apostles explain to the people that the way of the cross was intended by God in order to "give him the throne of his father David" (as Gabriel promised to Mary in Luke 1:32). On Pentecost, Peter preaches that the crucified and risen Jesus fulfills the promises made to *David* (Acts 2:22–36). And the community of believers confesses in its prayer that Jesus is the Anointed Son of "our father David" (Acts 4:25–27). And Paul, after his conversion, also preaches that Jesus is the promised Son of David (Acts 13:22–24, 32–39). In his letter to the Romans, he characterizes Jesus' descent from David's house as fulfillment of the promises (Rom. 1:2–3)—it is part of the Good News that "Jesus Christ, raised from the dead, descended from David" (2 Tim. 2:8). Finally, the Evangelists provide more concrete information on how Jesus actually descended from David: his mother was betrothed to Joseph, a man of Davidic origins, and God entrusted the child of Mary to him as offspring (Matt. 1:1–25; Luke 1:27, 32; 2:4; 3:23–38). This genealogical connection with David constitutes the background for the reality that seems inescapable: Jesus is the Promised One, irresistibly anointed with the Spirit of God.

According to some, the title *Son of David* was only a later response to the resurrection.[27] Thus Burger writes that Jesus "entered the line of David not by birth but by Easter and through the community's confession of faith."[28] This theory fails to do justice to the facts as reported by the Evangelists. However, the moments of resurrection *and ascension* are indeed significant for the outspokenness with which the title *Son of David* is preached. It seems that Jesus did allow the title to be attributed to him during his life on earth, but that he did not use it himself because he first wanted to lay the foundation for his heavenly rule as David's

27. Duling, "Promises to David and Their Entrance into Christianity."
28. Burger, *Jesus als Davidssohn*, 178.

Son by suffering and dying. He did not deny that he was "the Son of David," and he pointed the people in that direction by his miracles and his authority. He himself, on the other hand, made little of his Davidic descent, and he did not aspire to a throne. This Son of David would indeed come to judge the earth, but first he must enter Jerusalem "riding on the colt of a donkey." Israel must learn to understand the *timetable* of this promised king!

5.3 God's Anointed

As stated, the descriptive phrases *Christ* and *Son of God* are inextricably linked, and they refer to the same figure as the term *Son of David*. The three phrases are all indirect translations of Immanuel (God with us). We now come to the second term, *Christ*.

5.3.1 Confessing Jesus as the Christ

Jesus is "the Anointed One, the Son of the living God." This was the name the disciples gave him, through Simon Peter (Matt. 16:16; "Christ" in NIV). They stand by this affirmation despite the fact that most of the people in Israel never quite rose to that level of affirmation when they spoke of Jesus (Matt. 16:13–14). It is not a confession the disciples came to embrace gradually.[29] Even in the very beginning, when they were still the disciples of John the Baptist, Andrew already said to his brother Simon, "We have found the Messiah!" (John 1:41). Andrew said this as one of the two disciples who heard these words from John (John 1:40). The Baptist had pointed Jesus out to them with the words "Look, the Lamb of God!" (John 1:36), and thus they knew from the very beginning: Jesus is God's Anointed, the Messiah! They did not allow themselves to be dissuaded from their faith, not even when later many disciples dropped out and turned their backs on him (John 6:66). At that point Jesus asked the Twelve if they too wanted to turn away, and Simon Peter responded, "Lord, to whom shall we go? You have the words of eternal life. We believe and know that you are the Christ, the Son of the living God" (John 6:68–69; NIV, following other manuscripts, has, "that you are the Holy One of God"). This confession of the disciples who love Jesus is echoed by Martha: "I believe that you are the Christ, the Son of God, who was to come into the world" (John 11:27).

There were even a number of Samaritans who came to recognize Jesus as the Messiah (John 4:29, 42): "We have heard for ourselves, and we know that this man really is the Savior of the world, the Christ" (in

---

29. See van Bruggen, *Matteüs*, on Matt. 16:16.

NIV, following a small number of manuscripts, the word *Christ* appears only in 4:29 and not in 4:42).

The confession that Jesus is the Christ sometimes comes from very unexpected corners: the demons who are cast out all call Jesus "the Christ, the Son of God" (Luke 4:41; in NIV, following a small number of manuscripts, the phrase *ho christos* is absent, but all end this verse with the remark: "they knew he was the Christ").

So it was no secret in Israel that Jesus was laying claim to the title *Messiah*. We see this from the reactions of his opponents. In response to the spreading recognition of Jesus as the Christ, the leaders feel at last compelled to stem the tide, so they declare that any Jew who confesses that Jesus is "Christ" will be thrown out of the synagogue (John 9:22). The cause of this disciplinary measure was the increasing number of people who were making this confession (John 7:26, 31, 41, 48–49). The key question during his trial is therefore whether Jesus really thinks that he is "the Christ, the Son of God" (Matt. 26:63). And when the leaders bring him before Pilate, the charge is that he claims to be "Christ, a king" (Luke 23:2). So Pilate refers to him as "Jesus who is called Christ" (Matt. 27:17, 22). Later, at the cross, the same leaders ridicule such a presumption: "Let this Christ, this King of Israel, come down now from the cross, that we may see and believe" (Mark 15:32), and "He saved others; let him save himself if he is the Christ of God, the Chosen One" (Luke 23:35; compare 23:39).

Jesus is the Messiah, the Son of God. He has accepted this recognition as something that those who made this confession had learned from his Father in heaven (Matt. 16:17). And he himself declares to the Sanhedrin that he indeed is Christ, the Son of God; they will see him sitting at the right hand of the Mighty One and coming on the clouds of heaven (Matt. 26:64).

5.3.2 The Christ: An Expected Savior

What do the people actually mean when they call Jesus *the Christ*? They apparently base their confession on certain existing expectations concerning an *Anointed One*. Jesus appears to fulfill that expectation. Jesus did not begin by announcing a type of new program for an Anointed One and then follow it up with an explanation as to how *he* has come to fulfill it. He assumes that the program for the coming one from God was already known. The question now is only whether he meets the *already existing* expectations: May he be welcomed as "the expected one"? The answer to that question divides disciples and leaders, but they nevertheless share the same pattern of expectations concerning the one who is to come.

We learn from the Gospels that there is an existing frame of reference for the title "Christ, the Son of God." John the Baptist emphatically declares to the crowds and to the committee of inquiry that he is *not* the Christ (Luke 3:15–17; John 1:20, 25; 3:28). So at that point there is an expectation of a coming Christ against whom the prophet can be measured. The same happens with Jesus; his ministry is also compared with the generally held concept of the coming Christ. The people make this comparison (John 7:27, 41–42, 52; 12:34), as do the confessing disciples, who are of the opinion that suffering and dying are not appropriate for the Christ (Matt. 16:21–23). Even John the Baptist in prison makes this comparison (Matt. 11:2–3). Conversely, Jesus himself invites the leaders to measure his ministry against everything that the Scripture says about the Christ, the Son *and* Lord of David (Matt. 22:42–45).

Even the Samaritans know that a *messiah* is coming: "When he comes, he will explain everything to us" (John 4:25). For this reason Jesus can be succinct with the Samaritan woman. He does not need to explain to her what *Christ* means; he need only say, "I who speak to you am he."

The Gospels show clearly that there was already an expectation of a coming divine redeemer. It was not a matter of later Christians recognizing their leader as "*an* anointed one" to indicate that he was *a* holy personality among so many other holy things and persons. According to Karrer, we must see the title *Christ* within the context of Jewish and Hellenistic *cultic* practices of anointing; that which is anointed is sanctified and withdrawn from the profane, so that it is close to God.[30] By calling Jesus an anointed one, the Christians were supposedly expressing the fact that *for them* he was someone consecrated to God. From this designation the *title* "Christ" finally arose *within Christianity*. Not only is this theory in conflict with the information in the Gospels (where the title is already presupposed), but it is also based on a mistaken idea of the value attributed to anointing in the Hellenistic world.[31] In addition, Jesus' disciples were being called *christianoi* very early on (Acts 11:26). The formation of this title was analogous to the formation of party names ("followers of Christ"; compare *Hērōdianoi*), and those who spoke Greek at that time apparently regarded *Christos* (perhaps without full understanding) as a *personal name* and not as a qualifier ("anointed and consecrated"). But the word *Christ* could have

30. M. Karrer, *Der Gesalbte: Die Grundlagen des Christustitels*, FRLANT 151 (Göttingen: Vandenhoeck & Ruprecht, 1991).

31. R. D. Anderson, "Graeco-Roman Religious Anointing and Its Possible Implications for the Understanding of the Christos in the First Century: A Critical Evaluation of Sections from Martin Karrer's 'Der Gesalbte'" (doctoral thesis, Theological University, Broederweg, Kampen, Netherlands, 1993).

become a *personal name* so quickly only because it was already a *title* (not *"an* anointed" but *"the* Anointed").

5.3.3 Messianic Expectations in Judaism

The Gospels show that there was already an expectation during the ministries of John the Baptist and Jesus concerning the future appearance of a *messiah*. Is it possible to find and refine that expectation on the basis of extrabiblical data?

In this case it is not enough simply to refer back to the writings of the Old Testament. Certainly we find all sorts of prophecies there concerning the future of Israel and the world, and occasionally future personalities also play a role. But the relationships between these prophecies are not clear: should they be correlated in a particular way, and are different titles sometimes used to refer to the same future redeemer? With the key of Jesus Christ's later revelation in hand, it certainly is possible to arrange the various Old Testament data into a coherent pattern. This is the approach in, for example, Van Groningen's study of messianic revelation in the Old Testament.[32] The problem is, however, that this type of approach looks at the Old Testament *from a later perspective.* In doing so it is easy to forget that, while the Old Testament provided direction and hope long before the coming of Jesus Christ, it was obscure when it came to concrete images of the future (compare 1 Pet. 1:10–12).

So we should not be surprised to discover that Jewish writings from the centuries before the Christian era (insofar as they say something about the future of God) do not always agree in terms and concepts. According to some, this lack of agreement has a religio-sociological explanation: there was not just one Judaism but many kinds of Judaism existing side by side, and each kind generated its own messianic notions.[33] But this view is not supported by the New Testament writings. There we see that there was a diversity of ideas concerning the future, but that this diversity was contained within one kind of Judaism. This is apparent from the question posed by one priestly commission of inquiry to John the Baptist: "Are you Elijah? Are you the prophet? Are you Christ? If not, then why are you baptizing?" (John 1:19–25). The commission is not sure if this baptism that claims to be carried out in preparation for the coming of the kingdom of heaven is the work of the prophet, of Elijah, or of the Christ. On the other hand, they are unani-

---

32. G. van Groningen, *Messianic Revelation in the Old Testament* (Grand Rapids: Baker, 1990).
33. See the collection edited by Neusner and others with the telling title *Judaisms and Their Messiahs at the Turn of the Christian Era,* ed. J. Neusner, W. S. Green, and E. S. Frerichs (Cambridge: Cambridge University Press, 1987).

mous in their understanding that such a baptism can only have legiti-
macy within these models of expectation, which are derived from the
Holy Scriptures. From the perspective of extrabiblical sources it is also
incorrect to trace the diversity of expectations to a diversity in Jewish
faith communities—this underestimates the foundational and unifying
value of "the Law and the Prophets" during this period (including the
statements found there concerning the future). Thus the idea of the
coming of an Elijah, for instance, is not the product of a particular faith
community but a conviction people maintain on the authority of the
scribes (see Matt. 17:10).[34]

The vagueness of the sources should make us suspicious of any effort
to make the Jewish messianic expectations *too specific*. For a long time
the prevailing idea was that during the first century the Jewish people
were obsessed by the expectation of a *political* messiah. According to
some scholars, first-century Jewish messianic expectations had become
disconnected from their religious, prophetic roots and had become en-
tangled in the this-worldly problems of the political situation. Under
the Romans the people had lost more and more of their freedom, which
heightened the expectation that the messiah would come and liberate
them from this dominating power. Mowinckel sees the rise of chiliasm
as a compromise between the old prophetic expectation—a heavenly
kingdom—and the later expectation of an earthly liberator-king, who
would usher in the earthly thousand-year reign.[35] According to Pickl,
Jesus' own ministry can be seen as a complete refashioning of the this-
worldly expectations; the people must be converted to a divine and suffering messiah, as promised by the prophets.[36] Others claim that Jesus'
own messianic concept did not differ significantly from the prevailing
political notions of his day. Eisler believes that Jesus only separated
himself from these notions by opting for a nonviolent and liberating exodus to the wilderness.[37] Brandon sees the circle of followers gathered

34. In response to Neusner et al., Thoma points out that, although the messianic notions at the beginning of the Christian era were diffuse, they nevertheless form a cohesive
cluster that can serve as the basis for later Jewish and Christian messianic thought. As focal
points he sees (a) predominantly kingly-prophetic concepts; (b) predominantly priestly-
heavenly concepts (C. Thoma, "Entwürfe für messianische Gestalten in frühjüdischer
Zeit," in *Messiah and Christos: Studies in the Jewish Origins of Christianity*, Texte und Studien zum antiken Judentum 32, ed. I. Gruenwald et al. [Tübingen: Mohr, 1992], 15–29).

35. S. Mowinckel, *He That Cometh*, trans. G. W. Anderson (Oxford: Blackwell, 1956;
Norwegian ed. 1951).

36. J. Pickl, *The Messias*, trans. A. Green (St. Louis and London: Herder, 1946).

37. R. Eisler, *Iesous Basileus Ou Basileusas: Die messianische Unabhängigkeitsbewegung vom Auftreten Johannes des Täufers bis zum Untergang Jakobs des Gerechten, nach
der neuerschlossenen "Eroberung von Jerusalem" des Flavius Josephus*, 2 vols. (Heidelberg: Winter Universitätsbuchhandlung, 1929).

around Jesus as para-Zealots; Jesus criticizes not only the foreign rulers but also the leaders of his own people.[38] Thus in the end he is condemned as a rebel by both the Jews and the Romans.

These divergent reconstructions are based on the idea that in Jesus' day the party of the Zealots and a unilateral political messianic expectation were both very important. But this idea is incorrect (see sec. 1.2.3 on the Zealots, and sec. 5.2 on the Son of David). There is nothing to support the idea that the Jews of the first century nourished a this-worldly, political messianic expectation.

In order to somewhat reduce the confusion that has developed around the reconstruction of the Jewish messianic expectation, there have been repeated calls in recent years for the use of clearly delineated concepts. The vague term "messianic expectation" must be dropped. Methodologically a distinction must be made between a variety of Jewish expectations and concrete expectations of a messiah. The latter then may only be reconstructed from texts in which the word *messiah* specifically appears.[39] The material that remains after applying these delimitations turns out to be scarce—which is why many prefer to write about both messiah *and* messianic expectations. The latter then include eschatological expectations in which one or more end-time figures play a central role.[40] Such a point of departure is defensible, but if we want to examine the Jewish background for the New Testament use of the *title* "Christ," we must nevertheless limit ourselves to the explicit use of that title. Even in the New Testament we find other eschatological persons who play a role (the Prophet, Elijah), but *the Jews* distinguished them from *the Christ*. For an accurate answer to the question of what people were thinking, we must concentrate on extrabiblical texts that contain explicit references to *the Messiah*.

But then we face the curious fact that such texts are exceedingly rare, while at the same time it appears that people definitely expected that in one way or another God would send them a final redeemer (or redeemers) at the end of time.

The most important data can be summarized as follows:

1. *Psalms of Solomon.* This collection of eighteen psalms, ascribed to Solomon, was almost certainly produced during the first century B.C.

38. S. G. F. Brandon, *Jesus and the Zealots: A Study of the Political Factor in Primitive Christianity* (Manchester: Manchester University Press, 1967).

39. M. de Jonge, "The Use of the Word 'Anointed' in the Time of Jesus," *Novum Testamentum* 8 (1966): 132–48.

40. G. S. Oegema, *De messiaanse verwachtingen ten tijde van Jezus: Een inleiding in de messiaanse verwachtingen en bewegingen gedurende de hellenistisch-romeinse tijd* (Baarn: Ten Have, 1991); C. J. den Heyer, *De messiaanse weg*, vol. 1, *Messiaanse verwachtingen in het Oude Testament en in de vroeg-joodse traditie* (Kampen: Kok, 1983).

The seventeenth and eighteenth psalms include prayers for the coming of the promised redeemer from the house of David: he will restore all things. This saving king of God is called an "anointed ruler" in 17.32: "In those days there will be no injustice among them, for all men will be holy and their king will be an anointed ruler." Because this future king is "mighty in the Holy Spirit" (17.37), he will be wise and righteous. The inscription for the eighteenth psalm explains that this hymn also (*eti*) has to do with "the anointed ruler" (*tou christou kuriou*). The article thus refers back to Psalm of Solomon 17: the eighteenth hymn continues to speak of the "anointed ruler" mentioned there. The promised king of the LORD God is now described as "*his* anointed" (18.5). The people will submit to the rod of "an anointed ruler" (18.7). It is not necessary to translate the phrase as "*the* anointed ruler" here, as M. De Jonge does.[41] The purpose of the verse is to indicate the qualities of the promised ruler. Because he is an *anointed one (of God)*, he has reverence toward *his* God and he acts with wisdom of spirit, righteousness, and might (18.7b). Both psalms express the expectation of a future redeeming king from the house of David; he will be anointed by God with the Spirit and will thus be a great blessing for all.

It would be incorrect, however, to read these psalms from the perspective of the later, fixed term *messiah, christos*. These psalms are not a description of "*the* Messiah"; rather, they express the notion that the king of the future will be "one anointed by God." The word of the angel in Luke 2:11b is in close keeping with this hope: "Today an anointed ruler has been born to you" (author's translation).[42] The Psalms of Solomon show us the climate in which the title "messiah" will be able to develop, but that stage has not yet been reached. And this may be related to the fact that there was as yet no full clarity on the question whether the future king would be the *only* "Anointed One" of the end times (as is clear from the Qumran fragments).

2. *Qumran.* In an essay on the messianic expectations in the Qumran manuscripts, García Martínez deals with all the fragments (including those not published until 1992) that directly or indirectly refer to a messianic figure.[43] He calls the resulting picture "fragmentary and kaleidoscopic."[44] The highly fragmentary state of many of the texts precludes

---

41. M. De Jonge, "Use of the Word 'Anointed' in the Time of Jesus."

42. See also J. van Bruggen, *Lucas: Het evangelie als voorgeschiedenis*, Commentaar op het Nieuwe Testament, 3d series (Kampen: Kok, 1993), on Luke 2:11.

43. García Martínez, "Messianische Erwartungen in den Qumranschriften." See also C. A. Evans, *Jesus and His Contemporaries: Comparative Studies*, Arbeiten zur Geschichte des antiken Judentums und des Urchristentums 25 (Leiden: Brill, 1995), 83–154.

44. See also F. García Martínez and J. Trebolle Barrera, *The People of the Dead Sea Scrolls: Their Writings, Beliefs, and Practices*, trans. W. G. E. Watson (Leiden: Brill, 1995).

the possibility of definite pronouncements about the messianic expectations in the documents to which the fragments once belonged. Neither is it certain whether all fragments had the same spiritual background. García Martínez does not limit himself to passages in which an "anointed one" is explicitly mentioned; he includes fragments that also point to a "messianic figure." He concludes that at least three messianic figures can be distinguished: the royal, the priestly, and the prophetic.[45] But it cannot be determined whether these figures stand side by side or whether, for example, the prophet is to be a forerunner of the messiahs from Aaron and Israel.

When we limit ourselves to occurrences of the *title* "messiah," we are forced to accept a much more modest conclusion. Several figures can be referred to as "anointed ones," but it is incorrect to assume that "messiah" can indicate only one figure. If we read that "the anointed ones of Aaron and Israel" (1QS 9.10–11) are expected in addition to "the prophet," we cannot conclude that the people in Qumran were expecting a "double *messiah*." This would suggest that *messiah* was already an established term for the savior of the end times. The variations in the use of the words in the Qumran fragments, however, prove that the term *anointed* was not yet reserved for one figure alone. Thus the formulation "the anointed ones of Aaron and Israel" seems not to have been derived from a general terminology concerning *"the* messiah." It is rather a formulation based on Zechariah 4:14 (the two olive branches are the two anointed ones who stand before the Lord: Zerubbabel as representative of Israel and Joshua as priest of the house of Aaron). M. De Jonge is correct in insisting that the use of the word *messiah* instead of *an anointed one* in the translation of the Qumran fragments is far too suggestive.[46]

3. *1 Enoch.* In the second book of the Ethiopic 1 Enoch, we find two instances of the name "his anointed" (48.10 and 52.4). This refers to the same figure who in this second book is also called "the Chosen One" and more frequently "the son of man." The way this last title functions in 1 Enoch 37–71 was discussed in section 4.2.2.b, where it was concluded that this second book of 1 Enoch speaks of the "son of man" in such a way as to suggest that it must be a Christian document. That also means that 1 Enoch cannot be regarded as a source for the pre-Christian use of the term *his anointed one.*

---

45. Collins even distinguishes four messianic paradigms: king, priest, prophet, and heavenly king or son of man. (J. J. Collins, *The Scepter and the Star: The Messiahs of the Dead Sea Scrolls and Other Ancient Literature* [New York: Doubleday, 1995].)

46. M. de Jonge, "The Role of Intermediaries in God's Final Intervention in the Future according to the Qumran Scrolls," in *Jewish Eschatology, Early Christian Christology, and the Testaments of the Twelve Patriarchs: Collected Essays,* Novum Testamentum Supplement 63 (Leiden: Brill, 1991), 28–47.

4. *4 Ezra*. The Fourth Book of Ezra (= 2 Esdras NRSV), which has been preserved in Latin, is a Christian document, but the greater part of the book (chaps. 3–14) is also known as an independent apocalypse in Syrian, Ethiopian, Armenian, and Arabic versions. This apocalypse is generally considered a *Jewish* document from the first century A.D. In 12:32 there is mention of "an anointed one." In 7:28–29 we read about "my anointed son" (at this point the versions disagree: "my anointed one," "the anointed of God," and, in Latin, "my son Jesus"). Elsewhere we hear God speaking about "my son" as the future savior (13:37, 52; 14:9).

Considering the dating of the apocalypse, it is not unlikely that the document is Jewish-*Christian* or that as a Jewish document it was influenced by the terminology relating to Christ that became current within Jewish circles at that time. In any case, in the circles in which it was transmitted it was always read as a document that dealt (indirectly) with Jesus Christ (for an explicit reference, see the Latin version of 2:47: "He is the son of God, whom they confessed in the world").

Even when we regard the apocalypse as a document using original Jewish terminology, it is difficult to see it as support for the existence of the title *Messiah* in the first century *before* Christ. Even in this later document there are only two references to "being anointed," and then only as qualifiers for the future figure and not as a reference to a title.[47]

5. *Philo*. The Jewish philosopher and biblical exegete Philo of Alexandria, writing at the beginning of the Christian era, never uses the term *Messiah*. Nevertheless, he lived with the expectation that one day God would intervene in world history on a vast scale—the Jewish slaves throughout the world would be freed and would return to the Holy Land, and then a "change to virtue" would take place among all peoples.[48] When this happened, a world ruler would play a central role. This is the general Jewish expectation, which Philo shared, as is apparent from his exegesis of Balaam's prophecy. In Numbers 24:7a the Hebrew text reads, "Water will flow from their buckets; their seed will have abundant water." But the Greek translation, which Philo used, is quite different: "From your seed a man will appear and he will rule over many nations." In his exegesis of these words, Philo emphasizes that this world conqueror will accomplish a *bloodless* conquest by personal appeal and respect, thanks to the help that *God* will give his people.[49]

---

47. For the idea of the messiah in 4 Ezra, see also M. Stone, "The Concept of the Messiah in IV Ezra," in *Religions in Antiquity: Essays in Memory of E. R. Goodenough*, Studies in the History of Religions 14, ed. J. Neusner (Leiden: Brill, 1970), 295–312.

48. Philo, *On Rewards and Punishments* 28–29 §§164–72.

49. Ibid., 16 §§95–97.

6. *Josephus.* The Jewish historian Josephus, who wrote at the end of the first century A.D., uses the words *ho Christos* twice, both times in reference to Jesus. For many this is evidence that the passages are inauthentic—how could the Jew Josephus ever give Jesus the title *Messiah*? This topic is dealt with in more detail in *Christ on Earth*, section 1.2.2.1, where it is concluded that Josephus did not intend to recognize Jesus as the Messiah here but wanted to clarify for his Roman readers the fact that the *Jesus* he is describing is the same man as the one they have come to know as *Christ*—the *personal name* by which Jesus was best known in the Greek-speaking world because his followers were known as *christianoi.* The extent to which he himself was expecting the coming of a *Messiah* is still unclear.

This is less odd than it seems, because Josephus expressly presents himself as a historian, and when it comes to the future he is silent. He explicitly states this when he refuses to comment on the stone that will demolish the statue of the world rulers in Daniel 2.[50] It is plausible, however, that, on the basis of the Scriptures, he shared in the general expectation that a future world ruler would come from the Jewish people. This is suggested in *Jewish Wars* 6.5.4 §312, where Josephus reports that the chief provocation for the Jewish War was "an ambiguous oracle, likewise found in their sacred scriptures, to the effect that at that time one from their country would become ruler of the world." So there is a distinction between the contemporary oracle—which specifies "at this time"—and a prophecy in the Scriptures to which the oracle conforms in choice of words, but without any specific time reference.

Den Heyer incorrectly claims that Josephus traced the cause of the revolt to the Scriptures (Den Heyer mentions Num. 24:17),[51] and that this reveals a messianic tendency among the Zealots. Josephus does no more than *compare* the oracle with a scriptural passage foretelling the coming of a future world ruler from Israel. The oracle appeared to apply this promise to *this particular time.* At least that is how most of his contemporaries understand it—as referring to the imminent arrival of the promised world ruler *from among the Jews.* But the oracle does not state this in so many words. And the people identified it incorrectly with the biblical promise of a *Jewish* world ruler. Josephus himself understood that the oracle (which is *similar to* the biblical prophecy) must be seen as a prediction of Vespasian's rule as emperor: he was appointed world ruler (emperor) while he was in Palestine. This shows indirectly that all Jews (including Josephus) saw a promise in the Holy Scriptures about the coming of a future world ruler from Israel. But

---

50. Josephus, *Antiquities* 10.10.4 §210.
51. Den Heyer, *De messiaanse weg.*

there is nothing in Josephus's works to suggest any name or titles that he or others used in reference to the expected ruler. Josephus did not consider expectations about the future to be part of his task as historian. And it is not likely that for him *the Christ* was an established *title*, reserved for the expected world ruler from among the Jews. The ease with which he writes that Jesus was the bearer of the name *Christ* proves that he was not concerned about any potential confusion among his Roman readers.[52]

To sum up, we can conclude that within Judaism, on the basis of the prophecies in the Law and the Prophets, people were counting on the arrival in the last days of one (or more) savior figures who were *anointed by God*. The terminology, however, is not yet fixed. This savior was described as "someone coming from God" (anointed by God), but such a description had not yet led to a fully defined *title* ("the Christ").

When we compare this result with the New Testament data, we run into something of a problem. The New Testament also appears to reflect an existing expectation, but it seems that that expectation already had a fixed terminology—which is not confirmed and is even made improbable by the extrabiblical sources. We are thus led to the conclusion that in the period *directly preceding* Jesus' ministry a development must have occurred to explain the more fixed use of the title *the Christ*. And this is where the ministry of John the Baptist comes in (see chap. 2). This prophet and herald of "the one to come" revived in a short time all dormant expectations. He also gave direction to those expectations: "But one more powerful than I will come, the thongs of whose sandals I am not worthy to untie. He will baptize you with the Holy Spirit and with fire" (Luke 3:16). It is clear that John the Baptist is talking about someone who is coming from God and who is empowered by God. He will usher in the kingdom of heaven, so he must be the promised one. That means that the promised figure is *this one* person! John's ministry turned the vague expectation of "*an* Anointed One" into a concrete looking forward to "*the* Anointed One."

In the period before John's ministry, the term *anointed* is usually accompanied by other qualifying terms. Simeon is living in expectation of "the Lord's Anointed One" ("Christ" in NIV; Luke 2:26). The angel says to the shepherds, "Today in the town of David a Savior has been born to you; he is *an anointed* Lord" ("Christ the Lord" in NIV; Luke 2:11).[53]

---

52. For the future expectation as found in Josephus, see F. Dexinger, "Ein 'Messianisches Szenarium' als Gemeingut des Judentums in nachherodianischer Zeit?" *Kairos* 17 (1975): 249–78; M. de Jonge, "Josephus und die Zukunftserwartungen seines Volkes," in *Jewish Eschatology, Early Christian Christology, and the Testaments of the Twelve Patriarchs: Collected Essays*, Novum Testamentum Supplement 63 (Leiden: Brill, 1991), 48–62.

53. See van Bruggen, *Lucas*, on Luke 2:11.

"Anointed" here is still an attribute, not yet a title. Matthew 2:4 seems to be an exception, when Herod asks "where the Christ was to be born." In this context, however, he appears to be referring back to the question of the wise men about "one who has been born king of the Jews." They clearly point to the ruler promised by the prophets. This is why Herod asks the teachers of the law where "the *anointed* [king]" is to be born. Here "the anointed" is an independent (substantival) adjective, used to indicate what sort of king is being referred to.

It seems that under the influence of the ministry of John the Baptist, people in Israel began to speak about *the* Anointed One. The Samaritan woman knows that "an Anointed One is coming" (*hoti messias erchetai*), but Andrew, who has heard John the Baptist, is more concrete: "We have found *the* Anointed One [*heurēkamen ton messian*]" ("Messiah" in NIV; John 1:40–41).

The frequent occurrences of the *title* "the Christ" in the Gospels are, as far as content is concerned, in keeping with Judaism's scripturally based expectations about a coming divine savior (anointed by God). And its use as an honorific reflects a focusing of the more general meaning of the word, brought about by the imposing ministry and message of the prophet John the Baptist.

It is not impossible that the more titular designation "the Anointed One" was part of John the Baptist's own vocabulary. A close reading of John 1:19–24 shows that John, when visited by the priestly committee of inquiry from Jerusalem, immediately declared, *without being asked*, "I am not the Anointed One" ("Christ" in NIV; John 1:20). He seems to take the initiative and use the occasion to *direct* the attention of the inquirers to the Anointed One about whom he preaches (this is, after all, part of his mission: John 1:23, 26–27). Then the committee members ask him whether he is Elijah or the Prophet. They do not use the title "the Christ" until their summary of the conversation: "Why then do you baptize if you are not 'the Anointed One' ['Christ' in NIV], nor Elijah, nor the Prophet?" (John 1:25). The formulation in Luke 3:15 also suggests that John preached in so many words "the coming of *the Anointed One*," since some time later the people ask themselves whether John "himself might possibly be the Anointed One" ("Christ" in NIV). They do not simply ask "if he is the Anointed One," but if "he *himself*" (*autos*) is the Anointed One. This would seem to show indirectly that in his preaching about the one who is to come John used the title "*the* Anointed One."

5.3.4 Christ, Anointed with the Spirit of God

What do the Jews mean when they say they are expecting an "anointed" savior? In the Old Testament, anointing is a symbol of divine appointment. The priest, king, or prophet, anointed by order of God, was sent by God, which gave his office a certain inviolability. Although we never read that the patriarchs were anointed with oil, they are still referred to in Psalm 105:15 as "anointed ones": "Do not touch my anointed ones." This figurative usage illustrates how "the anointed one" is under God's special protection. He is not a product of human endeavor but a manifestation of God himself in history.

Thus an "anointed lord" ("Christ the Lord" in NIV; Luke 2:11) is a regent who comes from God and who can count on God's support.[54] The Old Testament contains promises concerning the coming of a person who can be regarded as God's anointed in a unique way—not because he was anointed with oil but because "the Spirit of the LORD God" ("Sovereign LORD" in NIV; Isa. 61:1) came upon him and anointed him. The most important aspect of being anointed is therefore not *the purpose* for which one comes (to be a prophet, priest, king, or something else), but *from where* one comes (sent from God).

Thus John preaches about the one who comes from God, who will baptize with the Spirit. This individual will be legitimized from above, as was foretold to the Baptist: "The man on whom you see the Spirit come down and remain is he who will baptize with the Holy Spirit" (John 1:33). And John can testify that he really saw it happen: "I saw the Spirit come down from heaven as a dove and remain on him" (John 1:32). This is Jesus' "public" anointing. It shows that he is not "from below" but "from above." Against this background it is all the more plausible that it was John the Baptist who began to use the more titular "*the Anointed One*" and that use of this title spread rapidly under his influence (see the conclusion of sec. 5.3.3).

At the beginning of his Galilean ministry, Jesus himself announces that he is the fulfillment of Isaiah 61: he has been anointed by God's Spirit! This is the message he preaches in the synagogue in Nazareth.[55] As God's Anointed, he has been *sent* (Luke 4:18) to proclaim the year of the LORD's favor.

For the Jews, calling Jesus "the *Anointed One*" means that he is the long-promised savior for the end times, *sent by God*, anointed with the Spirit, and recently announced by the prophet John the Baptist.

5.3.5 The Image of the Christ in Focus

The preaching of John the Baptist and the ministry of Jesus himself made the rather vague expectations concerning the savior of God more concrete.

54. Ibid.
55. See ibid., on Luke 4:16–30.

John the Baptist witnessed the anointing with the Spirit after Jesus' immersion in the Jordan. He spoke of this event, and through his testimony it became clearer that the expected Redeemer is one who has been anointed with the Spirit (John 1:32–34). The same is true of the voice from heaven that was heard after Jesus' baptism. It proclaimed who Jesus is: God's beloved Son! The great prophet is also a witness to this event (John 1:34; compare Matt. 3:16–17 = Mark 1:9–11).

Later, in prison, John the Baptist begins to hesitate: is Jesus really the one who is to come, or should we wait for another (in addition to Jesus, the Anointed)? The answer his disciples bring him proves that John's original expectation is correct, and that only one messiah is being sent (not two or three, as was believed in the Qumran community; see sec. 5.3.3, point 2). But there are two *phases* in Jesus' work: the current, priestly phase and the later, kingly one.[56]

Gradually it also becomes clear that this messiah is the same as "the prophet" (see sec. 5.1). On the other hand, the disciples begin to realize that the coming Elijah as forerunner must be distinguished from the Messiah, and that the prophecy concerning his appearance is fulfilled in John the Baptist (Matt. 17:13; for a more detailed discussion, see sec. 2.3.4).

Finally, the teaching about the Passion adds something completely new to the expectation of the coming savior (see chap. 6).

5.3.6 The Messiah Hides Nothing

Under Wrede's influence, twentieth-century Christology has often assumed a certain secrecy on Jesus' part regarding his messiahship during his earthly stay. Wrede himself saw this climate of secrecy as a Markan attempt to cover up the fact that Jesus never regarded *himself* as "Messiah." He believed that Jesus' disciples began to worship him as such only later, in retrospect. Other scholars toned down this critical view of Mark by claiming that Jesus *hid* his messiahship, revealing it to all after Easter. This concealment of his majesty then was related to his humiliation.[57]

These theories do not fit the reality presented in the Gospels, however. Jesus did not entrust everyone with the proclamation of his title, but he never made any attempt to conceal the fact that he was the Messiah.[58]

---

56. See van Bruggen, *Matteüs*, on Matt. 11:2–6.

57. H. N. Ridderbos, *Zelfopenbaring en zelfverberging: Het historisch karakter van Jezus' messiaanse zelfopenbaring volgens de synoptische evangeliën* (Kampen: Kok, 1946).

58. Compare P. H. R. van Houwelingen, "De strekking van het evangelie naar Marcus," in *Verkenningen in de evangeliën*, Theologische Verkenningen, Serie Bijbel en Exegese 5, ed. G. van den Brink et al. (Kampen: Kok Voorhoeve, 1990), 16–24.

The demons he exorcised know all too well that he is the Messiah. They shout at the top of their lungs that he is the Holy One, the Son of God (Mark 1:24; 5:7; Luke 4:41). Jesus allows them to do so, but then he orders them to be still (Mark 1:34; 3:11–12). He never denies that what they say is true, however; they *know* who he is (Mark 1:34; Luke 4:41)! Apparently he does not want this confession to be broadcast by his enemies in a *fearful* way. His purpose is to inspire the children of Israel to make a *trusting* acknowledgment of his messiahship. He is, therefore, not motivated by secrecy or concealment but by the desire to evoke an *appropriate* acknowledgment of the Savior of the world.

In Caesarea Philippi, when Peter and the other disciples are told to keep silent after their renewed confession that Jesus is the Christ (Matt. 16:20), it is because of the unsuitability *of that moment*. Now begins their instruction in the necessity of Jesus' suffering (Matt. 16:21), but for the time being this is something the disciples radically reject (Matt. 16:22; Mark 9:32; Luke 18:34). Only when they have learned to accept the fact that the man they have confessed as the Messiah must also suffer and die will they be fit messengers of the Christ (Luke 24:45–49; Acts 3:18–19). During their training they are told to remain silent—not in order to maintain secrecy about Jesus' messiahship, but to maintain the *purity* of the message. During the period preceding the Passion, the disciples are not suitable as preachers of the Messiah. They want to call down fire from heaven to destroy an inhospitable town (Luke 9:54). They are preoccupied with questions of rank in the kingdom of God (Luke 9:46; Mark 10:35–37).

But Jesus has continually presented himself through *the works of the Christ* (Matt. 11:2–6), and he has never been secretive about the fact that he is *the Son of God* (John 10:36). His ministry leads to the jubilation of the people at the triumphal entry and to the question of the high priest: "Tell us if you are the Christ, the Son of God" (Matt. 26:63). Throughout his ministry, he presents himself as the one anointed with the Spirit (Luke 4:18–21). He denies that he has come from Beelzebub—anyone who says that he has, misunderstands the Spirit of God who lives and works in him (Matt. 12:27–32). Jesus hides nothing.

Yet he never carries, so to speak, a sign that *proclaims* "I am the Messiah." He *asks* for that title! His opponents are well aware of it, but they refuse to make that confession. That is why they say irritably, "If you are the Christ, tell us plainly" (John 10:24). The response is crystal clear: "I did tell you, but you do not believe. The miracles I do in my Father's name speak for me" (John 10:25). It is part of Jesus' pedagogic method to invite others, through his ministry, to speak the word *Christ* as confession and to honor the Father.

5.4 The Son of God

The manifestation of God in Israel (*Immanuel*) is acknowledged when people begin to call Jesus "the Son of David" or "the Christ" and "the Son of God." These closely related designations are discussed separately here for practical reasons only. We now come to the designation "Son of God."

5.4.1 Christ, the Son of the Living God

In the New Testament, the title *Messiah* implies the designation "Son of God" ("Holy One of God"). The demons know that Jesus is the Christ, and they call him "the Son of God" (Luke 4:41). Peter confesses with the other disciples that Jesus is "the Christ, the Son of the living God" (Matt. 16:16). And the high priest asks whether Jesus is "the Christ, the Son of God" (Matt. 26:63).

In pre–New Testament Judaism we do not encounter the link between these two terms. Here we are faced with a development in terminology that is quite new, one that certainly cannot be explained on the basis of Hellenistic parallels.[59]

This development did not take place without any preparation, however. In the Old Testament we find the promise of Psalm 2 concerning the *son of God* who is *anointed* to be king of Zion (Ps. 2:2, 6–7).[60] And in Psalm 45 we read about a king *anointed* by God who is also addressed as *God* (Ps. 45:2–8). The Immanuel (son of a woman; Isa. 7:14) is called *Mighty God* (Isa. 9:6) on whom the *Spirit* of God rests (Isa. 11:2). But as far as we can determine, none of this led to the development among the Jews of a fixed terminology about "the Anointed One, the Son of God," or to an established expectation concerning a coming "Son of God."[61]

---

59. M. Hengel, *The Cross of the Son of God*, trans. J. Bowden (London: SCM, 1986); J. R. Brady, *Jesus Christ: Divine Man or Son of God?* (Lanham, Md.: University Press of America, 1992).

60. See van Bruggen, *Marcus*, on Mark 1:11.

61. In a Qumran fragment (4Q246; see E. Puech, "Fragment d'une apocalypse en araméen [4Q246 = pseudo-Dan[d]] et le 'royaume de Dieu,'" *Revue biblique* 99 [1992]: 98–131), we come across the term *Son of God* relating to an eschatological person. According to Mattila, the eschatology of 4Q246 deviates radically from that of 1QM and other writings that are representative for Qumran. J. J. Collins ("The *Son of God* Text from Qumran," in *From Jesus to John: Essays on Jesus and New Testament Christology in Honour of Marinus de Jonge*, ed. M. C. De Boer, JSNTSup 84 [Sheffield: JSOT Press, 1993], 65–82) believes the fragment demonstrates the pre-Christian roots of the fusion of messianic expectation with the term *son of God* (compare Collins, *Scepter and the Star*). But whether this fragment is pre-Christian is not certain, and the remaining context is too limited to permit conclusive statements concerning the value of the phrase (E. Puech, "Notes sur le fragment d' apocalypse 4Q246—'le fils de dieu,'" *Revue biblique* 101 [1994]: 533–58).

The preaching of the Baptist reactivated the prophetic promises of a *divine* redeemer and evoked the lively expectation of such a savior. John announced the coming of "the more powerful one"—a designation for someone who is more than a man (Mark 1:7). He would come after John, but he was before him (John 1:15, 27). The great prophet is not worthy even to carry the sandals of this one who is coming after him (Matt. 3:11). He will bring the Spirit to Israel (Mark 1:8), and he is the judge of the whole world (Luke 3:17). The preaching of John the Baptist refers to the approaching appearance of God himself: "Prepare the way for the Lord" (Mark 1:3). The extraordinary thing is that in announcing the coming of God, John at the same time mentions human attributes such as sandals; the LORD God will come in human form (see the more detailed discussion in sec. 2.2.2).

At the baptism of Jesus, John heard the heavenly voice say, "This is my Son, whom I love; with him I am well pleased" (Matt. 3:17; John 1:34). Jesus, who comes from Galilee, was born on earth. He wears sandals on his feet. He is of human birth, yet he is more than a human being: he is the Son of God. This does not refer to the *kind* of person he is—he is not *huios theōn*, a son of the gods. Rather, it refers to his *origin*—he is *huios theou*: he has God as his Father, so he also has a divine nature.

When Luke tells us how Jesus was addressed as the Son of God by the voice from heaven at his baptism ("my Son, whom I love; with you I am well pleased"; Luke 3:22), he then immediately mentions that the people on earth took this Jesus (contrary to the heavenly pronouncement) for "the son of Joseph." Here it is clear that for Luke the title "Son of God" indicates that the father of the man Jesus is not a man (Joseph) but God, as was also described in the birth narrative (Luke 1:31–35, 43, 48, 69, 76; 2:11).

The way in which Jesus is called "Son of God" is unique. God's people are sometimes called "his son" in the Old Testament, and the righteous are called "children of God," but in Jesus' case it apparently involves something special. The circumstances in which the name is given are

---

According to some, it is a presumptuous term of self-reference used by a Syrian king who is elevating himself above the LORD (J. T. Milik, "Les modèles araméens du livre d' Esther dans la Grotte 4 de Qumran," *Revue de Qumran* 15 [1992]: 383ff). According to others it is a messianic title, referring to an angel (García Martínez, "Messianische Erwartungen in den Qumranschriften") or to the Messiah (Collins, "*Son of God* Text from Qumran"). Still others see a positive designation here but not a messianic one: a name for a Davidic king not viewed as the Messiah (J. A. Fitzmyer, "4Q246: The 'Son of God' Document from Qumran," *Biblica* 74 (1993): 153–74) or possibly a collective designation for the entire people (Hengel, *Cross of the Son of God*, 71–72).

exceptional (an announcement by Gabriel; a voice from heaven). Furthermore, the response to this name by both disciple and opponent clearly indicates that in this name they do not see a new application of a familiar metaphor for God's people or for believers. They were "sons" or "children" by adoption. The awe, the surprise, and the irritation and indictments show that everyone in Jesus' day regarded the title "Son of God," as applied to Jesus, as a designation for a man who has God as his father and who is equal to God.

The preaching of John the Baptist concerning the one who is to come, as well as the works of Christ himself, clearly shows who Jesus of Nazareth is (John 5:33–36): the Son of God, the Son of the Father (John 5:20–23).

Because Jesus approaches Israel through the gateway of John's preaching and baptism, there was from the beginning a connection between the messianic presentation and being the "Son of God."

The people must come to faith on the basis of Jesus' works, on the basis of the testimony of God, and on the basis of the preaching of the Baptist. That is why during his humiliation Jesus never talks about being born of the *virgin* Mary. The miraculous birth was certainly not entirely unknown, because the shepherds had spread the word throughout Judea, and the prophetess Anna had talked about it in Jerusalem. Even so, Bethlehem plays no role in the presentation of Jesus (John 7:41–42); Galilee is in the foreground. It is as though he wants to be accepted on the basis of his works; they must see that he comes *from God* by seeing his works!

Later the stories of his birth were handed down within the circle of believers. They showed how it was possible that a human being could be called *Son of God:* the Spirit of God overshadowed Mary, so that the virgin became pregnant and bore a son (Luke 1:31–35; Matt. 1:20).[62] Thus he may truly be called Immanuel (Matt. 1:22–23). This name is not a status symbol for Jesus, however—it is a mission. For this reason Bethlehem remains in the background during his ministry and his saving work is in the foreground. He *is* Immanuel.

5.4.2 God Himself on Earth

If Jesus is the Son of God, he should be addressed as *God* as well. The Spirit dwelling in God dwells also in him. Often the designation "*Son* of God" is abbreviated to "*the* Son" (Matt. 11:27; 24:36; John 3:35–36; 5:23; 8:35–36). On a few occasions we also find the direct designation "God." Thus John the Evangelist speaks of Jesus as the Word that was with

---

62. See J. van Bruggen, *Christ on Earth: The Gospel Narratives as History* (Grand Rapids: Baker, 1998), sec. 3.2.

God and that *is* God (John 1:1, 18), and Thomas cries out, "My Lord and my God!" (John 20:28).[63]

The principal objection that the Jewish leaders have against Jesus is that he "makes himself equal with God" or "claims to be God" (John 5:18; 10:33). We should not infer from this that it would have been impossible for the Jews to imagine a human manifestation of the Lord.[64] Man is made in God's image, and in the Old Testament the Lord comes in human form to visit Abraham (Gen. 18:1–2). The leaders, however, refuse to see more than a human being *in Jesus*. They are absolutely convinced that he is nothing but a man; anything beyond that is presumption on his part. It is striking that the leaders never argue on the basis of rational impossibility. Jesus is never asked how God could come to the people in human form. The leaders' problem is that they cannot accept that *this Jesus* could be God. Such acknowledgment is too much for them. At the very least it would put an end to their days of boasting and seeking honor from people. The leaders have thrown up a blockade from behind which they operate and that cuts off the way to Jesus, and they have therefore no choice but to accuse Jesus of being *guilty of blasphemy* or being influenced by Beelzebub.

This reaction makes them guilty to the extent that they close themselves off against the testimony of the Baptist and the testimony of Jesus' own works. It is on the other hand an understandable reaction: the appearance of God on earth in the person of a man of human birth, Jesus of Bethlehem, is a mystery that was unknown until the day it actually happened. This unthought-of mystery is *now* revealed; what has been hidden from the wise and learned is now being revealed to children (Matt. 11:25).

In the Old Testament there is no revelation of an "only begotten Son of God." It is a phrase that is not appropriate until after the birth of Jesus, a person whose Father is not a man but God. The Spirit of the Lord came upon his mother, and thus Jesus is the Anointed One, the Son of God. He became recognizably human: the Nazarene! Nevertheless, as God, this only begotten from Bethlehem existed before Abraham (John 8:58). And the man Jesus, born here below, can say that, as a person, he "came from heaven" (John 3:13)—he comes "from above"

---

63. For other passages in the New Testament where Jesus is called *God*, see M. J. Harris, *Jesus as God: The New Testament Use of Theos in Reference to Jesus* (Grand Rapids: Baker, 1992). Harris does not mention John 6:27. There Jesus himself speaks of his divinity—if we translate the verse as "On him (the Son of Man) the father has set his seal: *God*." God's own seal on the Son makes him God as well. On John 6:27, see P. H. R. van Houwelingen, *Johannes: Het evangelie van het Woord*, Commentaar op het Nieuwe Testament, 3d series (Kampen: Kok, 1997).
64. Hengel, *Cross of the Son of God*.

(John 3:31). Christ's eternal divinity is an *implication* of the sonship of Mary's child Jesus. The *term* "Son of God," however, does not *explicitly* refer to the reality before the incarnation but to the factuality of the incarnation. This is why John the Evangelist does not say "the Son" became flesh but "the Word" became flesh and that "the Word" was with God and is God (John 1:1–3). It is precisely because the only begotten of Bethlehem is the incarnate *Word of God*, and because the *Spirit of God* dwells in him, that his earthly ministry has the radiance suiting an only begotten *of the Father* (John 1:14). And later, John writes that the only begotten Son (some manuscripts have "only begotten God") has made the Father known to us; as the only begotten Son, he rests in the bosom of the Father (John 1:18 KJV). John is not talking about the past here; he is not writing that Jesus *was* (*ēn*) in the bosom of the Father, but that he *is* there (*ōn*). Jesus was God's intimate confidant on earth (see Matt. 11:25–26; Luke 6:12; John 11:41–42), and after his resurrection he goes to the Father (John 14:28; 16:7, 27–28; 20:17). John does not apply the word "son" to the Word that is from eternity, but he indicates what the relationship of the Son (the incarnate Word) is to the Father. When we read in John 3:16–17 that God sent his only begotten Son into the world so that the world would be saved through him, it is a statement about the task the only *begotten* Son must fulfill on earth. Just as Abraham had to be prepared to sacrifice his only son on Mount Moriah (Heb. 11:17), so the Father allowed Jesus to be born to send this Son from Bethlehem to Golgotha (compare 1 John 4:9–11). This "sending" of the Son is here related to his mission, for which he receives life on earth from God. In the same way it can be said that John the Baptist appeared as "a man sent from God" (John 1:6). The "only begotten Son of God" describes the man called Jesus Christ. By believing in the *name* of this only begotten Son of God everyone must be saved (John 3:18). What is meant here is the name *Jesus Christ*—which is not the name of the Word "in the beginning" but the name of the one born in Bethlehem. In the New Testament, the expression "*Son* of God" cannot be abstracted from Jesus of Bethlehem conceived by the Holy Spirit and born of the Virgin Mary. Jesus is the only *begotten* Son of God!

It is important to note that the *name* "Son of God" came into the world after the incarnation. Only then can we understand how for Jesus' contemporaries the terms "Christ" and "Son of God" virtually coincide. He who was visibly and audibly anointed with the Spirit (from the moment of conception) is, as a man (as a son), apparently born *of God*, for God granted him the fullness of his Spirit and gave everything into his hands (John 3:34–35). God the Father grants the disciples this confession of Jesus: he is the Christ, the Son of the living God, no less than God himself (Matt. 16:16–17). The eternal Word became through the Virgin Mary

"*Son* of God" among humanity (Luke 1:35). That is why the mother of the Lord will be blessed among women for ever (Luke 1:42–43).

5.4.3 The Son of God in the New Testament

As a supplement to the previous section we offer a short survey of the most important passages in the New Testament where we encounter the expression "Son of God."

In Hebrews 4:14 we read about "Jesus, the Son of God." He is the great high priest who "has gone through the heavens." In this verse, "Son of God" is an extension of the name Jesus, just as Bar Jonah is an extension of Simon. This is understandable, since the angel Gabriel also announced to Mary that her son would be called *Jesus* (Luke 1:31) and that he would be great and would be called "*Son of the Most High*" (Luke 1:32). This designation is possible because the power of the Most High will overshadow Mary; therefore that which is to be born will be called "the Son of God" (Luke 1:35).

When Jesus is baptized in the Jordan, the Most High acknowledges him as his beloved Son through a voice from heaven (Luke 3:22). John the Baptist vouches for the fact that Jesus really is the Son of God (John 1:34). At that time, people were not yet accustomed to the creedal formulations of the later church, in which "Son of God" often suggested primarily the eternal second person in the Godhead and only secondarily the incarnation. The pronouncements at the Jordan had to do with the man Jesus and his origins; truly, his Father is God!

In the confession of Peter and the other disciples—that Jesus is the "Anointed One, the Son of the living God"—Peter does not apply an aspect of the doctrine of the Trinity to Jesus. By using the name "the Anointed One" he recognizes that God's Spirit is in Jesus, not a human spirit. And he recognizes that this Jesus does not have a human father, but that God himself is his Father. That is why Jesus is such an extraordinary person to whom people can entrust themselves completely (John 6:68–69).

Jesus himself more than once shows the intimate relationship that he has with his heavenly Father. As Son, he is in daily contact with the Father. He echoes the Father's words ("Yes, Father," Matt. 11:26), and while he is speaking with the people he continues to maintain direct contact with his Father (John 12:28). The Son, to whom everything has been given by the Father, is the man Jesus Christ, who speaks to all those who are weary and burdened (Matt. 11:27–28).

The people around him, hearing his allusions to the Father and to himself as the Son, understand them as references to his lineage. When Jesus talks about his Father, the Jews say, "Abraham is our father"

(John 8:38–39). And yes, through Abraham they have *one* Father, and that is God—but he is the Father whom they are to honor as his *adopted* people (John 8:41). Those who are part of the people of Israel were not born of fornication (idolatry); God himself took the people of father Abraham and made them his own people by covenant. The Jews understand full well, however, that Jesus means more than that God is his Father in the covenantal sense. Jesus calls God his Father in the same way the Jews call Abraham their father, which is why they mockingly say that he is not yet fifty years old, that he certainly has not seen Abraham, and that therefore he should not presume to be greater than Abraham. But Jesus says, "Before Abraham was, I am." As the Son of God on earth, he himself is also God by nature, and therefore he is older than Abraham—just as we read in John 1 that the Word became flesh and yet existed from eternity. That is why, as far as Jesus' person is concerned, there is no separation between the Word and the earthly born Son of God, born of Mary—he who always was and is becomes son through Mary and can therefore now be called Son of God by virtue of his incarnation, in which he remained God.

Understandably, when the title "Son of God" was used, the main accent soon came to rest on what that title implied: to call him Son of God is to suggest that he himself is God. And thus this name is also used retroactively to refer to him as one who always was with God and is himself God (compare Heb. 1:2–3a)! We see the same thing happen with the name "Christ." Yet the name "Son of God" could only come to be used after the Spirit of God took up residence in the human being who was conceived in Mary's womb, so that Jesus can call himself the Anointed One, the Son of God, sent, recognized, and glorified by him (compare Heb. 1:3b–13).

We must put ourselves back into the first century to be able to hear the name "Son of God" again as it sounded and was intended when it came into use in the New Testament. Thus 1 John 4:9 is often read from the perspective of Christ's preexistence: "This is how God showed his love among us: He sent his one and only Son into the world that we might live through him." But we can also hear this passage as dealing with the incarnation as an act of God and with God's purpose behind it. He had Jesus conceived by the Holy Spirit, and he sent this Son, born in Bethlehem, into the world of Israel to be crucified so that we might live through him. This sending of the Son must not be reduced to his birth alone. It includes Jesus' entire mission, including the birth and the judgment on Golgotha. God sent his Son (born of Mary) as an atoning sacrifice for our sins (1 John 4:10).

In his first letter, John spoke about that which existed from eternity and was revealed to us, yet he speaks of "his Son Jesus Christ." The identification as "Son" is tied to the historical names Jesus and Christ (1 John 1:3). See also 1 John 3:23: "believe in the name of his Son, Jesus Christ." The believer does not confess that the Son of God *became* "Jesus," but that *Jesus* is the "Son of God" (1 John 4:15; 5:5). In 1 John 5:20, the statement "we are in him who is true—even in his Son Jesus Christ" is followed by "he is the true God and eternal life." Because the man Jesus is the Son of God and the child of Mary, he is the true God ("Son *of God*") and eternal life ("*Son* of God" as a result of the incarnation).

In 1 John 2:22, the confession that "Jesus is the Christ" is parallel with acknowledging the Son of God. To refuse to recognize that the Spirit of God lives in Jesus is to deny the Son. See also 2 John 9: anyone who "continues in the teaching [of Christ] has both the Father and the Son."

In Romans 1:3–4 we read that "his Son" (1:3a), "as to his human nature," was a descendant of David. It does not say that human characteristics were added to the son, but that he became the *Son* from the house of David. The qualifier "as to his human nature" is necessary because according to the Spirit his origin is elsewhere.

The phrase "the gospel of his Son" (Rom. 1:9) indicates that Son and gospel are linked. The content of the Good News is that Jesus is God's Son!

Romans 8:3 ("For what the law was powerless to do in that it was weakened by the sinful nature, God did by sending his own Son in the likeness of sinful man to be a sin offering") is sometimes read as if the reference here is to the sending of a preexistent *Son* to the world of sinful men. But Paul is not writing of "sinful man" as the place where the Son was sent. He is only characterizing the *way* in which the Son was manifested to us, not in a glorified body but with a body *like* that of fallen sinners, vulnerable and mortal (*en homoiōmati sarkos hamartias*). The sending of the Son here relates to the fulfillment of Jesus' entire earthly mission—the rest of the verse deals with the cross. When God does not spare his own Son, it does not point to the fact that he sent a Son to earth who was present in heaven, but that he gave the earthly born Son to die (Rom. 8:32). Thus in Galatians 4:4, "God sent his Son" is qualified with the phrase "born of a woman, born under law," referring to the man Jesus who has come to redeem us, for which he was sent to earth (Gal. 4:5).

Are there any statements about the Son of God in the Gospel of John in which the incarnation is not implied? In John 5:18 the Jews fully realize that Jesus is calling God "his *own* [or *real*] Father" and thereby makes himself equal with God. Jesus confirms this. He is completely at home with the Father in heaven; he watches what the Father does and he imitates him (John 5:19–20). Here the verbs are in the present tense. This is therefore not a memory of preexistent times, but a reference to the current relationship between the Son and the Father. John 6:46 speaks of "having seen" the Father, followed by the designation "the one who is from God." There is thus certainly an eternal communion of knowledge and love between the Father in heaven and the man called Jesus since his birth in Bethlehem. That is why the church in its creeds rightly speaks of the *eternal* Son of God. In this, the confessing church refers back to the revealed mystery of the only begotten Son in the flesh. But in reading the New Testament, we must be careful not to allow the implications of the revelation that appear in later confessions to be applied to identical phrases in the New Testament. In John 5:26, we read that the Father has granted the Son to have life in himself. This granting of "life in himself" must not be isolated from the incarnation. In verse 27, this granting of life, together with the authority to judge, is connected to the fact that Jesus is the "Son of Man" (*huios anthrōpou*). He may be a child of Mary, who was a daughter of human beings, but because God's Spirit lives in him, Jesus has been granted life in himself. He is a human, but he is a uniquely different human: God of God, who has become Son. In John 10:36 Jesus, stating that he is the Son of God, refers to the fact that the Father has sanctified him and sent him into the world. He has come into the world and worked there as someone who has "proceeded from the Father." When he leaves this world he will return to his Father, who is his source (John 16:27–28; for the movement of the *Son* to the Father, Jesus does not use the verb *hypostrephein*, "return," but the verb *poreuesthai* or *hypagein*, "depart." So when he speaks here, it is also from the perspective of the incarnation.)

In John 17:1–5, the Son prays to be glorified with the glory that he possessed with God before the world began. He who speaks was with God and is God, but the son of Mary (with God as his Father) has not yet been glorified. Now God will cloak this incarnate Son in the glory that he already possessed with the Father before his incarnation. In Revelation 2:18, the Son of God is also the glorified Jesus, with eyes like blazing fire and feet like burnished bronze.

John 3:34–35 is also quite clear. He who was sent into the world by God speaks the words of God, for God gives the Spirit to him without limit; the Father loves his Son and has placed everything in his hands. Here Jesus is speaking about himself as a human being existing in time; he speaks the words of God as a result of the gift of the Spirit (received from the Spirit) and of the trusting surrender of all things into the hands of the incarnate Word. The Son *remains* forever in God's house (John 8:35). Because Jesus is not a servant but has been born into the house as a Son, he will remain there forever.

The conclusion that can be drawn is that "Son of God" is used in the New Testament to refer to Jesus as the eternal Word *who became man.*

6

Rejection and Suffering:
The Path of Sacrifice

Jesus came to the people with the works of God. He preached the Good News and healed all those who were sick. But he used the power of God's Spirit only for others, never for himself (chap. 3). It is also clear from his use of specific terms that although he was entitled to divine honor, he quietly submitted to being treated as nothing more than a man (chap. 4). He expected others to recognize him as "the Christ, the Son of the living God," but he did not flaunt his titles (chap. 5).

As we read the Gospels, we keep encountering this extraordinary tension: Jesus can do anything on earth, and he is everything for everyone else, but he never uses his abilities for his own gain. At the center of the breathtaking display of power stands an unpretentious man who refuses to exploit his popularity, and who because of this refusal sees the tide turn against him in the end.

Such a reversal was unavoidable because his person and his ministry did not go unchallenged. Conflict between him and the Jewish leaders grew increasingly acute. The combination of his enemies' growing aggression and Jesus' own gentleness finally resulted in his crucifixion. It became inevitable. But why did Jesus, through his attitude, allow it to reach that point?

This question is the focus of this sixth chapter: first, the fact of rejection and conflict (sec. 6.1); second, Jesus' own attitude of acceptance (sec. 6.2); and finally, an examination of the meaning Jesus attached to the course of his life (sec. 6.3).

6.1 A Path of Conflict

The path of rejection and suffering was willed by Jesus—but he did not instigate it. He does not come with a plan of self-destruction but with a rescue operation for Israel. But in carrying out this plan, a path of rejection and hostility opens up before him. Jesus does not evade this path of conflict—this is the path he *must* take.

6.1.1 The Nazarene

The *name* that is most commonly used in Israel to refer to Jesus already hints at his rejection by others and at his own gentleness. It was normal to name people after their father (Simon, son of Jonah, for instance; and John and James, the sons of Zebedee). In Jesus' case, however, people deviate from this rule. He is addressed with the name of the place where he grew up: Nazareth, a virtually unknown village in northern Galilee. The epithet "Nazarene" has a condescending ring: "the villager from Galilee."

This condescension is emphasized when "Nazarene" is pronounced with a pseudo-Galilean accent by people in Judea. In Galilean Aramaic, the vowel *a* is often muted into a *u* or an *o*.[1] The Judeans imitated this in their pronunciation of "Nazarene" (*Nazarēnos*), turning it into Nazorene (*Nazōraios*). The name "Nazarene" characterized Jesus as a man from the border region, and the mocking tone of the pronunciation betrays a measure of contempt.[2]

The use of the name "Nazarene" seems to reveal a certain displeasure with the fact that Jesus used neither the temple city of Jerusalem as his base of operations nor the city of Bethlehem, where David had come from. This becomes evident in various ways during the Feast of Tabernacles in John 7. Jesus' brothers (7:3–4) are surprised that on the one hand Jesus wants to attract the attention of the people, while on the other hand he stays on the periphery (Galilee). The crowds (7:42) wonder why he does not choose Bethlehem as his base of operations. And the leaders (7:52) tell Nicodemus that a prophet does not come from Galilee!

Irritation over this unpretentious and modest behavior is apparent in the name that the people give him: Jesus *of Nazareth*. The name *Nazorene* is well chosen; after all, the striking thing about this great teacher

---

1. H. Odeberg, *The Aramaic Portions of Bereshit Rabba with Grammar of Galilaean Aramaic*, vol. 2, *Short Grammar of Galilaean Aramaic* (Leipzig: Gleerup, 1939), 154.

2. The name *Nazōraios* is an implicit reference, via the place name and the pseudo-Galilean pronunciation, to the district of *Galilee*. Jesus is "the Galilean" (Matt. 26:69), and his disciples are also regarded as "Galileans" (Mark 14:70; Acts 2:7). Peter belongs with the *Nazarene* because his accent reveals that he *also* comes from *Galilee* (Mark 14:67, 70). And Jesus can be called a *Nazarene* (compare John 18:5–8) because his parents settled in *Galilee* (Matt. 2:22–23).

Later the Jews in Judea refer to the Christians as "the Nazarene sect" (Greek: "the sect of the *Nazōraioi*; Acts 24:5). This indicates that *Nazōraios* had become the common term (compare Matt. 2:23). The somewhat caustic exaggeration of the dialect pronunciation is omitted in a few cases; in Galilee itself the surname *of Nazareth* was used (Mark 1:24; Luke 4:34). In Mark 14:67, a Jerusalem slave girl uses the more neutral *Nazarene*, but here it is not a surname (which always *follows* the proper name) but strictly a reference to the place Nazareth, which *precedes* the proper name ("the Nazarene Jesus" instead of "Jesus the Nazarene").

and miracle worker is his reticence. He astonishes the world, but he wanders around the backwaters of Galilee. Isn't that proof of weakness? The fact that Jesus *allowed* people to call him this is a sign of his defenselessness. He can be addressed, without fear of contradiction or punishment, with a slightly mocking name that puts him in his place.[3]

6.1.2 The Conflict

Because Jesus, the Son of God, presented himself as a humble and vulnerable son of man, his life was threatened from several sides.

Rulers in Israel threatened his life. Shortly after his birth, Herod the Great ordered that all the children in Bethlehem, the place of his birth, be murdered, and Jesus escaped only because his parents fled with him to Egypt (Matt. 2:13–18). On their return, Herod's son Archelaus proved to be a threat in Judea, so the family had to flee to Galilee (Matt. 2:19–23). Later, another of Herod's sons, Herod Antipas, was afraid of Jesus (whom he regarded as a reincarnated John the Baptist) and at the same time eager to kill him (Luke 13:31–32; 23:8–12). Understandably, the Herodians were welcome accomplices in the attempts to corner Jesus and to kill him (Mark 3:6; 12:13).

Non-Jews occasionally also showed signs of aggression toward Jesus. The Samaritans refused to extend him hospitality when he chose to go to Jerusalem rather than Shechem (Luke 9:52–53). The population of the Decapolis region asked him to leave their country (Luke 8:37).

Yet Jesus is not the victim of kings or foreigners. It is the attitude of the leaders in Jerusalem that turns out to be decisive for the end of his earthly life (Luke 13:34–35; Matt. 23:37–39). They are the ones who finally arrest him and officially convict him of blasphemy before the Sanhedrin. And they are the ones who deliver him to the Roman governor to be crucified.[4]

The execution at the end is the conclusion of a long conflict. An overview of the several stages in this conflict will help clarify the *core* of the hostility that culminated in Golgotha.

3. The theory that the epithet originally had nothing to do with the place name Nazareth has generally been abandoned (J. A. Sanders, "*Nazōraios* in Matthew 2.23," in *The Gospels and the Scriptures of Israel*, JSNTSup 104, ed. C. A. Evans and W. R. Stegner [Sheffield: Sheffield Academic Press, 1994], 116–28). For a critical discussion of various theories about the positive, additional value the name supposedly had or had acquired (*nazarene*: dedicated to God; *nēṣer*: the shoot of Isaiah 11) and for an overview of the theories that do not derive the epithet from the place name Nazareth but from a pre-Christian baptismal sect (the Observants), see J. van Bruggen, "Nazoreeërs: De oudste naam voor christenen," in *Almanak Fides Quadrat Intellectum 1973* (Kampen: Kok, 1973), 147–67.

4. For a detailed description of the trial, see J. van Bruggen, *Christ on Earth: The Gospel Narratives as History* (Grand Rapids: Baker, 1998), chaps. 14–16.

1. *Sabbath conflicts.* At an early stage Jesus faces conflicts over his ministry on the Sabbath. He allows himself liberties on that day that are in conflict with the law. He not only heals in acute crisis situations but cures non-emergency cases on the Sabbath as well. A vivid example is the man who had been ill for thirty-eight years and who could easily have waited one more day (John 5:5–10). Jesus does not deny taking liberties (Matt. 12:2–6), but he claims that those liberties are his to take as Lord of the Sabbath (Mark 2:28) and as the master of Israel (Luke 13:14–16). His Father works without interruption, and so does he (John 5:17).

It is this claim that the Jews find so offensive. They attempt to kill him not only because he has repudiated the Sabbath but also because he has called God his own Father, making himself God's equal (John 5:18; compare 7:19–25)!

Nevertheless, Jesus makes this great claim without attaching any sanctions against the leaders, who now harass him with their criticism and even try to lure him into a trap on the Sabbath (Mark 3:2; Luke 14:1–6). Through his actions he stands before them as Israel's Lord and Master—but he allows himself to be treated like a deer that can be hunted.

2. *The Beelzebub interpretation.* The religious center, Jerusalem, is alarmed by the healing that has taken place on the Sabbath at the pool of Bethesda (John 5), so a group of teachers of the law travel from the city to look for Jesus in Galilee, the region where he ministers (Mark 3:22). Since his power and authority are undeniable, they try to destroy the admiration of the crowds by declaring that he must derive his power over demons from a pact with the devil (Matt. 9:34; 12:24; John 8:48, 52). Part of the crowd eventually accepts this theory (Luke 11:15); they wonder in all sincerity how a righteous healer could violate the Sabbath. The conclusion is that something must be wrong with the source of Jesus' miracles.

Although this is an open rejection of the Spirit of God dwelling in Jesus and of the Father who sent him, Jesus does nothing to interfere with those who are spreading such slander. His powerful ministry has led to aggressive opposition, but his tolerance of this aggression makes him look weak.

3. *The questions to trap Jesus.* The insinuation about Beelzebub was not sufficient to break Jesus' influence on the people, so the leaders are forced to engage in a more direct confrontation with him in front of the crowds. We now see how the leaders with some regularity try to convince the crowds, by means of various questions designed to entrap Jesus and by criticizing the behavior of Jesus' disciples, that they are confronted with a false prophet who ought to be indicted and killed (Luke 11:53–54). Jesus never puts an end to this activity, which must have made him feel besieged and misunderstood.

The Gospels contain several detailed examples of this approach.

a. A group of teachers of the law and Pharisees travel from Jerusa-lem to Galilee to find out why the disciples eat without washing their hands (Matt. 15:1–2; Mark 7:1–5). On this occasion Jesus tells the crowds that the dietary laws are not of essential impor-tance (Matt. 15:10–11; Mark 7:14–16). He acts like someone who stands *above Moses*. Nevertheless, he does not shield himself from those who are trying to undermine his authority. Whereas Korah, Dathan, and Abiram disappeared into the earth when they challenged Moses' authority, the teachers of the law and the Phar-isees can calmly return to Jerusalem!

b. On more than one occasion Jesus is asked for a direct sign from heaven. First the Pharisees and the Sadducees insist on a sign (Mark 8:11; Matt. 16:1), but later the question is taken up by the crowds (Luke 11:16). It is a question based on a misunderstand-ing of the heavenly origin of Jesus' deeds. They assume that he is working through Beelzebub (Luke 11:15), and they want to dem-onstrate this (Luke 11:16) by showing that no legitimizing sign from *heaven* will occur. Jesus interacts with this challenge in his teaching, but he does not ask the Father for a special voice from heaven at that time. He thereby accepts the fact that his oppo-nents will continue to repudiate and challenge him.

c. In Capernaum, the collectors of the temple tax try to accuse Jesus and his disciples of being contemptuous of the temple. Appar-ently, as Son of the Father, he had not paid his temple tax.[5] Jesus is not approached directly; rather, Peter is confronted about his Master's behavior. Jesus does not argue the point but, though not obligated to do so, pays the temple tax to avoid being a stumbling block to those who raised the issue. The repudiated Son takes the place of the servant!

d. During the confrontation in Jerusalem in the last days before Jesus' death, the questions asked by the teachers of the law, the Pharisees, and the Sadducees come at a much faster pace (Matt. 22:15–46). Jesus knows that these are not honest questions that are part of the teaching process. These questions are being asked to trap him. Even so, he does not evade the questions, nor does he be-come angry with those who try to catch them with their questions.

Everything the leaders do to make a case for charging Jesus with a capital offense (Luke 11:54) shows that they prefer to have him put to

---

5. See J. van Bruggen, *Matteüs: Het evangelie voor Israël,* 2d ed., Commentaar op het Nieuwe Testament, 3d series (Kampen: Kok, 1994), on Matt. 17:24–27.

death by means of a formal trial and not through a devious assassination (Mark 3:6; John 5:18; 7:1). A shadow of fear spreads over the people whenever they gather in Jerusalem; they do not dare speak of Jesus openly (John 7:13). At a certain point the leaders of the Pharisees even announce that anyone who confesses him as the Anointed One will be thrown out of the synagogue (John 9:22; 12:42). This inhibits not only the common people but also some of the leaders from openly recognizing him as the one sent by God (John 12:42). Jerusalem becomes a perilous place for the disciples (John 11:8, 16).

The conflict that leads to the crucifixion is not a misunderstanding that gets out of hand. It is a carefully deliberated controversy that evolves over a long period—not the result of a lack of understanding between Jesus and the crowds, but the result of the leaders' rejection. They have understood his claim completely, but at this point they refuse to accept it.

Why are the leaders of the Pharisees in particular so hostile to Jesus, even though they must acknowledge his miraculous power? Jesus' own explanation is that their pride and self-importance block their view (John 5:41–44; Luke 18:9–14; Matt. 23:5–12). God sent a humble son from Nazareth in Galilee. To bow down before him seems dishonorable. Why should the children of Abraham humble themselves before a "Nazarene"? The only ones prepared to make such a move are those who are aware of their own shortcomings and guilt. The tax collectors and sinners are sufficiently aware of their guilt and sufficiently without pretense to receive Jesus, but for the Pharisees he is too small and insignificant to be true.

The conflict, in fact, did not begin with Jesus but with John the Baptist. He taught the people that they must repent because the LORD would soon be coming. The Pharisees and Sadducees gathered at the Jordan, but they would not submit to the baptism of repentance. They trusted in their descent from Abraham (Matt. 3:7–12). But by refusing to respond to John's invitation, they rendered themselves unworthy to receive Jesus. Thus we read Luke 7:29–30, "All the people, even the tax collectors, when they heard Jesus' words, acknowledged that God's way was right, because they had been baptized by John. But the Pharisees and experts in the law rejected God's purpose for themselves, because they had not been baptized by John." And much later Jesus says in Jerusalem, "I tell you the truth, the tax collectors and the prostitutes are entering the kingdom of God ahead of you. For John came to you to show you the way of righteousness, and you did not believe him, but the tax collectors and the prostitutes did. And even after you saw this, you did not repent and believe him" (Matt. 21:31–32). At the root of the conflict over Jesus' authority is the question, "John's baptism—where did it come from? Was it from heaven, or from men?" (Matt. 21:25).

6.2 A Path Accepted

Jesus did not refuse to walk the path of rejection and enmity. He put up with the epithet "Nazarene." And he did not make himself immune from hostile treatment—which is remarkable, since he clearly had the power to do so.

We must even say that Jesus took this path of rejection, which forced itself upon him, and turned it into the path of his own choosing. He was not an unresisting victim: on more than one occasion he escaped attempts to stone him. His timing is his own! Even so, at his own pace he travels the path that must lead to his arrest and execution. And he makes it clear to his disciples that this path is God's program for his life.

6.2.1 The Acceptance of Enmity

The actual acceptance of this enmity can be seen in the peculiar way in which Jesus travels through Palestine. His journeys can be viewed as evasive movements that lead in the direction of the leaders who are waiting to kill him.

On the one hand he often evades his enemies. When the Pharisees begin to keep a closer eye on him because of the many people who begin to follow him, he retreats to Galilee (John 4:1–2, 43–44). Later, on several occasions in Galilee, he escapes the growing hostility (Luke 4:28–30; Matt. 12:14–16), and once he even goes across the northern border to the neighboring country for a time (Matt. 15:21–28; Mark 7:24–37); the result is that his opponents often have to travel to remote regions to search for him.[6] When the plans to kill him assume an increasingly more definite shape, he goes to the Feast of Tabernacles, not with the crowds but more or less incognito (John 7:10–14). And during the final months he retreats once more from Judea to the mountains of Transjordan and later to mountains of Judea (John 10:40–42; 11:54).

On the other hand, despite all sorts of evasions he always comes back into the public eye and always moves again toward his enemies. He postpones the escalation of the confrontation, but he does not make himself inaccessible. On the contrary, in the end he enters Jerusalem amidst cheering crowds, can be found daily in the temple (which for him is as dangerous as a robbers' den), and finally surrenders himself to the servants of the Sanhedrin.

Typical of Jesus' behavior is the way he once reacted to the threat that Herod Antipas wanted to kill him. He was in Perea, the tetrarch's territory. Jesus left a few days later, but not to escape death. His goal was Jerusalem—because *that* was the proper place for a prophet to be killed (Luke 13:31–35).

---

6. See van Bruggen, *Christ on Earth*, sec. 10.2.

This combination of withdrawal and head-on encounters with the enemy indicates that Jesus does not avoid the consequences of hostility but insists on following the path to arrest and death according to his own time frame. He also hints more than once at having his own schedule, and speaks of "his hour" or "his time" which is yet to come (John 7:30; 8:20; 12:23; 13:1; 17:1).

Some studies of Jesus assume that the same significance is attached to his suffering by himself or by others as to that of the persecuted prophet or the oppressed (and suffering) righteous person.

The theme of the *persecuted prophet* is the subject of a study by Schoeps,[7] who claims that gentile Christians expressed their anti-Jewish sentiments by holding the people of Israel responsible for the murder of Jesus the prophet. In reaction to this, Steck shows that even in the Old Testament, Israel as a whole is held responsible for the killing of prophets; in part of the New Testament this responsibility is then assumed to have been extended to include Jesus in order to explain why the Jews prevented missionary work among the Gentiles.[8]

The theme of the *oppressed righteous man* is addressed by E. Schweizer.[9] He argues that Jesus can be compared to the Old Testament righteous man who after his (martyr's) death is glorified by God. Ruppert challenges Schweizer for wrongly linking the apocalyptic notion of the oppressed *righteous man* with the rabbinical notion of the atoning power of martyrdom.[10] According to Ruppert, Jesus combines the oppressed righteous man (who will be raised up by God) and the prophet who suffers for his people (as Moses was prepared to do). Kleinknecht is also of the opinion that Jesus himself saw his messianic task within the framework of the suffering righteous man.[11] According to Den Heyer, it was the Christian community that, reflecting on the suffering and death of Jesus, was able to use the model of the suffering righteous man in combination with the suffering servant of

---

7. H. J. Schoeps, "Die jüdischen Prophetenmorde," in *Aus frühchristlicher Zeit: Religionsgeschichtliche Untersuchungen* (Tübingen: Mohr, 1950), 126–43.

8. O. H. Steck, *Israel und das gewaltsame Geschick der Propheten: Untersuchungen zur Überlieferung des deuteronomistischen Geschichtsbildes im Alten Testament, Spätjudentum und Urchristentum*, Wissenschaftliche Monographien zum Alten und Neuen Testament 23 (Neukirchen: Neukirchener Verlag, 1967).

9. E. Schweizer, *Lordship and Discipleship*, translated from the German with revisions by the author (London: SCM, 1960).

10. L. Ruppert, *Jesus als der leidende Gerechte? Der Weg Jesu im Lichte eines alt- und zwischentestamentlichen Motivs*, Stuttgarter Bibelstudien 59 (Stuttgart: Katholisches Bibelwerk, 1972).

11. K. T. Kleinknecht, *Der leidende Gerechtfertigte: Die alttestamentlich-jüdische Tradition vom "leidenden Gerechten" und ihre Rezeption bei Paulus*, WUNT 2/13 (Tübingen: Mohr, 1984), 367.

the LORD.[12] In this case it is not the pattern that is new but only the name of the person involved.

These comparisons with the Old Testament[13] fail to address the decisive difference between on the one hand the murder of a prophet or the oppression of a just man and on the other hand the suffering of Jesus. The persecuted prophet and the aggrieved righteous man wait for God's justification, but Jesus consciously lives toward his suffering and death. This is why he has come (Mark 10:45). He is not the victim of his surroundings! The murdered prophet and the oppressed righteous man endure the inevitable, but Jesus himself determines the hour for what he sees as the goal of his life. A comparison can certainly be made between the *attitude people often assume toward* prophets and righteous people, and their attitude toward Jesus. Jesus' *own* position, however, is different from that of the defenseless prophets and the powerless righteous. We see this in the fact that he does not eagerly await God's *punishment* of his enemies or *revenge* for what has been done to him by those who reject him. On the contrary, he declares that he has come for their salvation, and on the cross he prays for forgiveness for those who execute him (Luke 9:52–56; 23:34). Thus he accepts his suffering, not as a powerless individual who trusts that God will do right by him or her, but as the Ruler who thinks it necessary to allow himself to be bound and killed.

6.2.2 Death as a Plan for Life

From the beginning of his public ministry, Jesus was certain that as a human being he had to perish. This was apparent when he appeared before John the Baptist to be symbolically immersed in the waters of the Jordan. At first the great prophet refused to perform this humbling rite on Jesus. But he responded, "It is proper for us to do this to fulfill all righteousness" (Matt. 3:15). The descent into the water was an indication of the direction of his life and work.

And at a very early stage he made his disciples understand that a time for fasting was coming, when the bridegroom would be taken from them (Mark 2:18–20).

In the Passion announcements, Jesus teaches emphatically and systematically about the path he is to take that will lead to his death. These announcements are reported almost identically in the first three Gospels. Even though the disciples thought this teaching strange, it made a

---

12. C. J. den Heyer, "Jezus, de lijdende rechtvaardige en de knecht des HEREN," in *De knechtsgestalte van Christus: Studies door collega's en oud-leerlingen aangeboden aan Prof. Dr. H. N. Ridderbos* (Kampen: Kok, 1978), 54–64.

13. For a more detailed description, see M.-L. Gubler, *Die frühesten Deutungen des Todes Jesu: Eine motivgeschichtliche Darstellung aufgrund der neueren exegetischen Forschung*, Orbis Biblicus et Orientalis 15 (Freiburg/Göttingen: Universitätsverlag, 1977).

deep impression on them and they remembered the words with great accuracy. In the first announcements the focus is on the fact that the *leaders in Jerusalem* will be the ones to kill Jesus (Matt. 16:21; Mark 8:31; Luke 9:22). The second announcement adds that he will be *betrayed* (Matt. 17:22; Mark 9:31; Luke 9:44). And in the third announcement (which is confidential in nature and meant only for the Twelve), Jesus tells them that the leaders will hand him over *to the Gentiles* (Matt. 20:18–19; Mark 10:33–34; Luke 18:31–33). In Matthew 26:1–2 we read that two days before his arrest Jesus even tells his disciples the *time* at which the third announcement will be fulfilled!

The fact that this program of suffering and death was told to the disciples well in advance and in increasingly greater detail proves that Jesus accepted this path and consciously set out to follow it. In Gethsemane it will appear that this acceptance went hand in hand with an inner struggle. Jesus goes to his death willingly, but not without emotion. He prays to the Father that this cup, if possible, be taken from him, but he submits to what God asks him to do (Matt. 26:36–46).

6.2.3 Jesus' Death as Necessity

Jesus adds further explanations to the announcements of his suffering. He tells his disciples not only that this *will* happen, but he quite clearly explains that it *has to* happen. His path to perdition is based on divine necessity (Matt. 16:21).

This necessity has its basis in Scripture (Matt. 26:54; Luke 24:44). Apparently an explanation is needed, for the disciples consider the suffering of the Messiah, the Son of God, as completely incompatible with their own ideas. The Gospels make no secret of the fact that the apostles at first had enormous difficulty accepting the gospel that they would later preach. Until Easter they *refused* to believe Jesus *on this point*, and they were not even prepared to blindly resign themselves to it. For open-minded Jewish Bible readers of the time, the suffering of the Messiah was certainly not self-evident.

In the Gospels we find no indication of the scriptural teachings Jesus passed on to his disciples by way of explanation. But there is every reason to assume that the apostles' use of the Scriptures after Easter goes back to Jesus' use of the Scriptures before Easter. Where else would it come from? Many modern biblical scholars theorize that the Christian church, in retrospect and of its own accord, wanted to legitimize Jesus' suffering and death by appealing to passages from Scripture. This is not very plausible, however, when we note that the disciples refused to *accept* Jesus' suffering. Yet from the day of Pentecost on they are ready and willing to preach Jesus' suffering, making their appeal to the Law and the Prophets. There must have been some kind of preparation for this rapid reversal.

Their use of scriptural passages to explain the death of Christ must have been based on the teaching of Jesus himself, which they received but initially rejected because they did not understand it. When their mind is opened after Easter, so they can understand the Scriptures (Luke 24:45), they quickly catch up with what Jesus had been trying to explain to them.

In only a few places in the Gospels do we read of Jesus referring to specific scriptural passages. In Mark 12:10–11 he quotes Psalm 118:22–23 ("The stone the builders rejected"). Zechariah 13:7 is quoted in Mark 14:27 ("Strike the shepherd, and the sheep will be scattered"). Psalm 41:9 and 69:4 point to Judas ("He who shares my bread": John 13:18) and the world ("They hated me without reason"; John 15:25). Finally we read in Luke 22:37 a brief quote from Isaiah 53:12 ("And he was numbered with the transgressors"). Obviously Jesus must have made more frequent use of passages from the Bible.

Yet it is striking that appeals to the Scriptures are often referred to in more general rather than specific terms. It seems as if the *entire Bible* must provide proof for the necessity of Jesus' dying. It is "the Scriptures" that must be fulfilled (Mark 14:49). "The Scriptures" that the Jews study "testify to me," says Jesus (John 5:39). On the road to Emmaus he explains "what was said in *all* the Scriptures" concerning himself, "beginning with Moses and all the Prophets" (Luke 24:27). He *opens* "the Scriptures" to them (Luke 24:32), and later he *opens* the minds of the apostles "so they could understand the Scriptures" (Luke 24:45).

These are not just a few forgotten passages that have to do with the Messiah. What is needed is a different *perspective on* the Scriptures. This does not mean that Jesus adds a brand-new interpretation to an old document. Rather, the haze that covers the eyes of the readers must be removed. That is why Jesus can reproach them with, "How foolish you are, and how slow of heart to believe all that the prophets have spoken!" (Luke 24:25).

Apparently the believers, including Jesus' own disciples, have never grasped what the Scriptures are ultimately all about. They have read without understanding. It never occurred to them that the promises concerning the coming Savior could not possibly be fulfilled immediately—which is precisely what John the Baptist had come to say. Without repentance it is impossible to enter the kingdom. Without going under in the Jordan there can be no pardon. Something must be made right before the LORD can come to his people; the way must be prepared and made level, and a path must be made straight in the wilderness.

During the desert period after the exodus it became clear how unsuited the people were for an encounter with God in the Promised Land. During the period of the judges we see the powerlessness and the obstinacy of the entering tribes. The chronicles from the age of the kings overflow with sin and apostasy, resulting in the exile. And after the temple is rebuilt, the prophets from Haggai to Malachi once again begin calling for conversion. The ancient Scriptures are the pride of Israel, but in fact they reveal the scandal of the congregation of Israel. No connection is possible between that history and the kingdom of heaven. That is why John prophesied about the amnesty that would be brought about by the one who is to come. Yet his preaching did not get through to the Jewish people or to the disciples. They recognized their guilt and submitted to the baptism of repentance, but they did not fully realize that such a symbolic baptism could not save them. Only the actual perishing of someone else could do that.

The "necessary" suffering of Jesus is like the deficit or debit the book-keeping of the Scriptures shows. Stephen explains the reality of that deficit in his speech to the Sanhedrin (Acts 7), and Paul demonstrated it in the synagogue in Pisidian Antioch (Acts 13:13–49). Anyone in Israel who opposes the suffering of the Savior has a lot to learn about his or her own biblical history.

It is only within this appeal to Scripture *as a whole* that specific scriptural passages can find their proper place. Then the eye falls on those passages (often treated as marginal) that actually refer to a shepherd who will be killed for the straying sheep (Zech. 13:7), to a rejected stone that will become the capstone (Ps. 118:22–23), and a servant beloved of the Lord who will be numbered with the transgressors (Isa. 53:12). This use of biblical passages presupposes an openness toward the ultimate outcome of Israel's history as a whole. Jesus corrects the people's pride in their biblical history when he says to the teachers of the law and the Pharisees, "You testify against yourselves that you are the descendants of those who murdered the prophets" (Matt. 23:31). The history of the Law and the Prophets is a long trail of spilled blood, "from the blood of righteous Abel to the blood of Zechariah son of Berekiah, whom you murdered between the temple and the altar" (Matt. 23:35).

Those who shut their eyes to this view of history remain blind to the *necessity* of Jesus' suffering. They will miss the clues to this suffering that can be found here and there in the Old Testament. A history of sinners and a sacrifice belong together! God's people cannot walk straight into the messianic age. The Jordan separates them from him. They need a baptism of repentance. Jesus makes it clear that John's baptism is a symbol of his own earthly fate (Mark 10:38).[14]

An overview of the Old Testament passages the Evangelists used in writing about Jesus' suffering or alluded to can be found in Moo and in

14. See J. van Bruggen, *Marcus: Het evangelie volgens Petrus*, 2d ed., Commentaar op het Nieuwe Testament, 3d series (Kampen: Kok, 1992), on Mark 10:38.

Brown.[15] According to Moo, Jesus and the Evangelists refer most frequently to Isaiah's prophecies concerning the servant of the LORD (besides references to Zechariah 9–14, the Psalms, and texts about sacrifices). According to Brown, most of the allusions in the Gospels come from the Book of Psalms, especially Psalm 22. It is difficult to determine whether the apostles found these references themselves, after their minds had been opened, under the direction of the Spirit who had been poured out on them, or whether they had been alerted to them by Jesus during the periods of instruction between his resurrection and ascension. These detailed connections between Jesus' suffering and the Old Testament, however, are not the *basis* for the certainty that he *had to* suffer. Rather, the certainty is the basis for the *elaboration*.[16]

6.3 The Path to Amnesty

How does Jesus, as a willing victim of a proud people of God, bridge the gap between sinful people and the coming kingdom of heaven? He is the Son of God who is killed after a long line of God's servants, who were sent as he was, had been assaulted and murdered before him (Matt. 21:33–46). The process of opposition to God had reached its ultimate conclusion (Matt. 23:32), but how could this be of any positive value for the future of so many?

It is clear that the path of rejection and suffering will in the end serve a great and good purpose. Jesus says this before it happens. On the third day after his death he will rise again and precede the disciples to Galilee (Matt. 26:31–32). Through his suffering he will fulfill the Scriptures in a positive sense (Matt. 26:54).

In the Gospels, the point of Jesus' death is indicated by the language of atonement: this death confers pardon to all who believe! Immediately before his death, the atoning nature of the event is made explicit in the last Passover celebration with his disciples. For all those years, the personal name *Jesus* ("the LORD saves"; Matt. 1:21) had formed the hidden program of his life! These are the topics to be considered in the next four sections.

6.3.1 The Lamb of God

After Jesus' immersion in the Jordan, John the Baptist refers to him as "the Lamb of God, who takes away the sin of the world" (John 1:29,

---

15. D. J. Moo, *The Old Testament in the Gospel Passion Narratives* (Sheffield: Almond, 1983); R. E. Brown, *The Death of the Messiah: From Gethsemane to the Grave: A Commentary on the Passion Narratives in the Four Gospels*, 2 vols., Anchor Bible Reference Library (New York: Doubleday, 1993).

16. See also sec. 6.3.2, the discussion of the possible influence of Isaiah 53 on the development of the notion of a *suffering* Messiah.

36; this name was discussed in sec. 2.4.2). Apparently John the Baptist was taken by surprise when the More Powerful One expressed a desire to descend into the Jordan "to fulfill all righteousness" (Matt. 3:15). At that moment he came face to face with Jesus' intention to begin his work humbly, as one of the sinners. He would, as John had preached, bring amnesty for sins. The lambs that people normally offered as a sacrifice for sin were not sufficient. Now it seems that the humble, unpretentious Jesus (a lamb, not a lion) will become the lamb *of God* through whom this amnesty *will* be attained.

We do not know how much John already knew about the necessity of suffering and dying, but here he uses an image of Jesus as the one who, *humiliated* and *in his own person*, will be God's means of bringing about atonement. It does not make much difference whether he was thinking of the lamb that the priests sacrificed daily in the temple or the Passover lamb that the Israelite families killed once a year. What is important is that in Jesus, God *himself* was offering a lamb *for atonement*.[17]

The use of this image is also in line with the way in which the Holy Spirit came to Jesus after his baptism: the Spirit descended on him

17. Du Plessis is of the opinion that Jesus was called "Lamb of God" to indicate the intimate relationship between the Father and the Son ("his lamb, his own heart, his own Son"). This is undeniably a factor. God is delivering up his *own* lamb! But the choice of the word "lamb" (not only "son"), in the context in which John the Baptist uses the word, would remain incomprehensible if it did not refer in some way to the humble appearance of the Son and his destiny as sacrifice—it is for this very reason that he can be said to "take away the sins of the world" (P. J. du Plessis, "Zie het lam Gods: overwegingen bij de knechtsgestalte in het evangelie van Johannes," in *De knechtsgestalte van Christus: Studies door collega's en oud-leerlingen aangeboden aan Prof. Dr. H. N. Ridderbos* [Kampen: Kok, 1978], 120–38).

On the basis of several texts from the targums, Van Staalduine-Sulman claims that the name "lamb" was already in circulation within Judaism as a title for the coming Davidic messiah. In a hymn text, David is repeatedly referred to as a *lamb* in contrast to the *bear* Goliath. But no texts have been discovered yet in which this *comparison* is found independent of the specific David-Goliath context and used as a more or less fixed term or title for an expected messiah. Van Staalduine-Sulman sees "the symbolism of the messianic lamb" worked out differently in Christianity (where via Isa. 53 the sacrifice of the lamb is dominant) than it is in Judaism (where the weak lamb is strong in the power of the Lord). But then the "song of the lamb" in Rev. 15:3 could refer to the Jewish song handed down in the targum tradition about the coming (messianic) lamb. It is questionable, however, whether a song about David and Goliath in which the "bear-lamb" metaphor occurs a few times could have become known by the standard title "Song of the lamb." It would seem more plausible that neither the Jews in general nor John the Baptist refers to an existing title—"lamb"—for the Davidic messiah, and that John the Baptist's "Behold, the Lamb of God" is his own way of describing the path that Jesus will take (making use of the fact that lambs were well known as weak sacrificial animals; compare Isa. 53). See E. van Staalduine-Sulman, "The Aramaic Song of the Lamb," in *Verse in Ancient Near Eastern Prose*, Alter Orient und Altes Testament 42, ed. J. C. de Moor and W. G. E. Watson (Neukirchen: Neukirchener Verlag, 1993), 265–92.

"like a dove" (Matt. 3:16). In Israel, the dove was known especially as the most frequently used sacrificial animal in the temple. The visualization as a *dove* is appropriate for the descent of the Spirit from above (Luke 3:22). John "translates" this image of a sacrificial animal and applies it to Jesus, who is walking toward him, referring to him as the *"Lamb* of God."

There is no reason to see any special reference here to Genesis 22. When it turns out that Isaac does not have to be killed, God shows Abraham a *ram (krios)* in a thicket. John the Baptist is not speaking about a "ram," however, but about a "lamb." Understandably, later Christians interpreted Genesis 22 as a foreshadowing of the sacrifice of Christ: "God himself will provide the lamb for the burnt offering" (Gen. 22:8). The animal in Genesis 22, however, should be seen as an earthly ram (Gen. 22:13) and not a sacrifice that later would descend from heaven. There is no reason to assume that John the Baptist already understood Genesis 22 typologically and was thinking of this chapter when he called Jesus "the Lamb of God" after the baptism in the Jordan.

In the twentieth century, Genesis 22 has been used in a very different way as background for understanding Jesus' suffering and death as *atonement*. The focus is then on the interpretation this chapter acquired in the Jewish tradition about the binding of Isaac (the *aqedah*). In Genesis 22, the emphasis is on the fact that Abraham did not spare his son but was prepared to sacrifice him to God (Gen. 22:16). In the later targums, however, attention is also paid to *Isaac's* contribution: he allowed himself to be bound and was the willing *sacrifice*, and sacrificial blood may even have flowed during the binding. Influenced by this Jewish tradition, Jesus would then have come to be seen as a *sacrifice*, analogous to Isaac.[18]

Jesus is "the Lamb of God." John the Baptist already refers to him with these words as the man who embodies the means of pardon. But the term does not tell us much about the *path* he will use to bring about this amnesty. A later statement by Jesus himself says more about this.

---

18. G. Vermes, "Redemption and Genesis XXII: The Binding of Isaac and the Sacrifice of Jesus," in *Scripture and Tradition in Judaism: Haggadic Studies*, Studia Post-Biblica 4 (Leiden: Brill, 1961), 193–227. See Gubler for an overview of the study of the so-called *aqedah* motif (Gubler, *Die frühesten Deutungen des Todes Jesu*). The usefulness of the motif has been contested from many sides: (1) there are no sources demonstrating the existence of an independent sacrificial view of Isaac for the period of the New Testament (Brown, *Death of the Messiah*); (2) any New Testament allusions to Gen. 22 have to do with the parallel with Abraham, who did not spare his son (Rom. 8:32; James 2:21–23), and not with Isaac as a willing sacrificial victim (N. A. Dahl, *Jesus the Christ: The Historical Origins of Christological Doctrine* [Minneapolis: Fortress, 1991]).

6.3.2 A Ransom for Many

John the Baptist was immediately struck by Jesus' humble and serving attitude. This proves henceforth to be the Son of Man's permanent attitude toward life. As he himself later says, "[I] did not come to be served, but to serve" (Mark 10:45). Jesus then adds something. The extent of his service is far-reaching indeed—he will even *give his life as a ransom* for many." These words are closely related to his baptism in the Jordan. In the preceding passage Jesus had spoken of "the baptism I am baptized with" (Mark 10:38–39)—a striking expression. Was the humble immersion in the Jordan not sufficient? Was that merely a reference to another "baptism"? This appears to be the case. He who in the spirit of servitude submitted to baptism in water will in the end give up his life in the river of death to the service of many. His life of service will continue to the bitter end!

This life of self-sacrifice unto death proves to be a ransom for many. The Greek word *lutron* is not the customary translation of *guilt offering* (Heb. ʾāšām in Isa. 53:10). Nevertheless, the term "ransom" implies that there is a claim against the lives of "many" that will be settled by Jesus. The ransom will be paid for liberation from guilt, slavery, or imprisonment.[19] Jesus thereby sets the "many" free for God, so that his serving and dying mean liberation for others. His one death makes the deaths of many others unnecessary.

"Many" here is not a limiting word, in the sense of "not all." Rather, it sets the one who dies as a ransom in contrast to the many who are thereby made free.[20]

In Mark 10:45, Jesus himself characterizes his path of rejection and suffering as a necessary means for rescuing *others* from death and giving them life. His words presuppose a relationship of indebtedness between God and the many—which was exactly what the prophet of repentance, John the Baptist, had preached. By his death, Jesus himself plans to undo that indebtedness through the promised amnesty, in which everyone who had humbly submitted to immersion by John in the Jordan had placed their hope.

Jeremias believes that Jesus saw himself as the *"servant* of the LORD" as mentioned in the second part of Isaiah.[21] Through this identification

---

19. G. Sevenster, *De Christologie van het Nieuwe Testament* (Amsterdam: Holland, 1946).
20. See van Bruggen, *Marcus*, on Mark 10:45.
21. J. Jeremias, *"Pais (theou)* im Neuen Testament," in *Abba: Studien zur neutestamentlichen Theologie und Zeitgeschichte* (Göttingen: Vandenhoeck & Ruprecht, 1966), 191–216. Compare O. Cullmann, *The Christology of the New Testament*, trans. S. C. Guthrie and C. A. M. Hall (Philadelphia: Westminster, 1959); and F. F. Bruce, *This Is That: The New Testament Development of Some Old Testament Themes* (Exeter: Paternoster, 1968). See

with the "servant of Yahweh," both suffering and the idea of a ransom (Isa. 53) would have found a place in Jesus' plan.[22] Initially Jeremias was of the opinion that in certain pre-Christian Jewish circles the idea already existed of a suffering savior, the suffering "son of man." He reached this conclusion mainly because he saw the "son of man" in the Ethiopian Enoch as the glorified "son of the LORD." After being challenged by Sjöberg, he dropped this identification of the suffering servant with the glorified son of man. Neither is there a pre-Christian application of Isaiah 53 to a suffering messiah figure in the Testament of Benjamin 3.8; this is certainly a Christian passage.[23]

Therefore, because there is no trace in pre-Christian Judaism of Isaiah 53 being applied to a suffering *savior*, Jeremias now must limit himself to the idea that Jesus himself introduced this interpretation within the intimate circle of disciples. He has been challenged on this point especially by Hooker.[24] She concludes that Jesus talks in general about the necessity of his suffering and dying, but insofar as he himself quotes supporting texts, they are not taken from Isaiah 53 (Mark 12:10–11; 14:27). Hooker is correct here, but her conclusions exceed the data. In Luke 22:37, Jesus himself quotes from Isaiah 53! Hooker is correct when she observes that the quote in this case does not refer to *vicarious* death, but at the same time it cannot be denied that Jesus saw his own particular path of suffering as being in keeping with Isaiah 53.[25] In addition, the Evangelists all note that the prophecy of the humble *servant* of the LORD was fulfilled in the way Jesus lived (Matt. 8:17; 12:17–21; John 12:37–38). The preaching of the apostles also makes clear reference to Isaiah 53 whenever they talk about Christ (for example, Acts 8:32–35; 1 Pet. 2:24). There is every reason to assume that this use of Isaiah 53 by the Evangelists and the apostles was built on Jesus' own teaching. Because as a prophet John the Baptist saw himself in light of Isaiah 40 (John 1:22–23), it would seem natural to assume that the

---

Grimm for a survey of the investigation (W. Grimm, *Die Verkündigung Jesu und Deuterojesaja,* 2d ed., Arbeiten zum Neuen Testament und Judentum 1 [Frankfurt: Lang, 1981]).

22. Also see J. Jeremias, *New Testament Theology* (London: SCM, 1971), 274–84.

23. S. K. Williams, *Jesus' Death as Saving Event: The Background and Origin of a Concept,* Harvard Dissertations in Religion 2 (Missoula, Mont.: Scholars Press, 1975); M. de Jonge, "Test. Benjamin 3:8 and the Picture of Joseph as 'a Good and Holy Man,'" in *Die Entstehung der jüdischen Martyrologie,* ed. J. W. van Henten et al., Studia Post–Biblica 38 (Leiden: Brill, 1989), 204–14.

24. M. D. Hooker, *Jesus and the Servant: The Influence of the Servant Concept of Deutero-Isaiah in the New Testament* (London: S.P.C.K., 1959).

25. Ibid., 86. Ridderbos refers to the allusion to being despised (Isa. 53:3) in Mark 9:12 and to the mention of the "many" (Isa. 53:11–12) in Mark 10:45. H. Ridderbos, *The Coming of the Kingdom,* trans. H. de Jongste, ed. R. O. Zorn (Philadelphia: Presbyterian & Reformed, 1962), 165.

prophecies of Isaiah in particular would be read as illumination for the ministry of Jesus who was to follow.

Hooker is correct, however, when she states contra Jeremias that the meaning of Jesus' suffering as a whole is not simply the result of Jesus' identifying himself with the "servant" from Isaiah. He does not call himself "the servant of the LORD" but appears as the Son of God, although he comes in the form of a servant. Jesus asserts the divine necessity for his suffering directly and without any explicit reference to Isaiah 53. Even though that chapter is an early pointer to the necessity of the Servant's suffering, Jesus does not suffer because he read Isaiah 53 in the Bible. Isaiah 53 helps us see that Jesus' suffering was not a new idea but the fulfillment of ancient prophecies. On the other hand, it should not be characterized as the *origin and source* of the notion of a suffering *Messiah*. The prophecies concerning the servant of the LORD were in the centuries prior to the Christian era usually applied to the suffering people of God or to the persecution and liberation of the righteous.[26] Insofar as Isaiah 53 was read with an Anointed One in mind, no real attention was focused on the theme of suffering, nor is it clear whether this Messiah-Servant was understood individually or collectively.[27] Such an "open" reading of Isaiah 53 (compare Acts 8:34) is not surprising, since the Servant in the servant prophecies is not identified and is referred to more than once as "Jacob" or "Israel."[28] The direct application of the passage to the suffering *people* or *individual members of the people* only became impossible when John the Baptist called the entire people (without exceptions) to repentance. Apparently there is not yet among the people of Israel the new servant with whom the LORD is well pleased and on whom his Spirit rests. Another, more powerful one must come to effect the pardon. But at Jesus' baptism, God from heaven points out his Son as the Beloved with whom he is well pleased (Mark 1:11). This prophetic rejection of the people and the heavenly acceptance of the Son clearly demonstrate that the prophecies concerning the servant of the LORD ultimately can only be fulfilled through this unique son of Abraham.

According to some authors, the background for Mark 10:45 should not be sought in Isaiah 53 ("the many") but in Isaiah 43 (where the notion of "a ransom" is found). In Isaiah 43:3–4, the LORD says that he gives "Egypt for your ransom, Cush and Seba in your stead. Since you

---

26. Williams, *Jesus' Death as Saving Event*, 111–20.

27. H. Haag, *Der Gottesknecht bei Deuterojesaja*, Erträge der Forschung 233 (Darmstadt: Wissenschaftlicher Buchgesellschaft, 1985), 34–43.

28. J. C. Bastiaens, *Interpretaties van Jesaja 53: Een intertextueel onderzoek naar de lijdende Knecht in Jes 53 (MT/LXX) en in Lk 22:14–38, Hand 3:12–26, Hand 4:23–31 en Hand 8:26–40*, TFT-Studies 22 (Tilburg: Tilburg University Press, 1993).

are precious and honored in my sight, . . . I will give men in exchange for you, and people in exchange for your life." In the later rabbinical literature, these verses are applied to a final judgment in which the Gentiles constitute the "ransom" for chosen Israel. According to Grimm, Jesus must deal with this commonly held notion.[29] He then let it be known that it is not the people who will serve as a means of exchange for Israel, but he himself will be the ransom for many, both within Israel and among all the peoples of the earth.[30] The following objections can be made to this exegesis: (1) Isaiah 43:3–4 does not speak about the final judgment, nor about all gentile nations, but about a change in the balance of power whereby a few specifically mentioned nations will go under. (2) In Isaiah we find many promises concerning the ultimate salvation of the nations (or of many people from them). (3) The rabbinic literature dates from the period after the New Testament. (4) The context of Mark 10:45 does not support the theory that Jesus here contrasted his own ministry with the prevailing Jewish ideas about the Gentiles; the context is tension in the circle of disciples, who had incorrect views about the way of the Messiah.

6.3.3 God's Atonement Supper

John the Baptist had already said that Jesus' *humility* was of positive value. He is the Lamb of God, sent to bring about the amnesty that had been promised. Jesus himself presented his ministry in terms of his readiness to give his life as a ransom for many—the pardon would be achieved through his death. Now the disciples must learn to *accept* this rejected and dying Master as the price paid for their lives. This is what it came down to when Jesus instituted the supper of his body and blood on the night before his betrayal.

He already had let his disciples know, in strong statements, that he had come down from heaven so that "his flesh" might serve as food for the world (John 6:51). After the multiplication of the loaves and fishes he invites the disciples to "eat the flesh of the Son of Man and drink his blood." Only by doing so can they have life (John 6:53). These drastic formulations already pointed to the fact that it would be by *dying* that he would become food for humankind, and that people therefore would

---

29. Grimm, *Die Verkündigung Jesu und Deuterojesaja*, 231–77.
30. P. Stuhlmacher, "Existenzstellvertretung für die Vielen: Mk 10,45 (Mt 20,28)," in *Versöhnung, Gesetz und Gerechtigkeit: Aufsätze zur biblischen Theologie* (Göttingen: Vandenhoeck & Ruprecht, 1981), 27–42; V. Hampel, *Menschensohn und historischer Jesus: Ein Rätselwort als Schlüssel zum messianischen Selbstverständnis Jesu* (Neukirchen: Neukirchener Verlag, 1990); H. Baarlink, "Jezus, uw verzoenend sterven . . . : Hoe kunnen wij over de verzoening (s)preken?" in *Jezus' visie op zichzelf: In discussie met De Jonge's christologie* (Nijkerk: Callenbach, 1991), 85–99.

have to learn to accept and love him as the Rejected and Dying One. It is true that Jesus intended these statements as attempts to move on-lookers to *believe in him*, but it is also clear that this belief would have to be in a *Sacrificed One* (compare John 10:15–18).[31]

At the last Passover he celebrated with his disciples, Jesus distributed bread and wine to them as symbols of his body and blood. The now im-minent betrayal and execution take on a positive value. The disciples must accept this offering of Jesus' life as food for their own lives. His blood will be spilled for many for the forgiveness of sins (Matt. 26:28). When eating the bread one should think of him ("in remembrance of me," Luke 22:19), and when drinking the wine one should celebrate the joy of this memory of his death. The event becomes a supper of atone-ment with God.[32]

It is precisely by this conferring of the forgiving power of his death to the believing disciples that Jesus unequivocally distinguishes himself from every other person in history who has ever offered him- or herself up for faith or nation. No hero or martyr first instituted a supper in order to distribute his death as food. At a later point others may have gratefully remembered the suffering and death of other martyrs and profited from the consequences. But Jesus does not ask his disciples to simply think of him sometime in the future—he turns his death before-hand into the *food* and the *joyous drink* meant for his own disciples. He is not the hero or the martyr who is prepared to give up his life in the interest of others. He distributes his death as a positive fact. He is not *taken*, nor does he *allow* himself to be taken; rather, he *gives* his body and blood. His death does not create new chances for others, but his sacrifice as such *is* the new chance and eternal life. The disciples do not offer a toast for a good conclusion after Good Friday; rather they cele-brate the meal *of* Good Friday. As the exodus from Egypt, celebrated in the Passover, was a redeeming act of God, so will this exodus to the cross be the definitive redeeming act of God's Son. The Lamb of God gives himself as a ransom *to the believers*.

This unique supper held before the fact becomes for later Christians the meal celebrated after the fact (1 Cor. 11:20–29). The church's Lord's Supper owes its special significance, however, to the *moment* when Jesus gave bread and wine to his disciples as a symbol of his body and blood. It occurred *during the night in which he was betrayed!* The

31. For comments on John 6:48–59 and a discussion of what some regard as the sac-ramental aspect of this passage, see P. H. R. van Houwelingen, *Johannes: Het evangelie van het Woord*, Commentaar op het Nieuwe Testament, 3d series (Kampen: Kok, 1997): "John 6 is not about the Last Supper, but the Last Supper is about the fulfillment of John 6!"

32. For comments on Mark 14:22–26 and a more detailed treatment of the events that took place at the new meal during the night of Jesus' betrayal, see van Bruggen, *Marcus*.

sacrifice of his life as atonement for sins was therefore Jesus' own, prior goal!

The meaning of this death therefore cannot be derived solely from the circumstances of the prevailing conflict, which merely constitutes the earthly context for a heavenly event. Ultimately, Jesus alone is the main character who dominates the events, while the chief priests, teachers of the law, and Pharisees are mere bit players; their whole point in being there is to hand Jesus over. When this is accomplished, they are free to abandon their enmity and to believe in Jesus as God's Son and Anointed One (Acts 2:22–40). In this, too, Jesus' death is different from that of people who give up their lives for faith or nation. Their dying benefits the oppressed—but not the oppressors. Their death can resolve an impasse—but it cannot eliminate the underlying conflict.

It is possible to describe the bread and wine in the night of the betrayal as a sacrificial meal. Those present participate in the redemptive power of the sacrifice. Yet there is a difference. At sacrificial meals, people ate the animal that they *themselves* had brought and sacrificed. At the meal Jesus arranged during this last night, the focus is on a sacrifice that the participants did not bring themselves and that, at that moment, they *did not want to be brought at all.*

It is at this meal that the meaning of Jesus' dying is revealed as unique and unlike any other death on earth. Disciples who refuse to accept what will happen are served beforehand with symbols of that which they are not yet willing to embrace.

The terminology of surrender, which at first glance seems unique to the gospel, can also be found in the Greek world in connection with people who die for the good of the state, their family, or their friends. This suggests that it is *not* Jesus' *surrender for the good of others* that is unique. First, the fact that Jesus' *whole life* is devoted to this goal is quite unusual. Surrender is not merely forced on him and accepted; rather, it is part of his life's goal and explains the humility displayed by the Son of God throughout his time on earth. Second, it is unique that surrender is not a necessary means of averting disaster and thereby creating a better situation. Specifically in Jesus' case, death was not necessary as a means of warding off disaster and demons.[33] Jesus could triumph over everyone else's diseases and demons during his life and thereby conquer disease and death. His death is not a *pharmakos* for warding off evil; instead, his surrender has positive value *in and of itself.* For Greek listen-

33. For the function of the human sacrifice as "medicine" (*pharmakos*), see H. S. Versnel, "Quid Athenis et Hierosolymis? Bemerkungen über die Herkunft von Aspekten des 'Effective Death,'" in *Entstehung der jüdischen Martyrologie*, ed. J. W. van Henten et al., 188–92.

ers, the foolishness of the gospel did not lie in the fact that someone allowed himself to be killed for the good of others (compare Rom. 5:7), but that this death by crucifixion *itself* would be salvation in which people must put their trust, and that this death by crucifixion would serve as an unsolicited sacrifice on behalf of enemies and strangers.

The notion of a person's *atoning* (substitutionary) death does not fit in with the Old Testament, to the extent that it stresses each individual's personal responsibility before God (Exod. 32:31–33; Deut. 24:16). There is even something preeminently pagan about such a death; it is idol worshipers who toss Jonah into the raging waves to appease the gods (Jon. 1:15), and a Moabite ruler sacrifices his own son, to the horror of the Israelites (2 Kings 3:27). The only place where the notion of a sacrificial death on behalf of others is mentioned in a positive sense is in Isaiah 53:4–12, in the description of the servant of the LORD. For this reason many scholars regard Isaiah 53 as distinctly out of place in the Old Testament. Whether influenced by this passage or not, it was not until the second century B.C. or even later that the idea of an atoning *human* death finally arose. The occasion for this may have been the figure of the Jewish martyr.[34] According to some, the idea of the "atoning" death in Jewish "martyr theology" was strongly influenced by Hellenism.[35] Others believe that the development of this notion fits in Palestinian Judaism.[36] This dilemma is rather unproductive, however, because no clear dividing line can be drawn between Jewish and Greek culture due to the fact that there was a great deal of mutual influencing of cultures during the Hellenistic period.[37]

It is clear that special significance was attached to the deaths of the martyrs in 2 Maccabees (second century B.C.) and 4 Maccabees (late

34. For a survey of this research, see M. de Jonge, "Jesus' Death for Others and the Death of the Maccabean Martyrs," in *Text and Testimony: Essays on New Testament and Apocryphal Literature in Honour of A. F. J. Klijn*, ed. T. Baarda et al. (Kampen: Kok, 1988), 142–51. For an evaluation, see J. S. Vos, "Vragen rondom de plaatsvervangende zoendood van Jezus in het Nieuwe Testament," *Gereformeerd Theologisch Tijdschrift* 93 (1993): 210–31.

35. K. Wengst, *Christologische Formeln und Lieder des Urchristentums*, Studien zum Neuen Testament 7 (Gütersloh: Mohn, 1972). Williams sees this influence specifically and only in 4 Maccabees (Williams, *Jesus' Death as Saving Event*).

36. E. Lohse, *Märtyrer und Gottesknecht: Untersuchungen zur urchristlichen Verkündigung vom Sühnetod Jesu Christi*, 2d ed. (Göttingen: Vandenhoeck & Ruprecht, 1963), 66–72; J. Gnilka, "Martyriumsparänese und Sühnetod in synoptischen und jüdischen Traditionen," in *Die Kirche des Anfangs: Für Heinz Schürmann*, ed. R. Schnackenburg et al. (Freiburg: Herder, 1978), 223–46.

37. M. Hengel, *The Atonement: The Origins of the Doctrine in the New Testament* (Philadelphia: Fortress, 1981); J. W. van Henten, "De joodse martelaren als grondleggers van een nieuwe orde: Een studie uitgaande van 2 en 4 Makkabeeën" (doctoral thesis, University of Leiden, 1986).

first century A.D.). Does this mean that their deaths also took on a reconciling and substitutionary significance? This is doubtful where 2 Maccabees is concerned. The verb "reconcile" is used only in 2 Maccabees 7:33. The youngest of the seven brothers condemned to death says to King Antiochus:

> What are you waiting for? I will not obey the king's command, but I obey the command of the law that was given to our ancestors through Moses. But you, who have contrived all sorts of evil against the Hebrews, will certainly not escape the hands of God. For we are suffering because of our own sins. And if our living Lord is angry for a little while, to rebuke and discipline us, he will again be *reconciled* with his own servants.
>
> (2 Macc. 7:30b–33 NRSV, italic added)

These words testify to trust in God, but in and of themselves they do not suggest a connection between this anticipated reconciliation and the death of the martyr. Van Henten, however, is of the opinion that, based on the total context, the intention here must have been a reconciling *death*.[38] He refers to the end of the speech given by this seventh son: "[I appeal to God] through me and my brothers to bring to an end the wrath of the Almighty that has justly fallen on our whole nation" (2 Macc. 7:38 NRSV). Van Henten sees the words "through me and my brothers" as instrumental: "*by means of* [the death] of me and my brothers." He points out that after their martyrdom, the tide did indeed turn (2 Macc. 8:1ff.). But in this view there is a danger of conflating two things: "the martyr's prayer for reconciliation" and "the issuing of the reconciliation by God." The *prayer* does have effect,[39] mainly because the strength of the faith behind it was evident in the martyr's surrender to death. His dying reinforces the prayer, and God listens to him. This is also apparent from the fact that Judas does not appeal to the *fact* of the martyrdom of the seven brothers but rather asks God "to hearken to the blood that cried out to him" (2 Macc. 8:3 NRSV). This is essentially quite different from the Greek concept of a death that *as such* has the power to exorcise and purify.

Much closer to this Greek idea is 4 Maccabees. It is a sort of funeral oration in which the death of the seven brothers is described in much greater detail. Thus Eleazar prays, "Be merciful to your people, and let our punishment suffice for them. Make my blood their purification, and

---

38. Van Henten, "De joodse martelaren als grondleggers van een nieuwe orde."

39. U. Kellermann, "Zum traditionsgeschichtlichen Problem des stellvertretenden Sühnetodes in 2 Makk 7,37f," *Biblische Notizen* 13 (1980): 63–83; H. J. Klauck, "4. Makkabäerbuch," in *Unterweisung in lehrhafter Form*, Jüdische Schriften aus hellenistisch-römische Zeit 3.6 (Gütersloh: Mohn, 1989), 670.

take my life in exchange for theirs [*antipsychon autōn*]" (4 Macc. 6:28–29 NRSV). Even so, it is not the dying as such that elicits mercy. Eleazar implores God to *endow* his death with the significance of a sacrifice. At the end of the book, the author writes that the martyrs received honor because "on account of them" the enemies could no longer be victorious. The "homeland was purified" of its enemies because the martyrs became "as it were, a ransom [*antipsychon*] for the sin of our nation. And through the blood of those devout ones and their death as an atoning sacrifice, divine Providence preserved Israel that previously had been mistreated" (4 Macc. 17:20–22 NRSV). These phrases betray the strong influence of Greek thinking: the dying man as an atoning sacrifice for others. Yet even here, "divine Providence" remains the decisive factor. The sacrifice *acquires* redemptive power, which is *ascribed* to it by God. We see this in 4 Maccabees 18:3–4, where the martyrs not only are admired for their faithfulness, but God also honors them by granting peace to the people. It is not very likely that someone like Paul took his view of Jesus' death from 4 Maccabees, as Williams claims. He is forced to assign a very early date to 4 Maccabees (A.D. 35–40) and place it in Antioch in order to support his claim of the book's influence on Paul.[40] There is another point to consider. The Book of 4 Maccabees is a literary speech about the power of pious circumspection by which one controls one's appetites and desires (4 Macc. 1:1–8; 18:1–2). Its literary format and style make it difficult to determine the theological weight of various rhetorical turns of phrase and contemporary metaphors. Does the writer really mean that the martyrs were a redemptive sacrifice, or does he use the phrase as a metaphor?

Finally, with regard to the overall comparison with the Jewish martyrs, we can conclude that the differences between Jesus' death and that of the Jewish martyrs in 2 and 4 Maccabees are significant. (1) Jesus dies not only for the good of his people, but he also dispenses his death to his disciples before the fact as something valuable. (2) Jesus' death concerns not only his own faithfulness to God and the welfare of the people of Israel, but it is also aimed at the salvation of his enemies. (3) Jesus was not powerless in the face of powerful enemies—he willingly surrendered himself to them. (4) Jesus' substitution was not desired by his followers; Jesus' disciples ran away, whereas the mother of the seven sons of Eleazar encouraged her sons and even gave them up.

The reactions of Jews and Greeks show that, whatever comparable terminology and parallels may exist, they were most affected by the *unique* aspects of Jesus' death. For Jews it is a stumbling block, for Greeks foolishness. This would not have been true if it had been easy to

40. Williams, *Jesus' Death as Saving Event.*

establish connections between the story of Jesus' death and the deaths of much-admired martyrs or of fellow citizens and friends.

The gospel of Jesus' death did not come into being through a gradual evolution from older myths or theologies. It is the message of a miracle from heaven that suddenly came to earth. It is for this very reason that it is not impossible that reflections of the mystery of Jesus' substitutionary sacrifice can be found in myth and theology. We can think specifically of the meaning of human sacrifice in other cultures (the Hittite culture, for example). Another example is the older literary tradition of the Greeks concerning dying vicariously (especially Euripides) and the devotion (*devotio*) with which people at the beginning of the Christian era wanted to give their lives for a general or an emperor.[41] Such vague analogies,[42] however, can only be compared to Jesus' vicarious death to a very limited extent. When the totality of his life is compared with the totality of the lives of these mythic figures or of sacrificially minded citizens, the differences are many times greater than the similarities. Furthermore, these analogies provide no explanation for the notion of the atoning effects of Jesus' death. On the other hand, these analogies may represent memories of the truth of God, which was hidden for centuries until the Son appeared on earth. The gospel was not born out of myth or contemporary history—but that does not preclude the possibility that myth or history may contain hints of the gospel. The sun is not born of the dawn, yet there is a connection between the early morning light over the mountains and the approaching sunrise.

6.3.4 Jesus—Liberator from Sins

Mary's son bore the name *Jesus* when he walked on earth. In and of itself there was nothing unusual about this name; it was fairly common at that time. In the house of David, however, it was an uncommon name, so Joseph was given special orders in a dream to give this name to Mary's child (Matt. 1:21). She herself had already heard the name from the angel Gabriel when he came to announce the conception and birth (Luke 1:31). So on the day of the circumcision, the child was given "the name the angel had given him before he had been conceived" (Luke 2:21). Because of this unusual prehistory, Jesus' name takes on a hidden, programmatic significance: hidden because the name was not conspicuous in Israel; programmatic because it appears to express the child's lifework. At the very least, the name was a signpost for Joseph and Mary, and thus for Jesus as well. And for the Christians who later heard about the origin of the name, it confirmed in ret-

41. Versnel, "Quid Athenis et Hierosolymis?"
42. For a complete overview, see Hengel, *Atonement*.

rospect the direction of Jesus' life on earth. He himself spoke of sacrificing his life as ransom for many. He distributed the symbols of his body and blood for the benefit of his own during the night in which he was betrayed. He promised to return on the clouds of heaven and to lead all believers into the heavenly kingdom. In retrospect, it appears that the name *Jesus* was fulfilled in all this. With this name, heaven set the pitch for his life's song.

The angel says to Joseph, "He will save his people from their sins" (Matt. 1:21). Apparently he has a people of his own! He will not only bring them forgiveness, but he will also save (*sōsei*) them from the domination of sin. They are not only acquitted, they are completely liberated from the destructive influence of sin. This therefore does not refer only to the atoning sacrifice, but also to the outpouring of the Holy Spirit and the restoration of all creation. He will bring all this about for his people by his coming to earth, by becoming flesh, and by what he will do as a human being. He will be called *Immanuel* (Matt. 1:23)— God is with humankind! By beginning with a humble and unremarkable human name, he will effect the reunification of God and humanity. In the end Jesus will be acknowledged as Immanuel.

The connection of the name *Jesus* with the *salvation of sins* recalls the prophecies of Zechariah, in which the promised liberation from sins is twice symbolically connected with the figure of the high priest Jesus (which is the Greek form of the name Joshua, the son of Jehozadak). The name of this high priest became a clue for the future. And the angel reminds Joseph indirectly of the promises in Zechariah by using the name of the high priest connected with those promises: *Jesus* (Joshua in Hebrew).[43]

In the description of the name, we are not told *in what way* Jesus will save people from sin. The focus is on the fact that *he himself* will accomplish this. His person stands center stage (Jesus, Immanuel). The angel announces not merely events (liberation from sins) but above all a person: the Liberator! This Liberator will devote his life to his goal, but even after his death and resurrection he *himself* will remain the Liberator. He saves through his death, but ultimately he *himself* saves. Jesus is a personal name! And he saves through his death *and* life. His death is necessary as the final result of our obstinacy and as the apex of God's love. Because it is *his* death (the death of the Son of God), this is not the last word. He comes to life again, and after silence has fallen over the battlefield, he comes to raise the dead through his Spirit and in his name. God permits it. God permits Jesus all things, because he is a man who was obedient unto death. His faithfulness to God was tested to the

43. For a much more detailed discussion of the name *Jesus* and its relation to the prophecies of Zechariah, see van Bruggen, *Matteüs*, on Matt. 1:21.

very core of death. The Savior who died and arose is a man who can save us in his name. The gospel contains the forgiveness of sins because it is the Liberator from sins who preaches it.

Soteriology is only possible because of Christology! Anselm, in his *Cur Deus homo?* clearly showed that the key question is not why Jesus had to *die* but why God had to become *man* (which included humiliation unto death). The Anselmian theory of rational necessity and the inevitability of God's incarnation for the sake of divine satisfaction is a particular way of organizing elements of the gospel. But when Anselm's conception is seen as an absolute, it gives rise to the problem that the reasonableness of the incarnation as payment of an immeasurable debt replaces God's *good will*, which is unfathomable, precedes human reason, and surpasses that reason. Anselm wanted to leave no room for the question of whether it might have happened otherwise, but this question cannot be silenced rationally. It only melts away at the higher temperatures of humility and gratitude for what has been given. And Jesus' death was exactly what was needed to bring about that higher temperature of the Spirit in his disciples and later followers.

It is striking that Jesus does not speak of himself as a sacrifice (*thysia*). This is because neither the people nor the disciples offer him as a sacrifice. Furthermore, he is not consumed on the altar. He has not experienced dissolution, and he is resurrected on the third day. He offers himself up to God (Hebrews), and God brings his Son as a sacrifice for the world—but from our perspective he is not a substitute offering. We do not offer him. We stand on the outside and watch what God does. We then accept the total of this humbled life, but this acceptance is always assimilated into the acceptance of the living Savior in heaven.

Those who embrace the incarnation as an act of humiliation and who kneel before the Nazarene and his cross of sacrifice are thereby reconciled with God. This is what God says; apparently we must accept it without first knowing why it happened as it did, or whether it could have happened otherwise. Experiencing the reality (being) comes before reflecting on it! Apparently this is how God wants to make peace with us—in a way that permanently denies us any active role in the making of that peace (God allowed us to go to the bitter end of killing and denying and abandoning the Son) and in a way that makes God permanently visible as ultimate love.

We are reconciled by *Jesus*, the self-effacing Savior—this is how God chooses to put things right. This goes far above and beyond the idea of a formal demand for covering a debt in the Anselmian sense. Besides, we must not forget that Jesus forgave sins even *before* his death.[44] He

---

44. Williams, *Jesus' Death as Saving Event*, 230–31.

appears to be the Forgiver.[45] He is truly able to forgive. But what is needed is the complete amnesty and the *removal* of the sin and the renewal of heaven and earth. By offering himself, Jesus—as a human being—has received the reward of glorification, and with that the Spirit who renews all humanity. And as a human being he has received the place at the right hand of God, from where he looks after the affairs of humankind. Thus he not only heals and forgives, but he liberates as well—permanently!

45. Chong-Hyon Sung, *Vergebung der Sünden: Jesu Praxis der Sündenvergebung nach den Synoptikern und ihre Voraussetzungen im Alten Testament und frühen Judentum*, WUNT 2/57 (Tübingen: Mohr, 1993).

7

A New Phase for the People of God

Jesus preached and performed many miracles during his ministry in Israel, presenting himself as the powerful Son of God, the Anointed One. But this presentation came with strings attached: he laid a claim on the people. The rest of his ministry shows that this was done deliberately. He clearly did not want to be a loner, but a leader. He was looking not for an audience but for a following.

For this reason, a survey of Jesus' life and teaching cannot be confined to a description of his person and the course of his life. Attention should be given also to the manner in which he wanted to form a party or a community. The Christian community is not a group of people who came together later to honor the memory of the person of Jesus. He himself laid the foundation for this community during his life on earth. Jesus is not the lonely victim of his contemporaries, but the new organizer of Israel who offered up his life for his people.

In this chapter we describe a few aspects of this that are clearly visible. First, Jesus expressly addressed himself to *all* of Israel, sinners included. Second, he presented himself as the people's new focal point, the new center. And third, he saw this newly organized Israel as the basis for bringing in many baptized Gentiles.

7.1 All Israel

The prophet John the Baptist addressed himself emphatically to *all* of Israel: all were called to let themselves be baptized by him (see sec. 2.2.3). By this John let it be known that when God came, he wanted *the whole nation* to be ready, repentant, and expectant.

Jesus' approach is the same. He is the one who comes after John to perform divine works throughout Israel, and he has come for everyone. He addresses himself to the entire people.

7.1.1 All Synagogues

That Jesus has come searching for the entire nation of Israel is apparent from his preaching in all the synagogues. This is where he launches his work. He addresses the community of God in the places where they gather officially, on every Sabbath, throughout the country.

The Evangelists point out again and again that Jesus' traveling from synagogue to synagogue served as it were as the string on which his words and miracles were threaded, like beads. Everything that Jesus does is thus determined by that orientation toward the people.

Along with this goes the fact that whenever he visited Jerusalem— from the beginning (John 2:13–25) to the end (Luke 21:37–38)—he spoke openly in the temple court. There he addressed all of gathered Israel. There he also reached many Jews from the Diaspora.

Matthew writes that Jesus journeyed "throughout Galilee, teaching in their synagogues, preaching the Good News of the kingdom, and healing every disease and sickness among the people" (Matt. 4:23; compare Mark 1:39 and Luke 4:15, 44). Later Matthew repeats this statement to express the idea that this is a continuing approach, and he provides more detail: Jesus visited not only the synagogues in the cities, but also those in the villages (Matt. 9:35). Many healings thus took place in a synagogue (Mark 1:21; Matt. 12:9; Luke 13:10, etc.). Jesus ministered openly and publicly, and he later appeals to this fact when, standing before the former high priest, Annas, he says, "I have spoken openly to the world. I always taught in synagogues or at the temple, where all the Jews come together. I said nothing in secret" (John 18:20).

We know from the Gospels that Jesus also met frequently with the crowds in the open field. But this must not lead us to see Jesus primarily as a type of camp-meeting preacher or as someone who tried to gain influence over all or some of the people by going outside the normal channels. Ministering out in the fields or along the Sea of Galilee was not his first choice. He began his ministry on the Sabbath and in the synagogues, but he attracted such crowds that on more than one occasion he was forced to perform his healings in the marketplace (Mark 6:53– 56) or outside the city (Mark 1:45). The crowds ran after him and gave him no rest (Matt. 13:2). These are the moments when his compassion shows: he is prepared to keep on talking to the people and to heal their diseases (Matt. 9:36; 14:13–14; Mark 3:7–10). But this work "outside the gates" must be seen as an *extension* of his speaking to Israel in the synagogues. (For the moments in which Jesus withdraws with the crowds, see sec. 7.2.2).

7.1.2 All People

Israel was a divided nation in more ways than one. There were social lines of demarcation between the poor and the rich, but there were also religious differences between the law-abiding Pharisees on the one hand, and prostitutes, tax collectors, and sinners on the other. It is striking that throughout his ministry Jesus never identified himself with any one of these social strata or religious groups. He spoke with and welcomed all people, regardless of their social standing or religious affiliation. This openness toward everyone sometimes made him suspect in the eyes of those who belonged to a specific group or stratum, who expected him to distance himself from certain other persons or groups; when he did not keep those other persons or groups at arm's length, they were quick to assume that he had chosen the other side. Upon careful consideration, however, it becomes apparent that Jesus came for all people *without exception*, and this means the whole of the (divided) nation.

In the twentieth century, Jesus has more than once been characterized as siding with the poor and oppressed.[1] Indeed, the amount of attention that he pays to the poor and needy is quite striking. He fulfills the prophecy, "The blind receive sight, the lame walk, those who have leprosy are cured, the deaf hear, the dead are raised, and the good news is preached to the poor" (Matt. 11:4–5). Unlike so many healers, Jesus performs healings completely free of charge. He also notices the widow who, with her few coins, puts everything she owns into the temple treasury, while the rich give relatively little (Mark 12:41–44). When widows and orphans are the victims of the Pharisees and the teachers of the law, Jesus does not withhold comment (Mark 12:38–40). And he has compassion on the widow of Nain and raises her only son from the dead (Luke 7:12–15).

Yet he does not appear to be an opponent of the wealthy. He warns them that it is extremely difficult for wealthy people to enter the kingdom of heaven, but at the same time he points out that the impossible is possible with God; even for the wealthy there is room (Matt. 19:23–26)! We read that Jesus loved the rich young man (Mark 10:21), and he took up lodgings in the home of the wealthy tax collector Zacchaeus (Luke 19:2, 5). His burial was arranged by a wealthy follower, Joseph of Arimathea (Matt. 27:57). Jesus' concern for the poor is not based on a dislike of the wealthy. He does not side with any particular class, but he demonstrates God's precepts and mercy to everyone, rich and poor. Because the rich are more apt to bypass the kingdom of heaven and to abuse their position, they receive relatively more admonitions. And because the poor, in their dependence, are sometimes quicker to seek shelter with Jesus, we notice how he accepts them and encourages them. That Jesus focuses his attention on the rich as well as on the poor only emphasizes the reality of Jesus' attention for *everyone*.

1. C. H. Lindijer, *De armen en de rijken bij Lucas* (The Hague: Boekencentrum, 1981).

Jesus is also frequently regarded as having a one-sided preference for sinners, tax collectors, and sinful women. The Pharisees often stumbled over the fact that he did not simply ignore these people. And this reaction later evoked a counter-reaction in which Jesus is actually admired for his openness toward the less accepted members of society.[2]

In the context of Israelite society, it was decidedly striking that a teacher like Jesus was often a guest at the dinners held by tax collectors and that some of his admirers were prostitutes. Did this not indicate a measure of contempt for the established religious order of the teachers of the law and the Pharisees?

Certainly not. When Jesus begins to preach and perform miracles, he makes no distinctions. He does not reject the Pharisees. In his foundational sermon on the kingdom of heaven, we hear no criticism of this party. On the contrary, Jesus even dines with Pharisees (Luke 7:36; 11:37; 14:1), and until the end he praises their scrupulousness in keeping the law and the good commandments they hold before the people (Matt. 23:2–3a). There is no anti-Pharisaic sentiment in his teaching. Only later, when the teachers of the law and the Pharisees become hostile toward Jesus and try to draw the people away from him, does the tension increase. Then come the grave and harsh words about their behavior. This is not because they are *Pharisees*, but because as Pharisees they take a stand *against Jesus*. It is significant that on Good Friday his body is laid in the grave by two followers, one a wealthy man, the other a Pharisee (Nicodemus, John 3:1; 19:39). Jesus does not take sides against the Pharisees, but many of them side against him! His contact with the sinners can thus certainly not be explained on the basis of a reactionary preference for people who were less acceptable in the eyes of the Pharisees.

It would also be one-sided to fail to take into account that in Jesus' contact with sinners and tax collectors, he aggressively calls them to repentance. He does not simply spend his time with sinners, prostitutes, and tax collectors. That was the slander circulated by his opponents: "He is a friend of tax collectors and sinners" (Matt. 11:19; compare Luke 15:2). The reality is, however, that Jesus associates with those tax collectors and sinners who believe in the words of repentance preached by John the Baptist (Matt. 21:32) and with those who now let themselves be called to be his followers. The requirement for following Jesus is to sin no more and to rejoice in the mercy of God.

The banquet in the home of Matthew is held after Matthew, a tax collector, is called by Jesus and agrees to follow him (Matt. 9:9). Referring to the tax collectors and sinners who are also among the guests, Jesus

---

2. For a broader discussion of the place of tax collectors and sinners in Israel, see above, secs. 1.2.4 ("Tax Collectors") and 1.2.2 ("Sinners").

says that they are the "sick" who need a doctor (Matt. 9:12). He has compassion on them because he has come to call sinners to repentance (Matt. 9:13). The tax collectors and sinners in Jesus' company, who so annoy the Pharisees and teachers of the law, have come "to hear him" (Luke 15:1). And in the parable that follows, Jesus clearly describes the joy in heaven over "one sinner who repents" (Luke 15:7, 10). The repentant sinful woman who anoints Jesus' feet is granted forgiveness of sins because of the great love she shows (Luke 7:44–50), and to the adulterous woman he says, "Go now and leave your life of sin" (John 8:11). When Zacchaeus the tax collector repents and promises to generously repay anyone whom he has cheated, Jesus says, "Today salvation has come to this house" (Luke 19:9). Before Zacchaeus's repentance, Jesus regarded him not as a "friend" but as someone who was "lost" (Luke 19:10). Thus in the parable of the Pharisee and the tax collector, Jesus describes the tax collector as being justified by God because he humbled himself, beat his breast, and confessed his sins (Luke 18:13–14).

The attention Jesus pays to tax collectors and sinners does not mean that he has a one-sided preference in his contacts with Israel. His interest in and concern for them underscore his desire to save *everyone* in Israel, no sinner excepted. They are all Abraham's sons and daughters (Luke 13:16; 19:9). Some of the people of Israel wrongfully use their descent from Abraham to justify their self-confidence before God (Luke 3:8; 16:24–30; John 8:33, 39). John the Baptist had already pointed this out with great insistence: "And do not think you can say to yourselves, 'We have Abraham as our father'" (Matt. 3:9). The great prophet of repentance called *all* of Israel (Pharisees and teachers of the law included) to humble themselves before the coming Lord. Many tax collectors and sinners were among the baptized, but the teachers of the law and the Pharisees refused baptism (Luke 7:29–30; Matt. 3:7–10; compare 21:24–26, 32; John 1:19, 24). They regarded themselves as "healthy." It is against this background that we must read Jesus' words about coming for the sick and not for the healthy (Matt. 9:12), and about calling the sinners and not the righteous (Matt. 9:13; compare Luke 15:7). These statements might suggest that he has come for a special *portion* of Israel. But Jesus is being mildly ironic. The teachers of the law and the Pharisees *think* that they are healthy and righteous (Luke 18:9; 20:20). Apparently they have no need of repentance and forgiveness. Can they then blame Jesus for deciding to deal with people who *do* consider themselves "sick" and "unrighteous"? This, after all, is why he came to earth. Jesus does not use these words to distance himself from the teachers of the law and the Pharisees; rather, these words are part of his effort to get through to them as well. It is crystal clear that when he speaks in the synagogues he has a message for the *entire* people, and that he also has the leaders in mind. They can remain detached as "healthy people who have no need of a doctor," but it would be far better for them to take a seat in the doctor's waiting room and go in for treatment (Matt. 21:32). In this regard the sinners and tax collectors are an example to them! Jesus' association with sinners who turn to him throws light on his intentions for all of Israel. He comes in the midst of this people to prepare a table of the new covenant, where the wine is a symbol of his blood, "poured out *for many* for the forgiveness of sins" (Matt. 26:28).

7.1.3 Everywhere

During his travels through Israel, Jesus visited many cities and villages. Unlike John the Baptist, who had people come to him in the desert, Jesus traveled to them, bringing the gospel to them wherever they lived. This took time and energy. Palestine is not a big country, but every mile had to be traveled on foot. Then there were interruptions, such as journeys to Jerusalem, surging crowds who came to him with their sick, and brief retreats in Capernaum or on the mountain. It would have taken a number of years to visit all the Jewish cities and villages in Palestine in this way. But Jesus' time was limited: the hour of his death had been appointed.

Yet he was not satisfied with working in only part of Israel. When the crowds came to him with their sick, taking up much time, Jesus decided to intensify his campaign by enlisting his twelve leading disciples. He sent them out two by two, and he gave them access to the power that he himself possessed to heal illness and drive out demons (Matt. 9:35–10:10). In this way, the majesty of God's kingdom was spread in Jesus' name throughout all the cities and villages of Israel (Matt. 10:11, 23). The light penetrated the most remote corners of Palestine.

The sending out of the Seventy (or Seventy-two; Luke 10:1–20) should also be mentioned here. In this case, however, these disciples were to head for the areas where Jesus himself was planning to go on his way to Jerusalem to die and be resurrected (Luke 10:1). Their participation served to focus more attention on this last journey. It became impossible for Jesus to travel unnoticed to the temple city to accomplish his decisive act in Israel.

The mission of the Twelve had to do with extending the gospel throughout *all* of Israel, even in places that Jesus did not visit personally. The mission of the Seventy(-two) is different: they are to be followed by Jesus himself.[3]

---

3. For a more detailed discussion of the Seventy(-two) and the Twelve, see J. van Bruggen, *Ambten in de apostolische kerk: Een exegetisch mozaïek*, 2d ed. (Kampen: Kok, 1987).

7.1.4 A Preference for Israel

This orientation toward *all* of Israel is really an orientation toward *Israel*. We see this in the way Jesus defines the boundaries of his work. Although there are many who come to him from neighboring countries (Matt. 4:24), Jesus always makes it clear in his association with non-Israelites that he has come for the house of Israel. He heals the son of a gentile woman in the region of Tyre and Sidon because of her persistence and faith, but his first words are, "I was sent only to the lost sheep of Israel" (Matt. 15:24). In Samaria Jesus does not let the interest of many go unanswered, but first he clearly tells them, "You Samaritans worship what you do not know; we worship what we do know, for salvation is from the Jews" (John 4:22). And the twelve apostles are emphatically instructed, "Do not go among the Gentiles or enter any town of the Samaritans. Go rather to the lost sheep of Israel" (Matt. 10:5–6). This focus on Israel reaches a highly emotional pitch with Jesus' repeated cry, "O Jerusalem, Jerusalem, you who kill the prophets and stone those sent to you, how often I have longed to gather your children together, as a hen gathers her chicks under her wings, but you were not willing!" (Luke 13:34–35; Matt. 23:37).

At the same time, Jesus also had positive things to say about the faith of non-Israelites, and he alluded more than once to a future influx of believers from all nations. Does this mean that there are two trajectories in his ministry, the particular and the universal? Or should we conclude, as some do, that these two lines of thought can be reduced to the divergent perspectives of the editors/Evangelists? There is actually very little to support the existence of this dilemma.

Jesus' work is unambiguously oriented toward all of Israel. Everything he does for non-Israelites falls within the parameters of Israel's history as a whole. The Old Testament expresses openness to anyone from any other nation who wants to recognize and serve the God of Israel. And the Jews themselves are the ones who recommend to Jesus the Roman centurion in Capernaum: "This man deserves to have you do this, because he loves our nation and has built our synagogue" (Luke 7:4–5). So the leaders' criticism of Jesus does not include the accusation that he ministers to the Gentiles at the expense of the people of Israel. Some people do call him a Samaritan (John 8:48), but by this they mean that he, an Israelite, seems to be just as careless with Jewish tradition as the Samaritans. Jesus heals people from outside Israel only when they accept him as the prophet of Israel (Matt. 15:26–28). And in the Decapolis Jesus clearly acts like someone from the Israelite side of the Sea of Galilee—he permits the demons to enter the *unclean* pigs and to destroy them (Mark 5:11–13).

Sometimes Jesus talks about the future influx of the nations: "Many will come from the east and the west, and will take their places at the feast with Abraham, Isaac and Jacob in the kingdom of heaven" (Matt. 8:11). Such a coming of the nations into Israel had already been prophesied by Isaiah, however, and had earned a place in the Jewish people's future expectations. When Jesus says that "the gospel must first be preached to all nations" (Mark 13:10), this remark is not out of place in the context of a Judaism that had many proselytes—people who had come from other nations and had let themselves be circumcised. The Jews even made an effort to spread propaganda to other nations in support of faith in the God of Israel (Matt. 23:15; compare Acts 19:13–17; Rom. 2:17–20).

What is striking is that Jesus regards himself as the gateway to the nation, the gateway of Israel. He himself is the light of the *world* (John 8:12). The Samaritans discover that *he* is the savior of the *world* (John 4:42). The influx from the nations that was foretold by the prophets will take place because of the person of Jesus. As Simeon prophesied, God has sent *him* as "salvation . . . for all people" (Luke 2:30–31). It is faith in Jesus that is decisive. When the Greeks come to see Jesus, just before his death, he makes a connection between their coming and his approaching glorification (John 12:20–36).

The obverse of this is that Israel, insofar as it does not believe in him, voluntarily goes to its destruction. Jesus reproaches them: "You were not willing" (Matt. 11:16–24; 23:37b). His appearance before the *whole* nation now leads to a crucial division within Israel (Matt. 10:11–15; 11:25–30; 13:18–23). Ultimately, the kingdom will be taken away from the unbelieving leaders and given to a nation that will produce fruit; this refers to two "nations" now existing *within* Israel.[4] While those who repudiate Jesus, both people and leaders, stumble over the stone that was rejected by the temple builders, there is another *nation* remaining: the nation that consists of all believers from Israel who acknowledge the Messiah and follow him.

Jesus maintained this perspective on Israel throughout his life on earth. This demarcation of his territory shows that later, when the nations come flocking toward him, he will not stand *next to* Israel but *in the midst of* Israel, and that he, together with the believing descendants of Abraham, becomes the center around which the nations and Israel will be unified.

---

4. See J. van Bruggen, *Matteüs: Het evangelie voor Israël*, 2d ed., Commentaar op het Nieuwe Testament, 3d series (Kampen: Kok, 1994), on Matt. 21:43.

7.2 Jesus the Center

While Jesus addresses *all* of Israel, he presents himself as the center of the nation and the focus for the future. Israel saw itself as "a guide for the blind, a light for those who are in the dark" (Rom. 2:19), but Jesus concentrates this function in himself when he calls *himself* "the light of the world" (John 8:12). His entire ministry supports this view of his significance for Israel and the nations: (1) he is Israel's teacher; (2) he increasingly becomes a leader; (3) he acts as lawgiver; (4) he ends up traveling like a King surrounded by his own council of twelve; and (5) he is the good Shepherd for Israel and the nations.

7.2.1 Teacher of Baptized "Pupils"

Unquestionably Jesus was a teacher. He had his own "school," with a group of "pupils" or "students." The Greek word *mathētēs* is usually translated *disciple* and means "pupil" or "student." This group of people recognize Jesus as teacher and accept his teaching concerning the kingdom of heaven and his own mission. They confess that he is "the Christ, the Son of the living God" (John 6:60–71; Matt. 16:16), and they receive further instruction in the necessity of his suffering, death, and resurrection (Matt. 16:21–23).

How did one become a "disciple"? Not every Israelite who showed interest or who came for healing was immediately called a disciple. On the other hand, there were disciples right from the beginning, although we read nothing about their recruitment. In the stories of the Evangelists, the presence of "disciples" is simply a fact, the origin and background of which are no longer known.

Only in the Gospel of John, which covers this earlier period in greater detail, do we encounter a brief passage about the process of becoming a disciple. In John 4:1 we read that "Jesus was gaining and baptizing more disciples than John." This passage concerns the period between Jesus' baptism and the arrest of the Baptist and the beginning of Jesus' travels in Galilee that followed. During this time John the Baptist continued to preach and baptize, but Jesus' disciples began baptizing as well. They do this expressly as disciples *of Jesus*. People see this as a new baptismal movement associated exclusively with Jesus. So for the sake of clarity, John the Evangelist has to mention that this baptism was not administered by Jesus himself, but by his disciples (John 4:2). This does not alter the fact, however, that a second baptismal center had thus been formed in addition to, and clearly distinct from, that of John the Baptist (John 3:22–24). It was not the same baptism, administered at two locations; it even looks as if there is a kind of competition between the two baptisms. The disciples of the Baptist went to him and reported, "Rabbi, the man who was with you on the other side of the Jordan and about whom you testified—he's baptizing now, too, and everyone is going to him." And John responded with the words, "He must become greater; I must become less" (John 3:30). The baptism administered by Jesus and his disciples is not a carbon copy of John's. It is a new baptism, with its own essence (see also sec. *c* of the excursus at the end of this chapter). One could become a disciple of John and be baptized by him, but one could become a disciple of Jesus as well and be baptized *there* (John 4:1).

John's disciples ask their question in response to a dispute with a Jew "about *purification*" (John 3:25b KJV). The noun *katharismou* lacks the definite article, making it less likely that the passage concerns *Jewish ceremonial purification in general* (as in 2:6).[5] The topic of the discussion is determined by the participants, so it must have had to do with the baptism of John.[6] But it is also determined by the passage that follows, which concerns the baptism of Jesus. Otherwise the disciples of John would not have gone to their master in response to this disagreement and asked the question about *Jesus'* baptism.[7] So it is plausible that the disciples of John were drawn into a discussion with a Jew about *purification* ("How is Israel to be purified in anticipation of the one who is to come?"). John's disciples respond by referring to the baptism of their master (the baptism of repentance), but the Jew must have challenged their monopoly on baptism by mentioning the baptism through which one became a disciple of Jesus, the man who performed the great miracle in Cana and who attracted so much attention in the temple by performing a sign of purification without animal sacrifices (John 2:13–22). Is Jesus really the new Purifier (the alternative to the temple with its sacrifices)? If the argument about purification is an echo of the incident in the temple, and if John's disciples are now having to deal with the fact that more attention is paid to Jesus' baptism than to their master's, this conversation understandably leads them to ask what *right* Jesus has to do what he is doing.

John's answer confirms that the discussion is about this right. The great prophet of repentance stands by his own testimony, of which his disciples now remind him. They also have to learn to take it seriously

---

5. As rendered in the NIV ("over ceremonial cleansing") and argued by D. A. Carson (*The Gospel according to John,* Pillar New Testament Commentary [Grand Rapids: Eerdmans; Leicester: Inter-Varsity, 1991]); L. Morris (*The Gospel according to John,* New International Commentary [Grand Rapids: Eerdmans; London: Marshall, Morgan & Scott, 1972]); C. K. Barrett (*The Gospel according to St. John: An Introduction with Commentary and Notes on the Greek Text,* 2d ed. [London: S.P.C.K., 1956]); and others.

6. Compare G. R. Beasley-Murray, *John,* Word Biblical Commentary (Waco: Word, 1987).

7. Compare R. Bultmann, *The Gospel of John: A Commentary,* trans. G. R. Beasley-Murray (Oxford: Blackwell, 1971), 122–23, 125: "which in this context can only refer to the relationship between the baptism of Jesus and that of John."

and to accept its consequences—and with joy. John first says that a man may not presume on what has not been given him from heaven (John 3:27). This applies in two directions. John himself may not pretend to be greater than he is, and Jesus' own claim may not be dismissed as "presumptuous." This is why John has emphatically refused to be recognized as the Messiah and has said that he has only been sent to precede the Messiah (3:28). He is not the "owner" of Israel. The one who is to come after him has the true claim to "the bride" and is thus the bridegroom. John characterizes himself as the friend of the bridegroom who stands nearby and listens to him. He rejoices over the voice of the bridegroom (3:29). This bridegroom must become greater and John must become less (3:30). With these statements the Baptist makes it clear to his disciples that it is *good* if Jesus is becoming better known and if people are now going directly to this new Baptizer for purification and to become his disciple.

In 3:31–36, John elaborates further on his statement about Jesus. Jesus comes from above and is above all, but John comes from the earth and speaks as one from the earth. Jesus speaks about what he has heard and seen. Many do not accept his testimony, but when they do, they "certify" through their own faithful acceptance that God is truly present in Jesus. The verb "certify" (*esphragisen*, John 3:33) may refer to the baptismal confession. One was baptized to demonstrate belief in the one who has come, thus certifying through faith the truth of the preaching of the one who has come, he who has the Spirit of God—not with measure but in fullness. The full Spirit of God lives in him. He is the dwelling-place of God in Israel. He is more than the temple. Anyone who believes in the Son has eternal life, that is, all who (as was said in 3:26) come to Jesus and let themselves be baptized into him by his disciples.

This is how John (the forerunner who administers the baptism of repentance) legitimates the One who has come and his baptism, by which people become followers of Jesus and acknowledge him as the One sent by the all-powerful Father.

Here a tip of the veil is lifted. From the very beginning, and at first still more or less in the shadow of the imposing prophet John the Baptist, Jesus acted independently, and those who recognized him as Teacher were baptized. It is quite possible that a number of people were first baptized by John and later turned to Jesus, confessed him, and were also baptized by him (through his disciples). In any case, the disciples of Jesus were *baptized* with a *new* baptism (France even speaks of "Jesus the Baptist").[8]

---

8. R. T. France, "Jesus the Baptist?" in *Jesus of Nazareth, Lord and Christ: Essays on the Historical Jesus and New Testament Christology*, ed. J. B. Green and M. Turner (Grand Rapids: Eerdmans, 1994), 94–111.

Because Jesus clearly acted as the one about whom John had preached, acceptance of his teaching and his baptism also meant recognition of him as the Savior who had come, the promised Son of God from heaven (compare John 3:27–36). Thus from the very beginning, Jesus transmutes John's testimony about him into a presentation uniquely his own. And people who now, on the basis of John's advance announcement, accepted him as the Lord who has come to his people, also receive baptism into him. Through that baptism they become bound to him and are accepted as his disciples. That is why Jesus probably did not administer the baptism himself. John was a *witness*. He baptized people in anticipation of the one who was to come. Jesus himself *is* that One. He is the *content* of the baptismal confession, and perhaps for this reason Jesus' baptism was administered by his servants and not by Jesus himself. On the other hand, it is understandable that people considered themselves as having been baptized by Jesus because (unlike John's baptism) the dominating element was not the baptism by a specific person, but their faith in the Person to whom they now were bound through baptism.

When the curtain rises in the first three Gospels (after the arrest of the Baptist and at the time of Jesus' ministry in Galilee), there already *is* a circle of disciples. Nothing more is said about its formation. The remarks in the Fourth Gospel, however, clearly tell us that there was an important preliminary phase that led to its formation. The disciple *started out* with the confession of Jesus as the one come from heaven, the Christ, the Son of God. This was the baptismal confession. In the first three Gospels there is the danger of an optical illusion. When we hear the confession at Caesarea Philippi or at the Sea of Galilee, it seems as if this is the first time this confession is uttered. But these are in fact repetitions and reaffirmations made in the face of opposition and outward appearances. Some of the disciples appear not to let themselves be dissuaded from the testimony of the Baptist and from the confession by which they themselves became disciples.[9]

In conclusion we can state two things: (1) Jesus' teaching concerned himself and his work. The disciple bound himself to the person and authority of Jesus as the One come from God. (2) The increasing number of believers who were baptized during the initial phase of his ministry, when he stepped forward in the light of the Baptist's active witness, were baptized by Jesus' first disciples on the basis of this faith. These two conclusions make it clear that from the very beginning Jesus acted

---

9. See van Bruggen, *Matteüs*, on Matt. 16:13–16; P. H. R. van Houwelingen, *Johannes: Het evangelie van het Woord*, Commentaar op het Nieuwe Testament, 3d series (Kampen: Kok, 1997), on John 6:66–71.

as the center around whom a community of believers would form, a community characterized by faith and baptism.

This phase of "recruiting disciples *and baptizing*" was temporarily interrupted when Jesus withdrew to Galilee. Baptism was apparently not renewed until the day of Pentecost. To those accustomed to the later, regular administration of baptism, this seems strange. Yet we see something comparable in the Exodus. In Egypt the children were circumcised, but during the entire desert journey apparently no circumcision was performed, and the custom was not resumed until the Israelites entered Canaan (Exod. 4:24–26; Josh. 5:2–9). We cannot go beyond conjecture here, but perhaps the active recruitment of disciples (combined with baptism) was halted by Jesus at a propitious time because he was withdrawing into a period of voluntary humiliation and did not want to challenge the Jewish leaders. The "Pharisees heard that Jesus was gaining and baptizing more disciples than John," and it was *then* that he left Judea and went to Galilee (John 4:1, 3). The discontinuation of *baptismal* activity for the time being then would relate to the phases of Jesus' ministry during his humiliation. After his glorification, a kind of make-up baptism, so to speak, takes place on the day of Pentecost when God brings about three thousand Israelites to the baptism of Jesus in a single day (Acts 2:41).

7.2.2 Leader of Crowds That Follow

Jesus wants to have significance for all of Israel. We see this in his positive attitude toward the multitudes who come from all parts of the country to hear him and to have him heal their sick (Matt. 4:24–25). Moved by compassion, he always has time for them (Matt. 9:36; Mark 8:1–3). Even when he and his disciples are in need of rest and the crowds are following him, he does not send them away but has compassion on them and feeds them—in a very surprising way (Matt. 14:13–21). So it is hardly strange that almost the whole nation comes crowding around him during his entrance into Jerusalem. The multitudes who traveled with him and the crowds who now come out of the city to greet him meet each other, and their united "Hosanna" resounds across the temple court (John 12:12–18; Matt. 21:8–11, 14–16). The Pharisees draw a conclusion that is particularly painful for them: "See, this is getting us nowhere. Look how the whole world has gone after him!" (John 12:19).

This onrush of people might suggest that Jesus has set himself up as an agitator and as a leader of the people. But the opposite is true. He went to the people in the synagogues, but the crowds had to come to him on their own initiative in the open fields and in the temple court.

And sometimes they had to search long and hard, for Jesus seemed to withdraw from the crowds with regularity rather than waiting for them to come. By getting up at night and going to some lonely place to pray, Jesus causes Simon to exclaim somewhat irritably, "Everyone is looking for you!" But Jesus' reaction is evasive: "Let us go somewhere else—to the nearby villages—so I can preach there also. That is why I have come" (Mark 1:35–38).

Sometimes it is as if Jesus is playing a game of hide-and-seek with the crowds. Again and again he escapes them and allows himself to be found only with some effort (Mark 2:13; 3:7; 4:35–36; 6:31–34, 45–46, 54–56). Sometimes he withdraws across the border (Mark 7:24, 31; 8:27). Another time he insists on not letting people know what route he will take (Mark 9:30; John 7:10). More than once we read that the crowds *searched* for him in Jerusalem (John 7:11; 11:56–57). Jesus also *hides* from the crowds (John 8:59; 11:54). This attitude surprises his own brothers. They tell him, "You ought to leave here and go to Judea, so that your disciples may see the miracles you do. No one who wants to become a public figure acts in secret. Since you are doing these things, show yourself to the world" (John 7:3–4).

We must not conclude, however, that Jesus repeatedly withdrew because he did not really want to act as leader of the pressing crowds. His decision to heal *all* who were brought to him clearly shows that he saw himself as a savior of the *people*. Furthermore, he consciously assumes the position of a *leader* of the people. Again and again he teaches the people, clearly indicating that he is more than a healer. His teaching goes hand in hand with his healing (Matt. 13:1–23; John 6:26–29). At times Jesus emphatically acts as *leader* of the multitudes.

This happened very much programmatically when he went "up on a mountainside" with the gathered crowd (Matt. 5:1).[10] On this particular occasion, he goes to a place of his own choosing (lit. *"the* mountain") rather than to Jerusalem, and there shares his teaching and his commandments with the crowds. This exodus to the mountainside is very significant. It takes place in response to Jesus seeing the crowds: "When he *saw* the crowds, he went up on a mountainside." On the same day on which he preaches the Sermon on the Mount, Jesus also appoints the Twelve, and he presents himself with the Twelve to the crowds. We have here a glimpse of a new orientation: from going up to the temple to gathering around the person of Jesus.

Later something comparable occurs on this mountain. Around the time of the Passover, Jesus serves a meal here—a meal that was reminiscent of the manna in the wilderness. The new orientation shifts the

---

10. See van Bruggen, *Matteüs*, on Matt. 5.

attention from the manna of the fathers to the food of eternal life that Jesus brings and *is* (John 6:1–6, 32–35, 49–51).

Next we see Jesus (who had kept himself hidden while traveling to the city for the Feast of Tabernacles) finally appear in the temple court on the last day of the feast, crying out to the celebrating crowds, "If anyone is thirsty, let him come to me and drink. Whoever believes in me, . . . streams of living water will flow from within him" (John 7:37–38). The orientation shifts from the high priest, who pours water from the Siloam spring at the altar, to Jesus, in whom is the source of the abundance of God.

How do we explain that on the one hand Jesus often evades the crowds, while on the other hand he presents himself very emphatically as their leader? Apparently there is one thing he does not want: to be king. When he senses the risk that the crowds will take him by force and make him king, he withdraws into the mountains in solitude (John 6:15). He remains a Leader without a crown. This must have been puzzling for the crowds, just as it was strange for Jesus to choose an unpretentious donkey's foal for his great entrance into Jerusalem. Nevertheless, the people could have known what this all meant. The announcements of his suffering are directed at the disciples, but they are nevertheless delivered publicly. Only the "third announcement," in which he announced his execution by the Romans (the *cross*), was confidential (Matt. 20:17–19). The leaders are fully aware of Jesus' instruction concerning his Passion, such as the prediction of a resurrection on the third day (Matt. 27:63). Jesus also said "to them all," "If anyone would come after me, he must deny himself and take up his cross daily and follow me. For whoever wants to save his life will lose it" (Luke 9:23–24; also see 14:25–27). The idea of a king without a crown, a suffering leader, had become public knowledge. The soldiers even adopted it as the theme for a parody (the crown of thorns, etc.).[11]

In conclusion, it appears that Jesus tried to convey two messages to the crowds: (1) He is their *ultimate healer and authoritative leader*. This is why he always demands faith from those who want to be healed, and obedience to his teaching. Those who come to him must learn to be "followers." (2) He travels a path that *does not lead directly to a throne and crown*. That is why he is self-effacing and even withdrawing, and he asks the crowds to follow him along this path.

After Jesus' death and resurrection—and until he takes the throne at the time of his ascension—there comes an end to this phase. Yet for his representatives, the apostles, that which applied to Jesus during his

11. See J. van Bruggen, *Marcus: Het evangelie volgens Petrus*, 2d ed., Commentaar op het Nieuwe Testament, 3d series (Kampen: Kok, 1992), on Mark 15:16–28.

humble years on earth also applies to them. Although the gospel of Jesus is now the message of the Glorified One, for people on earth it remains a call not to look down on the suffering apostles of this king but to follow them in their willingness to suffer for a brief period of time.[12]

7.2.3 Israel's Lawgiver

In his role as leader of the crowds, Jesus acts with authority. The tone he uses in addressing them suggests that he has come to them as God himself. Typical of the way he speaks are such phrases as "I tell you," "Amen, amen, I tell you," "I am come," and "More than . . . is here!"[13]

But Jesus' authority is not limited to his tone. The *content* of what he says also involves a tremendous claim. He places himself beside and above Moses as the new and better Lawgiver. To Israel, this was very shocking. Who is this man who dares to replace Moses? Moses was God's personal servant. Only God himself could change or abolish the laws of this prophet. So when Jesus sets the law aside on several points, he is also making it clear that he is greater than Moses and that he personally represents God's authority—he does not appeal to new revelations but he gives new laws on his *own* authority. He does not take the place of Moses as God's servant, but he places himself next to Yahweh and turns to Israel with the authority of a divine lawgiver. The leaders realize this only too well: "We know that God spoke to Moses, but as for this fellow, we don't even know where he comes from" (John 9:29).

A striking example is Jesus' controversial teaching about divorce. It was known that he condemned divorce on any grounds other than adultery (Matt. 5:31–32; Luke 16:18). But this differed from Moses, who allowed divorce (Matt. 19:7). The Pharisees therefore use this as a trap to catch him as someone who places himself above Moses (Matt. 19:3).

Another example is Jesus' teaching about the meaning of clean and unclean food. He says that the dietary laws are no longer valid: "Nothing outside a man can make him 'unclean' by going into him" (Mark 7:15). He explains to his disciples that food enters the stomach and not the heart (Mark 7:18–19a). And for his non-Jewish readers, Mark then explains the tremendous significance of this statement: "In saying this, Jesus declared all foods 'clean'" (Mark 7:19b). Against this background we can also understand why Jesus had no objection to eating with tax collectors, even though he could never be sure that their food had been prepared in accordance with the stringent dietary laws.

Jesus' attitude regarding the temple (which was in principle the tabernacle of Moses) is also shocking. Even at the beginning of his ministry

---

12. See van Bruggen, *Matteüs*, on Matt. 25:31–46.
13. For the implications of these phrases, see the discussion in sec. 4.1.

he dared to say, "Destroy this temple, and I will raise it again in three days" (John 2:19). When his work on earth had come to an end, some people still remembered this statement, and the false witnesses repeated it in distorted form: "*I* will destroy this . . . temple" (Mark 14:58). But not long after making his controversial statement about the temple, Jesus explained to the Samaritan woman that he had not come to destroy the temple but to renew its worship: "A time is coming when you will worship the Father neither on this mountain nor in Jerusalem . . . but the true worshipers will worship the Father in spirit and truth" (John 4:21–26).

These are not simply incidental corrections of Moses' law or incidental changes in attitude toward the temple. Jesus is the new lawgiver across the board. We see this in the Sermon on the Mount, where he explains that he has come to fulfill the Law and the Prophets—while at the same time presenting himself as more than the Law. The law of Moses was given to the people of old, but Jesus counters it with "I tell you." The contrast is clear.[14] We also see it reflected in the actual content of the Law. Not only is Moses' certificate of divorce set aside, but the laws regarding murder, swearing an oath, and love of neighbors are also rewritten (Matt. 5:21–48). From now on, the commandments of Jesus (Matt. 7:24–29) serve as the foundation for the new phase of God's people.

We do not find a complete new set of laws in the Gospels. Jesus endorses the previous phase, that of Moses, but he then rises above it. The heart of his message is not a new law code but the authority of his own Person. This is not a matter of introducing an impersonal new law, but a new Lawgiver.[15] His person, he himself, is the law of faith: those who keep his commandments love *him* (John 14:15, 21; 15:10). Jesus' love for those who are his is the normative commandment for his followers in their relationships among themselves. This is the "new commandment" that he gives them, and this will identify them as Jesus' disciples (John 13:34–35).

Israel is being led from the law of Moses to the great prophet whom Moses had promised. From now on, people can listen to him and his commandments. On the Mount of Transfiguration, Moses himself passes, so to speak, the baton to Jesus, and the voice from heaven says, "This is my Son, whom I have chosen; *listen to him*" (Luke 9:30–31, 35). So Jesus warns the hostile leaders that Moses will be their accuser before God (John 5:45–47).

---

14. See the introduction preceding the discussion of Matt. 5:21–48 in van Bruggen, *Matteüs*.

15. Compare P. Stuhlmacher, *Biblische Theologie des Neuen Testaments*, Band 1, *Grundlegung: Von Jesus zu Paulus* (Göttingen: Vandenhoeck & Ruprecht, 1992), 96–107.

Following from Jesus' role as Lawgiver is the apostolic decision to exempt any Gentiles who come to Christ from the requirement of circumcision and from observing the law of Moses (Acts 15:6–29). For first-century Jewish Christians, this decision—certainly as it affected circumcision and dietary regulations—was a radical one and not easily accepted (Acts 11:1–18; 15:1–5). In the letters of Paul we notice how difficult it was for the Christian church to enter into this new phase. But this difficulty in acceptance cannot be explained as the result of a gradual, evolutionary process during the first century, as has often been assumed in the last two centuries. The opposite is true: Christians needed time to realize the full implications of a phase that Jesus had ushered in during his lifetime, but the consequences of which were not fully understood until many converts from the nations had entered Israel through faith and baptism. A gradual evolutionary process would never have led to the abolition of obligatory circumcision by people who had grown up with the tradition of the Pharisees. Apparently Jesus' own ministry provided a clear impetus for the struggle which people in the following decades could not escape.

7.2.4 The King with the Council of Twelve

In the midst of baptized disciples and admiring followers, a core group takes shape around Jesus that is referred to as "the Twelve." This was a group of twelve men from the wider circle of "disciples," *the* (familiar) twelve disciples (Matt. 10:1; 11:1; compare 28:16, after Judas's death: "the eleven disciples"). The most important point, however, is not that they are "disciples" (of whom there are many, for the Twelve were chosen from a larger circle of disciples, Luke 6:13). What is special is that there are *twelve* of them, which is why they are often simply referred to as "the Twelve" (Matt. 10:5; 26:14; etc.; Mark 3:14; 4:10; etc.; Luke 8:1; 18:31; etc.; John 6:71; 20:24).

This group is a sort of court council who are always with Jesus and to whom he can entrust special assignments (Mark 3:14). Within this group there is an even smaller group of three—James and John, the sons of Zebedee, and Simon Peter. The central figure of the three and of the Twelve is clearly Simon Bar-Jonah, whom early on Jesus had named Cephas (Greek *Petros*, Man of Stone; John 1:42).

The function of this court council can be determined from the number of its members. The number twelve symbolizes the nation that is made up of the twelve tribes of Israel. By providing himself with a permanent retinue consisting of precisely *twelve* chosen disciples, Jesus lets it be known that he is laying a new foundation for the new phase of God's people. On the broader foundation of the twelve sons of Jacob a superstructure will now be erected consisting of twelve disciples. The nation of Israel is thereby concentrated within the circle of those who accept Jesus and who gather around his twelve personal servants.[16]

What is taking shape here is a picture of a King with a court council. Jesus is not a single individual within Israel, as were the earlier prophets and John the Baptist. He is the beginning of a new configuration. The basis for this realignment of Israel is the Twelve, with Simon as the cornerstone.[17] We clearly see that this is Jesus' intent when the Twelve are sent out. They represent the authority of Jesus in Israel, and the acceptance or rejection of the Twelve is decisive for life and death in the future. Israel must enter the future of God by way of Jesus and the twelve servants he sends out (Matt. 10:5–14).

Just how decisive this is can be seen from the perspective of the future. Peter once states how he and the other eleven have left everything to serve Jesus (Matt. 19:27). Jesus responds by saying, "I tell you the truth, at the renewal of all things, when the Son of Man sits on his glorious throne, you who have followed me will also sit on twelve thrones, judging the twelve tribes of Israel" (Matt. 19:28). At their last Passover meal, Jesus also says, "You are those who have stood by me in my trials. And I confer on you a kingdom, just as my Father conferred one on me, so that you may eat and drink at my table in my kingdom and sit on thrones, judging the twelve tribes of Israel" (Luke 22:28–30).

While on the one hand Jesus often withdrew from the onrush of the crowds and refused to be crowned king, he also lets it clearly be known that he has royal aspirations by appointing a court council to whom he gives a large measure of authority. Apparently Jesus put together this group of twelve with an eye to Israel's future. They were well aware of it, which is why on more than one occasion they quarrel over which of them will occupy the most important position in the kingdom of heaven. The people were aware of it, too. Several people in the court of Caiaphas say to Simon Peter, "This fellow is one of *them*" (Mark 14:69–70). It is known that the Nazarene is the center (Mark 14:67), but it is also known that there is a Jesus *group,* consisting of permanent followers. The people who come to arrest Jesus by night arm themselves because they regard the Twelve as personal bodyguards who will defend their Master to the end (John 18:3–11). And after Jesus' burial, the leaders are afraid that these disciples will take action and possibly steal the body of their Master in order to give the appearance of truth to his statements about a resurrection (Matt. 27:64).

16. Compare Stuhlmacher, *Biblische Theologie des Neuen Testaments,* 1:83.

17. Compare N. A. Dahl, *Das Volk Gottes: Eine Untersuchung zum Kirchenbewusstsein des Urchristentums* (Darmstadt: Wissenschaftlicher Buchgesellschaft, 1962).

The council of the Twelve was a unique group, foundational for the new phase for God's people. The number *twelve* was indispensable here as an appeal to *all* of Israel (Acts 2:36; 3:20–26). For this reason, between the day of the ascension and the outpouring of the Holy Spirit, Simon Peter led the group of believers in electing a replacement for Judas (Acts 1:15–26). In this way Peter and eleven others (Acts 2:14) can stand together on the day of Pentecost as a group of twelve and preach the gospel of Christ the King to the whole nation of Israel (Acts 2:9–11).

7.2.5 The Good Shepherd for Israel and the Nations

While in Jerusalem, toward the end of what had become a highly controversial ministry in Israel, Jesus openly referred to himself as "the gate for the sheep" (John 10:7) and "the good shepherd" (John 10:14). The sheep go in and out through him and thereby find rich pasture (John 10:9). He even gives his own life for these sheep (John 10:11, 17), and he does all this in the service of his heavenly Father (John 10:15, 17).

Jesus contrasts himself here with "thieves and robbers" (John 10:8) who, rather than being a gateway to safe pasture, lead the flock to their doom, so that they are slaughtered or fall prey to wolves (John 10:10, 12). The notion that these thieves and robbers were actually references to the leaders of Israel must be rejected.[18] Jesus compares himself with others who try to lead the flock out of the pen *by going ahead of them*. There is a specific occasion for this comparison. The Jews had recently decided that anyone who confessed Jesus as Messiah would be thrown out of the synagogue (John 9:22). Thus the man blind from birth whom Jesus cured was excommunicated when he confessed Jesus (John 9:34), and many people (including elders) were afraid to openly express belief in Jesus (John 12:42). This caused Jesus to be branded as someone who stole the sheep from the safe pen of law and synagogue and led them astray: a thief or robber of the flock! Through the centuries, many Jews had been lost to Israel because they let themselves be lured away by the prophets of Baal or by the philosophers of Hellenism. Does Jesus represent the same kind of pitfall for the sheep?

This suggestion is raised by the leaders, and Jesus responds (John 9:35). Using a figure of speech (John 10:6), he explains that the actual situation is radically different. The sheep do follow behind him—but he leads through self-denial unto death, and he thereby grants life to the sheep. And why do people feel safe with Jesus and dare to follow him? Because from the beginning he distinguishes himself from all the others: his voice is familiar! The sheep *know* his voice. His role as Shepherd

18. See van Houwelingen, *Johannes*, on John 10.

and Savior is new, but the voice is that of the Father. It is the familiar voice of the God of Abraham, Isaac, and Jacob. That is why the sheep recognize the voice and allow themselves to be led by this One who is sent from the Father. His plan is to call others, from outside Israel, as well (John 10:16).

Under this image of the new—but good—Shepherd with the familiar voice, Jesus presents himself as the saving center of God's people, over against the leaders who brand him as a thief or robber. Anyone who is put out of the synagogue because of Jesus (like the man born blind) will not be lost, but he or she will be taken into the one flock owned by Jesus' Father. To Simon Peter (the cornerstone for the community of Christ: Matt. 16:18), Jesus later gives the order to care for the sheep of this flock (John 21:15–17).

7.3 God's People in Christ

Since Jesus is the gateway to God for Israel, every other nation must also come to God through this one door. Until now their only access to the Father had been indirect—by being incorporated into the people of Abraham. Gentiles were brought into the fold by circumcision, and as members of the people of Abraham they were subject to the religious laws of Israel (the law of Moses). Salvation was from the Jews. But now that there was a new door to the Father for the people of Israel, the other nations found they could also approach God through that same door. Jesus indicated this himself: (1) he sent apostles out to all nations and gave them a new teaching to take with them, and (2) he made individual baptism the sign of incorporation into God's people.

7.3.1 Apostles for the Nations

During his stay on earth, Jesus appointed *apostles* and sent them out. Through them he wanted to bring God's people together around his gospel of the kingdom of heaven. The apostles are those who invite everyone to participate in the new phase for God's people on earth. They bring the people to the Son of God, the savior of sinners and of the world.

The Twelve formed the core of this circle of apostles. They belonged to the disciples, but when they were chosen to become members of the council of twelve, they were given an apostolic task as well. Luke writes that Jesus chose twelve of his disciples "whom he also designated apostles" (Luke 6:13). The word *apostolos* means messenger or envoy; it is not a title in Greek. The twelve disciples are called "apostles" because they are sent out into Israel two by two (Luke 9:2, 10; Mark 6:7, 30; Matt. 10:1–5, 16; compare Luke 11:49). Jesus sends them on a mission;

thus they are "missionaries" (compare John 13:16). This name is used in connection with the actual mission of the Twelve to all Israel, but during the period when these Twelve serve as a sort of court council and are constantly in Jesus' company they are not referred to as the twelve "apostles" but as "the Twelve" or "the twelve disciples."[19]

In addition to the Twelve, there were the seventy(-two) others, also regarded as apostles, who later were sent out in preparation for Jesus' journey to Jerusalem to die and be resurrected. After Luke reports how Jesus sent out the Twelve (Luke 9:1), he describes how Jesus then appointed and sent out seventy(-two) *others* (Luke 10:1). These seventy(-two) are grouped together with the Twelve sent out earlier. Luke sees them as apostles, too. Similarly, the Seventy(-two) were also called "apostles" by Tertullian, Irenaeus, and Origen.[20]

The court council of the twelve disciples had a special position of trust, and their number constituted a plan for the future of Israel. At the same time, these Twelve are the active core of a larger circle of apostles in Israel. Together they are ambassadors, representing their Sender and bringing his message to the people. Anyone who takes them in also takes in Christ.[21]

Already during Jesus' time on earth it is apparent, however, that these apostles have another task: they must also bring the gospel to the *nations*. To begin with, the gospel must be preached to all Jews who lived outside Palestine but still belonged to the people of Israel, the Jewish Diaspora of that time. When Caiaphas says that it is better that one man die than that the whole nation perish, John elaborates, "He prophesied that Jesus would die for the Jewish nation, and not only for that nation but also for the scattered children of God, to bring them together and make them one" (John 11:51–52). But after that the gospel must be preached to all other nations. In his last address to the Twelve, Jesus foretells that the Good News *will* be preached to all nations (Matt. 24:14). It will happen because it is part of God's plan for the world; it belongs to the things that *must* become reality (Mark 13:10).[22] Thus after Jesus' resurrection we read the following explicit charge: "Therefore go

---

19. There are a few exceptions in Luke: "the apostles" (17:5); "Jesus and his apostles" (22:14; a majority of the manuscripts read "Jesus and his *twelve* apostles"). But here we must take into account that Luke considered not only the Twelve to be "apostles" but others as well. In Luke 24:9, we read that the women bring the message of Easter to "the Eleven and to all the others" (compare 24:33). In the next verse this is repeated in abbreviated form when Luke speaks of the women "who told this to the apostles." Also in Acts, Luke appears not to limit the group of "apostles" to the Twelve (Acts 14:4, 14).

20. For a more detailed discussion see van Bruggen, *Ambten in de apostolische kerk*.

21. See also sec. 7.1.3 for the mission to all places in Israel.

22. D. Bosch, *Die Heidenmission in der Zukunft Jesu*, Abhandlungen zur Theologie des Alten und Neuen Testaments 36 (Zürich: Zwingli, 1959), 159–74.

and make disciples of all nations" (Matt. 28:19). The whole of creation is now involved: "Go into all the world and preach the good news to all creation" (Mark 16:15). And that is what happened: "Then the disciples went out and preached everywhere" (Mark 16:20). Thus it was "written" in the Scriptures that "the Christ will suffer and rise from the dead on the third day, and repentance and forgiveness of sins will be preached in his name to all nations, beginning at Jerusalem" (Luke 24:46–47).

The apostles are set apart for this work. They are called Jesus' *witnesses* because they were always in his company and can therefore testify to what they saw and heard (Luke 24:48: "You are witnesses of these things").

The apostles are also given the authority to perform signs and miracles in Jesus' name to legitimate their message. They go forth and the signs go with them: "And these signs will *accompany* those who believe: In my name they will drive out demons; they will speak in new tongues; they will pick up snakes with their hands; and when they drink deadly poison, it will not hurt them at all; they will place their hands on sick people, and they will get well" (Mark 16:17–18). Jesus had already made this promise when the Seventy(-two) returned: "I have given you authority to trample on snakes and scorpions and to overcome all the power of the enemy; nothing will harm you" (Luke 10:19). The apostles will be empowered with the power from above (Luke 24:49).

The following points must also be considered part of the apostles' authority, although they are not discussed here in detail.[23] All disciples are in a unique position as eyewitnesses, and the apostles are prominent among them. They have been given special authority for their specific work as traveling apostles:

1. Christ has entrusted them with the gospel of the suffering and glorified Christ as the key to the kingdom of heaven, and with this key they can open the door for Jews and Greeks alike (Matt. 16:17–21).
2. Christ has given them the authority to bind and to loose for the entire people of God. Their combined preaching is decisive for the verdict in the Last Judgment (Matt. 16:17–21; 18:15–20).
3. Simon is the first among the apostles. He is the one on whom Christ will build his church (Matt. 16:17–21).

Although the Gospels are chiefly concerned with the earthly life of Jesus, they also report a series of statements by Jesus about the future

---

23. For a more detailed discussion of Matt. 16:17–21 and 18:15–20, see van Bruggen, *Matteüs*, and idem, *Ambten in de apostolische kerk*, 38–59.

of God's people. He has laid the foundation for the new phase. He has appointed the preachers and outfitted them for their task. And he has stated the goal: to all nations!

What does this mission to Israel's Diaspora and to all the nations mean? Is it a new impulse to revive the age-old attempt to incorporate the Gentiles into the Jewish nation? It is clear that the central focus of this preaching is not the Jewish nation, but the *Messiah* who has come from this nation. The Good News of God's heavenly kingdom and of his Son is what unites all those who are called. Jesus instructs the apostles to make all nations *his disciples*, "teaching them to obey everything I have commanded you" (Matt. 28:20). The law of Moses is not mentioned, which means that from now on Jesus as lawgiver will determine the law for God's people (see sec. 7.2.3). He is greater than Moses and *he* is the central figure; the nations will become disciples of *him*.

This paves the way for a gathering together of God's people in *Christ*, and no longer in *Moses*. This new phase is linked to the previous period in the person of Jesus himself, who was circumcised on the eighth day. But the change from Moses the lawgiver to Jesus as the unifying Savior and Teacher puts the law and rite of circumcision in another light for the Jews, while for the other nations access to God is no longer through a *people* but through a *Person* from among that people. After Pentecost, Jesus Christ had to give special revelations from heaven to Peter and Paul to make them aware of this. Accepting the implications resulted in considerable struggle in the church communities that consisted of both Jews and Greeks, but Jesus himself opened the way that led through that struggle!

7.3.2 Incorporation through Personal Baptism

When the apostles were sent out to all the nations, the Jewish rite of circumcision was not abolished but neither was it mentioned as a condition of entrance for the Gentiles. Jesus commands that everyone who becomes his disciple must be *baptized*. "Therefore go and make disciples of all nations, *baptizing them* in the name of the Father and of the Son and of the Holy Spirit, and teaching them to obey everything I have commanded you" (Matt. 28:19). This baptism of the faithful is also mentioned in Mark 16:16: "Whoever believes and is baptized will be saved, but whoever does not believe will be condemned."

Often this commandment to baptize all nations is understood as the point at which Christian baptism was *instituted*. The *inception* of this baptism would then have taken place during the period after Easter. Only then would Jesus have devised this ceremony for his future disciples. But if this is correct, then it is surprising that neither Matthew 28 nor Mark 16 provides us with a clear *institution* of this baptism. In Matthew 28 it is more or less mentioned in passing, as if it were an already familiar fact. The same is true for Mark 16:16, where baptism is not even singled out as a separate mandate. All that is said is that "whoever believes and is baptized" will be saved. The requirement of "faith" is not stated as something new, and neither is the requirement of "baptism."

This could be explained in part by assuming that Jesus took over John's already-familiar baptism and extended it into the future. Now the apostles must baptize just as John did. And just as repentance entailed accepting baptism in the Jordan, so belief in Jesus entails baptism from now on.[24]

But by equating Christian baptism with John's baptism, we fail to recognize the differences that exist between the two. Jesus does adopt the *ceremony* that had been instituted by the prophet John the Baptist (a one-time immersion in water), but he places that ceremony in a *new context:* people are no longer required to go to the Jordan. The character of the rite changes as well. The baptism of repentance administered in expectation of the coming of the Lord now becomes a baptism of faithfully confessing the Son of God who has already come. Baptism in the name of Jesus is in line with John's baptism, but it now takes on a new character of its own.

To explain how the Christian baptism of all nations could have been commissioned after Easter without any indication of a clear *institution* of baptism at that particular point, we have to go back to the period between the beginning of Jesus' ministry and John's imprisonment. Jesus' disciples were baptizing then, and even then their baptism was different from the baptism of John and his disciples. The *disciples* of Jesus who confessed him as the Christ during his ministry in Israel were

24. Bavinck writes, "The Divine institution of baptism thus begins with John, but Jesus took it over (after having undergone baptism himself) by having his disciples baptize (John 3:22; 4:1), and in Matt. 28:19 it was imposed as obligatory for all believers of all nations" (H. Bavinck, *Gereformeerde Dogmatiek*, 3d ed., 4 vols. [Kampen: Kok, 1918], 4:547). For Bavinck, John's baptism *is* in fact already the Christian baptism. On 4:545 he writes, "Furthermore, Jesus himself was baptized with John's baptism. He made essentially no distinction between the baptism administered by his own disciples and that administered by John (John 3:22, 23; 4:1). He invited the disciples baptized by John to join him without re-baptizing them . . . and in Matt. 28:19 he did not institute a new baptism but extended the existing baptism to include all nations. On this basis, the essential identity of the Johannine and Christian baptism, with slight differences, is adhered to by Reformed Christians and Lutherans. But it is contested by Roman Catholics, Anabaptists, Socinians, Arminians, and by many of the more recent theologians." Bavinck here markedly neglects the context, which in fact points out the *difference* between the "decreasing" Baptist and the "increasing" Jesus (John 3:30), and which associates becoming a disciple of Jesus with baptism by his disciples and not with baptism by John (John 4:1). For this difference, see also Acts 19:1–7.

themselves baptized in Jesus' name at an early stage.[25] That is why we find no *institution* of Christian baptism after Easter, but rather a *resumption and continuation* of the same rite, directed toward all nations. The recruitment of disciples seemed to have come to a standstill, and many people had even abandoned Jesus. But after Easter, Jesus initiates a new recruitment offensive. The entire world is invited to come to God in his name, and everyone must confess his or her faith openly by receiving baptism in Jesus' name.

Jesus' attaching a *ceremony of belonging* to the preaching of the gospel emphasizes his desire not only that all people believe in him but also that all believers join together into *one community*. Baptism establishes a *"nation"* of disciples. That this nation is united through *faith* and not through a ceremony is evident from the charge to "make disciples" of all nations and to "[teach] them to obey everything I have commanded you" (Matt. 28:19). This indicates that everyone who "believes and is baptized" will be saved. It is belief that is decisive. That is why Jesus does not say that everyone who is not baptized will be lost, but that everyone who "does not believe will be condemned" (Mark 16:16). Yet baptism is attached to this decisive belief as a confirming ceremony from God (confession of faith and baptism belong together, but they are distinct). Just as the people of Israel, united through their descent from Isaac, were distinguished by circumcision, so the people of Jesus Christ, united through faith in God's Son, are distinguished by baptism in his name. Those who believe must show their allegiance and be willing to receive the seal of baptism from God in Jesus' name.

The words in Matthew 28:19b ("in the name of the Father and of the Son and of the Holy Spirit") are not strictly intended as a *baptismal formula*. The focus of the baptism is *Jesus' name*. But access to the Father is obtained through Jesus, the Son, and the promised gift of the Spirit also comes through Jesus.[26]

Excursus: Origin of Christian Baptism

a. Baptism as an Authentic Ceremony

Although many scholars do not regard Matthew 28:19 as an original statement by Jesus, few deny that the rite of baptism was regarded as normative for the Christian community almost from the beginning.

---

25. See sec. 7.2.1, "Teacher of Baptized 'Pupils,'" for a broader discussion; see also sec. *c* of the excursus at the end of this chapter.

26. On Matt. 28:19b, see van Bruggen, *Matteüs*. Immersion in water at the confession of Jesus' name is different from receiving the Holy Spirit (also referred to as "baptism of the Spirit"). See chap. 8.

Hartman points out that Paul counts himself among the baptized as a matter of course (1 Cor. 12:13).[27] Thus there must have been a *baptizing* Christendom even before Paul's conversion, which takes us back in time to at most a year after Easter.[28]

Hartman asserts that the reason baptism is not mentioned in the sending out of the Twelve (Matt. 10; Luke 10) is the fact that the Christian community regarded baptism as a post-Easter institution, so they did not project it back into the charge to the Twelve. A more obvious explanation is that the Gospel authors were very good at differentiating between what was done and said before and after Easter, including matters concerning baptism.

But what is the origin of this rite? If it is authentic, there must have been some revelatory authority behind it that was accepted by everyone and that would explain both the institution of the rite of baptism and its rapid acceptance. If revelatory authority as the basis for the origin of baptism is rejected, however, then another basis must be found for the appearance of baptism. So at the end of the nineteenth century, when many rejected the New Testament as a source of revelation, studies appeared that attempted to explain the existence of church, baptism, and Last Supper on the basis of the religio-historical context of that period.

b. The Religio-Historical Explanation

Where baptism is concerned, an explanation was sought in the adoption of pagan initiations, or of Jewish purification rites, or in a link with Jewish proselyte baptism.

1. Otto Pfleiderer looked to the Eleusinian mysteries.[29] Initiation into these mysteries was seen as a kind of rebirth. The initiate was given a bath and a new name. Albert Eichhorn and Wilhelm Heitmüller endorsed this view.[30] According to Heitmüller, the world at that time was not ready for a purely spiritual acceptance of the gospel, so people had to resort to mystical union with the divinity through matter (water, food). "Faith" then is excluded and magic admitted. According to Reit-

---

27. L. Hartman, *Auf den Namen des Herrn Jesus: Die Taufe in den neutestamentlichen Schriften*, Stuttgarter Bibelstudien 148 (Stuttgart: Katholisches Bibelwerk, 1992).

28. Compare G. Lohfink, "Der Ursprung der christlichen Taufe," *Theological Quarterly* 156 (1976): 35–54.

29. O. Pfleiderer, *Das Urchristenthum, seine Schriften und Lehre, in geschichtlichem Zusammenhang beschrieben* (Berlin: Reimer, 1887).

30. A. Eichhorn, *Das Abendmahl im Neuen Testament*, Hefte zur Christlichen Welt 36 (Leipzig: Mohr, 1898); W. Heitmüller, *"Im Namen Jesu": Eine sprach- und religionsgeschichtliche Untersuchung zum Neuen Testament, speziell zur altchristlichen Taufe*, FRLANT 1.2 (Göttingen: Vandenhoeck & Ruprecht, 1903).

zenstein,[31] Paul is the father of the gnostics. The sacraments mediate between earthly man and the higher world. In a subsequent study of older, pre-Pauline gnostic material, scholars arrived at the Mandaeans, whose savior myth and baptism were alleged to have constituted the cradle of Christianity.

Further religio-historical studies showed, however, that the interest in the origins of Christianity caused the scholars of the time to be somewhat selective and also somewhat indifferent to dates. Thus the formula *renatus in aeternum* ("born again for eternity") only appears in combination with the taurobolium (bull sacrifice) of the Attis cult in Asia Minor, and the oldest documentation for this rite is dated A.D. 143. In addition, the formula *renatus in aeternum* only appears three times, and all three of those occurrences date from the fourth century! The Mandaean baptismal liturgy (as Lietzmann has demonstrated)[32] appears to have been derived from the Syrian Christian baptismal liturgy. Since the middle of the twentieth century not much is being heard concerning the pagan roots of Christian baptism.

2. The Jewish roots of baptism, on the other hand, are actively being considered. A general connection between Christian baptism and the Jewish purification baths has been frequently considered. Since the discoveries made at Qumran, many see a direct relationship between the purification baths found there and Christian baptism (via John). Erich Dinkler, however, advises restraint.[33] There are similarities (the linking of repentance and bath; the atoning character and the sacramental atmosphere), but the discrepancies are greater (repeated baths as opposed to a single baptism; in Qumran no prophet administered baptism, but people bathed themselves; in Qumran there was no connection between the purification and an anticipated coming of the LORD). For a discussion of the relationship between John's baptism and the purification baths at Qumran, also see section 2.2.3.

3. The idea that the Jewish proselyte baptism gave rise to Christian baptism is fairly generally accepted (also see sec. 2.2.3). But here, too, Dinkler is cautious (there is no proof of a proselyte baptism before the end of the first century; there is no connection between proselyte baptism and eschatology). Jeremias, on the other hand, spent a great deal of energy on the derivation from proselyte baptism.[34] On this he bases

31. R. Reitzenstein, *Hellenistic Mystery-Religions: Their Basic Ideas and Significance*, trans. J. E. Steely (Pittsburgh: Pickwick, 1978).

32. H. Lietzmann, *Ein Beitrag zur Mandäerfrage* (Berlin: de Gruyter, 1930).

33. E. Dinkler, "Taufe (im Urchristentum)," in *Die Religion in Geschichte und Gegenwart: Handwörterbuch für Theologie und Religionswissenschaft*, 3d ed. (Tübingen: Mohr, 1962), 2:627–37.

34. J. Jeremias, *Die Kindertaufe in den ersten vier Jahrhunderten* (Göttingen: Vandenhoeck & Ruprecht, 1958).

his argument for *infant* baptism (strongly contested by Aland).[35] According to Jeremias,[36] the Testament of Levi (14.6) is sufficient justification for the notion of a pre-Christian proselyte baptism ("you shall take the daughters of the Gentiles to wife, purifying them with unlawful purification"; *katharizontes autas katharismō paranomō*). According to Dockery, however, Jeremias's argumentation is inadequate and proofs for a proselyte baptism before A.D. 70 do not exist (either in the Old Testament or in Philo or Josephus).[37] In addition, Hartman, following G. Barth, rightly points out that proselyte baptism resembled an ablution that the person himself carried out without the mediation of an authorized prophetic baptizer.[38] The Testament of Levi is not compelling evidence for the notion of an initiation rite because it has to do with prostitutes and adulterers as well as gentile women. Having relations with them is likened to the behavior of Sodom and Gomorrah. The passage is about *mixed* marriages in which the appearance of a pious life was maintained by subjecting gentile women to certain purifying baths that were necessary before a Jewish man was allowed to have intercourse with a woman. Thus one safeguarded one's *own* purity by administering certain purification rites to women who had not become Jews at all. This hypocrisy is condemned. Although these women are Gentiles, there is no reason to see this practice as an initiation into Judaism.

4. About connections with Old Testament purification baths in general we can be brief. These are always repetitive and never occur only once. Versteeg, by way of the *bath* metaphor in Ephesians 5:26 and Titus 3:5, argues for a connection between baptism and the Old Testament ablutions.[39] But this is a major jump. To begin with, the term *bath* is not used exclusively for *ritual* ablutions. In addition, there is still the problem of comparing *one* bath with a multiplicity of Old Testament purifications. Finally, *bath* is a metaphor for baptism, but for the purifications in the Old Testament the word is not a metaphor but a description. Titus 3 concerns the outpouring of the Spirit. The image of a *bath* of rebirth and renewal arises quite naturally from the verb *to pour*. Thus this passage has more to do with water that washes over a person (a shower bath) than with water's ability to *purify*. And in Ephesians 5:26,

35. K. Aland, *Did the Early Church Baptize Infants?* (Philadelphia: Westminster, 1963). Compare J. Jeremias, *The Origins of Infant Baptism: A Further Study in Reply to Kurt Aland* (Naperville, Ill.: Allenson, 1963).

36. Jeremias, *Kindertaufe in den ersten vier Jahrhunderten*.

37. D. S. Dockery, "Baptism," in *Dictionary of Jesus and the Gospels*, ed. J. B. Green and S. McKnight (Downers Grove, Ill.: InterVarsity, 1992).

38. Hartman, *Auf den Namen des Herrn Jesus*.

39. J. P. Versteeg, "De doop volgens het Nieuwe Testament," in *Rondom de doopvont: Leer en gebruik van de heilige doop in het Nieuwe Testament en in de geschiedenis van de westerse kerk*, ed. W. van't Spijker et al. (Goudriaan: De Groot, 1983), 15.

the context refers to a washing off of dirt (the bride is washed clean; compare Ezek. 16:9–14). This purifying bath took place "through the word." Paul uses the word "bath" to allude to the purifying activity of preaching in combination with faith and baptism. There is no reason to understand the word "bath" here as an indication that baptism is a new form of the Old Testament baths that imparted ceremonial purity for participation in the temple cult.

It is striking that in surveys of recent New Testament scholarship there is little discussion of the historical background of baptism.[40] And the notion that baptism by immersion was an original institution in the case of John is contradicted less frequently than in the past.[41] The attempt made at the end of the nineteenth century and the beginning of the twentieth to explain baptism in the light of the history of religions has reached a dead end and has failed.

Here we come up against an indirect proof for the reliability of sources supporting the birth of Christianity (the New Testament writings, specifically the Gospels). In twentieth-century biblical scholarship there has been almost general agreement that the writings of the New Testament are for the most part retroactive projections of a number of heterogeneous Christian movements. The search focuses on the power of the charismatic person of Jesus, who might be able to explain the development of these movements. This is combined, however, with the denial that Jesus had any hand in establishing the rite of baptism. But if baptism had not been taken over from the mystery religions or Qumran, and if it is not an imitation of Jewish proselyte baptism, how do we explain the rapid and *general* acceptance of baptism throughout *all* of early (and supposedly still heterogeneous) Christianity? We can turn the question on its head. The existence of an original rite of baptism from the earliest moments of Christianity on indicates that there must have been a center of authority, and that everyone submitted to that authority. Jesus thus was more than a prophet or a miracle worker. He was also a *founder of the church*, from the very beginning. And he bound people not only to his example or his teaching, but first and foremost *to his person*. This image of an *authoritative church founder* who binds people *to himself* does not fit with the modern image of Jesus. It only fits if the New Testament is right and its image of Jesus is closer to re-

40. For example, E. J. Epp and G. W. McRae, eds., *The New Testament and Its Modern Interpreters* (Philadelphia: Fortress, 1989).

41. In support of the notion of a *new form* is the fact that John owed the epithet "The Immerser" to his apparently noteworthy ritual of immersion, as well as the fact that the word *baptisma* quickly arose as the technical term for something that is more than a *baptismos* (an immersion for the sake of purification).

ality than are the later reconstructions that result from historical and literary criticism. The presence of a generally accepted baptism testifies indirectly to the existence of a catholic Christology at this time!

c. When Was Christian Baptism Instituted?

Christian baptism was not instituted after Easter. It was already being administered by Jesus' disciples even before John's imprisonment (John 3:22–24). John the Evangelist reports that there was even some tension between the disciples of the Baptist and those of Jesus, because more and more people were going to Jesus (John 3:25–36). The Pharisees also noticed that Jesus was attracting more disciples and doing more baptizing through his disciples than John the Baptist (John 4:1–2). On the basis of these facts, sections 7.2.1 and 7.3.2 discussed how Jesus' disciples had already received Christian baptism during the time of his humiliation, and how the commission after Easter to baptize all nations can be seen as a *renewed* offensive now that Christ had been glorified.

In earlier centuries, an equating of the baptism by Jesus' disciples (John 3) with later Christian baptism was not unknown. Augustine appealed to this equality in his dispute with the Donatists in an effort to show that it is *Christ* who baptizes when his servants baptize—even though those servants (Judas!) are unworthy. Augustine does this by comparing John 3:22 (Jesus baptized) with John 4:2 (the disciples baptized). In *Epistula* 44.10,[42] Augustine says that the bridegroom did not baptize with the baptism of the bridegroom's friend or of his slave. And when the disciples baptized, they themselves also had to have been baptized. In *Epistula* 265.5[43] he adds that either they were baptized by John, as some believe, or with the baptism of Christ. He finds the latter far more likely (*"quod magis credibile est"*). In both letters, Augustine refers further to John 13:10 ("A person who has had a bath . . . is clean. And you are clean, though not every one of you") to conclude from this verse that Peter was baptized. This argument can only be maintained, however, if it is assumed that Judas forfeited the cleansing of his baptism by rejecting Christ. Maldonatus endorses the idea that Jesus himself must have baptized his disciples. Thomas Aquinas views the baptism administered by Jesus' disciples as Christian baptism.[44]

In many modern commentaries, the early baptismal activity of Jesus' disciples is emphatically *not* equated with (later) Christian baptism. This leaves us with two possibilities: either the early baptism by Jesus'

42. Corpus scriptorum ecclesiasticorum latinorum 34:117–18.
43. Ibid., 57:642–44.
44. *Summa Theologica* 3a.67.2.

disciples was the same as the baptism of John the Baptist, or this early baptism was a temporary, transitional form.

1. *The baptism by Jesus' disciples (John 3) was the same as that of the Baptist but different from later Christian baptism.* This theory can be found in various modern commentaries. Brown supports it because Christian baptism in the New Testament derives its power from the crucifixion and the resurrection.[45] Jesus then participated for a limited time only in the administration of John's baptism of repentance.[46] The ceremony is thus embedded in the preaching of repentance that was also adopted from John.[47] According to Hartman, Jesus distanced himself from this baptism relatively soon, which is why we do not see it mentioned later in the Gospels.[48] According to Maier, Jesus only "tolerated" this continuation of John's baptism on the part of his disciples.[49] He himself did not baptize and *only tolerated* what his disciples did. This baptism was a continuation of John's baptism (the baptism in the name of the triune God was possible only after Easter). Lagrange and Haenchen base their arguments on the fact that the Spirit had not yet been given (John 7:39).[50] Hoskyns even asserts that John the Evangelist writes about the participation of Jesus' disciples in John's baptism by water in order to offer a contrast: every baptism by water is insufficient as long as Christ does not bestow the invisible Spirit.[51]

2. *The baptism by Jesus' disciples (John 3) was not the same as that of the Baptist, but it was also different from later Christian baptism.* Some exegetes move somewhat more in the direction of Christian baptism. Thus Léon-Dufour is of the opinion that this early baptism was not identical to that of John the Baptist, as many critics maintain.[52] Even though the Spirit had not yet been poured out, the willingness to be bound to Jesus through this baptism establishes an openness to the Spirit.[53] Beasley-Murray regards the early baptism by the disciples as a

45. R. E. Brown, *The Gospel according to John*, Anchor Bible (Garden City, N.Y.: Doubleday, 1966–70), 151.

46. Morris, *Gospel according to John*, 237.

47. H. N. Ridderbos, *Het evangelie naar Johannes: Proeve van een theologische exegese*, 2 vols. (Kampen: Kok, 1987–92), 1:170.

48. Hartman, *Auf den Namen des Herrn Jesus*, 35.

49. G. Maier, *Johannes-Evangelium*, 2 vols., Bibelkommentar 6–7, edition C. (Neuhausen-Stuttgart: Hänssler, 1984–86), 1:131ff.

50. J. Lagrange, *Évangile selon Saint Jean*, Études Bibliques (Paris: Lecoffre, 1925); E. Haenchen, *John : A Commentary on the Gospel of John*, ed. R. W. Funk with the assistance of U. Busse, trans. R. W. Funk (Philadelphia: Fortress, 1984).

51. E. C. Hoskyns, *The Fourth Gospel*, 2d ed. (London: Faber & Faber, 1947).

52. X. Léon-Dufour, *Lecture de l'évangile selon Jean*, 3 vols. (Paris: Editions du Seuil, 1988–93), 1:322.

53. Compare R. Schnackenburg, *Das Johannesevangelium*, 4 vols. (Freiburg: Herder, 1965–84). By undergoing this baptism people showed their willingness to listen to Jesus.

sign of their obedient response to him who was busy establishing the kingdom of salvation.[54]

The frequently made distinction between the early baptismal activity of Jesus' disciples and Christian baptism seems to be based on two main motives.

First, it is maintained that the rites are not identical because the Spirit was not yet present. But this is based on an erroneous identification of water baptism with the (promised) baptism with the Spirit. The distance in time between the baptism by water in Jesus' name and the promised outpouring of the Spirit is, at the time of John 3, greater than it is after Pentecost, but even after Pentecost there is still a distinction between water baptism received in faith and the gift of the Spirit (see, for example, Acts 8 and 10).

The second reason for maintaining that it is impossible to view the early baptism as identical with later Christian baptism is that such a rite would not have been possible without the completion of the work of Good Friday and Easter. But this is based on an erroneous division between the person and the work of the Christ. Even *before* Easter, Jesus is the Christ, the Son of the living God, who grants life and forgives sins. If people could confess him with these words at that time, they could also be baptized in his name before Easter. The idea that Christian baptism can be understood only from the perspective of the cross and the resurrection, and not from the *divinity of Jesus as the one who is to come*, fails to acknowledge the decisive nature of the *incarnation* of the *Son of God*. Cross and resurrection make the meaning of the *name of Jesus* more and more explicit, but more important is the recognition of his heavenly power and majesty! Even before Easter, faith in his name brought healing to many and succeeded in driving out all demons. For this reason a circle was formed in Jesus' name of confessing and baptized disciples, and within that circle apostles were appointed who were to convey that faith and baptism to all nations.

54. Beasley-Murray, *John*, 52.

8

With Spirit and with Fire—
the Future of the Son of God

8.1 A Promised Future

In their preaching, John the Baptist and Jesus focus on the future. They proclaim God's time for this world—his kingdom is at hand!—and stress the need for a baptism of repentance. Belief in Jesus takes on a special urgency.

This focus on the future seems to have cooled off rather rapidly. John the Baptist dies in prison and Jesus is crucified. Is this the final curtain and does the world remain unchanged?

According to some, it does indeed appear that Jesus' expectations for the future ended in failure. Only his radical commitment serves us as example. The so-called radical-eschatological (or consequent-eschatological) school, with A. Schweitzer and J. Weiss as the leading proponents, sees Jesus as someone driven by the impulses of the apocalyptic movement in Judaism.[1] In Jesus the apocalyptic expectation reaches unprecedented heights, but he himself has become its victim in an environment that refuses to be drawn into this blazing hope in God. The same assessment was made, in a somewhat less romantic and less emotional form, at the end of the twentieth century. Thus H. J. de Jonge writes, "Viewed soberly, the expectation of the son of man never exceeds the level of misunderstanding or illusion. Why should it be any different for the expectation of Christ's second coming?"[2]

A somewhat more positive view of this kind of "future expectation" can be found among those who speak of a "realized eschatology." According to this idea, Jesus erased any distinction between the future

1. A. Schweitzer, *The Quest of the Historical Jesus: A Critical Study of Its Progress from Reimarus to Wrede*, with a new introduction by J. M. Robinson, trans. W. Montgomery (London: Black, 1931); J. Weiss, *Die Predigt Jesu vom Reiche Gottes* (Göttingen: Vandenhoeck & Ruprecht, 1892).
2. H. J. de Jonge, "De oorsprong van de verwachting van Jezus' wederkomst," in *Totdat Hij komt: Een discussie over de wederkomst van Jezus Christus*, ed. H. J. de Jonge and B. W. F. de Ruyter (Baarn: Ten Have, 1995), 31.

that lies before us and the present in which we now live. The future has already begun! The reality of God breaks through on earth and places humanity before the final decision. Dodd speaks of a realized eschatology,[3] and Jeremias later modified this idea somewhat by speaking of an "eschatology that is in the process of being realized."[4] In both cases, the fact that the anticipated future does not materialize is not regarded as a failure but as proof that that future is being realized *in the present*.

When Christ's expectations for the future are regarded as an illusion, there is always an accompanying rejection of the fact that he came from heaven with the ability and the desire to make the Father known to us. But in the case of a more positive view of his preaching about the future—such as those mentioned in the preceding paragraph—the historical reality of that future evaporates into a spiritualized reality.

Many New Testament scholars therefore choose a middle course. According to them, Jesus did anticipate an imminent future for heaven and earth (*Naherwartung*). Then later, when it became clear that he was not going to return so quickly, the church community was forced to come up with an answer to the problem of this delay (*Parusieverzögerung*). The period between Jesus' ministry and his second coming then would not have had a unique and new significance in Jesus' own view. The purpose of his preaching was to make it clear that the moment of decision had arrived. Time is eschatological, determined from the approaching end, and for this reason it no longer has any meaning as a time of progression and of continuing salvation history. Now people live, as it were, "between the times," balancing between the "already" and the "not yet." In Jesus' teaching, therefore, no provision is made for a longer interval between resurrection and second coming. The time after the decisive moment of Good Friday and the appearing of the Son of Man does serve an eschatological function, but it has no historic significance.[5]

Is it really true that Jesus, who taught his disciples so much, did not take into account a future of any length and significance? Why, then, did he train such disciples (Matt. 10) and prepare them to go out to every corner of the earth (Matt. 24:14; 28:19)? It is precisely the training of the apostles for a future mission to all nations that proves that Jesus himself must have taken into account an apostolic period that would have independent significance. It is therefore not accidental that the critical Reimarus, writing in the eighteenth century, began with the

3. C. H. Dodd, *The Parables of the Kingdom*, 2d ed. (London: Nisbet, 1936).

4. J. Jeremias, *New Testament Theology* (London: SCM, 1971).

5. Oscar Cullmann is an exponent of this line of thought; see O. Cullmann, *Salvation in History*, trans. S. G. Sowers et al. (New York: Harper & Row, 1967).

proposition that after Jesus' life ended with the failure of the cross, the apostles appointed themselves preachers of an entirely different gospel. But it would have been something entirely unique in the history of the world if the deception of twelve Galilean men had led to the establishment of a world church that has remained in existence century after century, despite persecutions and disputes, even in spite of Celsus and Reimarus!

When we listen carefully to the heart of John the Baptist's preaching, we see that the story *cannot* end with the crucifixion. The prophet of repentance announced the coming of someone who would baptize "with the Spirit and with fire." It is clear that Jesus' ministry, no matter how impressive its miracles and healings, is not the fulfillment of this announcement. There is no judgment, and Israel has certainly not yet been baptized with the Spirit, for many reject the Messiah. So John asks from his prison cell whether he should await someone else in addition to and after Jesus (Matt. 11:3). Even Jesus' disciples have the feeling, even after Easter, that the most important is yet to come. Right before the ascension they ask, "Lord, are you at this time going to restore the kingdom to Israel?" (Acts 1:6). On that day, it appears that Jesus himself still anticipates the promised future. He refers back to the preaching of John the Baptist about a baptism with Spirit and fire, and he announces that this promise will begin to be fulfilled in a few days, on the feast of Pentecost (Acts 1:5).

There were several occasions when the disciples should have noticed that more time lay before them. At the Last Supper, Jesus instructed them to celebrate this meal in his memory (Luke 22:19). He himself would be absent, "until that day when I drink the wine anew in the kingdom of God" (Mark 14:25).

Jesus also frequently used the image of a thief coming in the night or a bridegroom coming home late. These images are reminders of the call to be on guard and to persevere, because neither the day nor the hour is known (for example, Luke 12:35–48; Mark 13:28–37).

According to Cullmann,[6] Jesus makes *three* statements that show that he was counting on a speedy return, certainly within one generation: Matthew 10:23, Mark 9:1, and Mark 13:30. This is not, however, what these passage say or imply.[7] In Matthew 10:23, Jesus says that people must not live under the illusion that they will "finish going

---

6. Cullmann, *Salvation in History*, 188ff.

7. For special attention to this point, see each of these passages in J. van Bruggen, *Matteüs: Het evangelie voor Israël*, 2d ed., Commentaar op het Nieuwe Testament, 3d series (Kampen: Kok, 1994); and in idem, *Marcus: Het evangelie volgens Petrus*, 2d ed., Commentaar op het Nieuwe Testament, 3d series (Kampen: Kok, 1992).

through" the cities of Israel before the Son of Man comes. The issue here is not a time frame but a pattern of expectation. In Mark 9:1 Jesus says that some bystanders (the believers) will not "taste" of death before he comes. This statement is in line with his remark to Martha about believers who will live although they are dead. In Mark 13:30, Jesus says that "all these things" will happen within one generation, but "all these things" here has to do with the special signs of the times that will precede the second coming, not with the second coming itself.

In Jesus' own teaching, he talks not only about the present, about conversion and faith, but also about a future that had not yet become reality during his wanderings on earth: the promised future of Spirit and fire. Apparently Jesus' death, resurrection, and ascension were necessary to make that future a reality. The curtain does not fall at Golgotha. It was fully open only afterward!

In this last chapter it is our intention to describe the future perspective of Jesus' teaching and work. That future is inextricably bound up with Jesus himself. For this reason the remainder of the chapter is divided into two parts. The first part deals with Jesus' own future: his resurrection, ascension, and return (sec. 8.2). He appears to actively continue his work, but in a different way: no longer embattled on earth but mighty in heaven and coming on the clouds of heaven. The second part deals with the work Jesus does for this world: the baptism with Spirit and with fire. For the sake of clarity this second part is divided into two sections (with Spirit, sec. 8.3; with fire, sec. 8.4).

In this chapter we limit ourselves to what Jesus himself said about all this beforehand. The Book of Acts and the letters of the apostles were written when this future was becoming a reality. This later ministry of the apostles and their teaching does not fall within the scope of this book.

8.2 He Who Is Coming

8.2.1 The Announcement of Jesus' Future

Even before Good Friday, Jesus talked about his own future in his instruction to the disciples. He spoke about the period that was to come after his sentencing by the leaders to be crucified.

The *resurrection* from the dead was from the beginning the perspective for this instruction: "He then began to teach them that the Son of Man must suffer many things and be rejected by the elders, chief priests and teachers of the law, and that he must be killed and after three days rise again" (Mark 8:31). In the account in Matthew 16:21 is the phrase "on the third day be raised to life" (compare Luke 9:22). In the descent from the Mount of Transfiguration Jesus alludes to this teaching. There he says that Peter, James, and John must not talk about the appearance of Moses and Elijah "until the Son of Man had risen from the dead" (Mark 9:9). At that point the disciples do not seem to have absorbed this teaching. They ask themselves what Jesus means: "They kept the matter to themselves, discussing what 'rising from the dead' meant" (Mark 9:10). But the Master keeps on talking about his resurrection, even though his disciples fail to understand what he tells them—whenever he mentions his death they get too upset to hear what comes after that (Mark 9:31; 10:34). In the intimate circle of the Twelve, Jesus even adds a concrete plan of action: "But after I have risen, I will go ahead of you into Galilee" (Matt. 26:32).

This announcement of a resurrection has become rather widely known. The leaders know about it, and they try to silence the rumors about such a resurrection by having the tomb sealed: "We remember that while he was still alive that deceiver said, 'After three days I will rise again'" (Matt. 27:63). The angels who appear in the tomb remind the apostles, via the women, of what Jesus had said: "Remember how he told you, while he was still with you in Galilee: 'The Son of Man must be delivered into the hands of sinful men, be crucified and on the third day be raised again'" (Luke 24:6–7). The reference to Galilee (made privately a few days before) is given to the women as proof of authenticity: "But go, tell his disciples and Peter, 'He is going ahead of you into Galilee. There you will see him, just as he told you'" (Mark 16:7; compare Matt. 28:6–7).

The announcement of the resurrection on the third day is given in the context of Jesus' instructions about his Passion. Jesus thereby explains the nature of his death: not a demise, but a temporary task. His work continues—it does not come to an end. The thread of the journey to Galilee, after the feast, will be picked up again. Because the subject of the resurrection comes up as a clarification of his death, Jesus does not speak in this context about what will happen *after* the resurrection. But it must not have been difficult to make a connection with other moments in Jesus' teaching in which he speaks of a heavenly future.

The *ascension into heaven* is regularly mentioned in the farewell talks. Jesus says in no uncertain terms that he is going to the Father (John 14:1–3, 28; 16:5, 17) and is returning to the place from whence he came (16:28). People will look for him, but where he is going no one can follow (John 13:33, 36). The topic was not new. Jesus had already said that he would be raised and glorified. He would be lifted up from the earth and draw everyone to himself (John 12:32). His time had come "to leave this world and to go to the Father" (John 13:1), and he knows that he "had come from God and was returning to God" (John 13:3b). Finally, we see that this theme was present in personal conversations right from the beginning. During the first months of his public ministry, Jesus had already met with Nicodemus at night and told him, "No one has ever gone into heaven except the one who came from heaven— the Son of Man" (John 3:13). And to the disciples who had trouble with the hard sayings in his discourse about bread, Jesus says, "What if you see the Son of Man ascend to where he was before!" (John 6:62).

In the first three Gospels little of this aspect of Jesus' teaching has been preserved. Even so, there is no tension between these Gospels and the Gospel of John. The Synoptics not only end with a more or less descriptive reference to Jesus' ascension, but in the teaching of Jesus that has been preserved in these Gospels the ascension is also implicit—particularly in various statements about the place that he will occupy in heaven at the time of the last judgment.

Jesus declares to the Sanhedrin that he will be seated at the right hand of the Mighty One in heaven (Matt. 26:64). This statement is in line with what he taught the disciples about a period when he will appear before the Father on their behalf: "Whoever acknowledges me before men, I will also acknowledge him before my Father in heaven. But whoever disowns me before me, I will disown him before my Father in heaven" (Matt. 10:32–33). In the parable of the good and bad seed, the Son of Man is the judge who will "send out his angels" (Matt. 13:41). And the promise that Jesus will build his community on Peter and give his disciples the keys to the kingdom of heaven refers to a period in which he will not be with them: "whatever you bind on earth will be bound in heaven, and whatever you loose on earth will be loosed in heaven" (Matt. 16:19). In due course, the Son of Man will be seen "coming in his kingdom" (Matt. 16:28).

Toward the end of his ministry on earth, Jesus in no uncertain terms informs the teachers of the law who are trying to put him on the spot that he is the Son of David to whom the Lord has said, "Sit at my right hand until I put your enemies under your feet" (Matt. 22:44). In the discourse about the last days, Jesus presupposes that he will be absent from the earth. He warns against being confused by people who say, "Look, here is the Christ!" or "There he is!" (Matt. 24:5, 23). At the end of time the Son of Man will be "revealed" after people first "long to see one of the days of the Son of Man" (Luke 17:22–37). The parables of the ten virgins, of the talents, and of the sheep and the goats all assume that there will be a period in which the Master will be elsewhere (Matt. 25). And Luke writes in his Gospel, "As the time approached for him to be taken up to heaven . . ." (Luke 9:51).

It is not surprising that in John the ascension into heaven is mentioned more explicitly and in the other Gospels more indirectly. John presents the discourses in much greater detail, and he records many of the things Jesus said in private. The other three evangelists report more often Jesus' public teaching, where the accent lies on the day of judgment from heaven; Jesus' temporary absence, though implicit, is not a topic Jesus discusses directly with the crowds.

In his earthly instruction, Jesus spoke more than once about his *coming on the clouds of heaven*. Shortly after he began teaching about his Passion at Caesarea Philippi, he mentioned his coming in glory: "For the Son of Man is going to come in his Father's glory with his angels, and then he will reward each person according to what he has done" (Matt. 16:27). The discourse on the last days mentions the descent on the clouds: "They will see the Son of Man coming on the clouds of the sky, with power and great glory. And he will send his angels with a loud trumpet call, and they will gather his elect from the four winds, from one end of the heavens to the other" (Matt. 24:30–31). Jesus also tells the Sanhedrin that the Son of Man will be seen "coming on the clouds of heaven" (Matt. 26:64). This is the "coming [*parousia*] of the Son of Man" (Matt. 24:3, 27, 37, 39). This marks the beginning of the rebirth of all things, and at that time the Twelve will receive their reward: "I tell you the truth, at the renewal of all things, when the Son of Man sits on his glorious throne, you who have followed me will also sit on twelve thrones, judging the twelve tribes of Israel" (Matt. 19:28). The return will be the moment of the last judgment: "When the Son of Man comes in his glory, and all the angels with him, he will sit on his throne in heavenly glory. All the nations will be gathered before him, and he will separate the people one from another" (Matt. 25:31–32).

At the end of his controversies with the teachers of the law (Matt. 22:41–46), Jesus makes reference to his future heavenly glory by applying Psalm 110 to himself. The Christ is not only the son of David, but also David's *Lord*. God has said concerning him, "Sit at my right hand until I put your enemies under your feet" (Ps. 110:1; Mark 12:36).[8]

In summary it can be said that in Jesus' teaching there is clearly a perspective of a future for himself after his death. It is the future of a resurrection from the realm of the dead on the third day, a return to the Father, and a coming on the clouds as the judge of all nations. The disciples were not able to accept the announcement of Jesus' death, so they failed initially to understand this perspective of a future *after* his death, although they did grasp fragments of it. We see this, for instance, in their constant bickering over who will be greatest in the kingdom of

---

8. For the meaning of Psalm 110, see M. Hengel, "Psalm 110 und die Erhöhung des Auferstandenen zur Rechten Gottes," in *Anfänge der Christologie*, ed. C. B. Breytenbach and H. Paulsen (Göttingen: Vandenhoeck & Ruprecht, 1991), 43–73.

heaven. We see it also in the question raised by the sons of Zebedee (or their mother) about whether they might sit on the right and left of the King in his "glory" (Mark 10:37).

8.2.2 The Resurrection Life

Jesus' future after his death is different from his life on earth. It is the future in which the Son of Man will be glorified (John 12:23–24). Just as the heavens are above the earth, so will this future be exalted above the life lived in Galilee and Jerusalem. When Moses and Elijah appear from heaven on the Mount of Transfiguration, a radiant light can be seen around them—but not around the disciples. This is a sign: Jesus will be taken up into the glory of the heavenly light. His appearance will change, his face will shine like the sun, and his clothing will be as white as the light (Matt. 17:2). When Jesus returns to the Father, it means a transition to a higher order, for "the Father is greater than I" (John 14:28). It is therefore difficult for us, earth-bound humans, to give a concrete and detailed description of the reality in which Jesus is now living.

Jesus' future is greater and different, but it is not any less real than his life on earth has been. There is a kind of transformation that takes place from humiliation to glory, but there is a continuity of life and person. The connecting link is the bodily resurrection. The Evangelists speak unambiguously of a real resurrection, regardless of how wondrous and incomprehensible the sudden appearances of Jesus after his resurrection may be. The empty tomb is not what matters most; an empty tomb could also point to grave robbery. More important is the fact that the shroud, stiffened with ointment, was empty: the Master left behind the husk of his winding sheet![9] The disciples, when they see the risen Jesus, also think that they may be seeing a "ghost," but Jesus counteracts this impression by eating something—a piece of broiled fish and some honey.[10] He also invites Thomas to place his finger in the healing wounds on his hands, and to place his hand in the lance wound in his side (John 20:27).

If Jesus really rose from the realm of the dead, the statements about his ascension and return can not be interpreted as metaphors for a spiritual reality. The nature of Jesus' future is tied to his bodily resurrection. His glorification does not mean evaporation!

9. See J. van Bruggen, *Christ on Earth: The Gospel Narratives as History* (Grand Rapids: Baker, 1998), sec. 17.8.

10. See J. van Bruggen, *Lucas: Het evangelie als voorgeschiedenis*, Commentaar op het Nieuwe Testament, 3d series (Kampen: Kok, 1993), on Luke 24:36–43. The "honeycomb" mentioned in older translations does not appear in newer translations due to a preference for the reading of a smaller number of manuscripts.

Over the centuries, the bodily resurrection of Jesus has been challenged in a number of ways.[11] Frequently these challenges are combined with attempts at maintaining a "resurrection faith," which would involve a spiritual resurrection of which Peter became aware[12] or that was revealed to the disciples through visions they experienced after Jesus' death.[13] In recent decades, the idea has been propagated that Jesus' resurrection took place after the cross and in heaven. When Jesus died, his disciples were convinced that he, like the martyrs, would certainly be accepted by God and justified in heaven. His being given a place in heaven is the intended "resurrection." Only later was a period of three days inserted between the death and the "resurrection." The stories about appearances, like the Hellenistic appearance stories, would prove that according to the faith of his followers Jesus really has been resurrected in God's presence. Only then would the idea of a bodily, earthly resurrection be proposed, because Greek Christians (unlike the Jews) could not have imagined an assumption into heaven without the body disappearing from the tomb.

At first glance this idea seems to involve merely the details of the resurrection, but in fact it denies Jesus' entire future. The idea of a heavenly resurrection is indeed just an idea and not a reality. It is therefore understandable that the denial of the earthly resurrection is followed by the denial of a heavenly return.[14] It is, incidentally, paradoxical that an appeal to the Jewish *belief* in the heavenly justification of martyrs should result in *unbelief* in any kind of heavenly future!

For the Jewish belief in the heavenly assumption of martyrs (immediately after their death), H. J. De Jonge refers to 2 Maccabees 7.[15] The specific roots for this notion of a kind of heavenly resurrection can be found in publications on Jewish martyrology by Kellermann,[16] Van

11. See N. L. Geisler, *The Battle for the Resurrection* (Nashville: Nelson, 1989).

12. J. B. Spong, *Resurrection: Myth or Reality? A Bishop's Search for the Origins of Christianity* (San Francisco: Harper, 1994).

13. G. Lüdemann, *Die Auferstehung Jesu: Historie, Erfahrung, Theologie* (Göttingen: Vandenhoeck & Ruprecht, 1994). Compare Baum's critical review: A. D. Baum, "Auferstehung oder Vision? Gerd Lüdemanns Versuch, den christlichen Osterglauben zu erneuern: Ein Gutachten für die Gemeinde," *Diakrisis* 16 (March 1995): 23–34.

14. H. J. de Jonge, "Ontstaan en ontwikkeling van het geloof in Jezus' opstanding," in *Waarlijk opgestaan! Een discussie over de opstanding van Jezus Christus*, ed. F. O. van Gennep et al. (Baarn: Ten Have, 1989), 31–50. See also idem, "De opstanding van Jezus: De joodse traditie achter een christelijke belijdenis," in *Jodendom en vroeg christendom: Continuïteit en discontinuïteit*, Opstellen van leden van de Studiosorum Novi Testamenti Conventus, ed. T. Baarda (Kampen: Kok, 1991), 47–61; idem, "De oorsprong van de verwachting van Jezus' wederkomst," 9–36.

15. H. J. de Jonge, "Ontstaan en ontwikkeling van het geloof in Jezus' opstanding."

16. U. Kellermann, *Auferstanden in den Himmel: II Makkabäer 7 und die Auferstehung der Märtyrer*, Stuttgarter Bibelstudien 95 (Stuttgart: Katholisches Bibelwerk, 1979).

Henten,[17] and others. De Jonge incorporates all this into a comprehensive view of the evolution of the resurrection faith in the ancient church. According to this view, the verb *resurrect* would initially have been used for *being lifted up* to God, as would have been true in the case of the seven tortured brothers in 2 Maccabees 7. Reading this whole chapter, however, clearly shows that it speaks about a *future* resurrection. The mother of the seven sons offers encouragement to her last and youngest child at the time of his martyrdom: "Do not fear this executioner, but prove yourself worthy of your brothers, and make death welcome, so that *in the day of mercy* I may receive you back in your brothers' company" (7:29). The third boy calmly allows his hands to be cut off and says, "It was heaven that gave me these limbs; for the sake of his laws I disdain them; from him *I hope* to receive them again" (7:11). This is an expression of a *future* raising of the body (compare 7:14: "*God's promise* that we shall be raised up by him"). We find exactly the same Jewish expectation in the New Testament in the words of the sister of Lazarus: "I know he will rise again in the resurrection at the last day" (John 11:24). But a great deal of confusion and misunderstanding can be avoided by reading 2 Maccabees and other writings in their entirety. How, for instance, can one maintain that for the writer of 2 Maccabees, and the other Jews of that period in general, *raise up* or *rise again* meant a heavenly reward for martyrdom? Listen to what the writer of 2 Maccabees says in 12:43–44 about Judas the Galilean (and this is a *general* statement about the faith of the Jews at that time!): "After this he took a collection from them individually, amounting to nearly two thousand drachmae, and sent it to Jerusalem to have a sacrifice for sin offered, an altogether fine and noble action, in which he took full account of the resurrection. For if he had not *expected* the fallen to *rise again* it would have been superfluous and foolish to pray for the dead."

This is the same idea we also find in Hebrews: the martyrs hope for a future resurrection of the body (Heb. 11:32–40).

When it is reported that Jesus has been *raised*, it can have meant nothing other to Jewish listeners of that time than that he had returned bodily.

If speaking of *resurrection* in a Jewish environment would not have led people to think immediately of a *bodily* resurrection, how then is it possible that Herod and many other Jews thought that Jesus in fact was John the Baptist returned from the dead? The word *rise* carried with it a particular image, and in the case of John the Baptist that image was not of a man being taken from the dungeon (when he was beheaded) up

---

17. J. W. van Henten et al., eds., *Die Entstehung der jüdischen Martyrologie*, Studia Post-Biblica 38 (Leiden: Brill, 1989).

into heaven (as a Jewish martyr). Perhaps people did believe this of John, but they did not call it *resurrection*. People only bring up the subject of a possible resurrection when they look at Jesus: a man of flesh and blood, physically living on the earth. Was John supposed to have become a living *physical* man once again? Apparently this was part of the general Jewish notion of resurrection. But then it is to be expected that something similar is intended when it is said of *Jesus* that he is *risen*! For that matter, what else could people have imagined when they heard the stories of the *raising* of Lazarus? The crowds that heard this news did not look up to heaven, but traveled in throngs to Bethany to see for themselves. In this Jewish context it is implausible that a few weeks later people would have understood, even for a short time, the preaching about Jesus' *resurrection* as a reference to a heavenly acceptance of the Crucified One on Good Friday (when his body was entrusted to the tomb).

8.2.3 Between Ascension and Second Coming

What is the relationship between Jesus' future in the glory of his Father and his prior life and work on earth? This question easily gives rise to a falsified perspective. Christendom is fairly well informed about Jesus' life on earth: we have four Gospels that illuminate it from several angles. It is a life that has a certain closure, ending as it does with the cross and the cry, "It is finished." But, as we saw, it appears that even during his life on earth, Jesus was looking forward to a future life after his death. But what is the relationship between that future and what preceded it? Because we cannot follow the life and work of Christ in heaven, and no Gospels are written about it, this period in glory seems to be little more than a sort of appendix to the most important period, which we know so well from the Gospels. This future after his death seems like an interim that must be passed through before the purpose of Jesus' suffering and death is reached in peace on earth for those who earn God's pleasure. The principal function of this interim then seems to be *waiting* for each other: the gospel must be preached to all nations, and that takes time.

It is true that Jesus said that the end would not come until this preaching had been accomplished: "And this gospel of the kingdom will be preached in the whole world as a testimony to all nations, and then the end will come" (Matt. 24:14). And it was for this purpose that he commissioned his apostles after Easter: "Make disciples of all nations. . . . And surely I am with you always, to the very end of the age" (Matt. 28:19–20; compare Mark 16:15). Even so, carrying out this task is not the only activity with which Christ's heavenly time is filled. Jesus does indeed say that the preaching to all nations must take place before the end comes, but he does not say that his return will take place as soon as the last territory has been reached.

When Jesus speaks these words they sound incredible. The gospel is on the wane in Israel, and in a few days he will be dead. Will the apotheosis of the kingdom of heaven take place now, when not much of an audience is left? Jesus denies this. Contrary to every expectation people may have had at that moment, the gospel will see tremendous expansion. The apotheosis does not arrive unnoticed. Only after it is announced throughout the world will the day of the redemption of the world arrive. This is a statement about the *way* in which the end will come, but it is not a complete description of the *goal* of the coming period.

Jesus mentioned many other things that have a place in his heavenly period and that will occur before the end comes.

1. *The preaching of the gospel to all nations.* This command must certainly be mentioned first, because everything begins with that preaching. Just as so much began to happen around Jesus through the Baptist's preaching and his own ministry in the synagogues, so many things will be set in motion by the worldwide witness of the apostles.

Seen from the perspective of Jesus' own teaching about the preaching to all nations, it seems as if this commission will be accomplished within one generation and by those who were eyewitnesses of his ministry. The apostles are not told to *begin* this journey to all nations; they are told that they *themselves* must make disciples of all nations. Paul also works from this perspective (Col. 1:6: "All over the world this gospel is bearing fruit and growing"). The church of the first centuries also held the view that the gospel had been preached to the nations by the apostles, and that this work now must be maintained by a further christianization of the regions they had reached and by also reaching the barbarians outside the Roman empire.[18] The church that owes its foundations to the worldwide preaching of the apostles is aware of its obligation to continue speaking to others. But it would not be in line with Jesus' teaching to identify this later, non-apostolic work with the specific task of the apostles to convey the gospel to all nations.

2. *The great distress that will come to the Jewish people after the destruction of the temple.* In his shocking discourse about the fall of the temple Jesus did not only announce the total destruction of this house of God in Jerusalem, but he also linked it with a prophecy of the history of the Jewish people after the event. A period of great and unprecedented distress will come over them. This will affect non-Christian and

18. N. Brox, "Zur christlichen Mission in der Spätantike," in *Mission im Neuen Testament,* Quaestiones Disputatae 93, ed. K. Kertelge (Freiburg: Herder, 1982), 190–237.

Christian Jews alike,[19] so it is not a punishment for unbelief. Many of the people of Israel will be led astray, but the elect will persevere in their Christian faith. This suffering will not come to an end until Christ's second coming. Only then will the remaining believers be brought together from the four corners of the earth and be reunited (Matt. 24:29–31).

3. *The appearance of deceiving prophets and false messiahs among the Jewish people and of false christs among the Christians.* During the great distress, the Jewish people will have to deal with false messiahs and false prophets. Many will be deceived by them and kept from believing in the Messiah Jesus (Mark 13:21–23). Only the elect from within the Jewish people in the great Diaspora will remain true to this Messiah. The Christians will also be divided among themselves by people who come in Jesus' name and promote themselves (Mark 13:5–6). All this leads to the urgent appeal, "Watch out that no one deceives you" (Mark 13:5, 22b–23).

4. *Living in accordance with the commandments of Christ.* The future of Jesus will be characterized by the fact that he will leave his commandments behind on earth and that they must and will determine human behavior. Admission to the kingdom of heaven depends on whether one has done the will of Jesus' heavenly Father as stipulated in his commandments (stated in, among other places, the Sermon on the Mount, Matt. 7:21–27). Part of the apostles' mission is to teach all those who are baptized "to obey everything I have commanded you" (Matt. 28:20). In his farewell discourses Jesus repeatedly points out the importance of his commandments. Those who keep them are showing their love for Jesus (John 14:15, 21, 24; 15:10). These are the ones who bear fruit for him (John 15:5). The key commandment is to love one another (John 15:12, 17).

5. *Performing great works.* A hallmark of the great future of Jesus will be the great things that his disciples will accomplish on earth by faith: "If you remain in me and my words remain in you, ask whatever you wish, and it will be given you" (John 15:7). Shortly thereafter Jesus says, "I tell you the truth, my Father will give you whatever you ask in my name" (John 16:23; compare Matt. 21:22).

The power of faith makes possible the moving of mountains (Matt. 17:20; 21:21). This metaphor suggests that the impossible and inconceivable can be accomplished if necessary. A disciple of Jesus will never face insurmountable obstacles.

These promises are given especially to the apostles and the original disciples. Through prayer, they would have to overcome tremendous obstacles to spread the gospel everywhere, despite enormous resistance

---

19. See van Bruggen, *Marcus*, on Mark 13:14–23.

from the devil. Jesus himself worked with them and confirmed his word by the signs that accompanied it (Mark 16:20). The Book of Acts will prove that he really has given his apostles "authority to trample on snakes and scorpions" in their march against "the power of the enemy" (Luke 10:19).

It is not impossible that Jesus also authorized the postapostolic church to perform these works as often as necessary for the sake of the gospel. On the other hand, the works already performed (and reported in Acts) will be kept alive in sermon, hymn, and faith (even as the events from the wilderness period were kept alive in memory through the psalms that sang of them). These works are not the decisive element of the future, however. Jesus himself said, "Do not rejoice that the spirits submit to you, but rejoice that your names are written in heaven" (Luke 10:20).

6. *Increasing unbelief and worldly lifestyle.* A general hallmark of Jesus' heavenly period will be the increase of lawlessness on earth: "Because of the increase of wickedness [*anomia*, lawlessness], the love of most will grow cold" (Matt. 24:12). People will do little more than eat and drink, marry and be taken in marriage, as in the days of Noah and as in the city of Sodom (Luke 17:26–29).

7. *The perseverance of the saints.* Jesus speaks with assurance of the preservation of the elect. This is not a matter of course: the days will have to be shortened to accomplish this (Matt. 24:22), and Jesus prays urgently for this to his Father in his farewell prayer (John 17:12–26). The end, however, will prove that a faithful people has remained that is expecting the Master. These are people who were willing to "always pray and not give up," and because of them the Son of Man will find "faith on the earth" when he comes (Luke 18:1, 8). This is also the reason why he came to earth. As a good shepherd he gives up his life for his sheep in order to save many sheep in one flock with one shepherd (John 10:11–18). Now we come to the result of what Jesus had in view. He assures people more than once that he has come to seek and save the lost (Matt. 18:11; Luke 9:56 [in most manuscripts]; Luke 19:10), which causes rejoicing among the angels in heaven (Luke 15:7, 10, 32).

The heart of all this is the salvation of sinners by faith. The preaching of the gospel and the performing of great works are both undertaken in the service of this rescue operation. The warnings against increasing lawlessness and deceivers are intended to safeguard this work of salvation. The promise to preserve the elect gives them the courage they need to persevere. Jesus puts it succinctly and to the point when he says to Thomas, "Blessed are those who have not seen and yet have believed" (John 20:29).

Christ's stay with the Father is aimed at the gathering together of an elect people from the whole world. This means that he comes to "baptize with the Spirit" from heaven. The time when Jesus sits at the right hand of God after the completion of his earthly work is the period when he will fulfill the promise with which John the Baptist began: after me comes One who will baptize you with the Spirit!

In this way, through his ascension and through his taking his place in the glory of God's throne, Jesus will become "the One who comes with the Spirit and with fire." The heavenly period is not an appendix to the earthly period, but the earthly period was an introduction to the heavenly one. The words spoken on the cross, "It is finished," mean that now the conditions have been met for the actual work to begin. Now nothing stands in the way of baptism with the Spirit and with fire. During his stay on earth, it is clear that Jesus is the Son of God. He acts in Israel as God himself. On the other hand, there always seems to be something standing between him and God, an obstruction that serves as grist to the mockers' mill and that Jesus, in a conversation with John the Baptist, calls a stumbling block that must be accepted. Jesus resists using his divine power. He does use it on behalf of others, but not on his own behalf (see sec. 3.4). But this comes to an end when his life on earth is completed. The obstruction is removed. From that moment on, Jesus is the Son of God in glory, without any personal reticence. The period in the Gospels is a bitter exception that had to precede the splendor of his glory. The earthly life of Jesus is an occasion for endless astonishment and praise, but the heavenly life of the man Jesus, born of the Virgin Mary, is what it was about all along. The most important and abiding fact is the *future* of the Son of God.

8.3 The Time of the Spirit

8.3.1 Immersed in the Spirit

The great prophet John the Baptist presented Israel with a unique view of the future. He announced the coming of the Greater One who would "baptize with the Holy Spirit" (Mark 1:8). John uses the verb "baptize (immerse)" in order to make a comparison between his own work and that of the Man who was to come after him. The people were crowded along the banks of the Jordan to be immersed as a sign of repentance and expectation. John soon became known as "the Baptist." His work, however, remained limited. He did not go beyond plunging people under water so they could return, soaking wet, to the river bank. This water eventually dried. John prepared Israel for the great change, but he himself did not usher in this change. The Mightier One would do that. He will immerse people in the Holy Spirit. Those people will be dripping with the Spirit—they will never dry!

In later Christian usage, a noun came into circulation to typify this promise. People spoke of "the *baptism* in the Spirit." This noun easily suggests that (like water baptism) this is a one-time event, either the collective "baptism" of the universal church on Pentecost,[20] or the individual "baptism in the Holy Spirit" of each believer (the so-called second blessing).[21] It is significant, however, that the noun *baptisma* is only used in the New Testament in reference to the water baptism (the baptism of John or Christian water baptism). There is never any reference to a *baptisma* of the Spirit. This is not surprising. John used the verb *immerse* to depict the work of the Spirit in order to make a comparison between his own activity and that of the coming Mightier One. In the New Testament, therefore, the verb *baptizein* is used exclusively for the granting of the Spirit when a comparison is made between John the Baptist and Jesus (Matt. 3:11; Mark 1:8; Luke 3:16; John 1:33; Acts 1:5; 11:16). In all other cases (with the exception of 1 Cor. 12:13) other verbs are used ("to pour out" the Spirit when the prophecy of Joel is in view; "to give" and "to receive" the Spirit when there are no references to this prophecy).

John the Baptist does not compare two "baptisms" (one with water and one with the Spirit); he compares his own powerlessness with the power of Jesus. He himself can do no more than immerse in water, but Jesus comes to immerse in the Spirit. History has shown that Jesus does not replace water baptism but upholds it (Matt. 28:19). Added to that water baptism, however, is now the fulfillment of the promise that he would immerse in the Spirit (see Acts 2:38; 19:1–6).

The gift of the Spirit is God's work. John the Baptist announces the Man who will come after him as being clothed with the power of God himself. This man will be able to saturate people with the Holy Spirit. That Spirit also came to earth in the Old Testament. He spoke through the prophets (1 Sam. 10:10–11; 1 Kings 22:24–25) and came upon David, the prophet and king (Ps. 51:11). He was with the people in the desert, but there he became their opponent because the people resisted him (Ps. 106:33; Isa. 63:10). In that period, however, there was not a man on earth who could call down and dispense the Spirit. John the

20. R. B. Gaffin, *Perspectives on Pentecost,* 2d ed. (Phillipsburg, N.J.: Presbyterian & Reformed, 1980); N. H. Gootjes, "De doop met de Heilige Geest en de betekenis van Pinksteren," *Radix* 13 (1987): 139–58.

21. J. D. G. Dunn, *Baptism in the Holy Spirit: A Re-examination of the New Testament Teaching on the Gift of the Spirit in Relation to Pentecostalism Today,* Studies in Biblical Theology 2/15 (London: SCM, 1970).

Baptist now announces that there is a man coming who can "mediate" this Spirit on behalf of the people. This is something new.

The prophets of the Old Covenant had already promised a saving abundance of God's Spirit on earth. The restoration of the people of God will be accomplished by the outpouring of the Spirit of the LORD (Ezek. 37:14). Thus the generations will be united in praising God and thus they will be saved on the day of judgment (Joel 2:28–32). The Spirit will no longer be an outsider who comes and goes and moves people for a time. He will come and dwell in human hearts, and through that new covenant he will renew the people from the inside out (Jer. 31:31–34). Thus a new world will come into being in which the Spirit of God will fill the hearts of men and the righteousness of God will flood the earth as the waters cover the sea (Isa. 32:14–20; 44:1–5).

We learn from the preaching of the great prophet John the Baptist that the Mightier One, who will come after John, will fulfill this promise. In this way the failure of Israel's history will still result in the fulfillment of the promises made to Abram: in his seed, in Christ, all the nations of the earth will be blessed.

8.3.2 The Coming of the Comforter

This future, promised by John the Baptist, of immersion in the Spirit was not realized during Jesus' life on earth. Only at his ascension did the fulfillment begin. Then Jesus said to his disciples, "John baptized with water, but in a few days you will be baptized with the Holy Spirit" (Acts 1:5). John the Baptist was probably surprised that this future, which he had prophesied, initially failed to materialize. From his prison cell he asked Jesus himself if he should wait for someone else (Matt. 11:3).

During his life on earth, however, Jesus repeatedly said that he was the fulfillment of John's prophecy and that he was the one who would come after John. This means that he would also immerse in the Spirit and in fire. He clearly demonstrated his power to do this during his years on earth. He preached about himself that he was the one anointed with the Spirit of God (Luke 4:17–21), and he showed this by means of the many healing miracles and signs he performed (Luke 4:14–15; Matt. 12:28, 31–32). John the Baptist was aware of this; he saw the Spirit descend *and remain on him* and realized then that this Jesus would immerse in the Spirit (John 1:32–33) because God had given him the Spirit *without limit* (John 3:34). Although this immersion in the Spirit initially did not happen, Jesus let the people know that he had the power to distribute the Spirit to others. This was completely new. Under the Old Covenant, there were people who had been seized by the Spirit for longer or shorter periods of time, but no one had personal control over the Spirit of God and no one could pass it on to other people. In the case of Moses, the LORD God once took part of his own Spirit that was on Moses and laid it on seventy others (Num. 11:25). But Moses could only stand by when this happened and say, "I wish that all the LORD's people were prophets and that the LORD would put this Spirit on them!" (Num. 11:29). But Jesus is greater than Moses: he himself dispenses the powers of the Spirit of God. He does so with his twelve disciples and later with the seventy. Suddenly they are able do the works that he himself has done. They preach the gospel and heal and cast out evil spirits in Jesus' name (Matt. 10:1, 20; Luke 9:1; 10:17). Jesus has the Spirit of God at his disposal!

Yet while he is on earth, the immersion in the Spirit remains future. It is still a promise, but a promise of which the people are reminded again and again. Jesus himself takes responsibility for John the Baptist's predictions of the future.

This occurred most emphatically and publicly during a Feast of Tabernacles, when Jesus was already a subject of great controversy among the Jews. On the last day of the feast, he stood in the temple and cried aloud to the crowds, "If anyone is thirsty, let him come to me and drink. Whoever believes in me, as the Scripture has said, streams of living water will flow from within him" (John 7:37–38). This exclamation may allude to the pouring of water at the altar that took place during this particular feast. But the image of the abundance of water flowing from inside a person is reminiscent of the immersion in the Jordan by John the Baptist. This immersion left the outside of the person soaking wet as a sign of a future inner flooding by the Spirit of God. Jesus is the one who will fulfill this promise!

At another time, we read more or less between the lines that Jesus was intent on giving the Spirit. He teaches his disciples to pray with confidence to their heavenly Father: "If you then, though you are evil, know how to give good gifts to your children, how much more will your Father in heaven give the Holy Spirit to those who ask him!" (Luke 11:13).

Finally, in his farewell talks with the disciples, when the time of the Spirit was approaching, Jesus announces at length the coming of this Comforter or heavenly Helper (John 14:17).[22] And after his resurrection he gives them a sign of the imminent outpouring of the Spirit by blowing on them and saying, "Receive the Holy Spirit."[23]

22. For a more detailed discussion, see P. H. R. van Houwelingen, *Johannes: Het evangelie van het Woord,* Commentaar op het Nieuwe Testament, 3d series (Kampen: Kok, 1997), on John 14:17.

23. See Houwelingen, *Johannes,* on John 20:22.

Thus Jesus takes responsibility for the promise of John the Baptist. He also indicates what effects this giving of the Spirit will have.

1. *During the period of Jesus' bodily absence, the Spirit will be the Guide and Teacher for the apostles and for all who accept their words.* In situations of persecution, the Holy Spirit will inspire outspokenness and sound speech (Matt. 10:20; Mark 13:11; Luke 12:12). Thus the apostles will stand firm and will no longer flee, as they did in Gethsemane. The foundations of the church will be laid and the community will be built upon it. And the gates of hell will not prevail against it (Matt. 16:18).

The Spirit will also guide the apostles in the truth. This does not mean that Jesus did not preach the full truth. He revealed everything, but the disciples were only able to understand or accept it in part. The Spirit, however, will finish the work of Jesus and establish it in the hearts and mouths of the apostles. The Spirit will remind them of everything that Jesus had said (John 14:26). The Spirit is Jesus' witness (John 15:26–27), and he will make sure that Jesus receives his full due among the disciples. Thus the Spirit will "guide you into all truth" (John 16:13). This does not mean that Jesus' revelation would be incomplete without the additional revelation of the Spirit. The context of these words shows that the Spirit guides the way in the truth *that has already been made known.* Jesus has "much more to say" (John 16:12a), but not because he had kept much to himself. He made the Father completely known (John 17:6). Sadly, however, the Father is still not very well known among the disciples; during this last night, they ask the strangest questions about the Father (John 14:8–9). Jesus has said enough and has nothing to add, but nevertheless he cannot stop speaking because his audience has not yet completely understood and accepted what he is teaching. At the moment, however, it makes little sense to keep on talking. "I have much more to say to you, more than you can now bear" (John 16:12b). The disciples are not assimilating the content of his teaching. That is why the Spirit will come. He will guide (*hodēgēsei*) the disciples in the full truth, which at this point they want to enter into only in part (John 16:13a). In doing this, the Spirit will keep referring to what Jesus has already revealed: "He will bring glory to me by taking from what is mine and making it known to you" (John 16:14–15).

The special work of the Spirit among the disciples will benefit all believers. Because the apostles have been put and kept on the right path, everyone who accepts their words will also find themselves on the right path. The Spirit takes care of them through the commandments of the apostles and the prophets. In his last night, Jesus prays not only for the remaining disciples but also for everyone "who will believe in me through their message, that all of them may be one" (John 17:20). Even here, the Spirit stimulates future believers to be able to grasp a gospel that is strange to them and against which they, like the apostles, feel a great deal of resistance. The Spirit teaches them to enter deep into the world of a gospel that is a stumbling block to Jews and foolishness to the Gentiles. This Spirit teaches them to endure persecution and puts words in their mouths when they are taken into court.

2. *The Spirit comes to live in the hearts of believers with an abundance of heavenly gifts, which causes a profound change in their lives and gives them a completely different attitude toward God and their neighbors.* The streams of living water that flow from within them (John 7:37–38) are an image of the Spirit that believers will receive when Jesus is glorified (John 7:39). This Spirit changes the lives of believers. This does not involve the granting of faith but the fruits of faith. Those who confess Christ's name receive from him the gifts of the Spirit, which cause them to change and lead them into the kingdom of God's Spirit: the kingdom of heaven.

Christ causes rebirth in "water and the Spirit," through which people will see and enter the kingdom of God (John 3:3, 5). Jesus says this in so many words in his conversation with Nicodemus. He clearly alludes to the call to repentance and faith, sealed by baptism in the waters of the Jordan. The promise of immersion in the Spirit was linked to this baptism. If Nicodemus lets himself be called to faith (lets himself be baptized) by the Successor to John the Baptist, he will experience the subsequent work of the Spirit: the Spirit turns the believer into a changed person and leads him or her into the kingdom of God. In his conversation with the Pharisee Nicodemus, the accent is on *water.* The teacher of the law knows that God's Spirit is necessary for man, but now he must accept the fact that the way to that Spirit comes via the water of the new baptism that anticipates the coming Jesus. The immersion in the Jordan symbolized the death of the sinner. Only new birth can save his life!

John the Evangelist incorporates this teaching into the introduction to his Gospel. There he writes: "Yet to all who received him [Jesus], to those who believed in his name, he gave the right to become children of God—children born not of natural descent, nor of human decision or a husband's will, but born of God" (John 1:12–13).

8.3.3 *The Spirit Changes Borders*

Jesus' outpouring of the Spirit (after his ascension into heaven) ushers in a whole new period. This can become more apparent from a discussion of the Book of Acts and the apostolic epistles (which falls outside the scope of this volume). But the main features of this radical renewal can already be seen in the words Jesus spoke when he was living on earth.

1. The borders are opened. After the ascension, the disciples must serve as witnesses to the Resurrected One the world over. They will have to go forth and make disciples of all nations, baptizing them in the name of the Father, the Son, and the Holy Spirit. There is no mention here of circumcision (Matt. 28:19). This opening of the borders has everything to do with the outpouring of the Spirit: just before his ascension, Jesus tells them to wait in Jerusalem for the power from on high before going to Samaria and to the ends of the earth. They will receive this power "when the Holy Spirit comes on you" (Acts 1:8).
2. The pattern of worship changes. In his discussion with the Samaritan woman, Jesus indicates that the immersion in the Spirit will bring with it a change in worship. The Jews honored God in the temple in Jerusalem, and the Samaritans worshiped on Gerizim, but Jesus now says, "A time is coming when you will worship the Father neither on this mountain nor in Jerusalem" (John 4:21). The coming of Jesus brought with it the time "when the true worshipers will worship the Father in spirit and truth" (John 4:23). This is the fitting form of worship, for God himself is Spirit (John 4:24). The Mosaic form of worship, with its appointed places and times, its regulations of food and externals, was an aid in the true worship. But when Jesus pours out the Spirit, such aids will be superfluous. This means a change in law and custom, as Jesus alluded to elsewhere (for instance, in his comments on the dietary laws in Mark 7:18–19; see also sec. 7.2.3). These coming changes mean a transition to a new covenant, a covenant made possible by the direct bestowal of the Spirit on those who confess Christ's name.

8.4 The Day of Fire

8.4.1 Baptism with Fire

John the Baptist spoke not only of baptism in the Holy Spirit, but he also mentioned baptism with fire (Matt. 3:11; Luke 3:16). According to some exegetes, these both refer to the same baptism; fire is a metaphor for the previously mentioned Spirit of God. The flames of fire seen on the day of Pentecost (Acts 2:3) seem to support this idea. Yet taken as a whole, John's preaching requires another explanation. For him the "fire" points to God's imminent judgment. Shortly before his statement about baptizing with fire, John speaks of the judgment in which every tree that bears no fruit will be "cut down and thrown into the fire" (Matt. 3:10). And immediately after speaking of baptizing with fire, John says, "His winnowing fork is in his hand, and he will clear his threshing floor, gathering his wheat into the barn and burning up the chaff with unquenchable fire" (Matt. 3:12; compare Luke 3:17).[24]

As prophet of repentance, John warns the people of "the coming wrath" (Matt. 3:7). He who comes after John will execute judgment, and everyone who opposed God's word will be destroyed in overpowering fire. The result will be a great purification. The worthless chaff will be burned, and only the grain will remain. Already in the Old Testament, fire is a symbol of God's purifying and cleansing activity. This fire is not an uncontrollable, irrational natural disaster in which a great deal of value is lost, but a carefully planned trash incineration project to purify and preserve the environment of God's world.

John does not speak about this fire in purely informative terms. He issues a warning. The very reason he has come is to administer the baptism of repentance to prepare the people for the coming of the judge, so that they will be immersed in the Spirit and not in the fire. His speaking about the fire is intended to be preventative: God wants the people to escape the fire! The prophet of fire was sent, as his father Zechariah already prophesied, "to guide our feet into the path of peace" (Luke 1:79). The warning about the fire underscores how seriously the prophet of God and the One who will follow him must be taken.

8.4.2 Jesus Comes to Bring Fire to the Earth

Jesus takes up this aspect of the Baptist's preaching in his own sermons. In the Sermon on the Mount he even quotes John verbatim: "Every tree that does not bear good fruit is cut down and thrown into the fire" (Matt. 7:19; compare Matt. 3:10). Shortly thereafter Jesus connects with John's phraseology when he speaks of an "unquenchable fire" (Mark 9:43, 45, 47; compare Matt. 3:12). He also elaborates on the image of weeds that are burned (Matt. 3:12) in the parable of the weeds growing among the grain (Matt. 13:40, 42, 50; also compare John 15:6). More than once he warns, in his own words, against the danger of perishing in "the fire of hell" (Matt. 5:22; 18:9) or in "the eternal fire" (Matt. 18:8; 25:41).

Contrary to the expectations of the Baptist, Jesus does not usher in this fire immediately. But from what he says we realize that he has not abandoned John's future perspective. He affirms it and takes up John's warnings as his own.

---

24. For a more detailed discussion, see also van Bruggen, *Matteüs*, on Matt. 3:11–12.

His disciples understood this aspect of his teaching well, even though they were unclear about the time of its execution. When a Samaritan village refuses Jesus lodgings during his journey to Jerusalem, the "sons of thunder," James and John, ask if they should "call down fire from heaven to destroy them" (Luke 9:54), referring, according to many manuscripts, to the example of Elijah. But the fact that they immediately think of fire certainly also has to do with the preaching of the Baptist and of the Master himself. Jesus' answer (found in most manuscripts) is revealing. The Son of Man came to earth not to destroy but to save (Luke 9:56). His coming to earth is for the salvation of sinners, not for their destruction by fire. The purifying last judgment will only come when Jesus returns in the glory of the Father with all the holy angels (Mark 8:38).

On another occasion it seems as if Jesus has "come to earth" to bring fire. At one point he sighs, "I have come to bring fire on the earth, and how I wish it were already kindled!" (Luke 12:49). This indicates two things: (1) Jesus regards the purification with fire as an integral part of his coming to earth; (2) Jesus knows that this purification cannot take place immediately. He himself must first be immersed in death (Luke 12:50), and thereafter comes a period in which the distinction between the grain and the chaff must become very clear (Luke 12:51–53). The future will require time.[25] Yet Jesus longs for the day of purification by fire: then the righteous will shine like the sun in the kingdom of their Father (Matt. 13:43).

8.4.3 The Last Days and the Great Day

In the gospel of the Son of God, the great day of judgment is spoken of in terms of an *announcement*. The listeners are warned and encouraged. On the basis of the preaching about judgment by fire it is impossible to say with certainty whether many will be saved or few. The gospel is not a balance sheet of the future; it is a preparation. The question concerning profit or loss is addressed by Jesus with a personal appeal: "Make every effort to enter through the narrow door, because many, I tell you, will try to enter and will not be able to. . . . People will come from east and west and north and south, and will take their places at the feast in the kingdom of God. Indeed there are those who are last who will be first, and first who will be last" (Luke 13:24, 29–30).

The decision about the future is made today. Those who believe in the Son of God will not be judged; those who do not believe stand already condemned (John 3:18). These statements also are directed *at all*

---

25. See van Bruggen, *Lucas,* on Luke 12:49–53.

the people. When the gospel reaches them, the time of decision has come. Believing or not believing in Jesus Christ becomes possible only if one has heard the gospel. It is difficult for human beings to make definitive statements about God's dealings with those who have never heard of Christ. What was true in the circle of the disciples is even more true now. There the question was asked, "Lord, what about him?" (John 21:21). Jesus answered, "If I want him to remain alive until I return, what is that to you? You must follow me" (John 21:22).

Much of what Jesus says therefore has to do with being watchful. The disciples are called to be ready (Matt. 24:44; Luke 12:47). These appeals are a continuation of the preaching of the Baptist. His aim was to go before the Lord and "make ready" a people (*hetoimazein*; Luke 1:17). Jesus' concern is to increase their number by preaching the gospel to all people. His words are also aimed at ensuring that there will be a people who are ready to receive the Lord in faith when he returns (Luke 18:8).

It is not known when this day of liberation will take place. Even the Son does not know—only the Father (Mark 13:32). All we know are the hallmarks of the "last days" that will precede the time of harvest. Jesus described these hallmarks and said that they would become recognizable within a single generation (Mark 13:23, 28–30). The community of Christ is living during the last days, under a constellation that tells them that "it is near, right at the door" (Mark 13:29). And it encourages them to be watchful and to look forward to the great future of the Son of God (Mark 13:32–37): "What I say to you, I say to everyone: 'Watch!'"

APPENDIX 1
The Pharisees

The Pharisees were the most outspoken opponents of Jesus during his earthly life. The Gospels are filled with confrontations between them and Christ, and for this very reason it is difficult to gain insight into who the Pharisees actually were. Even so, the answer to this question is important because we have a tendency, consciously or unconsciously, to allow our notions about the party of the Pharisees to color our understanding of Jesus' ministry.

The letters of Paul also contain a considerable amount of material about this segment of the Jewish population. How does the ministry of this apostle relate to his earlier life as a Pharisee?

The general overview of the various Jewish groups in the first chapter of this book would have been skewed if one group had been discussed in too much detail. The party of the Pharisees may have been of relatively minor importance in the larger context of all the movements that were active at that time, but this group requires a disproportionate amount of attention—not only because the question of the sources is complicated but also because the reconstruction of the image of the Pharisees has become an area of controversy in recent years, and many divergent views have emerged. For this reason a separate appendix on the party has been added to this book.

1. The Problem of Historical Reconstruction

1.1 Party Name and Prejudice

The name "Pharisees" is no more than a neutral party designation—so neutral that in later years it came to function all too often as a negative characterization. For many people, the name is a designation for what the Pharisees *are*—it has taken on the meaning of "hypocrites" or "sanctimonious frauds." In later centuries, people who accused each other of being "Pharisees" thereby betrayed their own unfavorable opinion of this former party within Judaism. For them the name is negatively charged.

The name "Pharisees" even had a negative connotation to the fathers of the church and could be used to describe the stubborn Jews in the synagogues. Among the Reformers it was a prejudicial name for Roman Catholics who believed in salvation by works, and in the twentieth century it has become rather common to accuse those who argue on behalf of a Christian ethic of advocating "Pharisaism."

With so many centuries between us and the real Pharisees—the Jewish party that was active during the centuries around the beginning of the Christian era—it has become almost impossible for Christians to see the word in any kind of positive light. It is very difficult to talk about Pharisees impartially and without prejudice.

By way of exercise in neutralizing a term, it is helpful to use occasionally a different "working title" for a period of time, a label to which no indelible stigma has been attached. For the sake of convenience, and in pursuit of balance, one could try referring to this Jewish party with a foreign-sounding term such as *Pharseets*. It is a meaningless name, but that is precisely the point; historically speaking, the Greek name *Pharisaioi* is also meaningless.[1]

1.2 The Age of the Party

Nothing is known about the origins of the *party* of the Pharisees. From Josephus we do know that, in addition to the Sadducees and the Essenes, this group was already in existence by the second half of the second century B.C. Considering that the group had become influential by then, its origin must go back to at least the first half of the second century B.C.

The fact that the origin of the *name* can no longer be verified suggests that it came into being during a period about which little is known historically speaking. Since the period that began with the Maccabean uprising has maintained a prominent place in Jewish historical consciousness, it can be assumed that the three Jewish parties came into being during the period before that. Possibly these parties were formed during the third century, when Judea was still under the Egyptian Ptolemies.

1. A more detailed discussion of the problem of names can be found in an article by A. I. Baumgarten ("The Name of the Pharisees," *Journal of Biblical Literature* 102 [1983]: 411–28). He rejects the familiar interpretation of *perushim* (separatists), whether in the positive sense (J. Jeremias and L. Baeck, among others) or the negative sense (E. Schürer, L. Finkelstein, and E. Rivkin, among others). Baumgarten asserts that the claim of *akribeia* (precision in the law), found in Josephus and in the Book of Acts, may have been a claim connected with the meaning of the name. (In that case it remains uncertain whether this association of the name with "preciseness" implied a change or an improvement in regard to the original name. In any case, according to Baumgarten, during the first century after Christ, the party members called themselves *parushim* in the sense of "specialists in the law.")

In describing the party, our lack of knowledge concerning the name and origin makes it necessary to deduce the character of the group from later descriptions of the party and its functioning.[2]

1.3 The Sources of Our Knowledge

Over the past hundred years, many different conceptions of the party of the Pharisees have developed. A measure of bias is evident in these reconstructions.[3]

For Jewish researchers, who saw in this group one of the roots of later Judaism, the Pharisees are a group that on balance must be judged positively. Through continuing interpretation of the law, they passed on the legacy of the fathers in usable form to later generations.

Christian researchers are quicker to see the party in negative terms. The Old Testament faith was supposedly perverted by the Pharisees into legalism and a religion of works.

What are the sources on which these ideas are based? They are not only documents in which the Pharisees are explicitly mentioned but also the writings that are thought to have been written in the same spirit without referring to them by name. The Psalms of Solomon are a well-known example; until recently they were accepted by almost everyone as having been written within the ranks of this party.

In 1909, Schürer stated without hesitation, "The spirit with which the Psalms are suffused is entirely that of pharisaical Judaism."[4] But in 1986, the adapters of this part of Schürer's book (G. Vermes, F. Millar, and M.

2. It is a widely held idea that the Pharisees emerged from the Hasidim (the Pious Ones), who are mentioned in the time of the Maccabees. J. Bowker attaches an explanation for their name from this theory (*Jesus and the Pharisees* [Cambridge: Cambridge University Press, 1973]): the *perushim* were the more fanatical *separatists* of the orthodox party (which he calls the Chakamim). But this argument does not fully explain how Josephus could have referred to the party *by this name* as influential and active before the first half of the second century. For Hasidim and Pharisees, see J. Kampen, *The Hasideans and the Origin of Pharisaism: A Study of 1 and 2 Maccabees*, SBL Septuagint and Cognate Studies Series 24 (Atlanta: Scholars Press, 1988). This difficulty also applies to the theory advanced by W. W. Buehler (*The Pre-Herodian Civil War and Social Debate: Jewish Society in the Period 76–40 b.c. and the Social Factors Contributing to the Rise of the Pharisees and the Sadducees* [Basel: Reinhardt, 1974]). According to Buehler, the Pharisees were socially influential during the first half of the first century, when in their zeal to separate themselves from politics and in their piety they chose the side of the oligarchic patrician families, as opposed to the Sadducees, who chose the side of the monarchic and economically influential "nouveaux riches."

3. The history of the investigation has been carefully described by R. Deines, *Die Pharisäer: Ihr Verständnis im Spiegel der christlichen und jüdischen Forschung seit Wellhausen und Graetz*, WUNT 101 (Tübingen: Mohr, 1997).

4. E. Schürer, *Geschichte des Jüdischen Volkes im Zeitalter Jesu Christi*, 4th ed., 3 vols. (Leipzig: Hinrichs, 1901–9), 3:208: "Der Geist, welchen die Psalmen atmen, ist ganz des der pharisäischen Judentums."

Goodman) wrote: "The stress on obedience to the law, the doctrine of free will and faith in an afterlife are seen by many scholars as pointers to a Pharisaic origin of the Psalms. However, doubts have been voiced in recent years concerning an over-confident attribution of these poems to the Pharisees, because neither the doctrines listed, nor intense Messianism can be characterized as exclusively belonging to that group."[5]

The following arguments have been adduced for an exclusively pharisaic background of these Psalms of Solomon: (a) the opponents are the Hasmoneans; (b) the faith reflected in them is pharisaic (messianic hope, political quietism, a combination of predestination and free will); and (c) the dating fits (mid–first century B.C.). But these have been refuted by the following counter-arguments: (1) The religious convictions expressed in these Psalms can also be found beyond the party of the Pharisees.[6] Charlesworth himself therefore considers it unwise to ascribe the Psalms to a particular sect, all the more so because at the time of their composition many more sects existed than the three or four known to us, and because our knowledge of those known groups is deficient.[7] (2) In addition, Mason points out that it is open to question whether the Pharisees were opposed to the Hasmoneans and whether they were alone in their opposition.[8]

During recent decades, the areas of obscurity and the contradictions in the attempted reconstructions of the party have led to urgent requests for a fresh start, based on sources limited to the period before A.D. 70 and sources that stand in direct contact with that period, in which the Pharisees are explicitly named. This means limiting the current state of our knowledge to the New Testament, Josephus, and the rabbinic sources.

1.4 The Study of the Sources

Added to this limiting of the primary sources is a methodological consideration. From various directions concern has been expressed that the material from the sources not be taken out of context in the effort to reconstruct the party of the Pharisees. It is necessary to ask first *why* a particular source mentions the Pharisees and to what purpose. Only after

---

5. E. Schürer, *The History of the Jewish People in the Age of Jesus Christ (175 B.C.–A.D. 135)*, new English version, rev. and ed. G. Vermes, F. Millar, M. Black, and M. Goodman, 3 vols. (Edinburgh: Clark, 1973–87), 3.1:194–95.

6. Dupont-Sommer detects an Essene presence in these Psalms (see the introduction by R. B. Wright on the Psalms of Solomon in *The Old Testament Pseudepigrapha*, ed. J. H. Charlesworth, 2 vols. [Garden City, N.Y.: Doubleday, 1983–85]), 2:642.

7. Ibid.

8. S. Mason, *Flavius Josephus on the Pharisees*, Studia Post-Biblica 39 (Leiden: Brill, 1991), 8.

listening patiently to what the sources have to say can one begin work on a cautious sketch of the historical picture. The reason for this is that each source bears its own relationship to the group being researched, and no source limits itself to an objective recording of an impersonal reality.

Ellis Rivkin begins his book with this method of dealing with the sources individually, although he arrives rather quickly at a distillation of an overall picture from the sources.[9] Jacob Neusner,[10] concentrating on the rabbinic material, is more cautious in developing such a synthesis (only in *From Politics to Piety* does he briefly discuss the material from Josephus and the New Testament).[11] Steve Mason devoted an extensive study to Josephus and the Pharisees.[12] Thanks to these publications the sources outside the New Testament have been carefully explored. But even so, differences in interpretation are still possible, as evidenced by the differences between Neusner and Rivkin with regard to the rabbinic sources on the one hand and between Mason and Neusner with regard to the interpretation of Josephus on the other.[13]

a. For Rivkin the Pharisees are the ones who propagated the twofold law (written and unwritten). They constitute an apolitical movement that led Judaism to an internalization of spirituality. During the first century of the Christian era their influence was predominant among the people. According to Neusner, the Pharisees were involved in politics before the first century, and again after A.D. 70. In the intervening period they limited themselves to spiritual leadership under the influence of Hillel.

b. Neusner, following his teacher M. Smith, is of the opinion that a reversal took place in Josephus's attitude toward the Pharisees between the writing of the *Jewish War* and the *Antiquities*. In the former, Josephus does not emphasize their role and position (at least insofar as the first century is concerned), but in the *Antiquities* he implicitly advises the Romans to exploit in their own politics the great influence of this party among the population. A positive account of the discussion surrounding this thesis can be

9. E. Rivkin, *A Hidden Revolution* (Nashville: Abingdon, 1978).
10. J. Neusner, *The Rabbinic Traditions about the Pharisees before 70*, 3 vols. (Leiden: Brill, 1971). Abridged version: *The Pharisees: Rabbinic Perspectives*, Studies in Ancient Judaism 1 (Leiden: Brill, 1973).
11. J. Neusner, *From Politics to Piety: The Emergence of Pharisaic Judaism* (Englewood Cliffs, N.J.: Prentice-Hall, 1973), 45–80.
12. S. Mason, *Flavius Josephus on the Pharisees*, Studia Post-Biblica 39 (Leiden: Brill, 1991).
13. J. Neusner, "Josephus's Pharisees," in *Ex orbe religionum: Studia Geo Widengren* (Leiden: Brill, 1972), 1:224–44.

found in Goodblatt.[14] Mason, however, comes to the conclusion
that there is no essential difference between Josephus's treatment
of the Pharisees in the two works.

2. Josephus on the Pharisees

2.1 Was Josephus a Follower of the Pharisees?

Until recently many believed that Josephus himself belonged to the
Pharisees. This belief determined the interpretation of Josephus's data
concerning the Pharisees. These data are in part rather friendly and in
part less so. Some claim that the unfriendly passages were relatively unchanged borrowings from sources that were somewhat more critical of
the party than Josephus was. Others hypothesize a change of attitude
in Josephus himself, causing him to write more negatively about the
party in the *Jewish War* than in the *Antiquities*.

Mason opposes this hypothesis.[15] His main thesis is that Josephus
himself was never a member of the party of the Pharisees. The more fa-
vorable descriptions are found in passages in which Josephus portrays
the three parties as three "schools" within Judaism. In this portrait the
Essenes are presented most favorably, but the Pharisees are not depicted negatively, because Josephus's own religious convictions were
much closer to those of the Pharisees than of the Sadducees. The unfavorable descriptions that appear elsewhere do not have to do with the
party's religious convictions, however, but with their actions, which according to Josephus were often disturbing to the political order.

The idea that Josephus himself was a follower of the Pharisees is supposedly based on *Life* 2 §12.[16] Mason, however, has convincingly shown
that Josephus here says the following:

1. When he was sixteen years old he studied the three schools.
2. Dissatisfied, he then turns to the hermit Bannus and becomes his
   disciple for three years.
3. His longings satisfied, he returns to the city where he begins with
   politeuesthai (participation in public life; politics).
4. In doing so he follows the interpretation of the law and the practices of the Pharisees, not because he is a follower, but because

---

14. D. Goodblatt, "The Place of the Pharisees in First Century Judaism: The State of the
Debate," *Journal for the Study of Judaism* 20 (1989): 12–30.

15. Mason, *Flavius Josephus on the Pharisees.*

16. *kai diatripsas par' autō eniautous treis kai tēn epithumian teleiōsas eis tēn polin
hupestrephon. enneakaidekaton d' etos echōn ērxamēn (te) politeuesthai tē Pharisaiōn
hairesei katakolouthōn, hē paraplēsios esti tē par' Hellēsi Stōikē legomenē.*

anyone who wants to succeed in public life must go along with their customs (this was also true of the Sadducees, who could not introduce their own practices into public life but adopted those of the Pharisees for the sake of the people).

2.2 Josephus on the Pharisees (according to Mason)

Mason decided not to construct a comprehensive picture of the Pharisees. Methodologically this would not have fit in his book, which is devoted more to Josephus's way of writing than to the historical reconstruction of the Pharisees. Nevertheless, his work implicitly results in an image of the Pharisees:

a. The party of the Pharisees is as old as the other two schools, but it is the only one that enjoys the overwhelming support of the ordinary people.
b. The Pharisees are devoted to both the law *and* to the traditions of the fathers.
c. Predictions of the future and prophecies are found in their circles.
d. They appear to be extremely meticulous in their observance of the law, but in fact they are mainly interested in power, and they do not shrink from harsh measures and bribes in their pursuit of power. Although the Pharisees must be distinguished from the rigorous fourth party, which appeared much later (the Zealots, preceded by Judas the Galilean), they, like the Zealots, frequently disturbed the political equilibrium, even though this was not their intention. This would be especially apparent at the following moments: (1) According to Josephus, the downfall of the Hasmonean dynasty is to be blamed to a considerable extent on the fact that the Pharisees withdrew their support of John Hyrcanus, and that they exploited Alexandra in their own pursuit of power. (2) During the time of Herod they were the "opposition party" and were guilty of intrigue in court circles. (3) During the Jewish War, some Pharisees tried to have Josephus removed as commander of Galilee by devious means.

On a few points Mason goes too far or comes to erroneous conclusions: (1) his characterization of the members of the party of the Pharisees as "sanctimonious"; (2) his idea that the Pharisees were after power and thereby became a political nuisance; (3) his claim that Josephus believed that the Pharisees caused their party to go astray. In the following sections these three points will be discussed in more detail.

2.2.1 SANCTIMONIOUS?

Mason comes to the conclusion that according to Josephus the Pharisees *appeared* pious but were not. More than once they are said to "have the name" of being pious. This expression could be interpreted neutrally—it was how they were known. But it can also suggest that the reality was different than the reputation would lead one to suspect—they were pious "in name (only)." Mason is of the opinion that this suggestion is present in the wording, because *Jewish War* 1.5.2 §§110ff. gives an account of how merciless the Pharisees were during the time of Alexandra.

Josephus, however, does not say that the Pharisees were *regarded* as righteous without *being* righteous. He says that they had the reputation of being more precise in their understanding and application of the law than the others. The question whether they lived up to that claim or reputation is not addressed—there is no contrasting of "seeming" and "being."

Mason elaborates on a standard theme from Hellenistic moral philosophy: the contrast between "to seem" (*dokein*) and "to be" (*einai*).[17] In the passages he mentions, *dokein* is always used in explicit opposition to *einai*. But in Josephus, *dokein-einai* as a pair of contrasting words does not appear in the passages about the Pharisees. Mason's reference to Galatians 2:6, where *dokein* supposedly is used in the negative sense without opposition to *einai* (*hoi dokountes einai ti*), is incorrect. Paul speaks about the leaders in Jerusalem as people who either claimed or were reputed "to be something." Then he says that their *former* unimportance makes no difference; God is not a respecter of persons ("whatever they *were* makes no difference to me"). Paul himself regards the prominent people in Jerusalem (the *dokountes*) as real people who deserve to be included in the church. And the story about Alexandra *confirms* rather than contradicts their reputation of great precision in implementing the laws (see below).

In *Jewish War* 1.5.2 §110, we find the first mention of the Pharisees: "A group of Jews who think they are more pious than the others [*dokoun eusebesteron einai tōn allōn*] and interpret the laws more precisely." Does this concern their own *claim* or their *reputation*? It is difficult to say, and it really does not matter that much; these are two sides of the same issue. It would take a contrast between "to think/to seem" on the one hand and "to really be" on the other to really call the claim or reputation into question. But such a contrast is never an issue in *Jewish War*, nor in any of the other places where Josephus uses *dokein*

17. Mason, *Flavius Josephus on the Pharisees,* 111–12.

in his description of the Pharisees (*Jewish War* 2.8.14 §162; *Life* 38 §191).

Mason interprets *Antiquities* 17.2.4 §41 (*kai nomōn . . . prospoioume-non*) in a similar fashion.[18] Josephus supposedly distances himself in this passage from the subjective claim of the Pharisees that they are observers of the law. The reference mentioned by Mason (*Antiquities* 18.3.5 §81) *does* make an *explicit* distinction between "*to be* bad" and "to pose as an interpreter of the law"—but in *Antiquities* 17.2.4 §41 this kind of contrast is not made with reference to the Pharisees. In addition, it does not say that they *pose* as people who interpret the law, but that they "*claim* the law or *take it on themselves*." Perhaps the passage betrays Josephus's irritation with their claim to have a sort of monopoly on scrupulousness in interpreting the laws, but that is quite different from blaming them for being sanctimonious.

2.2.2 POLITICAL NUISANCE?

According to Mason, Josephus more than once indicates that the Pharisees, completely contrary to their claim or reputation, behaved in the political arena like people who pursue power with every justifiable and unjustifiable means. His account of Josephus's depiction of the actions of the Pharisees at the time of John Hyrcanus, of Alexandra, and under Herod, is far too negative, however. Mason loses sight of the fact that it was John Hyrcanus who alienated the Pharisees. In addition, he does not mention that in the case of Alexandra the Pharisees insisted on executions that were necessary *according to the law, without respect of persons*. At issue is neither revenge nor power, but the unconditional implementation of justice. Finally, Mason ignores the fact that the Pharisees, being a large group, stood in Herod's good graces, despite their pessimistic view of King Herod's coming to power (Herod's actions against Pharisees involved only certain individuals from their circle). The following sections provide a more detailed discussion of each of these three points.

2.2.2.1. In *Antiquities* 13.10.5 §288, Josephus writes that especially the Pharisees were hostile to John Hyrcanus. The issue here is not a general characterization, however, but a depiction of *rising* enmity. This is apparent from the context. The theme of the prosperity (*eupragia*) of the Jews at that time is pertinent. They were doing well, not only in Jerusalem but also in Egypt (13.10.4 §§284ff.). However, Hyrcanus (13.10.5 §288), unlike the successful Jewish generals of Cleopatra in Egypt, had to deal with the jealousy of his fellow Jews concerning his affluence and that of his sons. His relationship with the Pharisees was

18. Ibid., 265.

especially strained. This tension is not typical of Hyrcanus's whole administration, but it occurred when for him (and for the Jews in Egypt) a period of prosperity began. Their affluence evoked feelings of envy among the people (*phthonon ekinēse . . . hē . . . eupragia*). Such feelings arose all the more easily because something in Hyrcanus changed. At first he had been a disciple of the Pharisees and he was very dear to them (13.10.5 §289)! But during a friendly dinner with a group of Pharisee friends, a malicious Pharisee disrupted the mood by suggesting that Hyrcanus should step down as high priest because there were rumors that his mother had been a prisoner of war. This was a false rumor, and all the Pharisees were outraged. But when a Sadducee friend of Hyrcanus wrongfully suggested that *all* Pharisees agreed with this malicious remark, it became for Hyrcanus ultimately the reason to break ties with the Pharisees' party *on his part* and to switch to the Sadducees (13.10.6 §296). From that point on he followed their rules (based exclusively on the Torah) and fought against the observation of the patriarchal traditions in the style of the Pharisees, with their double law. *This* was the reason why the people began to hate him and his sons, because the people admired the Pharisees. Here we come full circle, from the introductory paragraph (13.10.5 §288) to the statement *"For this reason* the people developed a hatred against him and his sons" (13.10.6 §296). So it must be stated that the Pharisee John Hyrcanus switched to the party of the Sadducees (the party of the rich) during a period of affluence (using an annoying incident as an excuse), and that his abandoning of the traditions of the fathers estranged him from the Pharisees. This means that John Hyrcanus no longer sided with the common people but with the *rich* (this is why Josephus notes in 13.10.6 §298 that the Sadducees had followers among the *euporoi*). Thus it happened that this about-face caused him to lose the favor of the popular Pharisees, while at the same time evoking more and more envy among the common people because of his increasing wealth. The growing conflict certainly had also a social context, and in practice the latter may have been dominant in many people's experience. Certainly the social factor would have played a role in the attitude of the common people. In 13.10.5 §288, however, Josephus is sufficiently discreet to attribute the rising *envy* over wealth to the Jews in general, and of the Pharisees he says no more than that they were no longer on good terms with John Hyrcanus.

2.2.2.2. According to Mason, Josephus's criticism of the Pharisees at the time of Alexandra has to do with their arbitrariness. They acted contrary to their own intentions, morals, and ethics. But this is not a proper interpretation of the actual events. Why did the Pharisees demand the execution of such prominent citizens? Because they were guilty! They were accomplices in the unjust execution of eight hundred fellow Jews at the time of Alexander Jannaeus. These eight hundred were *not* by definition Pharisees. Alexander Jannaeus's offense was an offense against *the administration of justice*! In *Jewish War* 1.4.6 §97, Josephus himself notes that this ruler, in his rage, committed the sin (*asebeia*) of harshness (*ōmotēs*, absence of juridical precision) against these eight hundred and their families. The Pharisees talked the queen into retroactive punishment of the guilty in accordance with the law. Josephus's objection is that in interpreting the laws *regarding others* they failed to consider the consequences (Alexandra was saddled with the financial and political consequences). It is also striking that Aristobulus advised his mother not to go ahead with the execution demanded by the Pharisees "because it involves prominent men" (*dia to axiōma tōn andrōn, Jewish War* 1.5.3 §114). In other words, they are guilty according to the law, but because of their *position* it would be wise to avoid killing them! Instead they are banished. Thus Josephus is indeed critical, but more because the group of Pharisees was one-sided and thus failed to consider the interests of the people. It seems like a clash between one pious but realistic person and a group of pious people driven by mere enthusiasm.

2.2.2.3. In *Jewish War* 1.29.2 §571, we hear how Herod accused his sister-in-law of providing the Pharisees with financial support in order to oppose him. From this Mason infers a *general and active opposition* of the Pharisees against Herod. But here the context must be taken into account. It concerns a king who had a partially unreasonable aversion to his sister-in-law (Pheroras's wife) and left no stone unturned in his attempt to incriminate her. She was supposed to want to isolate Herod, and there were three groups whom she tried to turn against him: (a) his own daughters; (b) the Pharisees; (c) his own brother. Group (a) was intimidated, group (b) was set against him by her subsidies (*misthoi*), and person (c) was influenced by drugs. There was every indication that these three groups were regarded by Herod as his closest friends and relatives—so only a witch would want to come between them! In this context it is incorrect to conclude that the Pharisees were by definition against Herod. He himself apparently regarded them until shortly before this incident as people who were on his side.

In addition, the charge of subsidies or financial rewards (*misthoi*) was first turned against this woman and not against the Pharisees. Recalling that she paid the fines for the Pharisees that had been levied against them because of their refusal to swear the oath to Herod, we have here a situation in which this friendly gesture, extended to people who had received friendly and tolerant treatment from Herod, was *interpreted* by the furious ruler as money paid to induce alienation from him and to incite opposition to him. Mason seems to think Herod blamed the Pharisees for accepting money to support the opposition, but this is not the case. All we read in the passage is that *Herod* interpreted the events this way, but we cannot deduce from it whether the Pharisees themselves considered the subsidy as being political in nature or simply accepted it as helpful support, an act of mercy. Indeed, the fact that Herod had *only* fined them proves that he continued to be well-disposed toward them, despite their refusal to swear an oath of loyalty. This refusal had more to do with religious objections to taking an oath than with actual opposition to the reigning ruler.

At first glance, *Antiquities* 17.2.4 §§41–45 reveals a more somber picture: the Pharisees could have been of service to the king, but they were set on resisting and harming him (17.2.4 §41). Josephus describes how the Pharisees, with their strict interpretation of the law, gained the trust of the *women* in Herod's court and used this as a foothold for participating in court intrigues. But for a balanced evaluation of this passage, we must pay attention to what Josephus wrote earlier about the Pharisees and Herod.

To begin with, right from the start Herod had a weakness for Samaias, the *Pharisee* member of the Sanhedrin. Once, during the time of Hyrcanus, when Herod was called to appear before the Sanhedrin on charges of murder, he showed up with his soldiers in full regalia in order to intimidate the members of the court. Only Samaias had the courage to speak out openly against this intimidation, adding the prediction that if justice was not done to Herod now, he would kill his protégé Hyrcanus and the members of the Sanhedrin. This did indeed come to pass (*Antiquities* 14.9.4 §§172–76). Later, during the siege of Jerusalem, the Pharisee Pollion and his disciple Samaias advised surrender of the city to Herod. When Herod occupied the city, this Pharisee and his disciple were showered with favors (*Antiquities* 15.1.1 §§2–4).[19]

The Pharisees in general profited from this benevolent attitude. In *Antiquities* 15.10.4 §§368–72 we read how everyone who refused to take the oath of loyalty was persecuted, but when Pollion the Pharisee, Samaias, and most of their disciples continued to refuse, they were mercifully let off with a fine (as were the Essenes)! In 17.2.4 §42 we read that this involved more than 6,000 people. The attitude of Pollion and Samaias is thus rather representative of (a majority of) the Pharisees.

---

19. In *Antiquities* 14.9.4 §176, only Samaias is mentioned as the man who pointed out the sins of Jerusalem. In *Antiquities* 15.1.1 §4, Josephus ascribes the earlier incident in the Sanhedrin to Pollion and not to Samaias, as in *Antiquities* 14.9.4 §172. Because this concerns a master and his disciple, it may be that Samaias actually spoke the words that are attributed to Pollion.

For this reason, the hostile/friendly dilemma does not fit the relationship between the Pharisees and Herod. On the one hand they enjoyed Herod's favor because of their prophecies of the future and their non-revolutionary attitude, but on the other hand they were not friends of this punishing hand of God. Herod can feel the difference. As predictors of the future they could have been of great service to him, but because they are more devoted to the law than to the king, he suspects them of treachery—all the more so because his sister-in-law paid their fines. In exchange, they prophesied to her that Herod's throne would not endure.

It is striking that in 17.2.4 §44, only a *few* Pharisees are killed. Apparently these are individual Pharisees who are guilty of court intrigues. Their inside contact was the eunuch Bagoas (*ho pharisaios* in 17.2.4 §44). But it is obvious that the attitude toward the Pharisees as a group could not have been positively influenced by this incident.

So it can be said that the Pharisees did not obstruct Herod and perhaps gave him the impression that they were cooperating with his exercise of power. Their motive was religious, however (God punishes the sins of Jerusalem). For this reason it must sooner or later have dawned on Herod that despite their de facto acceptance of the king they were not true allies. The fact that his sister-in-law paid their fine (combined with other suspicions in court circles) could have led to increasing distrust of this group. When it was discovered that some Pharisees were involved in court intrigues, they were killed. Nevertheless, this does not sound like a general attack on the party of the Pharisees, nor do we read that the party had organized any active resistance against Herod. Mason leans too heavily on *Antiquities* 17.2.4 §41 by isolating it from the other data from this period.

2.2.3 A PARTY MISLED?

Josephus describes the party of the Pharisees in *Jewish War* 2.8.14 §§162–63. According to Mason, Josephus comments there that they "appear to interpret the laws with precision and to mislead the first sect." This is supposed to be a categorical condemnation of the party on Josephus's part. They are not only sanctimonious (see above), but they are also a *misled* party.[20]

The second clause of the introductory sentence in *Jewish War* 2.8.14 §162 (*kai tēn prōtēn apagontes hairesin*) has been a problem for translators. Does *prōtē* ("first") refer to the age (oldest sect), the rank (most influential party), or simply to the numerical order in the list contained in *Jewish War* 2.8.2 §119 (first-named)? Mason's choice is "most important," but in doing so he interprets *apagontes* as a negative word. If we

20. Mason, *Flavius Josephus on the Pharisees*, 125–32.

abandon the idea that Josephus must have been a Pharisee, then according to him the translation must be: "leading away/astray the foremost school of thought among the Jews"—an unfortunate comment![21] In this particular context, however, there is no reason for Josephus to issue such a condemnation, nor is there any explanation of this brief note. How should a Greek reader understand the way in which they were "leading the party astray"?

On page 132, section *c*, Mason suggests that the two elements of the introductory sentence in *Jewish War* 2.8.14 §162 provide a careful summary of what was said earlier: (a) the Pharisees seem meticulous, but they *are not* (*Jewish War* 1.5.2 §110: the passage about Alexandra); (b) the Pharisees mislead their party by getting involved in political intrigues (*Jewish War* 1.29.2 §571: the involvement of a few Pharisees in court intrigues under Herod). Thus the Greek reader was to understand that Josephus has provided a summary of how the Pharisees "led their party astray." The presuppositions of Mason's solution were shown to be incorrect in the last section, and thus his conclusion is unsatisfactory. Because *Jewish War* 1.29.2 §571 contains no indication of a *change* in the course of the party as a whole, the reader cannot be expected in 2.8.14 §162 to refer back to this episode in 1.29.2 §571 when reading about a party that had been led astray.

In interpreting *prōtē* ("first"), Michel and Bauernfeind opt for the third possibility ("first-named"), that is, Josephus refers to the numerical order in *Jewish War* 2.8.2 §119.[22] He is saying nothing more than that the Pharisees "constitute the first-named sect."

Arguments: (1) The translation of *apagein* as "to isolate, set apart, form" (Reinach: they established the first and oldest party) was considered possible by Mason[23] but not with reference to a one-time "charter of incorporation." The participle *apagontes* does not refer to a one-time event in the past (*apagagontes*), but to an enduring reality. But if the phrase is translated "that *constitute* the first-named party," there is no problem. Now the passage has to do with the permanent setting apart of a segment of the population as a separate party. (2) The phrase fits in an introduction. The actual information is still to come, but Josephus first recalls what he has said earlier about these people ("they are known for their meticulousness in interpretation of the law," see *Jewish War* 1.5.2 §110), and he then identifies them as the first of two parties initially mentioned by him in *Jewish War* 2.8.2 §119, before the Essenes,

---

21. Ibid., 132.
22. O. Michel and O. Bauernfeind, eds., *Flavius Josephus: De Bello Judaico; Der jüdische Krieg: Griechisch und Deutsch*, 4 vols. (Munich: Kösel-Verlag, 1959–69).
23. Mason, *Flavius Josephus on the Pharisees*, 129–30.

whom he had discussed extensively in 2.8.2–13 §§120–61. (3) The beginning of *Jewish War* 2.8.14 §162 recalls the *two* first parties; the Pharisees are then referred to as the *first* of those two and the Sadducees as the *deuteron tagma* (second group, *Jewish War* 2.8.14 §164). The use of *deuteron* in reference to the Sadducees also confirms that the *prōtēn* in reference to the Pharisees recalls the presentation of all three in *Jewish War* 2.8.2 §119.

On pages 130–31, Mason claims that in *Jewish War* 2.8.14 §162 Josephus's first words already indicated the connection with 2.8.2 §119 ("Of the two earlier [schools mentioned by me], the Pharisees ascribe . . . everything to God and Providence"). According to him there is then no reason why Josephus would repeat this phrase shortly thereafter in a subordinate clause ("Pharisees, known as meticulous interpreters of the law and establishing the first sect [mentioned by me]"). But Mason overlooks the fact that Josephus first refers back to the *two* schools he mentioned before the Essenes, reminding the reader that *two* discussions are still to come, and then indicates that the Pharisees were mentioned as the *first* of these two. (Josephus discussed the last-mentioned group, the Essenes, first, but he discusses the two earlier-mentioned parties in the order they were introduced: first the Pharisees [*Jewish War* 2.8.14 §162] and then the Sadducees [*Jewish War* 2.8.14 §164].)

2.3 The Pharisees according to Josephus (Conclusions)

Taking into account the results of Mason's study and the accompanying critical comments, the following picture emerges:

Pharisees—one of the three parties that already existed side by side by the second century B.C. (*Jewish War* 2.8.2 §119; *Antiquities* 13.5.9 §171; 18.1.2 §11; *Life* 2 §10: Pharisees, Sadducees, Essenes). The normal order for listing the three parties is: Pharisees, Sadducees, Essenes. *Antiquities* 18.1.2 §11 is an exception. There Josephus follows the reverse order, but in the description that follows he returns to the customary order. This order is not necessarily related to the age of the parties. It may refer to the level of importance in the lives of the people. If Josephus sometimes places the Essenes first (in a list, *Antiquities* 18.1.2 §11, or in a description, *Jewish War* 2.8.2 §§120ff.), this is because of his personal admiration for this group.

Claim/reputation—More strict than others in their interpretation of the law (*Jewish War* 1.5.2 §110; 2.8.14 §162) and in the God-fearing observance of that law (*Jewish War* 1.5.2 §110), in which the traditions of the fathers were honored in addition to the written

law (*Antiquities* 13.10.6 §297; 13.16.2 §408; 17.2.4 §41). The law
was *their* specialty (*Antiquities* 17.2.4 §41; *Life* 38 §191). Sanders
defends the position that the Pharisees did not regard the oral tradition as equal to the written laws of Moses; rather, as Pharisees
they set themselves apart in Judaism through their *own* laws.[24]
Hengel/Deines have soundly refuted this claim.[25] The Pharisees,
unlike the Sadducees, did not stop with the literal meaning of the
law but derived implications and consequences from it, and they
tried to win the entire nation over to this oral tradition because
they believed that it alone did full justice to the law of Moses.

Influence on public life—Not so much on the rich (who were closer to
the Sadducees, *Antiquities* 13.10.6 §298), but on large sections of
the population (*Antiquities* 13.10.5 §288; 13.10.6 §298; 13.15.5
§§401–2; 13.16.1 §406; in particular in the cities, 18.1.3 §15). Even
the Sadducees (as well as Josephus himself, *Life* 2 §12) were
obliged to observe the regulations of the Pharisees in public functions to avoid clashes with the people (*Antiquities* 18.1.4 §17).

Law—They support the observance of the law without respect of persons (executions during the time of Alexandra; their attitude toward Herod); they did not engage in deal making (John Hyrcanus).

Knowledge of the future—There is acceptance within their circles of
the possibility and practice of predicting the future (*Antiquities*
15.1.1 §4; 17.2.4 §43).

Doctrine—They combine the full attribution of all things to God and
his Providence with human responsibility (*Jewish War* 2.8.14
§163; *Antiquities* 13.5.9 §172; 18.1.3 §13). They believe in the im-
mortality of the human soul, the bodily resurrection of the righteous, and eternal suffering for the ungodly (*Jewish War* 2.8.14
§163; compare, with a somewhat different wording, *Antiquities*
18.1.3 §14).

Attitude—They live soberly and avoid luxury (*Antiquities* 18.1.3 §12).
They are friendly toward each other and seek the common good
for society (*Jewish War* 2.8.14 §166). They are mild in their penal-
ties (*Antiquities* 13.10.6 §294).

*A party with disciples and with the function of serving as an example
for the religious and moral life*—It must involve a kind of group or
party (there is a hierarchical structure of young and old, *Antiquities* 18.1.3 §12; there is reference to "the leading [*prōtoi*] Pharisees,"

24. E. P. Sanders, *Jewish Law from Jesus to the Mishnah: Five Studies* (London: SCM;
Philadelphia: Trinity Press International, 1990).

25. M. Hengel and R. Deines, "E. P. Sanders' 'Common Judaism,' Jesus and the Pharisees," *Journal of Theological Studies* 46 (1995): 17–41.

Life 5 §21). The people listen to their teaching and follow their example. A number of approximately six thousand is mentioned during the time of Herod. There is mention of the fact that certain Pharisees had disciples (John Hyrcanus was initially their disciple, *Antiquities* 13.10.5 §289; Pollion had his disciple Samaias, *Antiquities* 15.1.1 §3; a circle formed around both Pollion and Samaias, *Antiquities* 15.10.4 §370). What it is that distinguishes the admirers/followers of the Pharisees among the people from the Pharisees themselves and their disciples is unclear. It seems as if the Pharisees formed a group of associates, who had their own teachers who could sometimes also predict the future. The people admired and defended them because of their charisma and teaching. Was it the fact that they fully *observed* the regulations that distinguished the Pharisees from their admirers? In Luke 18:12, the Pharisee trusts mainly in the strict performance of works, and *Antiquities* 18.1.3 §§12, 15 is not only about their doctrine but in the first place about their *way of life*. The people were full of respect for these strict observers of the law, while they themselves could only comply with this extra *akribeia* (precision) to a lesser degree.

Individual variants—Not all Pharisees were alike. At the time of John Hyrcanus, there was a Pharisee named Eleazar with a bad character and an evil tongue (*Antiquities* 13.10.5 §§291–92). At the time of Herod, there were a number of Pharisees guilty of court intrigues (*Antiquities* 17.3.1 §46). Although the Pharisees were emphatically different from the politically aggressive Zealots (*Antiquities* 18.1.6 §23), Judas the Galilean still had the support of a Pharisee named Zadok (*Antiquities* 18.1.1 §4). A prominent man such as the Pharisee Simon did not hesitate to try to have Josephus removed as a commander in Galilee by offering bribes (*Life* 38–39 §§191–96), and at least three other Pharisees were involved in this plot (*Life* 39–40 §§197–203), in which even attempting an assassination was considered.

Conclusion—Josephus's reason for being less than positive in judging the Pharisees as a party is found in a matter that is not bad in and of itself. He reproaches them more for their impractical refusal to make (political) compromises than for any kind of immoral behavior (apart from a few individual cases). The power of the party lies in the extremely strict lifestyle of its members, in their propagation of such a law-abiding life according to tradition, and in their ability to predict the future.

In his book, Mason correctly warns against treating the negative remarks made by Josephus on the one hand and the criticism in the New

Testament on the other as equivalent. As we shall see, the New Testament essentially *confirms* the positive aspects of the picture presented by Josephus.

3. The Rabbinic Literature on the Pharisees

3.1 The Pharisees in the Rabbinic Literature

At the moment the most frequently discussed studies dealing with the Pharisees in rabbinic literature are those by Rivkin and Neusner. Since the results of their work are almost diametrically opposed to each other, we will look at them separately.

3.1.1 RIVKIN

Although Rivkin's study is not limited to rabbinic literature, this is where his focus lies, and his positive commitment to his subject is very clear. In his introduction Rivkin explains how he was raised by his parents in the tradition of the twofold law so admired by the Pharisees. In his study he also pays tribute to this party, who effected a silent revolution within Judaism. The Pharisees integrated certain Hellenistic ideas into Judaism and thereby managed to maintain a balance between preservation and renewal. They promised individual reward in the form of eternal life and the resurrection of the dead to all who remained faithful to the twofold law.[26]

Rivkin's study challenges the accepted picture of the Pharisees as a closed fraternity of Jews who set themselves apart from the *am-ha-aretz* (the people of the land) for the sake of a stricter observance of ritual purity (specifically *Hagigah* 2.7). This accepted picture is supposedly supported by the name *Perushim* (the isolated ones). The Pharisees must have been the same as the *haberim*.[27] It goes without saying that Rivkin must refute this picture of a closed, esoteric society by going to the source from which it appears to be mainly derived: the rabbinic literature.

Rivkin first discusses Josephus and the New Testament. He comes to the following conclusions regarding these two sources:

1. According to *Josephus*, the Pharisees constituted a *hairesis*—a school with its own philosophy. They had the support of the majority of the people. The *hairesis* was characterized by: (a) expert interpretation of the law; (b) a plea for moderation and reasonableness; (c) devotion to righteousness (*dikaiosynē*) and virtue (*aretē*); (d) the promotion of mutuality and friendliness; (e) belief

---

26. Rivkin, *Hidden Revolution*, 10–11.
27. Ibid., 27–28.

in retribution and punishment after death. In addition, man has freedom of choice, but the outcome is partly determined by Fate. Rivkin accepts that Josephus himself must have belonged to the Pharisees.[28]

A comparison with Mason clearly shows that Rivkin's picture of the Pharisees is a rather flattering one. This is possible because he allows for a great deal of anti-Pharisaic influence in certain sources Josephus supposedly consulted (in the Alexandra story, for instance).[29] He distinguishes between the pattern of the Pharisees' actions on the one hand and their religious convictions on the other. The latter is sympathetically and positively described by Josephus. The Pharisees were mainly champions of the two-fold law, which should be taken into account whenever the pattern of action comes up for discussion. Their actions were inspired by their convictions. They were apparently ready to act on their principles; but to what extent this led to problems is difficult to judge, given the bias of some sources.

2. In the New Testament, Rivkin begins with Paul, who himself was a follower of the Pharisees. From him we learn that they were strong in preserving traditions and in the struggle for righteousness. The Synoptics add to this that they were respected by the people, that they wielded great power, communicated with the rulers, opposed Jesus because of his lack of regard for tradition, persecuted the first Christians, and by means of excommunication shut them out of the synagogues. Rivkin notes that in the New Testament, designations such as lawyers, scribes, teachers of the law, or hypocrites more or less coincide with the designation Pharisees. These designations do not all refer to separate groups. Here Rivkin lays the groundwork for what he will draw from the rabbinic literature regarding the Pharisees as the *hakamim*.

3. In the rabbinic literature the question of name immediately comes up for discussion. Only here do we find the Hebrew *perushim*. But can this word, which means something like "separatists," always be identified with the Pharisees? There are places where the word certainly does not refer to them. As a working hypothesis, Rivkin assumes that the word *perushim*, when directly or indirectly contrasted with *Zedukim* (Sadducees), refers to the party of the Pharisees (designated as Separatists). He further observes that the name *Perushim* is sometimes replaced by *haka-*

28. Ibid., 73–75.
29. Ibid., 44–46.

mim. He also attempts to show that the *haberim* (the [separated] associates) form yet another group. Thus after eliminating the passages in which *perushim* or *parush* has nothing to do with the Pharisees, he arrives at the following picture:

> The Pharisees were a class of lawyers who defended the two-fold law—written and unwritten. They opposed the Sadducees, who only recognized the written law. Their *halakah* (system of rules for life) was operative in all areas (worship, property, jurisprudence, feasts, the actions of the high priest on the Day of Atonement, etc.). They promoted this *halakah* through their doctrine and their actions.
>
> The name "Pharisees" was used only in contradistinction to the Sadducees. In all other contexts they were called *hakamim* (the wise ones) or *sopherim* (scribes). The name *perushim* has a negative connotation. From the Sadducees' point of view these *hakamim* were "separatists, heretics." Thus when we look for use of the actual *name*, the rabbinic literature has little to say about the Pharisees (the name is only used out of sheer necessity as a hostile epithet from the Sadducees and in confrontation with them). In fact, however, the entire Mishnah is a source of information about the doctrine of the Pharisees—this is where the *halakah* of these *hakamim* and *sopherim* can be found! Simon ben Shetah, Shemaya and Abtalion, Hillel and Shammai, John ben Zakkai, and Rabban Gamliel are also representatives of the *hakamim*, despised by the Sadducees as *perushim*.[30]

Whatever is true of the connection between the Pharisees and the scribes, Rivkin draws the circle somewhat on the large side. Furthermore, he explains inadequately why this group is called *Pharisaioi* without reservation in Josephus and the New Testament, which would have been strange if *perushim* in fact is a term of disparagement used by the Sadducees. And within the Mishnah there certainly was no need to use the denigrating name *perushim* in reports of discussions with the Sadducees instead of the normal term *hakamim* for the party characterized by Rivkin.

3.1.2 NEUSNER

Neusner arrives at a very different picture.[31] While Rivkin takes the texts as they are, Neusner argues for the application of literary and historical criticism to the rabbinic literature. What has been the practice

---

30. Ibid., 176ff.
31. Neusner, *Rabbinic Traditions about the Pharisees before 70*.

in biblical scholarship for a century and a half has yet to be initiated in the study of the Talmud, he claims. Thus Neusner's publications consist of form analysis of the traditional material, an evaluation of possible origins, and an assessment of the redaction. This leads to profound atomization and considerable skepticism. Anyone interested in the motivation behind this unraveling of the sources is advised to read the appendix in the third part of his *Rabbinic Traditions* ("Bibliographical Reflections"). Neusner looks here at many publications from Jewish and Christians circles, and the discussion provides a demonstration of his own method. He takes a large number of Jewish authors to task for accepting all Talmudic data as historical without any discernment or for approaching their work far too apologetically. He blames the Christian authors for ignorance of the rabbinic literature and for often showing an anti-Semitic prejudice against what they consider barren, legalistic Judaism. Nor is Neusner too happy with the sympathetic Protestant view of E. P. Sanders.[32] He rightly asserts, "The history of the scientific study of the Pharisees cannot be seen apart from the history of Judaism and Christianity in the nineteenth and twentieth centuries, from the sociology of Judaism in Europe and the United States, and from the interrelationships that exist between both religious traditions."[33] The entire appendix is suffused with the spirit of a tormented man—only on page 330 does the sun break through for a moment. There Neusner praises the work of H. A. Fischel, who compares Talmudic and Hellenistic literature. He recognizes possibilities for fruitful research here, and as an example, he discusses an article about the function of the *chreia* in the Hellenistic world. The different traditions of many rabbinic utterances can be compared with the diverse *chreia* (aphorisms or anecdotal aphorisms) of the same single philosophical pronouncement. It is interesting that the figure of speech of the *chreia* appears at the same time in the study of the Talmud and in modern publications on the Gospels.

As might have been expected, Neusner arrives at a much more sober picture than Rivkin. In his summary,[34] he limits himself methodologically to the rabbinic traditions concerning the Pharisees that mention either individual masters from before A.D. 70 or the schools of Shammai and Hillel. This comprises approximately 371 items in about 655 pericopes. The majority are from Hillel and members of his circle (75 percent). Approximately 67 percent of all the material deals with dietary

32. J. Neusner, "Mr. Sanders' Pharisees and Mine: A Response to E. P. Sanders, *Jewish Law from Jesus to Mishnah*," *Scottish Journal of Theology* 44 (1991): 73–95.
33. Neusner, *Rabbinic Traditions about the Pharisees before 70*, 3:322.
34. Ibid., 3:301ff.

laws, ritual purity during meals, and agricultural laws with an eye to suitability for ceremonially clean consumption.[35]

The most striking result of Neusner's analysis is the assertion that the rabbinic traditions concerning the Pharisees as a whole typify them as "self-centered, the internal records of a party concerning its own life, its own laws, and its own partisan conflicts."[36] What is conspicuously absent is any connection to public or political events! These rabbinic data relate to the Pharisees as they lived at the end of Herod's administration and during the Roman period that followed. At that time they were a nonpolitical group. Their main objective was "the proper preservation of ritual purity in connection with eating secular (not Temple) food" and "the observance of the dietary laws of the day." Getting the party properly organized was a secondary consideration.[37]

The contrast with Josephus is considerable. But according to Neusner, Josephus describes the Pharisees primarily as they were under the Hasmoneans, when their position was different. On the other hand, the Pharisees of the Synoptics do display some similarity with these rabbis (tithing, purity, Sabbath, vows, etc.). It was with Hillel that the politically active party shrank to a meaningless, introverted sect with purity as its sole focus. The Pharisees worked at extending priestly sanctity to the whole people ("a holy priesthood"). Perhaps Hillel understood that the party would not survive under the Romans if, as during the Hasmonean period, it began meddling in politics once again.

3.1.3 RIVKIN AND NEUSNER COMPARED

When we look at the Pharisees first via Rivkin and then via Neusner, it is as if we were looking at the same people (orthodox but introverted Jews, mainly concerned with dietary laws and the Sabbath), but through totally different eyes. Rivkin is the uncomplicated admirer of

---

35. Rivkin is justifiably surprised that Neusner fails to discuss the aspects of the rabbinic material dealing with disputes between the Pharisees and the Sadducees. "In a massive treatise of 1207 pages, devoted to culling and analyzing the rabbinic traditions about the Pharisees, Neusner excludes the only tannaitic texts in which the term *perushim* as meaning Pharisees is confirmed by the juxtaposition of *Perushim* to *Zedukim*, 'Sadducees'!" (Rivkin, *Hidden Revolution*, 315). In *From Politics to Piety*, Neusner makes do in a footnote on page 1 with the laconic remark, "For pericopae in which Pharisees and Sadducees are juxtaposed, see Ellis Rivkin, 'Defining the Pharisees: The Tannaitic Sources,' *Hebrew Union College Annual*, 1970, pp. 205–49."

36. Neusner, *Rabbinic Traditions about the Pharisees before 70*, 3:304.

37. E. P. Sanders devotes two chapters to the Pharisees in his *Judaism: Practice and Belief 63 B.C.E.–66 C.E.* (London: SCM, 1992). He does not agree with Neusner concerning the Pharisees' concentration on ritual purity, but he does agree with the statement that the Pharisees of the first century were not as influential in society as Josephus suggests (for a comparison of the viewpoints of Sanders and Neusner, see also Hengel and Deines, "E. P. Sanders' 'Common Judaism,' Jesus and the Pharisees," 41–51).

traditional Judaism, but Neusner, also an orthodox Jew, is the critic of the naiveté within Judaism regarding its own literature and history. However, it looks as if Neusner, too, cannot escape from the same kind of involvement for which he so sharply criticizes others. Why doesn't he conclude that his material is not suitable for saying anything reliable about the Pharisees of the first century because the sources deal only with matters that have come through the filters of Jabne and Usha and were considered relevant *after* A.D. 70?

If Neusner's methodology were correct, the rabbinic material would in fact be almost meaningless in a reconstruction of the historical Pharisees. After all, it has never been established that the traditions he sees as *authentic* are *complete* in their presentation and characterization of the historical situation of the first century![38] It should now be clear that Neusner's view of Josephus and his study of the rabbinic literature fit together like the right and left hand.

Although Neusner comes to the conclusion that the Pharisees in their first-century version resemble (unfortunately) the Pharisees in the Synoptics (insofar as their data are not anachronistic), we must agree with Rivkin that nevertheless the New Testament as a whole presents a different picture (the Pharisees have great influence, they have contacts with the political leaders, they are an extroverted group).

3.2 Sotah 3.4

Yet we are faced with the remarkable fact that, despite all dissimilarity between Rivkin and Neusner, both scholars remove a considerable number of passages from the rabbinic literature from consideration (mainly those that are often used by Christians): Rivkin because he strictly limits the number of texts in which *perushim* is used to refer to the Pharisees, Neusner because his use of form and redaction criticism allows him to remove from consideration much data from the first century.

One such piece of data we will discuss here. The choice of the Mishnah *Sotah* 3.4 is related to the way in which this passage (along with the related Gemara) is used in the assessment of New Testament criticism of the Pharisees. Does the New Testament put the Pharisees in too

---

38. G. Stemberger, the authority on rabbinic literature, is of the opinion that much less can be deduced from this material concerning the Pharisees (and the Sadducees) than is often expected: "Diese Texte können zwar gewisse frühere Informationen ergänzen, illustrieren und bestätigen, helfen jedoch nicht, das Bild wesentlich aufzufüllen" [These texts, to be sure, can complement, illustrate, and confirm certain earlier data, but they do not help us by substantially adding to the picture] (G. Stemberger, *Pharisäer, Sadduzäer, Essener*, Stuttgarter Bibelstudien 144 [Stuttgart: Katholisches Bibelwerk, 1991], 64).

negative a light? In extrabiblical sources the Pharisees come off much
better. Silva has discussed this problem of apparently contradictory
sources. He suggests that the New Testament contains "informal generalizations" regarding the Pharisees. In fact, Jesus' criticism was directed at only a *segment* of the Pharisees, but in his rhetoric he speaks
as though what he says were true of all Pharisees. Silva then asserts
that the rabbinic sources also reveal a diversity among the Pharisees.
There were good Pharisees, but there were bad ones as well.[39] (Bowker's view is similar: Jesus' criticism was directed at the more fanatical,
separated group of the *perushim*, and not at the large group of orthodox teachers of the law and pious people. In the later Gospel tradition,
the designation *Pharisaioi* would be erroneously used to refer to this
larger group, whereby the specific aspects of Jesus' confrontation with
the small group of fanatics disappeared and misunderstandings became possible.)

In support of this theory Silva points to *Sotah* 3.4, a tractate from
Nashim that deals with the offering for jealousy in Numbers 5. Bietenhard renders the Mishnah in question as follows:

He (Rabbi Jehoshua[c]) used to say: "An ignorant holy man, a clever scoundrel, a pharisaic [*perusha*] woman, blows of the Pharisees [*Perushim*]—
see, these devastate the world."[40]

In Neusner's translation, however, the associations with the party of the
Pharisees have disappeared:

He (R. Joshua) would say, "A foolish saint, a smart knave, an abstemious
woman, and the blows of abstainers (*perushim*)—lo, these wear out the
world."[41]

The same is true of Neusner's translation of the Jerusalem Talmud on
Sotah 3.4: "an abstemious woman" and "blows of abstainers."[42]

39. M. Silva, "The Place of Historical Reconstruction in New Testament Criticism," in
Hermeneutics, Authority, and Canon, ed. D. A. Carson and J. D. Woodbridge (Grand Rapids: Baker, 1995), 115.

40. "Er (Rabbi Jehoschua[c]) pflegte zu sagen: Ein törichter Frommer, ein schlauer
Gottloser, eine pharisäische Frau, Schläge der Pharisäer—siehe, diese zerstören die
Welt." H. Bietenhard, *Sota: Die des Ehebruchs Verdächtige*, Die Mischna: Text, Überset-
zung und ausführliche Erklärung 3.6 (Berlin: Töpelmann, 1956).

41. J. Neusner, *The Mishnah: A New Translation* (New Haven, Conn., and London:
Yale University Press, 1988).

42. J. Neusner, *The Talmud of the Land of Israel: A Preliminary Translation and Explanation*, vol. 27, *Sotah*, Chicago Studies in the History of Judaism (Chicago and London:
University of Chicago Press, 1984), 92.

For a firm grasp of this passage it is necessary to understand its context. The discussion concerns the question of whether the "merits" of a woman can lead to her not swelling up and dying by drinking the water of jealousy. Simeon has stated that merits can serve as protection against judgment, and that they can therefore also protect when drinking the water of jealousy. But against Simeon's thesis it is argued that if this were true, women who drink the water and remain healthy could still get a bad name. After all, the exoneration provided by remaining healthy after drinking the water is weakened when it becomes known that a woman can remain healthy because of merits, even though she may in fact have committed adultery. Rabbi says that merits only postpone and delay the effect. The underlying premise was that merits can result in a postponement of one, two, or at most three years. For this reason it is important to teach your daughter the Torah (merit!). Eliezer says that he who teaches his daughter the Torah is like one who teaches her sexual fulfillment. Joshua says that a woman would rather have dry bread with sexual fulfillment than riches without it. Then follows the Mishnah already quoted.

The point under discussion here thus revolves around the usefulness of Torah study for women in relation to suspicion of adultery. On the one hand, Torah study is merit for her and it can make her realize that she is only given postponement of punishment because of the Torah study and not because God has not noticed her adultery. On the other hand it is really nothing but a waste of time, because if a woman is willing to sacrifice much and risk a great deal for sexual fulfillment, then Torah study will only help her slip through the loopholes. *Against* the true intention of the tradition, she will use the knowledge that Torah study as merit can postpone punishment. Thus there are pros and cons to both sides.

In this connection there is a proverb concerning the misery that results when two things that do not belong together are found in one person. The Jerusalem Talmud, like the Babylonian Talmud, uses examples to explain that a good thing (holy, clever, *perusha*, *perushim*) falls apart when combined with something that does not suit it (ignorant, scoundrel, woman, blows). The woman who learns the Torah and is bent on adultery is just like the following four groups that cause the world to fall apart (compare Proverbs).

1. A foolish saint who first wants to put away his tefillin before saving a drowning man; the man will be dead by the time he brings him to shore! Or a saint who finds the first fig but does not want to eat any first fruits, so he chases after the next person who comes along to give the fig away, and that person is a betrothed girl! He has landed himself in a painful situation!

2. A clever rogue who applies easy rules to himself and strict rules to others or who takes only the easy rules from both Shammai and Hillel.
3. An "abstemious woman" (an austere, sober woman) who sits down and suggestively quotes passages from the Bible, like Leah (Gen. 30:16). This woman *paid* her husband in order to get a son, and she was therefore "cool" or even "frigid." Perhaps this is the meaning: "a frigid woman." The discussion that follows shows that Jacob knew this: "The *only* thought in her mind is the desire to bear the founder of a tribe."
4. The blows of *perushim* (that is, blows that come from an unexpected source). *Perushim* are the people least likely to deliver such blows: for example, Torah authorities who advise the heirs to remove a widow from the estate, or students who give a fellow student who falls just below the poverty line a gift to deprive him of the subsidy for students living under the minimum standard.

This whole discussion is a reasonable case for concluding that it is not *Pharisaic* blows or a *Pharisaic* woman that is being referred to but treacherous blows of strict observers of the law and a woman with an attitude that is too modest (standoffish, prudish).[43]

What about the Babylonian Talmud? Here we find the familiar seven kinds of *perushim* as well as a reminder of something King Jannaeus said about them. This historic comment seems to recall the *Pharisees*.

The English translation of the Babylonian Talmud (Soncino) fails to do justice to the Mishnah when it translates "and *the plague* of the Pharisees." In the Hebrew text, the Mishnah passage is distinctly plural: "And *the blows* [plural] of the *Perushim*." This is important. The translation in the singular, combined with the translation "plague," suggests that the *Perushim* themselves constituted the plague. But what is being discussed here are the "blows" dealt by those *perushim*, people from whom you expect anything but underhanded behavior.

The following seven groups might easily be regarded as "the strict" or "the prudish" who adopt an aloof attitude. At issue here are not divi-

43. Rivkin had already contested the accepted translation of *Pharisees* in such sources as *Sotah* 3.4 and Babylonian Talmud *Sotah* 22b in a 1969 publication (E. Rivkin, "Defining the Pharisees: The Tannaitic Sources," *Hebrew Union College Annual* 41 [1970]: 205–49). In his *Rabbinic Traditions* (1971), Neusner bypasses the difficult question concerning the meaning of *perushim* in Babylonian Talmud *Sotah* 22b and other sources, but he does admit (*Rabbinic Traditions*, 1:2–3) to agreeing with Rivkin's abovementioned article, although he reproaches him for the rash acceptance of the historic value of material from the Mishnah. Rivkin also discusses this question of translation in *Hidden Revolution*, 168–71.

sions of the Pharisees but a more specific description of "strict observers of the law who may nevertheless strike you."

1. *Shikmi*. The Shechemite. Someone who let himself be circumcised like Shechem, yet his act *affects* Israel because the intent behind observing the law is stealing a daughter and promoting an
   illegal covenant.
2. *Nikpi*. Knocks his heels together. This probably refers to a strict
   observer of the law who expresses slavish or military submission.
   Such slaves or soldiers often say other things behind your back!
3. *Kizai*. Rabbi Nachman b. Isaac explains it this way: He lets his
   blood flow against the wall. A pointless matter. He is martyr *in the
   wrong place*.
4. *Pestle*. Rabbi b. Shila said, "bent like a pestle in the mortar." A
   pious man, but you are wise to avoid him. No consideration for
   others.
5. *Obtrusive*. Keeps on asking, "Now what should I do?" A good
   question, but an exhausting one.
6. *Interested*. Studies the Torah, but in order to improve himself in
   God's eyes by being rewarded. Disturbs unselfish Torah study by
   continuously asking, "What good will it do me, how can I benefit?"
7. *Faint-hearted*. Study of the Torah, but only to avoid punishment.
   Disturbs pure (scholarly) study. Even so, 6 and 7 can evolve into
   unselfish Torah students.

These seven groups are based on the wearisome experience of religious
instructors and ethicists working among the people. You hurt yourself
by dealing with people who want to be your followers in an inappropri-
ate manner.

The concluding passage that reminds us of Jannaeus can be translated without special reference to the "party of strict ones" (the Pharisees). It is striking that over against the *perushim* stands not another
party, but the *non-perushim*—the *non*-precise ones. Alexandra need
fear neither the ones who live modestly nor those who live in dissipa-
tion, but the ones who imitate the strict ones. Their deeds are like those
of Zimri, who committed adultery with a Midianite woman, yet they
want respect like that received by Phinehas, who killed him.

Even if this were all about the Pharisees, nothing attributed here to
these seven types could be ascribed to "*the* Pharisees." The focus here is
on "*pseudo* Pharisees."

Conclusion: The *Sotah* quote is not pertinent to the question concerning the doctrine and praxis of the Pharisees. Stemberger is of the

opinion that the passage about Jannaeus was later added by someone who erroneously understood the list of various *perushim* to refer to the *Pharisees*.[44] It is incorrect to use this *Sotah* passage in connection with the New Testament, because Jesus did not address a group of *pseudo* strict ones or *quasi* strict ones, but the Pharisees as such. The extent to which he made use of informal generalizations[45] must be determined by the exegesis of the New Testament itself.

4. The New Testament on the Pharisees

4.1 The Special Character of the Source

At first glance one has the impression that the Pharisees across the board were consistently and historically the natural opposites of Jesus. This impression has its origin in the fact that the New Testament is not concerned primarily with the Pharisees but with the life and teachings of Jesus. The New Testament indicates that he rather frequently enters into dialogue with the Pharisees or that they follow him with hostile intentions. But the special *relationship* between Jesus and the Pharisees who oppose him is not unqualifiedly suitable for constructing a historical picture of the Pharisees as such.

We see this within the New Testament. Although there are relatively few general statements made about the Pharisees, there are some, and they are invariably positive.

Neusner raises a very different objection to the unnuanced use of the New Testament data.[46] He believes that the New Testament writings project a later Pharisaism, which had become influential again after the year 70 (via Jabne), back onto the history of Jesus. Thus what we encounter in the Gospels are not the Pharisees of Jesus' time but the Pharisees the Christian church clashed with during the last decades of the first century. Nevertheless, Neusner concludes that the New Testament, like the rabbinic writings he has interpreted, also depicts the Pharisees before the year 70 as "a table-fellowship sect," concentrated on the laws of tithing and ritual purity, without any political influence.[47] But this raises the question whether it is correct to use *some* of the New Testament material to confirm the picture of the Pharisees before the year 70 as developed by Neusner while rejecting as anachronistic all material that does not fit into this picture.

---

44. Stemberger, *Pharisäer, Sadduzäer, Essener*, 44–46.
45. Silva, "Place of Historical Reconstruction," 115.
46. Neusner, *From Politics to Piety*, 67–68.
47. Ibid., 80.

According to Berger,[48] the Pharisaism of Jesus and Paul differs from the Pharisaism as it had been until then only in the replacing of a concept of protective, *passive* purity/sanctity with the concept of *aggressive* purity/sanctity. The ritually pure man now *makes* his environment pure and does not have to be protected against it. Thus association with sinners and preaching to the Gentiles takes on special meaning. Only in a later phase, when too little of this aggressive sanctity remained in the established church communities, was the other form of Pharisaism resuscitated within the Christian church. The conflict traditions in the Gospels come from this period.[49]

4.2 Paul, a Pharisee

In Philippians 3:5, Paul calls himself *kata nomon Pharisaios*, and he counts this among the attributes in which he could easily take pride (like his Jewish background and his circumcision; Phil. 3:4b, 7). He has abandoned his trust in these attributes, not because he discovered that they are perverted, but because he has received a greater treasure: Christ (Phil. 3:8). Through the grace of Christ he has been made aware that his earlier *self-confidence* was unjustified, even though he focused only on the good (even his sinful persecution of the Christian community was based in his well-intentioned zeal for God's people and must be regarded as a sin of ignorance). After many years of work as an apostle to the Gentiles, he still calls himself a follower of the Pharisees before the Sanhedrin (Acts 23:6: "I *am* a Pharisee"): he still confesses the resurrection of the dead! And in his defense before King Agrippa, Paul says, "According to the strictest sect of our religion, I lived as a Pharisee" (Acts 26:5). Even though Paul has now been given much more than a strict regard for the law, and even though he has learned not to trust in the flesh, his roots in the party of the Pharisees are part of a past of which he is not ashamed. On the contrary, the party as such can be mentioned with honor!

It would be strange if Paul continued to be able to speak entirely positively about his membership in the party of the Pharisees if as a Christian he had come to see them as a group of hypocrites.

4.3 Pharisaic Christians

Paul was not the only one to consciously maintain a certain continuity between his Pharisaic past and his present life as a Christian. In the church in Jerusalem were Christian believers who were also Pharisees.

48. K. Berger, "Jesus als Pharisäer und frühe Christen als Pharisäer," *Novum Testamentum* 30 (1988): 231–62.

49. Also see H. Falk, *Jesus the Pharisee: A New Look at the Jewishness of Jesus* (New York: Paulist, 1985).

In Acts 15:5 we read that some members of the party of the Pharisees who had become Christians were insisting that converted Gentiles be circumcised. Not all believing Pharisees insisted on this, but only a few of them. So there were a number of Christians who belonged to the community *as members of the Pharisees.* Although the name "Pharisee" is not specifically mentioned, they were certainly among the thousands of Jews who came to faith and were zealous for the law (Acts 21:20). Had Nicodemus not been their secret predecessor (John 3:1; compare 7:50; 19:39)? In any case, these thousands of Christians in Jerusalem who were zealous for the law *sympathized* with the party of the Pharisees, although they themselves may not have belonged to the party. This does not rule out that they had done away with misplaced self-confidence and arrogance, and that they had broken with certain practices. They were "born-again" Pharisees.

It is impossible to interpret the expression *tōn apo tēs haireseōs tōn Pharisaiōn* as meaning that they *came from* the party but had separated themselves from it in order to become Christians. Their being Christians is not denoted by the use of the preposition *apo*, but by the participle *pepisteukotes*. They were part of the Pharisees (compare Acts 12:1, where Christians are designated as *hoi apo tēs ekklēsias*). But these are Pharisees *who have come to believe in Jesus.*

Sanders takes a very different position.[50] He claims that in both his books, Luke has a negative attitude toward all Jews, while maintaining an ambivalent attitude toward the Pharisees. This betrays the *background* of his anti-Jewish sentiment, which is the result of his opposition to the sizable number of Jewish *Christians* who still advocated both the law and circumcision. On the one hand they are close to the gentile Christians, but on the other hand they are as hypocrites diametrically their opposites. In a sense Luke's Pharisees are a projection of the closest (Christian) Jews, with whom the sense of distance is the greatest precisely because they remain *Jewish.* This is the cause of a measure of "anti-Semitism" in Luke's writings.

Nicodemus, the Pharisee, did not have to break with the party. But he did have to be born again by accepting the baptism of John and expecting the promised baptism of the Spirit from the hands of the One coming from heaven (John 3:3, 5, 12–16). If the Pharisee Nicodemus rejects the love of God in Christ, then whatever works he does (however good they seem) stand condemned (John 3:18) because they have been soured by self-confidence. But if he accepts Christ in faith, whatever works he does (that seem good) have really been *done through God* (John 3:21).

50. J. T. Sanders, *The Jews in Luke–Acts* (London: SCM, 1987).

4.4 Pharisees and Christ

The assessment was not essentially different during the time *before* Jesus' death. The Pharisees were highly respected by the people. No one dared confess Jesus out of awe for them (John 12:42). Jesus himself is in agreement with the teaching of the teachers of the law and the Pharisees (Matt. 23:3), and when he says that the righteousness of his disciples must be greater than that of the teachers of the law and the Pharisees (Matt. 5:20), he implies that they are the most righteous group.

It is true that Jesus warns against the teaching of the Pharisees and Sadducees (Matt. 16:12), but this is not a reference to specific Pharisaic *dogmas* in general (the Sadducees, who followed a different teaching, are here grouped together with them). Jesus is talking about a specific teaching that was common to both groups at that time and that was being actively promoted among the people: that Jesus did not come from heaven but performed miracles as a confederate of Beelzebub. They taught this widely, and it is why the Pharisees came to Jesus and challenged him to prove the contrary by showing them a sign from *heaven* (Matt. 16:1). It is in that context that Jesus warns against their explanations or instruction.[51]

Matthew 5:20 is not about an inferior righteousness. In Matthew 5:17–48, the righteousness of the Law and the Prophets is called good, but Jesus now demands a perfection that exceeds that required by the Law and the Prophets. The teachers of the law and the Pharisees are extremely strict about doing everything that "was said to the people long ago" (the laws of Moses): this is their righteousness. But because Jesus now issues commandments that go beyond the law of Moses, the righteousness of the perfect children of God will also have to extend beyond the perfect—by Israelite standards—righteousness of the teachers of the law and the Pharisees. Thus Matthew 5:20 does not contain any criticism of this group, but it clearly explains that the commandments of Christ lead the people even further along the path to the perfect God.

The parable of the Pharisee and the tax collector also shows that the Pharisee does all the *right* things. The story would make no sense if that were not the premise. The major problem, therefore, is that not one of the Pharisees (with the exception of a few like Nicodemus) really believes in Jesus (John 7:47–48).

The fact that no Pharisees were included in the Twelve does not mean that Jesus passed them by—there were no rulers, priests, Sadducees, or Essenes represented among the Twelve either. Christ chose the

---

51. For *didachē* in the sense of "instruction," see Matt. 7:28; Mark 4:2; 12:38; Rev. 2:14. For the practice of giving this counter-instruction to the people, see Matt. 9:34; 10:25; 12:24.

humble and simple to illustrate that it is God's mercy and not human rank that leads us into the kingdom of heaven. But this message was subsequently delivered to all of Israel, *including* the rich and the Pharisees. In the composition of his council of Twelve, Jesus did not overlook some people or groups. His point was to lead *everyone* along the path of humility and faith.

It was the rejection of Jesus that led to the clashes. Belonging to the party of the Pharisees was not bad as such. In fact, we can say that for Jesus there was no party in Israel that was closer to the Scriptures, which he had come to fulfill. But when this party opposes him, they estrange themselves from the Son of God and thereby from their own roots (the Scriptures of God). It was not the character of the party that set the tone for this confrontation, but the person of John's successor.

This is apparent from several observations:

1. On more than one occasion, the Pharisees are named together with the Sadducees or the Herodians. It was not a perversity of *one* party that led to confrontation but their common refusal to undergo John's baptism (Matt. 3:7). And in one breath Jesus issues a warning against the yeast—the teaching—of both the Pharisees and the Sadducees (Matt. 16:1, 6, 11–12). Elsewhere he mentions the teaching of the Pharisees and the Herodians in one breath (Mark 8:15). At one point, when Jesus silences the Sadducees who had asked him a question to entrap him, the Pharisees immediately pick up the thread by baiting him with another (Matt. 22:34). Here the Pharisees and the Sadducees seem to be striving for the same goal. They also sometimes engage the help of the Herodians in their attempts to kill Jesus (Mark 3:6; Matt. 12:14) or to entrap him with questions (Mark 12:13). Perhaps the pressure the Pharisees exerted on Jesus to leave Perea is also based on collaboration between them and the party of Herod (Luke 13:31). During the last period of Jesus' ministry we also find regular mention of cooperation between the Pharisees and the chief priests (Matt. 21:45; 27:62; see also John 7:32, 45; 11:47, 57; 18:3).

2. In his early ministry, it was not *Jesus* who confronted the Pharisees. The confrontation only began when *they* started to become hostile. The hostility was based on a combination of well-intentioned zeal for the law and a denial of Jesus' claim to be the Son of God, Teacher, and Savior. This is apparent from their criticism of his eating with tax collectors and sinners (because of the possible violation of the dietary laws or the laws of ritual purity; Matt. 9:11) and also from the question of why Jesus' disciples fasted so

seldom compared to the disciples of John the Baptist and the Pharisees (Matt. 9:14; Mark 2:18; Luke 5:33). And then there is their suspicion of Jesus' attitude toward tradition when they ask about the washing of hands before eating (Matt. 15:12; see Mark 7:3). When they want to marshal their forces in establishing a charge against Jesus, it concerns a violation of the Sabbath law (Matt. 12:1; Mark 2:24; Luke 6:2 and then Luke 6:7). They do not deny the great miracles Jesus is performing, but—since he sometimes appears to violate the law—his power must be from Beelzebub (Matt. 9:34). This conviction stimulates them to become increasingly aggressive in working toward his downfall. By asking him about his controversial statements concerning divorce, they try to drive a wedge between him and the crowds (Matt. 19:3; Mark 10:2). And by asking him about the coming of the kingdom of heaven, they try to make it obvious that John the Baptist and Jesus are only chasing after illusions (Luke 17:20). Behind later questions is a deliberate plan to entrap him (Matt. 22:15) in order to find charges against him or to cause him to lose his popularity. In short, on the basis of revelation the Pharisees think that they have an obligation to God to try, condemn, and kill Jesus.

3. On more than one occasion Jesus receives and accepts invitations to dine with Pharisees (Luke 7:36–39; 11:37–38; 14:1).

4. The regular cooperation between the Pharisees and the scribes (often teachers of the law [*nomodidaskaloi*] in Luke) indicates that the latter regard the Pharisees' opposition as entirely legal and in conformity with the laws (Matt. 12:38; 15:1; Mark 7:1, 5; Luke 5:17; 6:7; 7:30; 11:53; 14:3; John 8:3). Some of these teachers of the law also lean in the direction of the Pharisees (Mark 2:16; compare Acts 23:9), but the category "teachers of the law" as such does not coincide with the party of the Pharisees (interpretation of the law is mainly the job of the priests and Levites).

5. There are moments when the Pharisees are divided among themselves as to whether Jesus really did come from God (John 9:16). This proves that they want to act *in accordance with set norms*. See also the doubt of Gamaliel, himself a Pharisee, concerning the apostles (Acts 5:38–39).

6. When it is said in Luke 16:14 that the Pharisees are *philarguroi* (avaricious), it does not mean that they led luxurious lives (in fact, Josephus tells us that they rejected luxury). It refers to a weakness that was also pointed out in the case of the rich young man. It is not a specific weakness, however, and certainly not the cause of the opposition against Jesus. Otherwise, there are no other negative comments about the Pharisees *as such* in the Gospels.

All the more striking are Jesus' harsh words spoken to the teachers of the law and the Pharisees in Matthew 23, as well as the comparable speech to the Pharisees in Luke 11, which is followed by a broadening that also includes the teachers of the law. These speeches are made in reaction to specific actions of the Pharisees; they are not suitable for establishing a general picture of this group. The balance now tilts far to the negative side, because it is they, who had been given the privilege of being leaders, who so definitively and mercilessly reject Jesus. In doing so, all their works lose their value. Instead of enriching the lesser by means of the Greater, they reject the Master, and now these lesser things become their downfall. The exegesis of Matthew 23, which cannot be discussed here, confirms this.[52]

4.5 The Roots of the Conflict between Christ and the Pharisees

Was a clash between Christ and the Pharisees not *unavoidable* because of the Pharisees' external religion (based on traditions), their casuistry, their distorted interpretation of the Bible, and their using the law as though it were a path to salvation?

For many Bible readers, it is simply inconceivable that in Matthew 23 Jesus might have meant that people had to live by everything that the teachers of the law and the Pharisees teach. After all, did he not harshly criticize their traditions when they challenged him over the fact that his disciples, after returning from the market, ate with unwashed hands? He became fiercely ironic: "You have a fine way of setting aside the commands of God in order to observe your own traditions!" (Mark 7:9). As an example, Jesus mentions the rule of Corban: by placing something under a vow it can no longer be used for taking care of, for example, father or mother. Thus they get around the fifth commandment ("Honor your parents")! And this is not merely a minor, external blemish on an otherwise flawless record: "You do many things like that" (Mark 7:13). Jesus' criticism is not directed at the tradition *as such*, however, but at the practice of playing the rules established by tradition against the primary laws of God. The Corban regulation is good: that which is dedicated to the Lord is withdrawn from human use. But when this regulation is used to avoid one's obligation to one's parents, the tradition is honored above the commandment of God. In the same way the Pharisees manipulate the rule about washing one's hands before eating after returning from the market in order to be rid of Christ, the Son of

52. For an in-depth treatment of Matthew 23, see J. van Bruggen, *Matteüs: Het evangelie voor Israël*, 2d ed., Commentaar op het Nieuwe Testament, 3d series (Kampen: Kok, 1994).

God. The tradition derived from the rule is turned against its own foundation: God and his commandment. But at the same time the validity of the ancient traditions *as such* never comes up for discussion.

Thus Jesus, in a conflict about the Sabbath, appears to agree with the rule that on the Sabbath one may not prepare a meal and thus may not pick heads of grain (Mark 2:23–28; Matt. 12:1–8). He defends the deviant behavior of his disciples not by dismissing the rule in question but by saying that in *his* service such a rule is subordinate to the commandments he himself—the Son of Man—has issued. So *in general* Jesus can also say in Matthew 23:3 that people must obey *everything* that the teachers of the law and the Pharisees teach. Even in Matthew 23 we see that his criticism is directed at the *attitude* with which one performs good works: failure to have compassion for one's neighbor and enjoying everyone's honor (Matt. 23:4–7). In the end that attitude leads to the *bad works* they performed in those days: the campaigns against Jesus, the slander, the baiting questions, the plotting with the other leaders, and so on.

Apparently the honest devotion of the party of the Pharisees (zeal for applying the biblical commandments in the concrete lives of God's people) gradually came to be accompanied by symptoms such as playing the later rules of tradition against the primary commandments, feelings of superiority, and a lack of love of neighbor. When John the Baptist calls on the whole nation to acknowledge their guilt and repent, the Pharisees and other leaders consider themselves too good for this. They trust in their descent from Abraham and in their good works. This self-confidence keeps them from receiving the grace of forgiveness through Jesus Christ. Thus there is an intrinsic connection between the general attitude of the leaders, especially the Pharisees, and their rejection of Jesus. But it would be incorrect to search for erroneous *teaching* in this connection, as if their zeal for the law and their development of a casuistic ethics (traditions of the fathers) were where they had gone wrong. Nor are there any indications that Jesus reproached them for a distorted exegesis of the Old Testament. The cause of the Pharisees' stumbling is not directly connected with their specific characteristics as an orthodox party, but rather with a more general, human attribute that also became a stumbling block for many non-Pharisee leaders and rich people: self-confidence before God.

4.6 The Pharisees according to the New Testament (Summary)

The New Testament essentially confirms the data provided by Josephus concerning the social status and the religious objectives of the

Pharisees. Neusner's thesis that the Pharisees of the first century were an introverted sect that focused on ritual purity should be rejected on the basis of the first-century sources in the New Testament. The negative pronouncements of Jesus concerning the Pharisees stem not from a negative judgment of their party as such or of their zeal for righteousness according to the law but from the fact that around the year 30 this party turned against the greatest prophet (John the Baptist) and against the Lord who came to call on his people (Jesus). In the resulting confrontation, Jesus exposes a hidden fatal weakness of the Pharisees: their trust in their good works and their sense of pride. We learn in the Book of Acts, however, that after his ascension Jesus nevertheless called many of the Pharisees to faith, not the least of whom was Saul of Tarsus. But during his life on earth, Jesus had to endure the fact that the very people who were closest to him in terms of their love of Scripture were precisely the ones who challenged and threatened him. It was not the enemies of God in Israel who caused him to suffer, but the friends of God! His own did not know him—not the Pharisees, not many of the disciples, not Judas. And in the end even his closest friends abandoned him. But afterward he received them as a reward for his work—some again, others for the first time.

5. Pharisees: The Natural Opposites of Christ?

The Pharisees *as Pharisees* are not the natural opposites of Christ. Jesus is not anti-Pharisaic! But his coming does reveal how even in the heart of the most righteous, the evils of self-preservation, egotism, pride, and self-confidence can dwell. The clash between the Pharisees and Jesus is a very special moment in salvation history—a moment that has passed. Paul is now in our midst. And not Paul alone. It has become apparent that even a member of the Pharisees cannot be saved without being born again. But this is something quite different from the claim that a member of the Pharisees *as such* is less eligible for faith than a non-Pharisee. Considering their love and zeal for God's law, they should have been the first!

Jewish orthodoxy, nourished by the Tanakh, Mishnah, and Talmud, can be viewed in many respects as heir to the party of the Pharisees (without their more aggressive orientation toward public life). To the extent that this is true, we cannot ignore in our evaluation of this orthodoxy the fact that this continuation has taken on an entirely different character by deliberately bypassing the greatest prophet of the Tanakh (John the Baptist) and the man prophesied in the Tanakh, who did come, the Angel of the LORD, Jesus Christ, the Son of God. Orthodox Judaism and Christianity are separated not by the legacy of legalistic or casuistic Pharisees, but by the One who came after John. Christians do not reject Pharisaism; in many respects they are the heirs of Pharisaism. The task of the Christian is to choose Christ. He alone makes them—Pharisees and Greeks—in his mercy once and for all the true heirs and children of Abraham!

Appendix 2
The Son of Man in 1 Enoch 37–71 and 4 Ezra 13

The Book of 1 Enoch in its entirety is known only in an Ethiopian version and consists of five parts. The second part, chapters 37–71, is usually known as the "Parables" or "Similitudes," based on the most characteristic material found there. In the "parables" there is with some regularity mention of a "son of man." This "son of man" is based on Daniel 7. When "someone like a man" is led before God (46.1), Enoch asks who this "son of man" is (46.2). He turns out to be the source of all wisdom and the future judge (46.3–8). This figure crops up regularly in the chapters that follow (48; 62–63; 69–71), sometimes under the name "chosen" (39–40; 45; 51–53; 55; 61–62) or "anointed" (48; 52).

The possible significance of these passages for the New Testament is categorically denied by some, in one of two ways:

1. When the Parables of Enoch are dated in the Christian era, they no longer have any direct bearing on the New Testament. The fact that this part is missing in Qumran where fragments of the other parts of 1 Enoch have been found has led some to conclude that this part must be from a later date. This conclusion is not compelling, however. Nevertheless, the dating of the parables—the last century before the Christian era or later?—continues to be a disputed question that is difficult to solve.[1]

2. If the son of man is to be identified with Enoch, the Parables of Enoch do not constitute a direct background for the way in which the New Testament speaks about the son of man. In 71.14, it seems as though Enoch (after being taken into heaven) is told, "Thou art the son of man."[2] In recent publications it is therefore often as-

---

1. See A. J. B. Higgins, *The Son of Man in the Teaching of Jesus*, Society for New Testament Studies Monograph Series 39 (Cambridge: Cambridge University Press, 1980), 12–17; and C. C. Caragounis, *The Son of Man: Vision and Interpretation*, WUNT 38 (Tübingen: Mohr, 1986).

2. Thus translated by S. Uhlig, *Das äthiopische Henochbuch*, Jüdische Schriften aus hellenistisch-römischer Zeit 5.6 (Gütersloh: Mohn, 1984).

sumed that "son of man" is a name for Enoch and not a title for an expected savior.[3] Charles tried to avoid this identification by "improving" the text and translating this passage as *"This* is the son of man."[4] Others chose to regard chapters 70–71 as an older tradition because of this identification of the son of man with Enoch,[5] or as a later addition[6] that differed from the rest. Isaac, however, points out that the phrase "son of man" in 71.12 uses a different Ethiopian wording than is usually used, and he translates without any textual emendations "Thou, son of man. . . ."[7] But according to Black,[8] the difference in wording is not important; it may have been the result of two different translators working on the same text. Apart from this disputed point, it is highly improbable that in 70–71, Enoch is equated with the heavenly, preexistent son of man. The fact that he is placed *"before* the son of man" in 70.1 does not fit with this idea,[9] nor that he fell prostrate when he arrived in heaven and had to be helped up by Michael (71.3). This angel shows him many secrets (71.4), but as "the son of man" Enoch would have known them all anyway (compare 49 and 52.4)! In 71.14 the phrase lacks the customary demonstrative pronoun before "son of man," and it is directed at Enoch, who in this context is clearly being differentiated from *"that* son of man."

The conclusion then is obvious: the phrase "son of man" is apparently not yet a title and is thus not reserved for the divine figure. Enoch,

3. E. Sjöberg, *Der Menschensohn im äthiopischen Henochbuch*, Skrifter utgivna av kungl. humanistiska vetenskapssamfundet i Lund 41 (Lund: Gleerup, 1946); H. Lichtenberger, "Messianische Erwartungen und messianische Gestalten in der Zeit des Zweiten Tempels," in *Messias-Vorstellungen bei Juden und Christen*, ed. E. Stegemann (Stuttgart: Kohlhammer, 1993), 9–20; M. Casey, *Son of Man: The Interpretation and Influence of Daniel 7* (London: S.P.C.K., 1979).

4. R. H. Charles, ed., *The Apocrypha and Pseudepigrapha of the Old Testament in English* (Oxford: Clarendon, 1913).

5. M. Black, "The Eschatology of the Similitudes of Enoch," *Journal of Theological Studies* 3 (1952): 1–10.

6. C. Colpe, "ὁ υἱὸς τοῦ ἀνθρώπου," in *Theological Dictionary of the New Testament*, ed. G. Friedrich, trans. G. W. Bromiley (Grand Rapids: Eerdmans, 1972), 8:400–477 ; C. J. den Heyer, *De messiaanse weg*, vol. 1, *Messiaanse verwachtingen in het Oude Testament en in de vroeg-joodse traditie* (Kampen: Kok, 1983).

7. E. Isaac, "1 (Ethiopic Apocalypse of) Enoch: A New Translation and Introduction," in *The Old Testament Pseudepigrapha*, ed. J. H. Charlesworth (London: Doubleday, 1983), 1:5–89.

8. M. Black et al., *The Book of Enoch or 1 Enoch: A New English Edition with Commentary and Textual Notes*, Studies in Veteris Testamenti Pseudepigrapha 7 (Leiden: Brill, 1985), 206–7.

9. J. J. Collins, "The Son of Man in First-Century Judaism," *New Testament Studies* 38 (1992): 448–66.

as a person, is also a "son of man." He is *born* for righteousness, but that does not therefore make him, who is a son of man, *that* son of man.

The study of the idea of the "son of man" in 1 Enoch 37–71 often focuses on the use of terminology and on the identification of the son of man, while less attention is paid to the content of the statements about this son of man. But when we read the entire second part of 1 Enoch, we discover that the son of man referred to here is not only a (still hidden) heavenly being, but that he also was and is important for the people on earth! This son of man has already been made known; he was hidden by God, but God revealed him to the saints or he himself made known God's righteousness to the saints (48.7). The son of man was hidden from the beginning, but God revealed him to his saints and chosen people (62.7). That is why he can also be called God's "anointed" (48.10; 52.4). He is the "chosen one, in whom he [the Lord of the Spirits] is well pleased" (49.4). The righteous are saved "in his name" (48.7). He already has a "house of his community"; at present the members of this community are being oppressed in the name of God, but when the son of man reveals his community, they will no longer be persecuted (53.6). Later the nations will be led before him, and then they will *acknowledge* him, they will beg him for mercy but will be condemned because of their lack of faith (62.1: "open your eyes . . . when you are able to recognize the chosen one"; 62.3: all kings will "see him and recognize him"; 62.9: they ask for mercy). The nations stand *ashamed* before the king of kings, whom they failed to recognize (63.11).

Because we know of no such revealed or revealing figure in Judaism, we must assume that the image of this son of man has been influenced by familiarity with the revelation of Jesus Christ. Aside from questions about the integrity of 1 Enoch 37–71 and the dating of the whole or of parts of the text, we must consider the document (or part of the document) as it now lies before us an echo of the gospel of Jesus Christ. For it deals with a "son of man" who has already been revealed to the saints, who has a community here, and who will be revealed to all people at the Last Judgment. His name is already known to the righteous, who are thereby saved. Because the entire document is projected onto the life of Enoch, the name *Jesus* is never mentioned. He is referred to only indirectly, when Enoch is told who the human figure is who is being led to God (Dan. 7). This figure is "that son of man" (in the Ethiopian a demonstrative pronoun is always used). The Parables of Enoch make use of Jesus' self-descriptions, connecting them with Daniel 7, and then describe how all the treasures of wisdom and knowledge are hidden in this rejected son of man and how he will appear as judge of all people. It is not improbable that a Jewish Christian chose to explain in this manner that the "descendant of man" who was rejected by his people now occupies the place of the figure from Daniel 7 in the heavenly reality. But even though we cannot speak with certainty about the origin and intent of the Parables, they seem to *presuppose* Jesus' self-designation as we know it from the Gospels and therefore provide us with no background information for the origin of that self-designation.[10]

We can be brief about 4 Ezra 13. Here we find no concept of a "son of man" who is to be expected. There is a vision in which the author sees something like a human form rising from the sea (= 2 Esdras 13:3 NRSV), but in the explanation this human figure is simply called "man" or "anointed" or "my son." However important this vision may be for clarifying the Jewish expectations of a Messiah, it does not make clear whether "son of man" is an existing title for this anointed one.[11]

10. For the *Christian* background of the Parables of Enoch, see also C. L. Mearns, "Dating the Similitudes of Henoch," *New Testament Studies* 25 (1978–79): 360–69; and R. Leivestad, "Jesus—Messias—Menschensohn: Die jüdischen Heilandserwartungen zur Zeit der ersten römischen Kaiser und die Frage nach dem messianischen Selbstbewusstsein Jesu," in *Aufstieg und Niedergang der römischen Welt* 2.25.1 (Berlin: de Gruyter, 1982), 220–64.

11. W. G. Kümmel, *Jesus der Menschensohn?* Sitzungsberichte der wissenschaftlichen Gesellschaft an der Johann Wolfgang Goethe-Universität Frankfurt am Main 20.3 (Stuttgart: Steiner, 1984).

Bibliography

Aland, K. *Did the Early Church Baptize Infants?* Translated from German. Philadelphia: Westminster, 1963.

Alexander, P. S. "Rabbinic Judaism and the New Testament." *Zeitschrift für die neutestamentliche Wissenschaft* 74 (1983): 237–46.

Allison, D. C. "Elijah Must Come First." *Journal of Biblical Literature* 103 (1984): 256–58.

Anderson, R. D. "Graeco-Roman Religious Anointing and Its Possible Implications for the Understanding of the Christos in the First Century: A Critical Evaluation of Sections from Martin Karrer's *Der Gesalbte*." Doctoral thesis, Theological University, Broederweg, Kampen, The Netherlands, 1993.

Aquinas, T. *Theologische Summa van den H. Thomas van Aquino. XXII: Over de Sacramenten (III, Q.60–72)*. Latijnsche en Nederlandsche tekst uitgegeven door een groep Dominicanen. Antwerp: Geloofsverdediging, 1932.

Baarlink, H. "Jezus, uw verzoenend sterven . . . : Hoe kunnen wij over de verzoening (s)preken?" In *Jezus' visie op zichzelf: In discussie met De Jonge's christologie*, 85–99. Leidse lezingen. Nijkerk: Callenbach, 1991.

Bachmann, M. "Johannes der Täufer bei Lukas: Nachzügler oder Vorläufer?" In *Wort in der Zeit: Neutestamentliche Studien*, edited by W. Haubeck and M. Bachmann, 123–55. Leiden: Brill, 1980.

Backhaus, K. *Die "Jüngerkreise" des Täufers Johannes: Eine Studie zu den religionsgeschichtlichen Ursprüngen des Christentums*. Paderborner theologische Studien 19. Paderborn: Schoeningh, 1991.

Badtke, W. B. "Was Jesus a Disciple of John?" *Evangelical Quarterly* 62 (1990): 195–204.

Bammel, E., and C. F. D. Moule, eds. *Jesus and the Politics of His Day*. Cambridge: Cambridge University Press, 1984.

Barrett, C. K. *The Gospel according to St. John: An Introduction with Commentary and Notes on the Greek Text*. 2d ed. London: S.P.C.K., 1956.

Barth, G. "Zwei vernachlässigte Gesichtspunkte zum Verständnis der Taufe im Neuen Testament." *Zeitschrift für Theologie und Kirche* 70 (1973): 137–61.

Bastiaens, J. C. *Interpretaties van Jesaja 53: Een intertekstueel onderzoek naar de lijdende Knecht in Jes 53 (MT/LXX) en in Lk 22:14–38, Hand 3:12–26, Hand 4:23–31 en Hand 8:26–40*. TFT-Studies 22. Tilburg: Tilburg University Press, 1993.

Bauckham, R. "The Son of Man: 'A Man in My Position' or 'Someone'?" *Journal for the Study of the New Testament* 23 (1985): 23–33.

Bauer, D. R. "Son of David." In *Dictionary of Jesus and the Gospels*, edited by J. B. Green and S. McKnight, 766–69. Downers Grove, Ill.: InterVarsity, 1992.

Baum, A. D. "Auferstehung oder Vision? Gerd Lüdemanns Versuch, den christlichen Osterglauben zu erneuern: Ein Gutachten für die Gemeinde." *Diakrisis* 16 (March 1995): 23–34.

Baumgarten, A. I. "The Name of the Pharisees." *Journal of Biblical Literature* 102 (1983): 411–28.

Bavinck, H. *Gereformeerde Dogmatiek*. 4 vols. 3d ed. Kampen: Kok, 1918.

Beall, T. S. *Josephus' Description of the Essenes Illustrated by the Dead Sea Scrolls*. Society for New Testament Studies Monograph Series 58. Cambridge: Cambridge University Press, 1988.

Beasley-Murray, G. R. *Jesus and the Kingdom of God*. Grand Rapids: Eerdmans, 1986.

———. *John*. Word Biblical Commentary. Waco: Word, 1987.

———. "The Kingdom of God in the Teaching of Jesus." *Journal of the Evangelical Theological Society* 35 (1992): 19–30.

Becker, J. *Johannes der Täufer und Jesus von Nazareth*. Biblische Studien 63. Neukirchen: Neukirchener Verlag, 1972.

Ben-chorin, S. *Broeder Jezus: De Nazarener door een Jood gezien*. Translated by F. van der Heijden. Baarn: Ten Have, 1971 (original German edition, 1967).

Berger, K. *Die Amen-Worte Jesu: Eine Untersuchung zum Problem der Legitimation in apokalyptischer Rede*. Beihefte zur Zeitschrift für die neutestamentliche Wissenschaft 39. Berlin: de Gruyter, 1970.

———. "Zur Geschichte der Einleitungsformel 'Amen, Ich sage euch.'" *Zeitschrift für die neutestamentliche Wissenschaft* 63 (1972): 45–75.

———. "Die königlichen Messiastraditionen des neuen Testaments." *New Testament Studies* 20 (1973–74): 1–44.

———. "Zum Problem der Messianität Jesu." *Zeitschrift für Theologie und Kirche* 71 (1974): 1–30.

———. "Jesus als Pharisäer und frühe Christen als Pharisäer." *Novum Testamentum* 30 (1988): 231–62.

Bernouilli, C. A. *Johannes der Täufer und die Urgemeinde*. Leipzig: Neue Geist, 1918.

Betz, O. "Was John the Baptist an Essene?" In *Understanding the Dead Sea Scrolls: A Reader from the* Biblical Archaeology Review, edited by H. Shanks, 205–14. New York: Random House, 1992.

Bietenhard, H. *Sota: Die des Ehebruchs Verdächtige*. Die Mischna: Text, Übersetzung und ausführliche Erklärung 3.6. Berlin: Töpelmann, 1956.

———. "Der Menschensohn—*ho huios tou anthrōpou*: Sprachliche und religionsgeschichtliche Untersuchungen zu einem Begriff der synoptischen Evangelien: I. Sprachlicher und religionsgeschichtlicher Teil." In *Aufstieg und Niedergang der römischen Welt*, part II, *Principat*, vol. 25, *Religion*, 1:265–350. Berlin: de Gruyter, 1982.

Billerbeck, P. *See* Strack, H. L.

Black, M. "The Eschatology of the Similitudes of Enoch." *Journal of Theological Studies* 3 (1952): 1–10.

Black, M., et al. *The Book of Enoch or I Enoch: A New English Edition with Commentary and Textual Notes*. Studies in Veteris Testamenti Pseudepigrapha 7. Leiden: Brill, 1985.

Blackburn, B. L. "Miracle Working *Theioi Andres* in Hellenism (and Hellenistic Judaism)." In *Gospel Perspectives*, vol. 6, *The Miracles of Jesus*, edited by D. Wenham and C. Blomberg, 185–218. Sheffield: JSOT Press, 1986.

———. "The Miracles of Jesus." In *Studying the Historical Jesus: Evaluations of the State of Current Research*, edited by B. Chilton and C. A. Evans, 353–94. New Testament Tools and Studies 19. Leiden: Brill, 1994.

Böcher, O. "Johannes der Täufer in der neutestamentlichen Überlieferung." In *Rechtfertigung, Realismus, Universalismus in biblischer Sicht: Festschrift für Adolf Köberle zum 80. Geburtstag*, edited by G. Müller, 45–68. Darmstadt: Wisschenschaftlicher Buchgesellschaft, 1978.

———. "Lukas und Johannes der Täufer." *Studien zum Neuen Testament und seiner Umwelt* 4 (1979): 27–44.

Borg, M. "The Currency of the Term *Zealot*." *Journal of Theological Studies* 22 (1971): 504–12.

Bosch, D. *Die Heidenmission in der Zukunft Jesu*. Abhandlungen zur Theologie des Alten und Neuen Testaments 36. Zürich: Zwingli, 1959.

Bousset, W. *Die Religion des Judentums im späthellenistischen Zeitalter*. 3d ed. Edited by H. Gressmann. Handbuch zum Neuen Testament 21. Tübingen: Mohr, 1926; reprinted, Tübingen: Mohr, 1966.

————. *Kyrios Christos: A History of the Belief in Christ from the Beginnings of Christianity to Irenaeus*. Translated from 1913 German edition. Nashville: Abingdon, 1970.

Bowker, J. *Jesus and the Pharisees*. Cambridge: Cambridge University Press, 1973.

————. "The Son of Man." *Journal of Theological Studies* 28 (1977): 19–48.

Brady, J. R. *Jesus Christ: Divine Man or Son of God?* Lanham, Md.: University Press of America, 1992.

Brandon, S. G. F. *Jesus and the Zealots: A Study of the Political Factor in Primitive Christianity*. Manchester: Manchester University Press, 1967.

————. *The Fall of Jerusalem and the Christian Church: A Study of the Effects of the Jewish Overthrow of A.D. 70 on Christianity*. 2d ed. London: S.P.C.K., 1978.

Brown, J. P. "The Son of Man: 'This Fellow.'" *Biblica* 58 (1977): 361–87.

Brown, R. E. "Three Quotations from John the Baptist in the Gospel of John." *Catholic Biblical Quarterly* 22 (1960): 292–98.

————. *The Gospel according to John*. Anchor Bible. Garden City, N.Y.: Doubleday, 1966–70.

————. *The Death of the Messiah: From Gethsemane to the Grave: A Commentary on the Passion Narratives in the Four Gospels*. 2 vols. Anchor Bible Reference Library. New York: Doubleday, 1993.

Brownlee, W. H. "John the Baptist in the New Light of Ancient Scrolls." *Interpretation* 9 (1955): 71–90.

Brox, N. "Zur christlichen Mission in der Spätantike." In *Mission im Neuen Testament*, edited by K. Kertelge, 190–237. Quaestiones Disputatae 93. Freiburg: Herder, 1982.

Bruce, F. F. *This Is That: The New Testament Development of Some Old Testament Themes*. Exeter: Paternoster, 1968.

Buehler, W. W. *The Pre-Herodian Civil War and Social Debate: Jewish Society in the Period 76–40 B.C. and the Social Factors Contributing to the Rise of the Pharisees and the Sadducees*. Basel: Reinhardt, 1974.

Bultmann, R. *Theology of the New Testament*. Translated by K. Grobel. New York: Scribner, 1951–55.

————. *The Gospel of John: A Commentary*. Translated by G. R. Beasley-Murray. Oxford: Blackwell, 1971.

Burger, C. *Jesus als Davidssohn: Eine traditionsgeschichtliche Untersuchung*. Forschungen zur Religion und Literatur des Alten und Neuen Testaments 98. Göttingen: Vandenhoeck & Ruprecht, 1970.

Burkett, D. *The Son of Man in the Gospel of John*. Journal for the Study of the New Testament Supplement Series 56. Sheffield: JSOT Press, 1991.

————. "The Nontitular Son of Man: A History and Critique." *New Testament Studies* 40 (1994): 504–21.

Caragounis, C. C. *The Son of Man: Vision and Interpretation*. Wissenschaftliche Untersuchungen zum Neuen Testament 38. Tübingen: Mohr, 1986.

Carson, D. A. *The Gospel according to John*. Pillar New Testament Commentary. Grand Rapids: Eerdmans; Leicester: Inter-Varsity, 1991.

————. "Do the Prophets and the Law Quit Prophesying before John? A Note on Matthew 11.13." In *The Gospels and the Scriptures of Israel*, edited by C. A. Evans and W. R. Stegner, 179–94. Journal for the Study of the New Testament Supplement Series 104. Sheffield: Sheffield Academic Press, 1994.

Casey, M. *Son of Man: The Interpretation and Influence of Daniel 7*. London: S.P.C.K., 1979.

———. *From Jewish Prophet to Gentile God: The Origins and Development of New Testament Christology.* Cambridge: Clarke; Louisville: Westminster/John Knox, 1991.

———. "The Use of the Term *bar (ʾ)nasi(ʾ)* in the Aramaic Translations of the Hebrew Bible." *Journal for the Study of the New Testament* 54 (1994): 87–118.

———. "Idiom and Translation: Some Aspects of the Son of Man Problem." *New Testament Studies* 41 (1995): 164–82.

Charles, R. H., ed. *The Apocrypha and Pseudepigrapha of the Old Testament in English.* 2 vols. Oxford: Clarendon, 1913.

Charlesworth, J. H., ed. *The Old Testament Pseudepigrapha.* 2 vols. Garden City, N.Y.: Doubleday, 1983–85.

Chilton, B. "Jesus *ben David*: Reflections on the *Davidssohnfrage.*" *Journal for the Study of the New Testament* 14 (1982): 88–112.

———. "The Son of Man: Human and Heavenly." In *The Four Gospels 1992,* edited by F. van Segbroeck, 1:203–18. Bibliotheca ephemeridum theologicarum lovaniensium 100. Louvain: Peeters, 1992.

———. "The Kingdom of God in Recent Discussion." In *Studying the Historical Jesus: Evaluations of the State of Current Research,* edited by B. Chilton and C. A. Evans, 255–80. New Testament Tools and Studies 19. Leiden: Brill, 1994.

Chilton, B., ed. *The Kingdom of God in the Teaching of Jesus.* Issues in Religion and Theology 5. Philadelphia: Fortress, 1984.

Collins, J. J. "The Son of Man in First-Century Judaism." *New Testament Studies* 38 (1992): 448–66.

———. "The *Son of God* Text from Qumran." In *From Jesus to John: Essays on Jesus and New Testament Christology in Honour of Marinus de Jonge,* edited by M. C. De Boer, 65–82. Journal for the Study of the New Testament Supplement Series 84. Sheffield: JSOT Press, 1993.

———. *The Scepter and the Star: The Messiahs of the Dead Sea Scrolls and Other Ancient Literature.* New York: Doubleday, 1995.

Colpe, C. "ὁ υἱὸς τοῦ ἀνθρώπου." In *Theological Dictionary of the New Testament,* edited by G. Friedrich, translated by G. W. Bromiley, 8:400–477. Grand Rapids: Eerdmans, 1972.

———. *Das Siegel der Propheten: Historische Beziehungen zwischen Judentum, Judenchristentum, Heidentum und frühem Islam.* Arbeiten zur neutestamentlichen Theologie und Zeitgeschichte 3. Berlin: Institut Kirche und Judentum, 1990.

Conzelmann, H. *An Outline of the Theology of the New Testament.* Translated by J. Bowden. London: SCM, 1969.

Cortés, J. B., and F. M. Gatti. "The Son of Man or the Son of Adam." *Biblica* 49 (1968): 457–502.

Craig, W. L. "The Problem of Miracles: A Historical and Philosophical Perspective." In *Gospel Perspectives,* vol. 6, *The Miracles of Jesus,* edited by D. Wenham and C. Blomberg, 9–48. Sheffield: JSOT Press, 1986.

Cullmann, O. *The Christology of the New Testament.* Translated by S. C. Guthrie and C. A. M. Hall. Philadelphia: Westminster, 1959.

———. *Salvation in History.* Translated by S. G. Sowers et al. New York: Harper & Row, 1967.

Dahl, N. A. *Das Volk Gottes: Eine Untersuchung zum Kirchenbewusstsein des Urchristentums.* Oslo: Dybwad, 1941; reprinted, Darmstadt: Wissenschaftlicher Buchgesellschaft, 1962.

———. *Jesus the Christ: The Historical Origins of Christological Doctrine.* Minneapolis: Fortress, 1991.

Dalman, G. *The Words of Jesus Considered in the Light of Post-Biblical Jewish Writings and the Aramaic Language.* Translated from German. Edinburgh: Clark, 1902.

Davies, S. L. "John the Baptist and Essene Kashruth." *New Testament Studies* 29 (1983): 569–71.

Deines, R. *Jüdische Steingefässe und pharisäische Frömmigkeit: Ein archäologisch-historischer Beitrag zum Verständnis von Joh 2,6 und der jüdischen Reinheitshalacha zur Zeit Jesu.* Wissenschaftliche Untersuchungen zum Neuen Testament 2/52. Tübingen: Mohr, 1993.

———. *Die Pharisäer: Ihr Verständnis im Spiegel der christlichen und jüdischen Forschung seit Wellhausen und Graetz.* Wissenschaftliche Untersuchungen zum Neuen Testament 101. Tübingen: Mohr, 1997.

Dexinger, F. "Ein 'Messianisches Szenarium' als Gemeingut des Judentums in nach-herodianischer Zeit?" *Kairos* 17 (1975): 249–78.

Dibelius, M. *Die urchristliche Überlieferung von Johannes dem Täufer.* Forschungen zur Religion und Literatur des Alten und Neuen Testaments 15. Göttingen: Vandenhoeck & Ruprecht, 1911.

Dinkler, E. "Taufe (im Urchristentum)." In *Die Religion in Geschichte und Gegenwart: Handwörterbuch für Theologie und Religionswissenschaft,* 3d ed., 2:627–37. Tübingen: Mohr, 1962.

Dockery, D. S. "Baptism." In *Dictionary of Jesus and the Gospels,* edited by J. B. Green and S. McKnight. Downers Grove, Ill.: InterVarsity, 1992.

Dodd, C. H. *The Parables of the Kingdom.* 2d ed. London: Nisbet, 1936.

Doeve, J. W. *Vertekende Beelden: Over de selectie van de bronnen bij de beoefening der Judaïstiek van de eeuwen rondom het begin onzer jaartelling.* Leiden: Brill, 1963.

Donahue, J. R. "Recent Studies on the Origin of 'Son of Man' in the Gospels." *Catholic Biblical Quarterly* 48 (1986): 484–98.

Duling, D. C. "The Promises to David and Their Entrance into Christianity: Nailing Down a Likely Hypothesis." *New Testament Studies* 19 (1973–74): 55–77.

———. "Solomon, Exorcism, and the Son of David." *Harvard Theological Review* 68 (1975): 235–52.

Dunn, J. D. G. *Baptism in the Holy Spirit: A Re-examination of the New Testament Teaching on the Gift of the Spirit in Relation to Pentecostalism Today.* Studies in Biblical Theology 2/15. London: SCM, 1970.

———. *Christology in the Making: A New Testament Inquiry into the Origins of the Doctrine of the Incarnation.* London: SCM, 1980.

Eichhorn, A. *Das Abendmahl im Neuen Testament.* Hefte zur Christlichen Welt 36. Leipzig: Mohr, 1898.

Eisler, R. *Iesous Basileus Ou Basileusas: Die messianische Unabhängigkeitsbewegung vom Auftreten Johannes des Täufers bis zum Untergang Jakobs des Gerechten, nach der neu-erschlossenen "Eroberung von Jerusalem" des Flavius Josephus und den christlichen Quellen.* 2 vols. Religionswissenschaftliche Bibliothek 9. Heidelberg: Winter Universitätsbuchhandlung, 1929–30.

Enslin, M. S. "John and Jesus." *Zeitschrift für die neutestamentliche Wissenschaft* 66 (1975): 1–18.

Epp, E. J., and G. W. McRae, eds. *The New Testament and Its Modern Interpreters.* Philadelphia: Fortress, 1989.

Ernst, J. *Johannes der Täufer: Interpretation—Geschichte—Wirkungsgeschichte.* Berlin: de Gruyter, 1989.

Evans, C. A. *Jesus and His Contemporaries: Comparative Studies.* Arbeiten zur Geschichte des antiken Judentums und des Urchristentums 25. Leiden: Brill, 1995.

Falk, H. *Jesus the Pharisee: A New Look at the Jewishness of Jesus.* New York: Paulist, 1985.

Farla, P. J. *Jezus' oordeel over Israël: Een Form- en Redaktionsgeschichtliche analyse van Mc 10,46–12,40.* Kampen: Kok, 1978.

Feine, P. *Theologie des Neuen Testaments.* 3d ed. Leipzig: Hinrichs, 1919.

Fiebig, P. *Der Menschensohn: Jesu Selbstbezeichnung mit besonderer Berücksichtigung des aramäischen Sprachgebrauches für "Mensch" untersucht.* Tübingen: Mohr, 1901.

Fisher, L. R. "Can This Be the Son of David?" In *Jesus and the Historian: Written in Honor of Ernest Cadman Colwell,* edited by F. T. Trotter, 82–97. Philadelphia: Westminster, 1968.

Fitzmyer, J. A. "4Q246: The 'Son of God' Document from Qumran." *Biblica* 74 (1993): 153–74.

Flusser, D. *Judaism and the Origins of Christianity.* Jerusalem: Magnes, 1988.

France, R. T. "Jesus the Baptist?" In *Jesus of Nazareth, Lord and Christ: Essays on the Historical Jesus and New Testament Christology,* edited by J. B. Green and M. Turner, 94–111. Grand Rapids: Eerdmans, 1994.

Gaffin, R. B. *Perspectives on Pentecost.* 2d ed. Phillipsburg, N.J.: Presbyterian & Reformed, 1980.

García Martínez, F. "Messianische Erwartungen in den Qumranschriften." *Jahrbuch für Biblische Theologie* 8 (1993): 171–208.

García Martínez, F., and J. Trebolle Barrera. *The People of the Dead Sea Scrolls: Their Writings, Beliefs, and Practices.* Translated by W. G. E. Watson. Leiden: Brill, 1995.

Geisler, N. L. *The Battle for the Resurrection.* Nashville: Nelson, 1989.

Gnilka, J. "Die essenischen Tauchbäder und die Johannestaufe." *Revue de Qumran* 3 (1961): 185–207.

———. "Der Täufer Johannes und der Ursprung der christlichen Taufe." *Bibel und Leben* 4 (1963): 39–49.

———. "Martyriumsparänese und Sühnetod in synoptischen und jüdischen Traditionen." In *Die Kirche des Anfangs: Für Heinz Schürmann,* edited by R. Schnackenburg et al., 223–46. Freiburg: Herder, 1978.

Goodblatt, D. "The Place of the Pharisees in First Century Judaism: The State of the Debate." *Journal for the Study of Judaism* 20 (1989): 12–30.

Goodman, M. *The Ruling Class of Judaea: The Origins of the Jewish Revolt against Rome A.D. 66–70.* Cambridge: Cambridge University Press, 1987.

Gootjes, N. H. "De doop met de Heilige Geest en de betekenis van Pinksteren." *Radix* 13 (1987): 139–58.

Goppelt, L. *Theology of the New Testament.* Edited by J. Roloff. Translated by J. E. Alsup. Grand Rapids: Eerdmans, 1981.

Grabbe, L. L. *Judaism from Cyrus to Hadrian.* One-volume edition. London: SCM, 1994 (original two-volume edition 1992).

Grimm, W. *Die Verkündigung Jesu und Deuterojesaja.* 2d ed. Arbeiten zum Neuen Testament und Judentum 1. Frankfurt: Lang, 1981.

Groningen, G. van. *Messianic Revelation in the Old Testament.* Grand Rapids: Baker, 1990.

Gubler, M.-L. *Die frühesten Deutungen des Todes Jesu: Eine motivgeschichtliche Darstellung aufgrund der neueren exegetischen Forschung.* Orbis Biblicus et Orientalis 15. Freiburg/Göttingen: Universitätsverlag, 1977.

Guevara, H. *La resistencia judia contra Roma en la epoca de Jesus.* Meitingen: Meitinger, 1981.

Haag, H. *Der Gottesknecht bei Deuterojesaja.* Erträge der Forschung 233. Darmstadt: Wissenschaftlicher Buchgesellschaft, 1985.

Haenchen, E. *John: A Commentary on the Gospel of John.* Edited by R. W. Funk with the assistance of U. Busse. Translated by R. W. Funk. Philadelphia: Fortress, 1984.

Hahn, F. *The Titles of Jesus in Christology: Their History in Early Christianity.* Translated by H. Knight and G. Ogg. London: Lutterworth, 1969.

Hampel, V. *Menschensohn und historischer Jesus: Ein Rätselwort als Schlüssel zum messianischen Selbstverständnis Jesu.* Neukirchen: Neukirchener Verlag, 1990.

Hare, D. R. A. *The Son of Man Tradition.* Minneapolis: Fortress, 1990.

Harnack, A. von. *What Is Christianity?* With an introduction by R. Bultmann. Translated by B. Saunders. Gloucester: Smith, 1957.

Harris, M. J. *Jesus as God: The New Testament Use of* Theos *in Reference to Jesus*. Grand Rapids: Baker, 1992.

Hartman, L. *Auf den Namen des Herrn Jesus: Die Taufe in den neutestamentlichen Schriften*. Stuttgarter Bibelstudien 148. Stuttgart: Katholisches Bibelwerk, 1992.

Hasler, V. *Amen: Redaktionsgeschichtliche Untersuchung zur Einführungsformel der Herrenworte "Wahrlich ich sage euch."* Zürich: Gotthelf, 1969.

Heitmüller, W. *"Im Namen Jesu": Eine sprach- und religionsgeschichtliche Untersuchung zum Neuen Testament, speziell zur altchristlichen Taufe*. Forschungen zur Religion und Literatur des Alten und Neuen Testaments 1/2. Göttingen: Vandenhoeck & Ruprecht, 1903.

Hengel, M. *The Atonement: The Origins of the Doctrine in the New Testament*. Philadelphia: Fortress, 1981.

———. *The Cross of the Son of God*. Translated by J. Bowden. London: SCM, 1986.

———. *The Zealots: Investigations into the Jewish Freedom Movement in the Period from Herod I until 70* A.D. Translated by D. Smith. Edinburgh: Clark, 1989.

———. "Psalm 110 und die Erhöhung des Auferstandenen zur Rechten Gottes." In *Anfänge der Christologie: Festschrift für Ferdinand Hahn*. Edited by C. B. Breytenbach and H. Paulsen, 43–73. Göttingen: Vandenhoeck & Ruprecht, 1991.

Hengel, M., and R. Deines. "E. P. Sanders' 'Common Judaism,' Jesus and the Pharisees." *Journal of Theological Studies* 46 (1995): 1–70.

Henten, J. W. van. "De joodse martelaren als grondleggers van een nieuwe orde: Een studie uitgaande van 2 en 4 Makkabeeën." Doctoral thesis, University of Leiden, 1986.

Henten, J. W. van, et al., eds. *Die Entstehung der jüdischen Martyrologie*. Studia Post-Biblica 38. Leiden: Brill, 1989.

Herrenbrück, F. *Jesus und die Zöllner: Historische und neutestamentlich-exegetische Untersuchungen*. Wissenschaftliche Untersuchungen zum Neuen Testament 2/41. Tübingen: Mohr, 1990.

Heyer, C. J. den. "Jezus, de lijdende rechtvaardige en de knecht des HEREN." In *De knechtsgestalte van Christus: Studies door collega's en oud-leerlingen aangeboden aan Prof. Dr. H. N. Ridderbos*, edited by H. H. Grosheide et al., 54–64. Kampen: Kok, 1978.

———. *De messiaanse weg*, vol. 1, *Messiaanse verwachtingen in het Oude Testament en in de vroeg-joodse traditie*. Kampen: Kok, 1983.

Higgins, A. J. B. *The Son of Man in the Teaching of Jesus*. Society for New Testament Studies Monograph Series 39. Cambridge: Cambridge University Press, 1980.

Hoehner, H. W. *Herod Antipas*. Society for New Testament Studies Monograph Series 17. Cambridge: Cambridge University Press, 1972.

Hogan, L. P. *Healing in the Second Temple Period*. Novum Testamentum et Orbis Antiquus 21. Freiburg: Universitätsverlag, 1992.

Hooker, M. *Jesus and the Servant: The Influence of the Servant Concept of Deutero-Isaiah in the New Testament*. London: S.P.C.K., 1959.

———. "John the Baptist and the Johannine Prologue." *New Testament Studies* 16 (1969–70): 354–58.

Horsley, R. A. "Josephus and the Bandits." *Journal for the Study of Judaism* 10 (1979): 37–63.

———. "Like One of the Prophets of Old: Two Types of Popular Prophets at the Time of Jesus." *Catholic Biblical Quarterly* 47 (1985): 435–63.

———. "The Zealots: Their Origin, Relationships, and Importance in the Jewish Revolt." *Novum Testamentum* 28 (1986): 159–92.

Horst, P. W. van der. *Ancient Jewish Epitaphs: An Introductory Survey of a Millennium of Jewish Funerary Epigraphy (300* B.C.E.*–700* C.E.*)*. Contributions to Biblical Exegesis and Theology 2. Kampen: Kok Pharos, 1991.

Hoskyns, E. C. *The Fourth Gospel.* 2d ed. London: Faber & Faber, 1947.

Houwelingen, P. H. R. van. "De strekking van het evangelie naar Marcus." In *Verkenningen in de evangeliën*, edited by G. van den Brink et al., 16–24. Theologische Verkenningen: Bijbel en Exegese 5. Kampen: Kok Voorhoeve, 1990.

———. *Johannes: Het evangelie van het Woord.* Commentaar op het Nieuwe Testament, 3d series. Kampen: Kok, 1997.

Hübner, H. *Biblische Theologie des Neuen Testaments.* Vol. 1, *Prolegomena.* Göttingen: Vandenhoeck & Ruprecht, 1990.

Hughes, J. H. "John the Baptist: The Forerunner of God Himself." *Novum Testamentum* 14 (1972): 191–218.

Isaac, E. "1 (Ethiopic Apocalypse of) Enoch: A New Translation and Introduction." In *The Old Testament Pseudepigrapha*, edited by J. H. Charlesworth, 1:5–89. London: Doubleday, 1983.

Jeremias, J. "Der Ursprung der Johannestaufe." *Zeitschrift für die neutestamentliche Wissenschaft* 28 (1929): 312–20.

———. *Die Kindertaufe in den ersten vier Jahrhunderten.* Göttingen: Vandenhoeck & Ruprecht, 1958 (3d rev. ed. of *Hat die älteste Christenheit die Kindertaufe geübt?* [1st ed., 1938; 2d ed., 1949]).

———. *The Origins of Infant Baptism: A Further Study in Reply to Kurt Aland.* Naperville, Ill.: Allenson, 1963.

———. "*Pais (theou)* im Neuen Testament." In *Abba: Studien zur neutestamentlichen Theologie und Zeitgeschichte*, 191–216. Göttingen: Vandenhoeck & Ruprecht, 1966 (revision of "παῖς θεοῦ" in *Theologisches Wörterbuch zum Neuen Testament*, edited by G. Friedrich, 5:698–713. Stuttgart: Kohlhammer, 1954).

———. *New Testament Theology.* London: SCM, 1971.

———. "Zum nicht-responsorischen Amen." *Zeitschrift für die neutestamentliche Wissenschaft* 64 (1973): 122–23.

Jonge, H. J. de. "Ontstaan en ontwikkeling van het geloof in Jezus' opstanding." In *Waarlijk opgestaan! Een discussie over de opstanding van Jezus Christus*, edited by F. O. van Gennep et al., 31–50. Baarn: Ten Have, 1989.

———. "De opstanding van Jezus: De joodse traditie achter een christelijke belijdenis." In *Jodendom en vroeg christendom: Continuïteit en discontinuïteit*, edited by T. Baarda, 47–61. Opstellen van leden van de Studiosorum Novi Testamenti Conventus. Kampen: Kok, 1991.

———. "De visie van de historische Jezus op zichzelf." In *Jezus' visie op zichzelf: In discussie met De Jonge's christologie*, edited by H. Baarlink et al., 48–64. Leidse lezingen. Nijkerk: Callenbach, 1991.

———. "De oorsprong van de verwachting van Jezus' wederkomst." In *Totdat Hij komt: Een discussie over de wederkomst van Jezus Christus*, edited by H. J. de Jonge and B. W. F. de Ruyter, 9–36. Baarn: Ten Have, 1995.

Jonge, M. de. "The Use of the Word 'Anointed' in the Time of Jesus." *Novum Testamentum* 8 (1966): 132–48.

———. "Jezus als profetische Zoon van David." In *Profeten en profetische geschriften*, edited by F. García Martínez et al., 157–66. Kampen: Kok, 1987.

———. "Jesus' Death for Others and the Death of the Maccabean Martyrs." In *Text and Testimony: Essays on New Testament and Apocryphal Literature in Honour of A. F. J. Klijn*, edited by T. Baarda et al., 142–51. Kampen: Kok, 1988.

———. "Test. Benjamin 3:8 and the Picture of Joseph as 'a Good and Holy Man.'" In *Die Entstehung der jüdischen Martyrologie*, edited by J. W. van Henten et al., 204–14. Studia Post-Biblica 38. Leiden: Brill, 1989.

———. "Jesus, Son of David and Son of God." In *Jewish Eschatology, Early Christian Christology, and the Testaments of the Twelve Patriarchs: Collected Essays*, 135–44. Supplements to Novum Testamentum 63. Leiden: Brill, 1991.

————. "Josephus und die Zukunftserwartungen seines Volkes." In *Jewish Eschatology, Early Christian Christology, and the Testaments of the Twelve Patriarchs: Collected Essays*, 48–62. Supplements to Novum Testamentum 63. Leiden: Brill, 1991 (originally published in 1974).

————. "The Role of Intermediaries in God's Final Intervention in the Future according to the Qumran Scrolls." In *Jewish Eschatology, Early Christian Christology, and the Testaments of the Twelve Patriarchs: Collected Essays*, 28–47. Supplements to Novum Testamentum 63. Leiden: Brill, 1991.

Kahl, W. *New Testament Miracle Stories in Their Religious-Historical Setting: A Religionsgeschichtliche Comparison from a Structural Perspective*. Göttingen: Vandenhoeck & Ruprecht, 1994.

Kampen, J. *The Hasideans and the Origin of Pharisaism: A Study of 1 and 2 Maccabees*. Society of Biblical Literature Septuagint and Cognate Studies Series 24. Atlanta: Scholars Press, 1988.

Karpinski, R. *Exousia: A la base de l'enseignement de Jésus et de la mission apostolique selon S. Matthieu*. Rome: Nilo, 1968.

Karrer, M. *Der Gesalbte: Die Grundlagen des Christustitels*. Forschungen zur Religion und Literatur des Alten und Neuen Testaments 151. Göttingen: Vandenhoeck & Ruprecht, 1991.

Kaufmann, Y. *Christianity and Judaism: Two Covenants*. Translated by C. W. Efroymson. Jerusalem: Magnes, Hebrew University, 1988 (originally appeared as chaps. 7–9 of vol. 1 of *Golah ve-Nekhar* [1929–30]).

Kautzsch, E., ed. *Die Apokryphen und Pseudepigraphen des Alten Testaments*. 2 vols. Tübingen: Mohr, 1900.

Kearns, R. *Vorfragen zur Christologie: Morphologische und Semasiologische Studie zur Vorgeschichte eines christologischen Hoheitstitels*. 3 vols. Tübingen: Mohr, 1978–82.

————. *Das Traditionsgefüge um den Menschensohn: Ursprünglicher Gehalt und älteste Veränderung im Urchristentum*. Tübingen: Mohr, 1986.

————. *Die Entchristologisierung des Menschensohnes: Die Übertragung des Traditionsgefüges um den Menschensohn auf Jesus*. Tübingen: Mohr, 1988.

Keck, L. E. "Toward the Renewal of New Testament Christology." *New Testament Studies* 32 (1986): 362–77.

Kee, H. C. *Medicine, Miracle, and Magic in New Testament Times*. Society of New Testament Studies Monograph Series 55. Cambridge: Cambridge University Press, 1986.

Kellermann, U. *Auferstanden in den Himmel: II Makkabäer 7 und die Auferstehung der Märtyrer*. Stuttgarter Bibelstudien 95. Stuttgart: Katholisches Bibelwerk, 1979.

————. "Zum traditionsgeschichtlichen Problem des stellvertretenden Sühnetodes in 2 Makk 7,37f." *Biblische Notizen* 13 (1980): 63–83.

Kim, S. *The "Son of Man" as the Son of God*. Wissenschaftliche Untersuchungen zum Neuen Testament 30. Tübingen: Mohr, 1983.

Klauck, H. J. "4. Makkabäerbuch." In *Unterweisung in lehrhafter Form*. Jüdische Schriften aus hellenistisch-römische Zeit 3.6. Gütersloh: Mohn, 1989.

Kleinknecht, K. T. *Der leidende Gerechtfertigte: Die alttestamentlich-jüdische Tradition vom "leidenden Gerechten" und ihre Rezeption bei Paulus*. Wissenschaftliche Untersuchungen zum Neuen Testament 2/13. Tübingen: Mohr, 1984.

Koskenniemi, E. *Apollonius von Tyana in der neutestamentlichen Exegese: Forschungsbericht und Weiterführung der Diskussion*. Wissenschaftliche Untersuchungen zum Neuen Testament 2/61. Tübingen: Mohr, 1994.

Kraeling, C. H. *John the Baptist*. New York: Scribner, 1951.

Kümmel, W. G. *Promise and Fulfillment: The Eschatological Message of Jesus*. Translated by D. M. Barton. London: SCM, 1961.

————. "Das Gesetz und die Propheten gehen bis Johannes—Lukas 16,16 im Zusammenhang der heilsgeschichtlichen Theologie der Lukasschriften." In *Verborum Veritas:*

Festschrift für Gustav Stählin zum 70. Geburtstag, edited by O. Böcher and K. Haacker, 89–102. Wuppertal: Theologischer Verlag, 1970.

———. *The New Testament: The History of the Investigation of Its Problems.* Translated by S. M. Gilmour and H. C. Kee. London: SCM, 1973.

———. *Jesus der Menschensohn?* Sitzungsberichte der wissenschaftlichen Gesellschaft an der Johann Wolfgang Goethe-Universität Frankfurt am Main 20.3. Stuttgart: Steiner, 1984.

———. *Vierzig Jahre Jesusforschung (1950–1990).* 2d ed. Edited by H. Merklein. Bonner Biblische Beiträge 60. Weinheim: Beltz Athenäum, 1994.

Kvanvig, H. S. *Roots of Apocalyptic: The Mesopotamian Background of the Enoch Figure and of the Son of Man.* Wissenschaftliche Monographien zum Alten und Neuen Testaments 61. Neukirchen: Neukirchener Verlag, 1988.

Ladd, G. E. *Jesus and the Kingdom: The Eschatology of Biblical Realism.* London: S.P.C.K., 1966.

Lagrange, J. *Évangile selon Saint Jean.* Études bibliques. Paris: Lecoffre, 1925.

Laperrousaz, E. M. *Les Esséniens selon leur témoignage direct.* Religions et Culture. Paris: Desclee, 1982.

Légasse, S. *Naissance du baptême.* Lectio Divina 153. Paris: Cerf, 1993.

Leipoldt, J. *Die urchristliche Taufe im Lichte der Religionsgeschichte.* Leipzig: Doerffring, 1928.

Leivestad, R. "Jesus—Messias—Menschensohn: Die jüdischen Heilandserwartungen zur Zeit der ersten römischen Kaiser und die Frage nach dem messianischen Selbstbewusstsein Jesu." In *Aufstieg und Niedergang der römischen Welt,* part II, *Principat,* vol. 25, *Religion,* 1:220–64. Berlin: de Gruyter, 1982.

Le Moyne, J. *Les Sadducéens.* Études bibliques. Paris: Gabalda, 1972.

Leon-Dufour, X. *Lecture de l'évangile selon Jean.* 3 vols. Paris: Editions du Seuil, 1988–93.

Lettinga, J. P. "De uitdrukking 'De zoon des mensen.'" In *Almanak Fides Quadrat Intellectum 1955–1957,* 141–49. Kampen: Kok, 1957.

Lichtenberger, H. "Messianische Erwartungen und messianische Gestalten in der Zeit des Zweiten Tempels." In *Messias-Vorstellungen bei Juden und Christen,* edited by E. Stegemann, 9–20. Stuttgart: Kohlhammer, 1993.

Lietzmann, H. *Der Menschensohn: Ein Beitrag zur neutestamentlichen Theologie.* Freiburg: Mohr, 1896.

———. *Ein Beitrag zur Mandäerfrage.* Berlin: de Gruyter, 1930.

Lightfoot, J. *A Commentary on the New Testament from the Talmud and Hebraica.* 4 vols. Grand Rapids: Baker, 1979 (reprint of the 1859 edition of *Horae Hebraicae et Talmudicae,* first published 1658–74).

Lindars, B. *Jesus Son of Man: A Fresh Examinaton of the Son of Man Sayings in the Gospels in the Light of Recent Research.* London: S.P.C.K., 1983.

Lindeskog, G. "Johannes der Täufer: Einige Randbemerkungen zum heutigen Stand der Forschung." *Annual of the Swedish Theological Institute* 12 (1983): 55–83.

Lindijer, C. H. *De armen en de rijken bij Lucas.* The Hague: Boekencentrum, 1981.

Lohfink, G. "Der Ursprung der christlichen Taufe." *Theological Quarterly* 156 (1976): 35–54.

Lohmeyer, E. *Das Urchristentum,* vol. 1, *Johannes der Täufer.* Göttingen: Vandenhoeck & Ruprecht, 1932.

Lohse, E. *Märtyrer und Gottesknecht: Untersuchungen zur urchristlichen Verkündigung vom Sühnetod Jesu Christi.* 2d ed. Göttingen: Vandenhoeck & Ruprecht, 1963.

Loos, H. van der. *The Miracles of Jesus.* Supplements to Novum Testamentum 8. Leiden: Brill, 1965.

Lövestam, E. "Jésus Fils de David chez les Synoptiques." *Studia theologica* 28 (1974): 97–109.

Lüdemann, G. *Die Auferstehung Jesu: Historie, Erfahrung, Theologie*. Göttingen: Vandenhoeck & Ruprecht, 1994.

Lundström, G. *The Kingdom of God in the Teaching of Jesus: A History of Interpretation from the Last Decades of the Nineteenth Century to the Present Day*. Translated by J. Bulman. Edinburgh: Oliver & Boyd, 1963.

Lupieri, E. F. "John the Baptist in New Testament Traditions and History." In *Aufstieg und Niedergang der römischen Welt*, part II, *Principat*, vol. 26, *Religion*, 1:430–61. Berlin: de Gruyter, 1992.

Luz, U. "Basileia." In *Exegetisches Wörterbuch zum Neuen Testament*, edited by H. Balz and G. Schneider, vol. 1. Stuttgart: Kohlhammer, 1980.

Maier, G. *Johannes-Evangelium*. Bibelkommentar, edition C. 2 vols. Neuhausen-Stuttgart: Hänssler, 1984–86.

———. "Zur neutestamentlichen Wunderexegese im 19. und 20. Jahrhundert." In *Gospel Perspectives*, vol. 6, *The Miracles of Jesus*, edited by D. Wenham and C. Blomberg, 49–88. Sheffield: JSOT Press, 1986.

Main, E. "Les Sadducéens vus par Flavius Josèphe." *Revue biblique* 97 (1990): 161–206.

Maldonatus, J. *Commentarii in quattuor evangelistas*. Edited by Sausen. Mainz: Kirchhemius, 1840–44.

Manson, T. W. "John the Baptist." *Bulletin of the John Rylands University Library* 36 (1953–54): 395–412.

Marshall, I. H. "The Synoptic 'Son of Man' Sayings in the Light of Linguistic Study." In *To Tell the Mystery: Essays on New Testament Eschatology in Honor of Robert H. Gundry*, edited by T. E. Schmidt and M. Silva, 72–94. Journal for the Study of the New Testament Supplement Series 100. Sheffield: JSOT Press, 1994.

Mason, S. *Flavius Josephus on the Pharisees*. Studia Post-Biblica 39. Leiden: Brill, 1991.

Mattila, S. L. "Two Contrasting Eschatologies at Qumran (4Q246 vs 1QM)." *Biblica* 75 (1994): 518–38.

McLaren, J. S. *Power and Politics in Palestine: The Jews and the Governing of Their Land 100 B.C.–A.D. 70*. Journal for the Study of the New Testament Supplement Series 63. Sheffield: JSOT Press, 1991.

McNamara, M. *Palestinian Judaism and the New Testament*. Good News Studies 4. Wilmington, Del.: Glazier, 1983.

Mearns, C. L. "Dating the Similitudes of Henoch." *New Testament Studies* 25 (1978–79): 360–69.

Meier, J. P. "John the Baptist in Josephus: Philology and Exegesis." *Journal of Biblical Literature* 111 (1992): 225–37.

Menken, M. J. J. "De 'zeloten': Een overzicht." *Vox theologica* 45 (1975): 30–47.

Merklein, H. *Jesu Botschaft von der Gottesherrschaft: Eine Skizze*. 3d ed. Stuttgarter Bibelstudien 111. Stuttgart: Katholisches Bibelwerk, 1989.

Meyer, A. *Jesu Muttersprache: Das galiläische Aramäisch in seiner Bedeutung für die Erklärung der Reden Jesu und der Evangelien überhaupt*. Freiburg: Mohr, 1896.

Meyer, R. *Der Prophet aus Galiläa: Studie zum Jesusbild der drei ersten Evangelien*. Leipzig: Wissenschaftlicher Buchgesellschaft, 1940.

Michel, O., and O. Bauernfeind, eds. *Flavius Josephus: De Bello Judaico; Der jüdische Krieg: Griechisch und Deutsch*. 4 vols. Edited by O. Michel and O. Bauernfeind. Munich: Kösel-Verlag, 1959–69.

Milik, J. T. "Les modèles araméens du livre d'Esther dans la Grotte 4 de Qumran." *Revue de Qumran* 15 (1992): 321–408.

Miller, P. D. "Moses My Servant: The Deuteronomic Portrait of Moses." *Interpretation* 41 (1987): 245–55.

Mills, M. E. *Human Agents of Cosmic Power in Hellenistic Judaism and the Synoptic Tradition*. Journal for the Study of the New Testament Supplement Series 41. Sheffield: JSOT Press, 1990.

Moe, O. "Der Menschensohn und der Urmensch." *Studia theologica* 14 (1960): 119–29.

Moo, D. J. *The Old Testament in the Gospel Passion Narratives*. Sheffield: Almond, 1983.

Moore, G. F. *Judaism in the First Centuries of the Christian Era: The Age of the Tannaim*. 3 vols. Cambridge, Mass.: Harvard University Press, 1927–30.

Morris, L. *The Gospel according to John*. New International Commentary on the New Testament. Grand Rapids: Eerdmans; London: Marshall, Morgan & Scott, 1972.

Mowinckel, S. *He That Cometh*. Translated by G. W. Anderson. Oxford: Blackwell, 1956 (original Norwegian edition published 1951).

Müller, M. *Der Ausdruck "Menschensohn" in den Evangelien: Voraussetzungen und Bedeutung*. Acta theologica danica 17. Leiden: Brill, 1984.

Neale, D. A. *None but Sinners: Religious Categories in the Gospel of Luke*. Journal for the Study of the New Testament Supplement Series 58. Sheffield: JSOT Press, 1991.

Nebe, G. *Prophetische Züge im Bilde Jesu bei Lukas*. Beiträge zur Wissenschaft vom Alten und Neuen Testament 127. Stuttgart: Kohlhammer, 1989.

Neugebauer, F. "Die Davidssohnfrage (Mark xii 35–7 parr.) und der Menschensohn." *New Testament Studies* 21 (1974): 81–108.

Neusner, J. *The Rabbinic Traditions about the Pharisees before 70*. 3 vols. Leiden: Brill, 1971.

———. "Josephus's Pharisees." In *Ex orbe religionum: Studia Geo Widengren*, 1:224–44. Studies in the History of Religions 21. Leiden: Brill, 1972.

———. *From Politics to Piety: The Emergence of Pharisaic Judaism*. Englewood Cliffs, N.J.: Prentice-Hall, 1973.

———. *The Pharisees: Rabbinic Perspectives*. Studies in Ancient Judaism 1. Leiden: Brill, 1973 (an abridgement of *Rabbinic Traditions*).

———. *The Talmud of the Land of Israel: A Preliminary Translation and Explanation*, vol. 27, *Sotah*. Chicago Studies in the History of Judaism. Chicago and London: University of Chicago Press, 1984.

———. *The Mishnah: A New Translation*. New Haven, Conn., and London: Yale University Press, 1988.

———. "Mr. Sanders' Pharisees and Mine: A Response to E. P. Sanders, *Jewish Law from Jesus to Mishnah*." *Scottish Journal of Theology* 44 (1991): 73–95.

Neusner, J., W. S. Green, and E. S. Frerichs, eds. *Judaisms and Their Messiahs at the Turn of the Christian Era*. Cambridge: Cambridge University Press, 1987.

Nielsen, H. K. *Heilung und Verkündigung: Das Verständnis der Heilung und ihres Verhältnisses zur Verkündigung bei Jesus und in der ältesten Kirche*. Acta theologica danica 22. Leiden: Brill, 1987.

Odeberg, H. *The Aramaic Portions of Bereshit Rabba with Grammar of Galilaean Aramaic*, vol. 2, *Short Grammar of Galilaean Aramaic*. Leipzig: Gleerup, 1939.

Oegema, G. S. *De messiaanse verwachtingen ten tijde van Jezus: Een inleiding in de messiaanse verwachtingen en bewegingen gedurende de hellenistisch-romeinse tijd*. Baarn: Ten Have, 1991.

Pelletier, M. *Les Pharisiens: Histoire d'un parti méconnu*. Paris: Editions de Cerf, 1990.

Perrin, N. *The Kingdom of God in the Teaching of Jesus*. London: SCM, 1963.

Pesch, R., and R. Schnackenburg, eds. *Jesus und der Menschensohn: Für Anton Vögtle*. Freiburg: Herder, 1975.

Pfleiderer, O. *Das Urchristenthum, seine Schriften und Lehre, in geschichtlichem Zusammenhang beschrieben*. Berlin: Reimer, 1887.

Philonenko, M. "Jusqu'à ce que lève un prophète digne de confiance (1 Machabées 14,41)." In *Messiah and Christos: Studies in the Jewish Origins of Christianity; Presented to David Flusser on the Occasion of His Seventy-Fifth Birthday*, edited by I. Gruenwald et al., 95–98. Texte und Studien zum antiken Judentum 32. Tübingen: Mohr, 1992.

Pickl, J. *The Messias*. Translated by A. Green. St. Louis and London: Herder, 1946.

Pixner, B. "Das Essener-Quartier in Jerusalem." In *Wege des Messias und Stätten der Urkirche: Jesus und das Judenchristentum im Licht neuer archäologischer Erkenntnisse*, edited by R. Riesner, 180–207. Giessen: Brunnen-Verlag, 1991.

———. "Bethanien bei Jerusalem—eine Essener-Siedlung?" In *Wege des Messias und Stätten der Urkirche: Jesus und das Judenchristentum im Licht neuer archäologischer Erkenntnisse*, edited by R. Riesner, 208–18. Giessen: Brunnen-Verlag, 1991.

Plessis, P. J. du. "Zie het lam Gods: Overwegingen bij de knechtsgestalte in het evangelie van Johannes." In *De knechtsgestalte van Christus: Studies door collega's en oudleerlingen aangeboden aan Prof. Dr. H. N. Ridderbos*, edited by H. H. Grosheide et al., 120–38. Kampen: Kok, 1978.

Porton, G. G. "Diversity in Postbiblical Judaism." In *Early Judaism and Its Modern Interpreters*, edited by R. A. Kraft and G. W. E. Nickelsburg, 57–80. The Bible and Its Modern Interpreters 2. Philadelphia: Fortress, 1986.

Puech, E. "Fragment d'une apocalypse en araméen (4Q246 = pseudo-Dan^d) et le 'royaume de Dieu.'" *Revue biblique* 99 (1992): 98–131.

———. "Notes sur le fragment d'apocalypse 4Q246—'le fils de dieu.'" *Revue biblique* 101 (1994): 533–58.

Purvis, J. D. "The Samaritans and Judaism." In *Early Judaism and Its Modern Interpreters*, edited by R. A. Kraft and G. W. E. Nickelsburg, 81–98. The Bible and Its Modern Interpreters 2. Philadelphia: Fortress, 1986.

Reicke, B. "Die jüdischen Baptisten und Johannes der Täufer." In *Jesus in der Verkündigung der Kirche*, edited by A. Fuchs, 76–88. Studien zum Neuen Testament und seiner Umwelt, series A/1. Linz: Fuchs, 1976.

Reimarus, H. S. *Apologie oder Schutzschrift für die vernünftigen Verehrer Gottes*. Edited by G. Alexander. 2 vols. Frankfurt: Insel, 1972.

Reiser, M. *Die Gerichtspredigt Jesu: Eine Untersuchung zur eschatologischen Verkündigung Jesu und ihrem frühjüdischen Hintergrund*. Neutestamentliche Abhandlungen, n.F., 23. Münster: Aschendorf, 1990.

Reitzenstein, R. *Die Vorgeschichte der christlichen Taufe*. Leipzig: Teubner, 1929.

———. *Hellenistic Mystery-Religions: Their Basic Ideas and Significance*. Translated by J. E. Steely. Pittsburgh: Pickwick, 1978.

Rengstorf, K. H. "λῃστής." In *Theological Dictionary of the New Testament*, edited by G. Kittel, translated by G. W. Bromiley, 4:257–62. Grand Rapids: Eerdmans, 1967.

Ridderbos, H. *Zelfopenbaring en zelfverberging: Het historisch karakter van Jezus' messiaanse zelfopenbaring volgens de synoptische evangeliën*. Kampen: Kok, 1946.

———. *The Coming of the Kingdom*. Translated by H. de Jongste. Edited by R. O. Zorn. Philadelphia: Presbyterian & Reformed, 1962.

———. *Het evangelie naar Johannes: Proeve van een theologische exegese*. 2 vols. Kampen: Kok, 1987–92.

Rivkin, E. "Defining the Pharisees: The Tannaitic Sources." *Hebrew Union College Annual* 41 (1970): 205–49.

———. *A Hidden Revolution*. Nashville: Abingdon, 1978.

Rogers, C. L. "The Promises to David in Early Judaism." *Bibliotheca Sacra* 150 (1993): 285–302.

Rose, W. H. "De 'Leraar der Gerechtigheid': Johannes, Jakobus, of X? De datering van de Dode-Zeerollen en de vroegchristelijke kerk." In *Een sprekend begin: Opstellen aangeboden aan Prof. Drs. H. M. Ohmann*, edited by R. ter Beek et al., 186–99. Kampen: Kok, 1993.

Ruppert, L. *Jesus als der leidende Gerechte? Der Weg Jesu im Lichte eines alt- und zwischentestamentlichen Motivs*. Stuttgarter Bibelstudien 59. Stuttgart: Katholisches Bibelwerk, 1972.

Saldarini, A. J. *Pharisees, Scribes, and Sadducees in Palestinian Society*. Edinburgh: Clark, 1989.

Sanders, E. P. *Jesus and Judaism*. London: SCM, 1985.

————. *Jewish Law from Jesus to the Mishnah: Five Studies*. London: SCM; Philadelphia: Trinity Press International, 1990.

————. *Judaism: Practice and Belief, 63 B.C.E.–66 C.E.* London: SCM, 1992.

Sanders, J. A. "*Nazōraios* in Matthew 2.23." In *The Gospels and the Scriptures of Israel*, edited by C. A. Evans and W. R. Stegner, 116–28. Journal for the Study of the New Testament Supplement Series 104. Sheffield: Sheffield Academic Press, 1994.

Sanders, J. T. *The Jews in Luke-Acts*. London: SCM, 1987.

Schlatter, A. *Johannes der Täufer*. Edited by W. Michaelis. Basel: Reinhardt, 1956 (original manuscript 1880).

Schlosser, J. *Le Règne de Dieu dans les dits de Jésus*. 2 vols. Études bibliques. Paris: Gabalda, 1980.

Schmithals, W. *Wunder und Glaube: Eine Auslegung von Markus 4,35–6,6a*. Neukirchen: Neukirchener Verlag, 1970.

Schnabel, E. J. *Das Reich Gottes als Wirklichkeit und Hoffnung: Neuere Entwicklungen in der evangelikalen Theologie*. Wuppertal: Brockhaus, 1993.

Schnackenburg, R. *Das Johannesevangelium*. 4 vols. Freiburg: Herder, 1965–84.

Schnider, F. *Jesus der Prophet*. Orbis Biblicus et Orientalis 2. Freiburg: Universitätsverlag, 1973.

Schoeps, H. J. "Die jüdischen Prophetenmorde." In *Aus frühchristlicher Zeit: Religionsgeschichtliche Untersuchungen*, 126–43. Tübingen: Mohr, 1950.

Schürer, E. *Geschichte des Jüdischen Volkes im Zeitalter Jesu Christi*. 4th ed. 3 vols. Leipzig: Hinrichs, 1901–9.

————. *The History of the Jewish People in the Age of Jesus Christ (175 B.C.–A.D. 135)*. New English version. Revised and edited by G. Vermes, F. Millar, M. Black, and M. Goodman. 3 vols. Edinburgh: Clark, 1973–87.

Schütz, R. *Johannes der Täufer*. Abhandlungen zur Theologie des Alten und Neuen Testaments 50. Zürich: Zwingli, 1967.

Schwartz, D. R. *Agrippa I: The Last King of Judaea*. Texte und Studien zum Antiken Judentum 23. Tübingen: Mohr, 1990.

————. "Scribes and Pharisees, Hypocrites: Who Are the 'Scribes' in the New Testament?" In *Studies in the Jewish Background of Christianity*, 89–101. Wissenschaftliche Untersuchungen zum Neuen Testament 60. Tübingen: Mohr, 1992.

Schwarz, G. *Jesus "der Menschensohn": Aramaistische Untersuchungen zu den synoptischen Menschensohnworten Jesu*. Beiträge zur Wissenschaft vom Alten und Neuen Testament 6/19. Stuttgart: Kohlhammer, 1986.

Schweitzer, A. *The Quest of the Historical Jesus: A Critical Study of Its Progress from Reimarus to Wrede*. With a new introduction by J. M. Robinson. Translated by W. Montgomery. London: Black, 1931.

Schweizer, E. *Lordship and Discipleship*. Translated from the German with revisions by the author. London: SCM, 1960.

Sevenster, G. *De Christologie van het Nieuwe Testament*. Amsterdam: Holland, 1946.

Sidebottom, E. M. "The Son of Man as Man in the Fourth Gospel." *Expository Times* 68 (1956–57): 231–35.

Silva, M. "The Place of Historical Reconstruction in New Testament Criticism." In *Hermeneutics, Authority, and Canon*, edited by D. A. Carson and J. D. Woodbridge, 109–33. Grand Rapids: Baker, 1995.

Sjöberg, E. *Der Menschensohn im äthiopischen Henochbuch*. Skrifter utgivna av kungl. humanistiska vetenskapssamfundet i Lund 41. Lund: Gleerup, 1946.

Smallwood, E. M. *The Jews under Roman Rule: From Pompey to Diocletian*. Studies in Judaism in Late Antiquity 20. Leiden: Brill, 1976.

Smit, J. *De daemoniacis in historia evangelica*. Dissertatio exegetico-apologetica. Rome: Pontificii Instituti Biblici, 1913.

Spong, J. B. *Resurrection: Myth or Reality? A Bishop's Search for the Origins of Christianity*. San Francisco: Harper, 1994.

Staalduine-Sulman, E. Van. "The Aramaic Song of the Lamb." In *Verse in Ancient Near Eastern Prose*, edited by J. C. de Moor and W. G. E. Watson, 265–92. Alter Orient und Altes Testament 42. Neukirchen: Neukirchener Verlag, 1993.

Stanton, G. N. *The Gospels and Jesus*. The Oxford Bible Series. Oxford: Oxford University Press, 1989.

Stauffer, E. *New Testament Theology*. Translated by J. Marsh. London: SCM, 1955.

Steck, O. H. *Israel und das gewaltsame Geschick der Propheten: Untersuchungen zur Überlieferung des deuteronomistischen Geschichtsbildes im Alten Testament, Spätjudentum und Urchristentum*. Wissenschaftliche Monographien zum Alten und Neuen Testament 23. Neukirchen: Neukirchener Verlag, 1967.

Stegemann, H. *Die Essener, Qumran, Johannes der Täufer und Jesus: Ein Sachbuch*. Freiburg: Herder, 1993.

Stemberger, G. *Pharisäer, Sadduzäer, Essener*. Stuttgarter Bibelstudien 144. Stuttgart: Katholisches Bibelwerk, 1991.

Stone, M. "The Concept of the Messiah in IV Ezra." In *Religions in Antiquity: Essays in Memory of Erwin Ramsdell Goodenough*, edited by J. Neusner, 295–312. Studies in the History of Religions 14. Leiden: Brill, 1970.

Strack, H. L., and P. Billerbeck. *Kommentar zum Neuen Testament aus Talmud und Midrasch*. Vols. 1–4. Munich: Beck, 1926–28 (vols. 5–6 edited by J. Jeremias and K. Adolph. Munich: Beck, 1963).

Stuhlmacher, P. "Existenzstellvertretung für die Vielen: Mk 10,45 (Mt 20,28)." In *Versöhnung, Gesetz und Gerechtigkeit: Aufsätze zur biblischen Theologie*, 27–42. Göttingen: Vandenhoeck & Ruprecht, 1981.

———. *Biblische Theologie des Neuen Testaments*, vol. 1, *Grundlegung: Von Jesus zu Paulus*. Göttingen: Vandenhoeck & Ruprecht, 1992.

Sung, Chong-Hyon. *Vergebung der Sünden: Jesu Praxis der Sündenvergebung nach den Synoptikern und ihre Voraussetzungen im Alten Testament und frühen Judentum*. Wissenschaftliche Untersuchungen zum Neuen Testament 2/57. Tübingen: Mohr, 1993.

Taylor, J. E. *The Immerser: John the Baptist within Second Temple Judaism*. Grand Rapids: Eerdmans, 1997.

Taylor, T. M. "The Beginnings of Jewish Proselyte Baptism." *New Testament Studies* 2 (1955–56): 193–98.

Taylor, V. *The Names of Jesus*. London: Macmillan, 1954.

Thoma, C. "Entwürfe für messianische Gestalten in frühjüdischer Zeit." In *Messiah and Christos: Studies in the Jewish Origins of Christianity: Presented to David Flusser on the Occasion of His Seventy-Fifth Birthday*, edited by I. Gruenwald et al., 15–29. Texte und Studien zum antiken Judentum 32. Tübingen: Mohr, 1992.

Tilborg, J. H. A. van. "The Jewish Leaders in Matthew." Doctoral thesis, University of Nijmegen, 1972.

Tödt, H. E. *Der Menschensohn in der synoptischen Überlieferung*. Gütersloh: Mohn, 1959.

Torrance, T. F. "Proselyte Baptism." *New Testament Studies* 1 (1954–55): 150–54.

Uhlig, S. *Das äthiopische Henochbuch*. Jüdische Schriften aus hellenistisch-römischer Zeit, vol. 5, *Apokalypsen*, part 6. Gütersloh: Mohn, 1984.

Van Bruggen, J. *De oorsprong van de kerk te Rome*. Kamper Bijdragen 3. Groningen: de Vuurbaak, 1967.

———. "Nazoreeërs: De oudste naam voor christenen." In *Almanak Fides Quadrat Intellectum 1973*, pp. 147–67. Kampen: Kok, 1973.

———. *Ambten in de apostolische kerk: Een exegetisch mozaïek*. 2d ed. Kampen: Kok, 1987.

———. *Marcus: Het evangelie volgens Petrus*. 2d ed. Commentaar op het Nieuwe Testament, 3d series. Kampen: Kok, 1992.

————. *Lucas: Het evangelie als voorgeschiedenis.* Commentaar op het Nieuwe Testament, 3d series. Kampen: Kok, 1993.

————. *Matteüs: Het evangelie voor Israël.* 2d ed. Commentaar op het Nieuwe Testament, 3d series. Kampen: Kok, 1994.

————. *Christ on Earth: The Gospel Narratives as History.* Grand Rapids: Baker, 1998.

Vawter, B. "Ezekiel and John." *Catholic Biblical Quarterly* 26 (1964): 450–58.

Vermes, G. "Redemption and Genesis XXII: The Binding of Isaac and the Sacrifice of Jesus." In *Scripture and Tradition in Judaism: Haggadic Studies*, 193–227. Studia Post-Biblica 4. Leiden: Brill, 1961.

————. "Jesus the Prophet." In *Jesus the Jew: A Historian's Reading of the Gospels*, 86–102. Philadelphia: Fortress, 1973.

————. "Jesus the Son of Man." In *Jesus the Jew: A Historian's Reading of the Gospels*, 160–91. Philadelphia: Fortress, 1973.

————. "The Use of Bar Nash/Bar Nasha in Jewish Aramaic." In *Post-Biblical Jewish Studies*, 147–65. Studies in Judaism in Late Antiquity 8. Leiden: Brill, 1975 (originally published in 1967).

————. "The Present State of the 'Son of Man' Debate." In *Jesus and the World of Judaism*, 89–99. London: SCM, 1983.

Vermes, G., and M. D. Goodman, eds. *The Essenes: According to the Classical Sources.* Oxford Centre Textbooks 1. Sheffield: JSOT Press, 1989.

Versnel, H. S. "Quid Athenis et Hierosolymis? Bemerkungen über die Herkunft von Aspekten des 'Effective Death.'" In *Die Entstehung der jüdischen Martyrologie*, edited by J. W. van Henten et al., 162–96. Studia Post-Biblica 38. Leiden: Brill, 1989.

Versteeg, J. P. "De doop volgens het Nieuwe Testament." In *Rondom de doopvont: Leer en gebruik van de heilige doop in het Nieuwe Testament en in de geschiedenis van de westerse kerk*, edited by W. van't Spijker et al., 9–133. Goudriaan: De Groot, 1983.

Vielhauer, P. "Gottesreich und Menschensohn in der Verkündigung Jesu." In *Aufsätze zum Neuen Testament*, 55–91. Theologische Bücherei 31. Munich: Kaiser, 1965 (originally published in 1963).

————. "Jesus und der Menschensohn." In *Aufsätze zum Neuen Testament*, 92–140. Theologische Bücherei 31. Munich: Kaiser, 1965 (originally published in 1957).

Vögtle, A. *Die "Gretchenfrage" des Menschensohnsproblems: Bilanz und Perspektive.* 2d ed. Quaestiones Disputatae 152. Freiburg: Herder, 1995.

Vos, J. S. "Vragen rondom de plaatsvervangende zoendood van Jezus in het Nieuwe Testament." *Gereformeerd Theologisch Tijdschrift* 93 (1993): 210–31.

Walker, W. O. "The Son of Man: Some Recent Developments." *Catholic Biblical Quarterly* 45 (1983): 584–607.

————. "The Son of Man Question and the Synoptic Problem." In *New Synoptic Studies: The Cambridge Gospel Conference and Beyond*, edited by W. R. Farmer, 261–301. Macon, Ga.: Mercer University Press, 1983. (This is an expanded version of the *CBQ* article.)

Webb, R. L. *John the Baptizer and Prophet: A Socio-Historical Study.* Journal for the Study of the New Testament Supplement Series 62. Sheffield: JSOT Press, 1991.

————. "John the Baptist and His Relationship to Jesus." In *Studying the Historical Jesus: Evaluations of the State of Current Research*, edited by B. Chilton and C. A. Evans, 179–229. New Testament Tools and Studies 19. Leiden: Brill, 1994.

Weiss, J. *Die Predigt Jesu vom Reiche Gottes.* Göttingen: Vandenhoeck & Ruprecht, 1892.

Wengst, K. *Christologische Formeln und Lieder des Urchristentums.* Studien zum Neuen Testament 7. Gütersloh: Mohn, 1972.

Westerholm, S. *Jesus and Scribal Authority.* Coniectanea Biblica, New Testament Series 10. Lund: Gleerup, 1978.

Williams, S. K. *Jesus' Death as Saving Event: The Background and Origin of a Concept*. Harvard Dissertations in Religion 2. Missoula, Mont.: Scholars Press for Harvard Theological Review, 1975.

Willis, W., ed. *The Kingdom of God in Twentieth-Century Interpretation*. Peabody, Mass.: Hendrickson, 1987.

Wink, W. *John the Baptist in the Gospel Tradition*. Society for New Testament Studies Monograph Series 7. Cambridge: Cambridge University Press, 1968.

Witherington III, B. *The Christology of Jesus*. Minneapolis: Fortress, 1990.

———. *Jesus the Sage: The Pilgrimage of Wisdom*. Edinburgh: Clark, 1994.

Wrede, W. *The Messianic Secret*. Translated by J. C. G. Greig. Cambridge: Clarke, 1971.

Yamauchi, E. "Magic or Miracle? Diseases, Demons, and Exorcisms." In *Gospel Perspectives*, vol. 6, *The Miracles of Jesus*, edited by D. Wenham and C. Blomberg, 89–184. Sheffield: JSOT Press, 1986.

General Index

Scripture Index

Old Testament

Genesis
18:1–2   145
22   165, 165 n. 18
22:8   165
22:13   165
22:16   165
30:16   261
49:10   124

Exodus
4:24–26   191
5:6   30
5:10   30
5:14   30
5:15   30
5:19   30
32:31–33   172

Numbers
11:16   30
11:17   117
11:25   229
11:29   229
24:7   135
24:17   124, 136

Deuteronomy
18   118, 119, 119
   n. 11
18:9–14   116
18:9–22   116
18:14   117
18:15   116
18:16–17   116
18:17–19   117
18:18   116, 117
18:18–19   115, 118
18:19   116
18:20–22   116

23:19–20   28
24:16   172
34:10–12   116–17

Joshua
5:2–9   191

1 Samuel
10:10–11   227

2 Samuel
7:10–16   121
7:25–29   121

1 Kings
20:35   107 n. 41
20:41   107 n. 41
22:24–25   227

2 Kings
2:3–15   107 n. 41
3:27   172
4:38   107 n. 41
5:22   107 n. 41
6:1   107 n. 41

Ezra
7:6   30
7:11–12   30
7:21   30

Psalms
2   124, 142
2:2   142
2:6–7   142
8:4   98
22   163
41:9   161

45   142
45:2–8   142
51:11   227
60:10   65
69:4   161
89:4–5   121
89:28–52   121
105:15   139
106:33   227
108:10   65
110   109, 218
110:1   124, 218
118:22–23   161,
   162
132:11–18   121

Proverbs
30:1–4   108

Isaiah
7:14   66, 121, 124,
   142
9:1–7   121
9:6   66, 124, 142
11   153 n. 3
11:1–5   124
11:1–10   121
11:2   142
32:1–8   121
32:14–20   228
40   55, 56, 64, 67,
   167
40:2   55
40:5   55
40:9   55
40:10–11   55
43   168
43:3–4   168, 169
44:1–5   228

53   163 n. 16, 164
   n. 17, 167, 168,
   172
53:3   167 n. 25
53:4–12   172
53:10   166
53:11–12
   167 n. 25
53:12   161, 162
61   79, 139
61:1   139
63:10   227

Jeremiah
23:5–6   124
23:5–8   121
31:31–34   228

Ezekiel
9   58 n. 35
16:9–14   208
34:23–31   121
37:14   228

Daniel
2   136
2:44   77
7   102 n. 19, 103,
   108, 109, 275,
   276
7:11–14   77
7:13   98, 101, 102,
   102 n. 19, 103,
   108, 109
7:13–14   101–2
7:27   102
9:24   77
9:24–26   77
12:8–13   77

297

Old Testament Apocrypha

New Testament

Index of Other Ancient Writings

Christian Writings

Classical Writing

Jewish Writings

Mishnah

Philo

Qumran Scrolls

Additional Writings

1 Enoch

Jakob van Bruggen is professor of New Testament at the Theological University in Kampen, Netherlands, where he has taught since 1967. He is the author of more than fifteen commentaries and monographs in Dutch and English, including *Christ on Earth*. He is the general editor of a major New Testament commentary series published by J. H. Kok, Kampen, Netherlands.